Jerry Bauer

About the Author

HELEN CASTOR, a fellow in history at Cambridge, has spent ten years working on the Paston letters. She lives in London with her husband and son.

HELEN CASTOR

Blood AND Roses

One Family's Struggle
and Triumph During the
Tumultuous Wars of the Roses

HARPER ● PERENNIAL

NEW YORK ● LONDON ● TORONTO ● SYDNEY

HARPER ● PERENNIAL

First published in a different form by Faber and Faber Limited in Great Britain in 2004.

A hardcover edition of this book was published in 2006 by HarperCollins Publishers.

HarperCollins books may be purchased for educational, business, or sales promotional use.
For information please write: Special Markets Department, HarperCollins Publishers,
10 East 53rd Street, New York, NY 10022.

FIRST HARPER PERENNIAL EDITION PUBLISHED 2007.

Designed by Kate Nichols

The Library of Congress has catalogued the hardcover edition as follows:
Castor, Helen.
Blood and roses: one family's struggle and triumph during England's tumultuous
Wars of the Roses / Helen Castor.—1st ed.
p.   cm.
Originally published: Blood & roses: the Paston Family in the fifteenth century.
London: Faber and Faber, 2004.
Includes bibliographical references and index.
ISBN-13: 978-0-00-714808-0
ISBN-10: 0-00-714808-9
1. Great Britain—History—Lancaster and York, 1399–1485.
2. Nobility—Great Britain—Biography. 3. Paston family. I. Title
DA245.C3687 2006
942.04092'2—dc22
2005055101

ISBN: 978-0-00-716222-2 (pbk.)
ISBN-10: 0-00-716222-7 (pbk.)

07 08 09 10 11 ❖/RRD 10 9 8 7 6 5 4 3 2 1

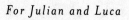

For Julian and Luca

CONTENTS

LIST OF ILLUSTRATIONS

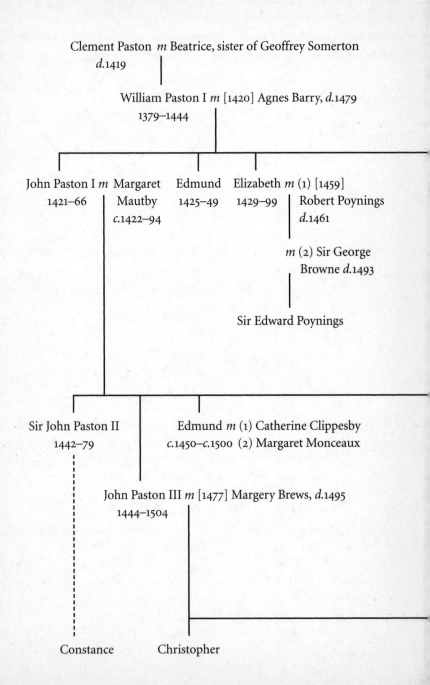

Clement Paston *m* Beatrice, sister of Geoffrey Somerton
*d.*1419

William Paston I *m* [1420] Agnes Barry, *d.*1479
1379–1444

John Paston I *m* Margaret
1421–66   Mautby
            *c.*1422–94

Edmund
1425–49

Elizabeth *m* (1) [1459]
1429–99   Robert Poynings
            *d.*1461

m (2) Sir George
Browne *d.*1493

Sir Edward Poynings

Sir John Paston II
1442–79

Edmund *m* (1) Catherine Clippesby
*c.*1450–*c.*1500 (2) Margaret Monceaux

John Paston III *m* [1477] Margery Brews, *d.*1495
1444–1504

Constance   Christopher

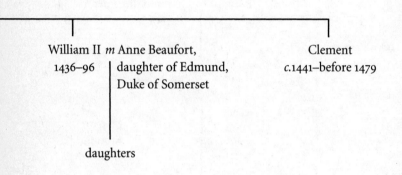

William II *m* Anne Beaufort,
1436–96   daughter of Edmund,
           Duke of Somerset

Clement
*c.*1441–before 1479

daughters

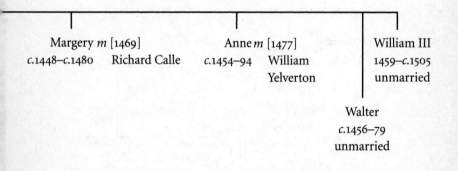

Margery *m* [1469]
*c.*1448–*c.*1480   Richard Calle

Anne *m* [1477]
*c.*1454–94   William
          Yelverton

William III
1459–*c.*1505
unmarried

Walter
*c.*1456–79
unmarried

William Paston IV *m* Bridget Heydon   Elizabeth *m* William Clere

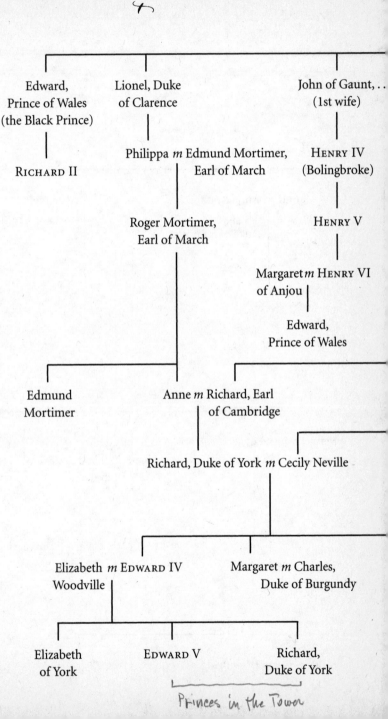

Edward,
Prince of Wales
(the Black Prince)

Lionel, Duke
of Clarence

John of Gaunt, . .
(1st wife)

RICHARD II

Philippa *m* Edmund Mortimer,
Earl of March

HENRY IV
(Bolingbroke)

Roger Mortimer,
Earl of March

HENRY V

Margaret *m* HENRY VI
of Anjou

Edward,
Prince of Wales

Edmund
Mortimer

Anne *m* Richard, Earl
of Cambridge

Richard, Duke of York *m* Cecily Neville

Elizabeth *m* EDWARD IV
Woodville

Margaret *m* Charles,
Duke of Burgundy

Elizabeth
of York

EDWARD V

Richard,
Duke of York

Princes in the Tower

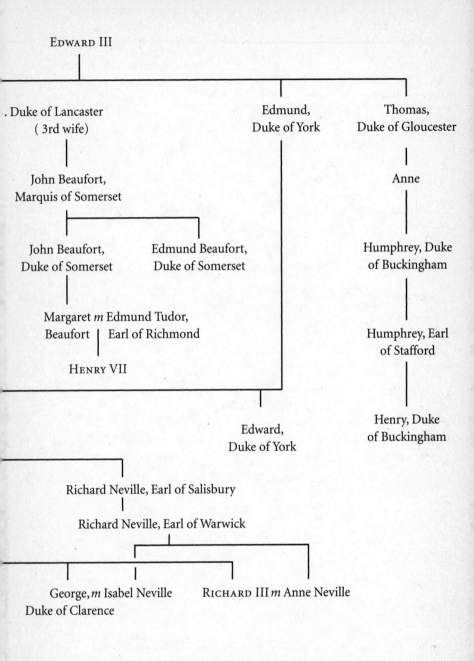

EDWARD III

. Duke of Lancaster
(3rd wife)

Edmund,
Duke of York

Thomas,
Duke of Gloucester

John Beaufort,
Marquis of Somerset

Anne

John Beaufort,
Duke of Somerset

Edmund Beaufort,
Duke of Somerset

Humphrey, Duke
of Buckingham

Margaret *m* Edmund Tudor,
Beaufort | Earl of Richmond

Humphrey, Earl
of Stafford

HENRY VII

Edward,
Duke of York

Henry, Duke
of Buckingham

Richard Neville, Earl of Salisbury

Richard Neville, Earl of Warwick

George, *m* Isabel Neville
Duke of Clarence

RICHARD III *m* Anne Neville

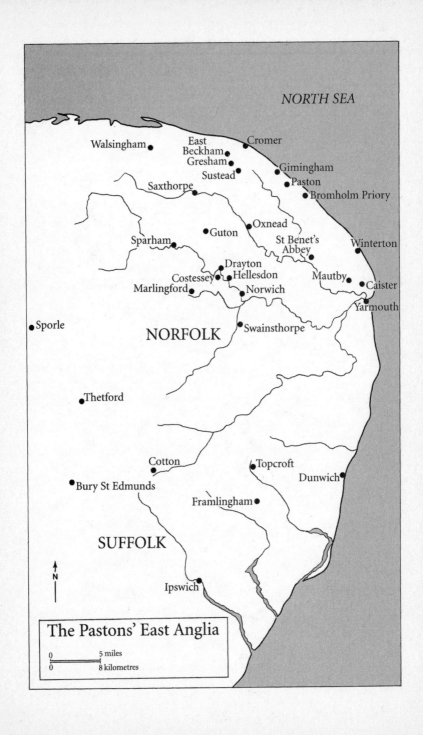

NORTH SEA

Walsingham

East
Beckham
Gresham
Sustead
Saxthorpe

Cromer

Gimingham
Paston
Bromholm Priory

Oxnead
Guton
Sparham
Drayton
Hellesdon
Costessey
Marlingford
Norwich

St Benet's
Abbey

Winterton

Mautby
Caister
Yarmouth

Sporle

NORFOLK

Swainsthorpe

Thetford

Cotton
Topcroft
Dunwich
Bury St Edmunds
Framlingham

SUFFOLK

N

Ipswich

The Pastons' East Anglia

0   5 miles
0   8 kilometres

AUTHOR'S NOTE

THE UNITS OF CURRENCY in late medieval England were pounds (£), shillings (s), and pence (d); there were twelve pence to the shilling and twenty shillings to the pound. Money could also be accounted in marks, each of which was equivalent to two-thirds of a pound (13s 4d). Among the coins in circulation were the groat, worth a third of a shilling (4d), and the noble, worth a third of a pound (6s 8d).

The spelling of all quotations from contemporary sources has been modernised. As far as possible, vocabulary has been left unaltered, but a few now-obsolete words have been substituted for ease of comprehension.

ACKNOWLEDGMENTS

I COULD NOT HAVE BEEN more fortunate in my agents, Patrick Walsh and Emma Parry: they have made the impossible happen, several times over. I owe heartfelt thanks to my editors, Courtney Hodell at HarperCollins, and Jon Riley and Walter Donohue at Faber; I have learned so much from working with all three of them.

Christine Carpenter introduced me to the Paston letters sixteen years ago; for that, as for so much else, I am profoundly in her debt. As always, she has been unfailingly generous with her expertise and her friendship, as have Richard Partington, Caroline Burt, John Watts, Benjamin Thompson, and Rosemary Horrox. Richard Beadle first made me think about telling the Pastons' story, and Colin Richmond offered kind encouragement along the way. Sidney Sussex College, Cambridge, has been a happy academic home for me for ten years, and I must thank everyone there—master, fellows, staff and students, and particularly the historians—for making it so.

I owe more than I can say to the people who have seen me through the writing of this book from its very beginnings: Rachel Aris, Lucyann Ashdown, Tony Badger, Gary Beggerow, Sarah Beglin, Nigel Blackwood, Katie Brown, Melissa Calaresu, Virginia Crompton, Russell Davies, John Foot, Robert Gordon, Harriet Hawkes, Grace Hodge, David Jarvis, Emily Lawson, Jo Marsh, Rosemary Parkinson, Barbara Placido, Anne Shewring, Keith Straughan, Catherine Taylor, Thalia Walters, and Simon Whiteman. Without Allison Weild, the book could not have been written: thank you.

My family, and especially my sisters, Harriet and Portia, have been a constant source of encouragement and inspiration. Very special thanks to my parents, Grahame and Gwyneth, for a truly extraordinary combination of emotional, practical, and intellectual support.

Julian Ferraro has helped in more ways than I can begin to describe. The book is dedicated to him and to Luca, with all my love.

BLOOD AND ROSES

then was a
good world

ASTON VILLAGE, NORFOLK. November 2004. A cold wind, heavy with salt, drags across the churchyard. The sea, less than a mile away, is invisible over the gentle rise of open fields, but its presence can be felt everywhere, in the vastness of the sky and the closeness of the wide horizon. Here, England's eastern coastline is austere even in summer. In winter, it has a bleak grandeur, the shore bellying out into slate-grey water that stretches four hundred miles northward, to the coast of Scandinavia. Across this North Sea, more than a thousand years ago, came the North Men, Viking warriors in their dragon-headed longships, to raid and plunder and, in time, to settle on the rich Norfolk soil. Now, though, both sea and land are quiet.

This has been a holy place for centuries. There was a church here already in 1066, when Norman knights—descendants of those Norsemen who had sailed on from English waters to overrun northern France—invaded England in their turn, and conquered it. But the church that now stands guard over the graves of generations was built three hundred years later, in the fourteenth century. It is at once stern and domestic, the severity of its flint tower, square-sided and battlement-topped, softened by the roof of steeply sloping thatch that covers the long nave. At first sight, the building seems defiantly solitary, turning its back on the road to the north and sheltering its gabled porch out of sight of passing travellers. But this is illusion born of historical accident, not ecclesiastical design: the road once curved south to the church door, until it was moved at the behest of a long-ago lord of the manor to protect his nearby home from curious eyes.

Through the heavy wooden door, the interior is equally spare, with white-painted walls beneath a simple raftered roof. Almost five hundred years ago, when King Henry VIII defied the authority of Rome to declare himself Supreme Head of the English Church, Protestant reformers made sure that the images of medieval Catholicism were swept away. In an orgy of zealous destruction, statues were burned and broken, paintings obliterated with plaster and whitewash. But, at Paston, tales of "pictures on the walls" persisted in local memory, and twentieth-century parishioners uncovered what their predecessors had been forbidden to look upon. Now spectral figures—fragments of a lost world—gaze down again for the first time in half a millennium. Directly opposite the door is a towering image of St. Christopher. Draped in the folds of an elegant cloak, with breeches ornately tied just above his well-turned calves, the saint strides across a river, fish swimming open-mouthed about his ankles. Nothing distracts his attention from the figure balanced neatly in his palm: the Christ Child, dressed all in red, his left hand carrying the weight of the world, his right raised in a gesture of blessing.

Even now, in faded outline, the tableau draws the eye of every visitor who steps into the church. Newly painted, with its red and yellow ochre luminously fresh, it must have been arresting—and deliberately so. "Cristofori faciem die quacumque tueris, illa nempe die morte mala non morieris," a fifteenth-century woodcut of the saint declared: "Whenever you look on Christopher's face, that day, surely, you shall not die a bad death."[1] A bad death was an unprepared one, an end too sudden to allow repentance and confession of sin, reconciliation with neighbours and loved ones, or the final ministrations of the Holy Church. Without such preparation, the human soul would face the unspeakable torments of eternal damnation—and as a result medieval men and women feared the unpredictability of death almost more than its inevitability. Despite the prophylactic power of St. Christopher's colossal presence, it was essential for the faithful at Paston to remember that the end might come at any moment, and to be ready.

That was the message of the elaborate memento mori which unfolds along the north wall toward the chancel: the legend of "Les Trois Vifs et les Trois Morts," The Three Living and the Three Dead. The painting survives only in faint, irregular patches, but its drama is urgent and unmistakable.

Three young kings enjoy the hunt, with hawks on their wrists and dogs at their feet. Their leader stares out confidently, even arrogantly, his beard fashionably forked into two neat points, his left hand resting casually on his hip, all the better to display one finely shaped leg in deep red hose. We gather from the nonchalance of his pose that he has not yet seen the dreadful apparition by which his terrified companions and attendants are transfixed. Three hollow-eyed skeletons stand before them, a ghastly vision of the kings' own future, and a reminder of the vanity of earthly dominion: "as you are, we once were; as we are, so shall you be."

Such fearful images were everywhere in medieval England, from this modest village church to the great cathedral of St. Paul's in London. There, the danse macabre gambolled round the cloister walls, a grim painted pageant in which king and pope, knight and peasant each found himself attended by a leering corpse. In the Middle Ages, life, it seems, was full of death. How could it be otherwise, when childbirth might all too easily kill mother and baby together; when the attentions of a physician might prove not only agonising but lethal; when one season of bad weather might leave famine and starvation in its wake? Every day, the experience of human suffering challenged medieval minds to contemplate the reality of the four "last things": death, judgment, heaven, and hell.

Even so, nothing could have prepared them for the apocalyptic horror of the epidemic that swept across Europe in the late 1340s—a disease that came to be known as the Black Death, although contemporaries called it simply "the pestilence," or "the great mortality." Victims found painful, darkly swollen lumps in their groins, armpits, or necks; most became feverish, many delirious, others comatose. Some died within a single day; most clung to life for three or four days more before finally giving up the ghost. In the rarest of cases, a patient exhibiting these excruciating symptoms might even recover—an insubstantial hope, but a consolation denied to those whose lungs were the principal seat of infection. Fighting for air and coughing up blood, they died quickly, and without exception.

This devastating plague had taken hold first in the steppes of central Asia, before spreading south, into China and India, and west, reaching the Crimea by 1345. In 1346, it all but annihilated Tartar forces besieging the Black Sea port of Caffa. No longer able to fight by conventional means, the few survivors embarked instead on biological warfare, using catapults to pitch infected cadavers over the walls. The handful of Genoese merchants who managed to escape the hell hole that Caffa soon became took the disease with them as they fled, first to Constantinople, and then home, to Italy. From there it picked up speed, racing in all directions along the myriad trading routes from the great commercial centres of Genoa and Venice. It reached the south coast of England in the summer of 1348. By the end of the following year, almost half of the country's people—perhaps three million men, women, and children—were dead.

It was a cataclysm on a scale so vast that it seemed the world was ending. A Franciscan friar named John Clynn left a haunting account of the epidemic's inexorable advance from England into his Irish homeland. He wrote, he said, as he sat "waiting among the dead for death to come," seeking only to record the terrors he had witnessed "in case anyone should still be alive in the future." At that point, his text falls silent. A copyist preserved his words for the future generations whose very existence Clynn had come to doubt, and appended one brief, final note: "Here, it seems, the author died." If the plague's reach was universal, its touch was brutally intimate. Homes and families were ripped apart, the chroniclers reported, not only by death but by the fear of contagion, so that husbands fled their dying wives, and parents their children, "as if from leprosy, or from a serpent." Others described the devotion of those who refused to abandon the ones they loved even in death. In the southeastern English town of Rochester so many people had perished that no one could be found to carry corpses to burial, but "men and women carried the bodies of their own little ones to church on their shoulders," having no choice but to consign the dead infants to mass graves whose stench made it scarcely tolerable for the townspeople to pass by the churchyards.[2]

By December 1349, it seemed at last as though the pestilence had done its worst. ". . . those of us who have survived and have been mercifully spared by Providence, although we do not deserve it, must break forth in praises," the archbishop of Canterbury declared.[3] His prayers were powerless, however, to prevent its return: before the end of the century, England would suffer four more outbreaks of plague and thousands more deaths. The consciousness of human mortality, difficult to escape even before the epidemic, was now ever-present, and the Church's teaching left faithful Christians in no doubt of what the fate of their souls would be once their time came. Only a very few people—the saintly, in the literal sense of the word—could expect immediate admission to the everlasting joys of heaven. The overwhelming majority of humankind, whose spiritual account books at the day of reckoning would show a surplus of sin and a deficit of penance, could not be admitted to the presence of God until their souls had been cleansed in purgatory, a shadowy, liminal place between the gates of heaven and the pit of hell. There, sin would be purged by suffering, with punishments exquisitely devised to mirror the sinner's offence. Those guilty of usury might be boiled in liquid gold; darts of anger would become the sharpest of spears to pierce the sides of the wrathful; and the proud, painfully bound onto great wheels, would find no peace, hurled precipitously upwards only to find themselves cast down once more in sickening perpetual motion.

In a world where death was always close at hand, this tortured vision of the afterlife evokes a mental landscape where the animated corpses sketched on the walls at Paston loom as a disturbing, ominous presence. But it is not so easy to know how these skeletal figures spoke to the villagers who gazed up at them when their paint was still fresh. Modern observers have been quick to characterise the fourteenth century as "a violent, tormented, bewildered, suffering and disintegrating age," an era of morbid obsessions and psychological extremes. "Living emotion stiffens," we are told, "amid the abused imagery of skeletons and worms."[4] But, at a distance of six hundred years, is it right to assume that this is how the people of Paston felt about their lives? Is it really so simple to extrapolate from threatening imagery to cowed, fearful response?

There are good grounds for believing that the answer is a forthright, even a resounding no. Without question, the people of the Middle Ages were acutely aware of death and its consequences. Thanks to the plague's appalling devastations, they experienced suffering and loss on an unprecedented scale. But to depict them shrouded in a repressive culture of pessimism, their emotional engagement with the world stunted by a ghoulish fascination with the macabre, is to overlook their vitality, their diversity, their sophistication, their ambition—fundamentally, to underestimate their humanity.

To contemporaries, the theological message of Les Trois Morts at Paston was not as morbid as their gruesome forms suggest to modern eyes. The prospect of purgatory, for all its disturbing violence, offered medieval Christians a redemptive vision of their souls' fate. The agony they faced after death, terrible though it might be, could be endured in the sure and certain knowledge of salvation. As one tract proclaimed, "the pain of purgatory is full of good hope and of grace": all who suffered there were assured of eternal bliss, however long the hideous process of purgation might take before their entry to paradise.[5] The distinction between purgatory's hellish pains and the tortures of hell itself was essential and absolute, and brought consolation and hope to all repentant sinners.

If purgatory served to liberate the faithful from the terror of damnation, then the Church's relentless emphasis on the physical horror of the purgatorial process was not an injunction to despair but a spiritual call to arms, an insistent reminder that the way to salvation could begin in the present moment. Repentance and absolution at the point of death could save even the most reprobate of evildoers from the devil's grasp, but such malefactors would face thousands of years of torment before their souls were purged of sin. Knowing what lay in store, who would not choose to act in this life rather than suffer in the next? It was only in purgatory that penance took the form of pain. In this world, sin could be expiated instead by works of charity and mercy, by living a good Christian life. And the scales were loaded in favour of those who chose to act for themselves while they still had the chance: a single day of patient endurance in the face of trouble or sickness before death would help a sinful soul on its journey toward God as much as an entire year of purgatorial agony. Those who devoted themselves to good works, the Church declared, might secure "so much pardon in this world that shall remove all the pains of purgatory and lightly bring them to bliss of heaven."[6]

It was this message—intended to goad the living into pious action, not to paralyse them with fear—that the Three Dead brought to the parishioners at Paston. Twenty miles away, in the Norfolk village of Sparham, it was made more explicit still. In the church there, painted on a wooden screen, stand a pair of modishly dressed skeletons, a man sporting a jaunty feathered cap with a rich chain around his neck, and a woman bedecked in an ermine-trimmed gown. Beneath their grinning skulls, bony fingers clasp a fragile flower and a burning torch. Any spectator struggling to interpret these symbols of transience and decay could read their meaning spelled out in Latin script below: SIC TRANSIT GLORIA MUNDI—"thus passes earthly glory."

But it was precisely because the glories of this world were so captivating that the Church harped so insistently on their fleeting and ephemeral nature. The ghoulish images which have convinced us that the people of the late Middle Ages were obsessed with their own mortality might just as easily reflect the Church's conviction that they did not think about it enough— that they were too deeply engrossed in earthly concerns, too easily distracted from contemplation of the consequences of sin. It was not that parishioners rejected the Church's teaching about the afterlife; they endorsed it wholeheartedly whenever age or infirmity made the prospect of death an uncomfortably pressing issue. Those with money to spend left elaborate bequests in their wills for the good of their souls; they paid for the building of new churches and the beautification of old ones, and specified intricate arrangements for the prayers and masses that would help to speed their souls through purgatory once they were gone. But the challenge was to persuade the faithful not only to die in a state of grace, but to live in one. If shock tactics were used in the attempt—tactics given putrefying flesh in the cadaverous forms that stalked across church walls—it was, in part at least, because so many people found the pleasures and pains of this world more immediately preoccupying than the principles upon which they would be judged in the next.

The plague, after all, had not only brought death to millions of people; it had also heightened the experience of life for those who escaped its ravages. The complex psychology of survival—a volatile amalgam of euphoria and denial, vulnerability and guilt—was intensified by seismic social shifts. Economic certainties that had held good for centuries disintegrated overnight. Suddenly, land was plentiful and hands to work it scarce. Most Englishmen and women found they had choices of a kind they had never known: they could eat more, drink more, work less, wear finer clothes. For the great landowners, it came as a rude awakening to discover that the abundant supply of cheap labour on which their lavish lifestyles depended had simply ceased to exist. Not only that, but the order of God's creation (as they saw the social structure that underpinned their power and privilege) was being subverted by the explosion of opportunities for those of humble birth to better themselves, first by making money and then by spending it to mask their lowly origins with the trappings of wealth and status.

The landed aristocracy—the nobility and gentry, with the king at their head—snapped into action in defence of their own interests within months of the plague's arrival. In June 1349, it was decreed that labour costs should be fixed by law at the "customary" level—that is, at the low rates that land-lords had been accustomed to paying before half the workforce died. This imposition of a maximum wage was justified with outraged denunciations of the "indolence" and "greed" of working people who were discovering, for the first time in their lives, that they had economic muscle. Government efforts to enforce the legislation were concerted and persistent, but landowners found that their public determination to stand shoulder to shoulder against the labourers' demands soon began to crumble in private. If their estates were to be tilled and their crops harvested, they had no choice but to compete, with ever-more-enticing terms of employment, for the services of a labouring class that was now discerning rather than desperate.

The futility of the attempt to hold back the economic tide by royal fiat was already becoming apparent by 1363, when a statute was passed specifying detailed restrictions to the "outrageous and excessive apparel" that many people were now affecting, "contrary to their estate and degree." If the aristocracy could not stop the lower orders earning more money, the reasoning went, they could at least prevent them from using it to drape themselves in finery as if they were gentlefolk. Agricultural workers were to dress only in blanket and russet, coarse woollen cloths in drab colours, while craftsmen and yeomen were forbidden to wear "any belt, knife, clasp, ring, garter, brooch, ribbon, chain, knot, seal or anything else of gold or silver, or any sort of embroidered, decorated or silk clothing." Their wives and daughters could trim their gowns with the skins of lamb, rabbit, cat, and fox, but were prohibited from buying more expensive furs or budge, an exotic variety of black lamb fleece imported from North Africa. The new law applied to fashion as well as to fabric: those below the rank of knight should have "no turned-back facings or fur linings in their garments," the statute declared, "and have no slashings, jagged edges or fripperies." Reserved for the very rich was the right to wear the finest furs, ermine, and lettice (the prized skin of the snow weasel), and to festoon their clothes with pendant jewels and pearls.[7]

In practice, of course, this battle too was already lost. Not only was the legislation unenforceable, but, behind the static façade of the medieval hierarchy, social mobility had been a fact of life for centuries. The trick, for the upwardly mobile, was to join the ranks of the landed classes by the practical means of buying land, and then to imitate the demeanour, style, and attitudes of those whose status was already established beyond question. Within a generation or two, such an impersonation might well—given enough luck, money, and influence to silence whispers of a humble past— turn into accepted reality. But the deadly intervention of the plague vastly increased the number of would-be gentlemen trying to scramble up the social ladder—gentlemen who, when they reached its upper rungs, turned to join the chorus of aristocratic indignation at those still snapping at their heels below.

The naked self-interest of the landowners' attempt to use their political power in defence of their economic privileges added another provocative ingredient to this already simmering brew of social tensions. It reached boiling point in 1381. Four years earlier, the same government which had insisted that "custom" should determine how much labourers could earn in the aftermath of the plague had perpetrated a radical break with tradition by levying a poll tax to pay for urgently needed defence against French raids on the south coast. By long-established convention, national taxation took the form of a charge on movable property and required the consent of parliament, in which the propertied classes who would bear the brunt of the tax were represented. Now—seeing the economic gains their social inferiors were making in this post-plague world, and feeling the pinch in their own purses—members of parliament moved to shift the burden of taxation downward by agreeing to the imposition of a flat-rate charge of four pence per head (or "poll") on all English men and women over the age of fourteen.

Despite the manifest unfairness of a tax that required the most impoverished peasant to pay the same amount as the wealthiest magnate in the land, revenue was collected in 1377 without serious incident, and again in 1379 when a second poll tax was granted, this time on an elaborate sliding scale designed to take at least some account of an individual's ability to pay. But this concession to social justice was abandoned only a year later. In 1380, when a third poll tax was levied, every one of the king's adult subjects was required to contribute twelve pence: in just three years, the rate had tripled. The first signs of defiance came as the money was totted up. If the tax returns are taken as a head count, a third of England's population had vanished between 1377 and 1381. Such concerted evasion was passive resistance on a massive scale, and the government would have been well advised to heed the warning. Instead, heavy-handed commissions were dispatched from London to extract payment from the recalcitrant. The result was violent insurrection.

Revolt began to stir at the beginning of June 1381. A commissioner named John Bampton arrived at Brentwood in Essex, twenty miles northeast of the capital, accompanied by two sergeants-at-arms, elite servants of the crown recruited for their military expertise and often used as royal enforcers. Bampton summoned before him the inhabitants of the town and its surrounding villages and demanded that they make up the shortfall in the local revenues collected so far. The reply came that they had already paid the tax, and would pay no more. Bampton persisted, threatening grievous retribution against anyone who would not contribute. Again the people "told him outright that they would not deal with him nor give him any money."[8] At that, Bampton lost his patience, ordering the summary arrest of those who had spoken for their friends and neighbours. But the sergeants-at-arms did not meet the mute compliance they expected. Rather than submit to demands they saw as unjust and unjustifiable, the villagers threatened to kill the king's officers, who fled back to London to save their own skins. Still the government did not see the danger, sending one of the chief justices of the realm to prosecute and punish the ringleaders of this insubordination. He, too, was sent packing, and this time violence began in earnest. Those who had cooperated with the commissioners were seized and murdered, their heads severed and carried aloft on spiked poles as a bloody warning of the dangers of collaboration.

Disturbances spread quickly across the southeast of England, fuelled by a potent mix of anger and fear: anger at the oppressions of lords who were abusing their political and judicial authority to exploit the "true commons" of England; and fear of the consequences if, having embarked on this perilous course, the rebels failed to sweep away the power of their oppressors. This was not a revolt of the destitute and disenfranchised; it was resistance born of hopes thwarted and expectations dashed. Its leaders were substantial figures in their villages and communities, men who knew something of the workings of law and government, and did not like what they had seen in the years since the plague had transformed the economic landscape. At every turn, their ambitions for themselves and their families had been checked by local magistrates seeking to enforce laws designed to benefit their own class, in their private capacity as rich landowners, at the expense of the wider community. Peasants, artisans, and labourers could see the prizes of greater wealth and greater freedom that should have been securely within their grasp, and they knew who was responsible for the attempt to keep those prizes tantalisingly out of reach.

The poll tax was the spark that set this tinderbox of grievances alight. Not only was the tax fundamentally inequitable, but the contemptuous manner in which it was levied added provocative insult to damaging injury. It was even alleged that some tax collectors indecently assaulted teenage girls in the villages they visited, on the outrageous pretext of establishing (in the absence of officially documented proofs of age) whether the girls were sexually active adults and therefore liable to pay the charge. Whether or not the reports were true—and they were all too plausible, either as a gratuitous abuse of power or a monstrously cynical ploy to bully families into handing over more money—the fact that they were widely believed goes a long way toward explaining the violent anger of the crowds who converged on London in the second week in June. If the rebels' fury unleashed terrible destruction on the city, as buildings burned and heads were hacked off, that did not mean that their call for justice was either shallow or groundless.

By Friday, 14 June 1381, the dead included the archbishop of Canterbury and the prior of the Hospital of the Knights of St. John at Clerkenwell, both men objects of loathing because of their government posts as chancellor and treasurer of England. They were dragged from the Tower of London, the chief royal residence within the city, and decapitated on Tower Hill, their heads paraded through the streets and then exposed to public view above the gate at London Bridge like the traitors the rebels claimed they were. To blame the king's chief ministers for the realm's ills was a well-worn strategy, allowing protesters to declare their loyalty and fidelity to the king himself. In this case, however, rhetoric reflected political reality. King Richard II was fourteen years old—an adult by the terms of the poll tax enacted in his name, but not yet in command of his own government. In the four years since he had succeeded his elderly grandfather Edward III, England had been ruled on his behalf by leading nobles and churchmen—and it was this magnate-dominated regime that had devised and imposed the new tax, blatantly prioritising landowners' interests over those of the mass of the king's subjects.

But the rebels' faith that their young monarch would right these wrongs proved to be their undoing. With enormous courage, Richard rode out to meet them on Saturday, 15 June, at Smithfield, the "smooth field" that lay outside the city walls to the northwest. He was guarded by a large entourage, but the fact remained that the rebels were in effective control of the capital, and the blood of the chancellor and treasurer had been spilled only twenty-four hours earlier. The royal party drew up on the east side of the field, the insurgents on the west, and the king rode forward to speak to the man who had emerged as their leader, a charismatic and articulate Kentishman named Walter (or, more familiarly, Wat) Tiler. Richard listened patiently as Tiler enumerated the rebels' demands: the great landowners should be stripped of their political and judicial powers, and village communities should instead be left to govern themselves, answering only to the crown. With extraordinary composure, the king played along, agreeing to all of Tiler's stipulations insofar as they might accord with "the regality of his crown." In the meantime, he said, the commons should disperse and return to their homes. But Tiler's bold manner—by one report, he addressed the king as "brother"—appeared insolently presumptuous to Richard's attendants. Heated words were exchanged, and a scuffle erupted between Tiler and the mayor of London, a merchant named William Walworth. Daggers flashed: Walworth was saved by his body armour, but Tiler toppled to the ground, streaming with blood.[9]

It was a heart-stopping moment. In horror, the rebels watched their leader fall. Many among their ranks notched the longbows they carried, ready to fight for their cause and their own survival. But the young king reacted with nerveless presence of mind, spurring his horse forward and calling them to follow him, crying, "I will be your king, your captain and your leader!"[10] He was little more than a boy, but he was their anointed sovereign, and they rallied to his command. As Richard led the rebels a few hundred yards northward to the open fields outside the Priory of St. John at Clerkenwell, Mayor Walworth seized his chance to muster armed support from inside the city. In the mêlée, Tiler had been spirited away to St. Bartholomew's Hospital nearby, but Walworth tracked him down and, rather than wait for his gaping wounds to do their work, ordered that the dying man be dragged outside and beheaded. It was over. At the king's insistence, the cowed commons were allowed to leave London without further reprisals—for the moment at least. As they streamed across London Bridge, exhausted, frightened and disconsolate, it was no longer the severed heads of the chancellor and treasurer that stared down at them from the city gate, but the sightless gaze of Wat Tiler, their dead leader.

London had not been the only place overwhelmed by violent protest, but once insurrection had failed in the capital, it could not hope to succeed elsewhere. An unsteady peace was restored across southeastern England three weeks after the tumultuous events of 15 June. Charges were brought in the royal courts against hundreds of alleged rebels in the following months, and many local rebel leaders were hanged. Overall, however, the judicial response was notable for its moderation and restraint; and it gradually became clear that, in defeat, the rebel movement had achieved a startling transformation in government policy. The message that the regime had directly provoked this terrifying convulsion in the social order was unmistakable, and Richard II's nobles and ministers were no fools. The poll tax was abandoned immediately. (Six hundred years would pass before another attempt was made to impose a regressive levy of this kind in England: in

1990, as in 1381, it provoked riots and mass resistance, which forced the government into retreat.) Further efforts to hold wages down at pre-plague levels were also quietly dropped. Although in theory landlords' powers stood unchanged, in practice, increasing numbers of great landowners now realised that the attempt to shore up their revenues by aggressively asserting their rights over their peasant tenants was dangerous and unsustainable. Instead, they sought the reassurance of a regular, dependable, undemanding, and uncontroversial income by leasing out their estates to tenant farmers—something that lifted many of the burdens and restrictions of direct seigneurial control from smallholders across the country.

The way was now open as never before for able and ambitious men to rise from poverty and obscurity to wealth and influence, to turn their names into lineages and their families into dynasties. The possibility of such social transformation was most apparent in the regions at the heart of the rising of 1381—unsurprisingly, given that it was the consciousness of thwarted opportunities which had so powerfully animated the rebel movement. Among those regions was the county of Norfolk. Disturbances had erupted all over the shire, but unrest had been particularly intense in the city of Norwich and the countryside to the north and east, stretching almost twenty miles to the coast on which the village of Paston lies. The Norfolk rebels, led by a local dyer named Geoffrey Litster, rampaged into Norwich on 17 June and held sway in the city for a week. Litster installed himself in style in Norwich Castle, where he was attended with great ceremony by his followers, and where he presided over court sessions to dispense the rebels' own brand of justice. They were forced to retreat on 24 June by the arrival of forces under the command of Norwich's bishop, Henry Despenser, an unusually bellicose priest who was himself a capable soldier. The rebels fled northward to North Walsham, less than four miles from Paston, where they fashioned a makeshift wooden fort out of tables, shutters, and gates bound together behind a hastily excavated ditch. But their rudimentary defences were no match for Bishop Despenser, who led his men into combat, one chronicler reported admiringly, "like a wild boar gnashing its teeth."[11] The rebel encampment was quickly overwhelmed by the force of Despenser's assault, and Litster was captured in the rout. The bishop sentenced him to death, and personally heard the condemned man's last confession before leading him to the gallows.

The revolt in northeastern Norfolk was scarcely less dramatic than the shocking events that had unfolded in London a week earlier—something which perhaps reflected the fact that few other places could come so close to matching the capital's dazzling wealth of commercial opportunities, and therefore the intense frustration of those excluded from the chance to reap the benefits. At the region's heart was the great city of Norwich. Its site, at the highest navigable point on the River Wensum, had been a place of settlement for centuries, but it was after the Norman Conquest of 1066 that the town began its rapid growth into one of the richest and most populous cities in England. That process was given tangible expression in the late eleventh century by the construction of two spectacularly contrasting buildings. Norwich Castle was conceived as a physical embodiment of Norman dominance: its squat, square keep, looking down from its steep mound, is a looming and muscular presence that speaks unambiguously of power and control. Norwich Cathedral, on the other hand, stands in the open space of its own vast precincts—the largest in England—and its soaring architecture reaches for the heavens, a confection of light and space combining coolly elegant lines with a dizzying sense of weightlessness.

Around these magnificent buildings, within city walls that enclosed meadows and orchards as well as an urban maze of narrow streets, lived a bustling, jostling, and fiercely competitive community. There were countless ways to make a living in Norwich. The inhabitants of every great city needed to be fed, clothed, and housed, and the tradesmen of Norwich included butchers, bakers, cheesemongers, candlemakers, shoemakers, hosiers, glovers, hatters, tailors, fripperers (who dealt in secondhand clothes), taverners, apothecaries, carpenters, masons, and smiths working in gold, iron, and latten (an alloy resembling brass). There were tradeswomen, too. Wives played their part in family businesses, and widows often ran them. Some occupations were almost exclusively in female hands: as elsewhere in England, much of the city's ale was produced by female "brewsters," while poorer women might eke out their income in one of the two oldest female professions by taking in other people's washing, or by turning tricks on the bluntly named "Gropecunt Lane."

But Norwich's trade, and its significance, reached far beyond its city walls. Its situation—an average of three days' ride across flat ground from London—meant that the city was in constant contact, economically, politically, and socially, with the capital. Bulky goods, however, could be transported more quickly and cheaply by water than by road, and Norwich's position on a navigable river just twenty miles from the seaport of Yarmouth gave it easy access not only to other ports on England's eastern coast, but also to trading posts in Europe and beyond, via Calais, the Low Countries, and the Baltic. The sophistication and variety of the city's shops, and of the laden stalls in the great rectangular market beneath the shadow of the castle, testified to the appetite of Norwich's consumers for the rarefied products of international trade—Mediterranean almonds, dates, and raisins; a piquant array of costly spices, including cinnamon, ginger, aniseed, and cumin; medical unguents such as aloe oil and calamine; and paper and wax of the finest quality—as well as the less esoteric commodities of Swedish iron and Latvian timber.

Once these cargoes had been unloaded, the ships that had carried them filled their hulls with the finest wares that Norwich and its hinterland had to offer—especially a woollen cloth that took its name, worsted, from a village twelve miles northeast of the city. Worsted was a versatile fabric that did not require fulling (the process of beating woollen textiles in water with soap or fine clay and then stretching them on "tenterhooks" to dry, to give the cloth a felted finish). As a result, it was less expensive to manufacture, and could be competitively priced even when it was sheared and pressed to a luxuriously glossy sheen. Worsted cloths were made in the villages of northern Norfolk, and increasingly in Norwich itself; they could then be sold for finishing elsewhere, or dyed in the city with imported pigments such as woad, an intense blue, or madder, a brilliant red. Thousands of such cloths were distributed across England and the Continent, driving forward the remarkable commercial success of the region from which they came.

But wool was not the only source of wealth for this part of East Anglia. Fertile Norfolk soils produced enough grain to supply the lucrative export trade, as well as feeding the urban markets on their doorstep. And the sea was as abundant as the land: fourteenth-century Norwich fishmongers piled their stalls high with cockles, crabs, eels, oysters, cod, sole, plaice, and whelks, while Yarmouth fishermen dominated the national trade in herring, a staple food that assumed particular significance during the six weeks of Lent, when the eating of meat was prohibited by the Church. The preservation of herring—as of other types of fish, meat, butter, and cheese— required enormous quantities of salt, which was not only imported from the Continent but produced locally, by evaporating seawater in large shallow pans. With such a range of opportunities in agriculture, fishing, shipping, manufacturing, trade, crafts, and commerce, the region's economy was vibrant in its diversity.

All in all, there were few better places to be, for those with the drive and determination to improve their lot, than Norfolk in the late fourteenth century. Here the double effect of the Black Death was laid bare in pitiless intensity, as the devastation it caused cleared a path for the ambitions of those who survived. The city of Norwich suffered unimaginably horrifying losses: probably two-thirds of its inhabitants perished, leaving a population of less than eight thousand where almost twenty-five thousand people had once lived. But while some other towns languished in economic depression after the plague, Norwich responded with extraordinary dynamism. It may already have been England's second most populous city in the early fourteenth century; it certainly became so during the fifteenth, in the process overtaking the wealthy regional centres of York in the north and Bristol in the southwest. Norwich was now the hub of one of the most prosperous counties in England. Norfolk men found that they could make their way in the world not only as tradesmen, craftsmen, and merchants, but also as soldiers and administrators, lawyers and priests.

But what we do not know—despite all the details that can be traced of their professions, their politics, and the practice of their religion—is how these people felt about their lives. In this crucial respect, the sources are opaque. The problem does not lie in the volume of evidence: in fact, the sheer number of records produced by the government of late medieval England is overwhelming, even without taking into account innumerable legal deeds and wills written by individual families, or the great contemporary works of scholars, chroniclers, and poets, from Gower and Langland to Chaucer and Lydgate. But in none of these texts can voices be heard speaking for themselves in private, without the constraints of technical form or the consciousness of a public readership. There is a void in the sources between the arid impersonality of formal administrative records and the melodramatic accounts of chroniclers writing for self-consciously moral or political ends, and as a result it is impossible to establish with any certainty what even the most eminent figures in medieval society—monarchs, nobles, and prelates—thought about their own experiences. Their characters remain in shadow, for the most part unknown and unknowable. In the case of less-exalted men and women, evidence even of their actions can be difficult to find and harder to interpret.

Small wonder, then, that the people of the Middle Ages have so often seemed like alien beings, so full of contradictions as to be almost incomprehensible. "The men of that time," the great historian Johan Huizinga wrote, "always oscillate between the fear of hell and the most naïve joy, between cruelty and tenderness, between harsh asceticism and insane attachments to the delights of this world, between hatred and goodness, always running to extremes."[12] But then, how would people of the twenty-first century appear to the eyes of posterity, if they were to be judged on the evidence of their legislation and litigation, a handful of novels and some tabloid newspaper headlines?

Miraculously, there is a single great exception to the rule that the inner lives of medieval men and women are irretrievably lost from view. Just five collections of private letters survive from fifteenth-century England. Their rarity makes all of them invaluable, but four are so limited in scale that they can offer only isolated glimpses of their authors' lives. But the fifth—a collection known as the Paston Letters—is unique in its depth and range. This astonishing archive—the earliest great collection of private correspondence in the English language—contains more than a thousand documents, written by three generations of a single family over a period of seventy years. They lived at Paston village in Norfolk: this trail of paper leads back to our beginning, at the door of Paston church. The family claimed, loudly and forcefully, that they had bestowed their name on the village as lords of the manor there; it was one of their number who diverted the road to the north of the churchyard to afford their grand home greater privacy. But the Pastons' claim stood the truth on its head: in fact, they took their name from the place where they had worked the land for generations in quiet obscurity. Like so many others in late medieval Norfolk, they were peasant farmers made good in the aftermath of the plague, an ambitious nouveau riche family striving to establish themselves in a world of cutthroat snobbery and vicious power struggles.

Extraordinarily, the chance survival of these letters opens a doorway into the Pastons' lives. At a distance of more than five hundred years, their individual voices still have the immediacy of an overheard conversation. They are people like us—husbands and wives, parents and children, friends and enemies—even if the world in which they lived is dramatically different. And the Pastons were far more than passive observers of their times. In the turbulent arena of fifteenth-century politics, they fought their own battles in the attempt to leave their humble origins behind and so secure their place in history.

This is their story.

a wise man
of the law

PASTON VILLAGE, NORFOLK. 1400. Against the immense East Anglian sky stood the imposing silhouette of a newly built church, its flint walls bearing witness to the prosperity, as well as the piety, of those who worshipped there. Beyond the churchyard lay a settlement of smallholdings, with barns, byres, and sturdy timber-framed houses of two or three rooms under roofs of thatched straw, their wattle-and-daub walls coated in plaster and lime. Their inhabitants farmed the open fields to the south, where rippling grain grew in the light soil, with wheat and rye sown each winter, and oats and barley in the spring. Among their number was a "good plain husbandman" named Clement, who took his surname, Paston, from the place where he lived.

Clement Paston was a peasant farmer, now in settled middle age, who held some arable land and "a little poor watermill running by a little river." That was the sum total of his estate; "other livelihood nor manors had he none, there nor in none other place." He was a careful man who devoted himself unstintingly to the relentless and sometimes back-breaking labour required to make his living from the land. The single surviving document describing his life tells how he "went at one plough both winter and summer, and he rode to mill on the bare horseback with his corn under him, and brought home meal again under him." After the harvest each year, he drove his cart the fifteen miles or so down the coast to the village of Winterton to sell his grain, "as a good husbandman ought to do."[1] Perhaps it was at Winterton market, almost a quarter of a century earlier, that he had met a young woman named Beatrice Goneld, whose family lived at Somerton, less than a mile away. Clement and Beatrice married, and in 1378 Beatrice gave birth to their only surviving child, a son named William.

At a distance of more than six hundred years, there is little else that can be said about the lives of Clement and Beatrice Paston. But the fact that these few details survive renders this ordinary couple extraordinary: most people of their time and class have left no trace in the written records that would allow even the sketchiest outline of their life stories to be drawn. So much remains that we cannot know about their characters, their relationship, their emotions, or their experiences, but one conclusion can be reached with confidence: Clement and Beatrice were determined to do everything they could to give their son greater opportunities than they had ever had.

Clement himself had been born under the looming shadow of the Black Death, only a few years after the plague had struck England's shores. Like so many of his generation, he resolved to seize with both hands the opportunities that the suffering of millions had opened up for those who survived. In 1381, as a young man and a new father, he also shared the violent anger that convulsed southeastern England at the blatant injustice of the poll tax and all that it represented. He was careful not to put his own life and his family's future in serious jeopardy by embroiling himself in Geoffrey Litster's occupation of Norwich, or in the rebels' battle with Bishop Despenser's army, which raged almost on his own doorstep at North Walsham; but there were other, smaller-scale demonstrations of protest and resistance. In many cases, outrage at the great landowners' attempt to protect their privileges and power at the peasantry's expense was directed at tangible representations of lordly authority. Documents were seized from seigneurial archives and piled onto bonfires; as the parchment crumbled into ash, so too did the landlords' ability to prove that their control over their peasant tenants was rooted in law by custom and precedent. The two greatest landowners in the region, and therefore the chief targets of these conflagrations, were John of Gaunt, duke of Lancaster, the young king's eldest uncle, who held a string of valuable estates across the north of the shire, and the Abbey of St. Benet's Hulme, a wealthy monastic foundation ten miles east of Yarmouth. Records of their local manor courts were burned in villages all over northeastern Norfolk, and Clement Paston was one of those who helped to hurl the vellum rolls on to the fires.[2]

Ironically, of course, these were radical actions in defence of utterly conventional aspirations. Clement was not seeking to overturn the social order but to climb into its upper ranks, or at least to achieve a financial position from which his son, William, might have a chance of doing so. Clement's diligence and acumen served him well—he probably ended up farming as much as 100 or 120 acres of arable land—but his dream was that his son should not have to follow in his footsteps behind the plough. If William's hands ever bore calluses, his father hoped it would be by the rubbing of a quill pen on his writing fingers, not by the weight of a scythe in his palm.

Education—then, as now—was the key to social mobility. Given hard-won access to schooling, a bright boy from a humble background might carve out a career for himself as a priest, a merchant, an administrator, or a lawyer. The results could be spectacular. William de la Pole was a merchant from the east Yorkshire port of Hull in the mid-fourteenth century who made a fortune in wine, wool, and war loans; his own origins were so obscure that even his parents' names are unknown, but he died a knight and a wealthy landowner, while his son rose so high in royal favour that Richard II created him earl of Suffolk. And the political and ecclesiastical talents of de la Pole's near contemporary Simon Langham took him from modest beginnings in the Rutland village with which his family shared its name to successive appointments as abbot of Westminster, treasurer of England, archbishop of Canterbury, and cardinal at the papal curia.

If William Paston were to have any hope of emulating these men's meteoric success, he would first of all need to learn how to read and write. Many children learned their ABCs at the knee of their parish priest, or at home, as more and more parents acquired a modicum of basic literacy. Writing with a sharpened quill on parchment or paper, however, was a technical skill that required specialist instruction; and any future professional advancement would depend on mastery of Latin, the formal language of the Church and the law. For tuition in "grammar," as the study of Latin was known, William would have to attend school. Such establishments were springing up in increasing numbers across the country: some were small private businesses run by a master who taught a handful of boys in his own home; while others were formal institutions established by a wealthy patron, often a monastery or cathedral. Their pupils—boys from the age of eight or nine—were instructed in Latin syntax, grammar, and verse and prose composition. They also learned the basics of French, the language of aristocratic society since the Norman Conquest three centuries earlier, which was now being superseded by English in everyday use even among the highest social classes, but which remained essential for the practice of trade, diplomacy, and law. For the most part, teaching was conducted orally, with emphasis on rote learning, and masters did not hesitate to use the birch on those whose attention wandered. The school day was a long one, eight or ten hours, and began early, soon after dawn: in this it was typical of working life in a world where the artificial light produced by candles, tapers, and torches was both dim and costly, and daylight had therefore to be exploited to the full.

The specific details of William's schooling are unknown; perhaps he studied at Bromholm Priory, a Cluniac foundation only a mile from his home at Paston, or perhaps he was sent to Norwich, almost twenty miles away. Either way, his education was expensive. Schools established for charitable purposes, offering free places, were not unknown in the late fourteenth century—Winchester College, for example, was founded in 1382 to provide a free education for seventy pupils—and were increasingly common in the fifteenth. But William's was not one of them, and Clement had to support him from the family's limited income. School fees were typically three shillings a year, but an additional and much more burdensome charge was levied for board and lodging, bringing the annual cost up to almost two pounds—probably half of Clement's yearly earnings. Under the circumstances, it seems hardly surprising that he struggled to find the cash: "often he borrowed money to fund him to school," the surviving account of Clement's life remarks.[3]

Given the sacrifices his parents had made, it was fortunate that William displayed both a promising intellect and a prodigious work ethic. As a result, when the time came for him to leave the schoolroom for more specialised training, Clement found a ready source of financial help close to home. Beatrice's brother Geoffrey Goneld, or Somerton, as he now called himself after their family's home village, was a modestly successful local attorney with no children of his own, and when it was proposed that William should follow in his uncle's professional footsteps, Geoffrey agreed to help with the cost of the boy's legal tuition in London.

Even for a young man accustomed to the diversity and sophistication of Norwich, England's second city, the capital offered an experience of urban life on an unfamiliarly grand scale. London's forty thousand inhabitants were packed into a square mile encircled by Roman and medieval city walls that stretched from Ludgate in the west to Aldgate in the east, from Moorgate in the north down to the riverfront wharves that marked the city's southern limit. The Thames could be crossed by foot or on horseback at only one point, where London Bridge—a three-hundred-yard span borne on nineteen slender arches and lined, Rialto-like, with shops and houses—carried a constant stream of traffic to and from the inns, mansions, churches, and brothels of Southwark, a sprawling suburb on the river's south bank. Elsewhere, the murky, reeking waters were themselves a teeming thoroughfare for passengers ferried in bustling skiffs and for cargoes brought to the quays on lighters and barges from deep-hulled trading ships. Many of the galleys that supplied the city with wine, spices, linen, silks, velvets, and furs, before returning to sea packed with yard upon yard of English woollen cloth, belonged to merchants from Venice, Genoa, Florence, and Lucca, or the cities of the Hanseatic League in northern Germany. Other "aliens" among the capital's population included men and women from the Low Countries—Flanders, Brabant, Zeeland, and Holland—who were skilled in leatherworking, dyeing, brewing, and the manufacture of bricks, clocks, and spectacles. French voices could also be heard in London's streets, and the occasional Greek accent: the Effamatos brothers, for example, built a thriving business on their expertise in making delicate gold wire to adorn the luxurious fabrics worn by the wealthy.

The capital's skyline was dominated by two extraordinary buildings. Near Ludgate in the west stood the vast cathedral of St. Paul's, one of the largest churches in Europe, its lead-covered steeple soaring almost five hundred feet into the city skies; and in the east, not far from Aldgate, the massive fortifications of London's royal palace, the Tower, rose from the riverfront. Its square Norman keep—nicknamed the "White Tower" because of the luminescent whitewash on its ninety-foot ragstone walls—had already kept guard over the capital for more than three hundred years. In between these two imposing edifices, representing the interlinked forces of church and state, lay a city of extremes. The town houses of well-to-do merchants and rich gentlemen were havens of peace and luxury, timber-framed halls rising from vaulted stone undercrofts built around small courtyards and gardens full of fruit and flowers, their chambers furnished with featherbeds, fine tapestries, and Venetian glass. The majority of Londoners, however, had more modest aspirations: perhaps a shop front ten or twelve feet wide from which to sell their wares, with truckle beds stored in a single room above—comforts for which the city's poorest inhabitants, crowded into the narrowest of alley tenements, would have been truly grateful. The wealthy enjoyed the use of private wells and cesspits, while the less well-off shared communal conduits and privies, and emptied refuse of every kind into the shallow open drains running down the middle of the streets. The city corporation made repeated efforts to compel householders to keep the frontage of their homes clean and sanitary ("no one shall throw dung into the king's highway, or before the house of his neighbour," ran one stern decree), and to prevent pigs escaping from urban backyards to scavenge for waste in the streets; but the very repetition of these ordinances testifies to their inadequacy.[4]

All in all, to a newcomer's eye, London was a noisy, restless, hectic place, full of promise and threat in equal measure. One such outsider is the protagonist of a contemporary satirical poem, "London Lickpenny," in which a countryman visits the capital to bring a complaint to the king's law courts, only to be baffled, bruised, and bewildered by the hurly-burly of the city. Finding that he is too poor to secure food, drink, transport, or the justice for which he came, he retreats to his rural home with a mournful refrain: "for lack of money I might not speed."[5] There is no way of knowing whether William Paston found his first experiences of London equally unsettling, or whether this ambitious and driven young man took the squalor and the glamour of the capital in his stride. Either way, the city itself was not his principal destination: like the narrator of "London Lickpenny," he was headed for Westminster, a mile and a half outside the city walls to the southwest, where the central courts of justice sat.

Westminster was a rich suburb, home to about two thousand inhabitants, which had grown up around the palace and abbey church established by the last Anglo-Saxon king, Edward the Confessor, in the 1040s. Edward's church—known as the "west minster" to distinguish it from St. Paul's to the east—had been replaced in the mid-thirteenth century by a new cathedral built to a sublimely elegant design in the Gothic style, in which the body of the dead king, now declared a saint, was laid in a dazzling shrine elaborately adorned with gold and jewels. His palace still stood, but in extended form: the largest great hall ever built in England—a colossal space 240 feet long and almost 70 feet wide—was constructed there at the end of the eleventh century on the orders of William Rufus, son of the Conqueror. When William Paston first set foot in Westminster Hall three hundred years later, the sight that met his gaze was awe-inspiring. The building had been freshly remodelled by Richard II: light flooded in through new windows, and richly painted statues of the king's royal predecessors stood in niches behind the dais on which the marble throne was set. Most impressively of all, the pillars that had previously punctuated the vast interior were gone, and a new roof of exquisite craftsmanship now enclosed the space without support from the ground. From the top of the walls along the hall's great length jutted huge timbers known as "hammer-beams," each one intricately carved to represent a horizontal angel with wings unfurled, and carrying the royal arms of Richard II impaled with those of Edward the Confessor. From the backs of these hovering angels sprang the series of pointed arches on which rested the span of the roof itself. It was a remarkable feat of engineering, and a breathtaking embodiment of royal power.

Here parliaments and councils met, and coronations were celebrated with days of banqueting. Here, too, sat the four great central law courts: the court of Common Pleas, which heard civil suits between the king's subjects, X on the west side of the hall; the King's Bench, the principal criminal court in the land, together with the Chancery, exercising equitable jurisdiction in cases that could not be heard under the common law, on the dais at the south end; and the Exchequer, which dealt with financial cases, in antechambers to the north. When all four courts were in session, the echoing space was filled with a cacophony of voices rising from the press of people to the magnificent new roof forty feet above their heads.

This was where William Paston came with his fellow students to sit in the "crib," the place reserved for lawyers-in-training to observe the courts in action. For the novice, legal proceedings could be a confusing spectacle. Until as recently as 1362, three languages had been in simultaneous use in the courts: judges and lawyers spoke in French, a language incomprehensible to the majority of English litigants; while the clerks filled long parchment rolls with notes taken exclusively in Latin. The Latin records remained, but now, at least, judges, lawyers, and litigants alike spoke in English, on the sensible grounds that the law would be better served and understood if it were conducted in a language comprehensible to all.

William and the other students were expected to take copious notes on the cases they witnessed, and on the explanatory asides that the judges from time to time aimed in their direction. But this practical observation of judicial process did not constitute a full-time course of study. The courts sat for only three hours each day, from eight to eleven in the morning, during four terms—Michaelmas, Hilary, Easter, and Trinity—divided by "vacations," when legal business was suspended for religious or practical reasons, with the most extensive breaks falling at Christmas and during the period of intensive agricultural activity (harvesting, stock-taking, rent-collecting, and accounting) in August and September. At the end of the courts' daily sessions the students left Westminster, wending their way through the prosperous shops and stalls that made small fortunes selling upmarket fare to the litigants and pilgrims who thronged the streets; the hungry plaintiff in "London Lickpenny" found that he could afford neither the "good bread, ale and wine" nor the "ribs of beef, both fat and fine" with which streetside hucksters tried to tempt him.[6]

The trainee lawyers took the road that led back in the direction of London via the suburb of "Farringdon Without," so called because the city ward of Farringdon—now distinguished as "Farringdon Within"—had expanded through Ludgate to create a thriving residential centre outside the city walls. Here, along Fleet Street and the Strand, were inns and taverns under signs such as the Sword and the Saracen's Head, and grand residences of bishops and noblemen (although the Savoy Palace, John of Gaunt's London home, was no longer among them, having been reduced to ashes by the rebel mob in 1381). Here, too, were the lawyers' lodgings, the four Inns of Court—Gray's Inn, Lincoln's Inn, and the Inner and Middle Temple. The Inns had first developed as a convenient form of accommodation in the capital for lawyers working away from home, and now provided a supplementary curriculum of lectures for the students who lived, two to a room, in their chambers. By the early fifteenth century they were also offering courses of instruction in the vacations between the legal terms. Students attended "readings" given by senior members of the Inn—seminars where statutes were discussed in detail, clause by clause, over a period of several weeks—and took part in "moots," mock trials in which they themselves had the chance to argue cases before their peers and their teachers. It was a rigorous and exacting training, and many students lacked the stamina or the acuity to last the course. William Paston, however, was not one of those who abandoned their studies. He had the sharp intelligence and voracious memory necessary to succeed as a lawyer at the top level; he also knew how much his parents and his uncle had invested in his education, and how great were the opportunities offered by a career in the law.

The English legal system—at this time probably the most centralised and sophisticated in Europe—derived its authority from the supreme power of the crown. The king's most fundamental responsibility was the defence of his realm and people, and he was therefore required to be a warrior, fighting to protect England's borders or even to extend them, wherever his rights or those of his kingdom had been infringed; but he also had to be a judge, shielding his subjects from violence and disorder by enforcing the law and offering justice to all. As a result, the courts at Westminster stood at the head of a network of royal officials that reached into every corner of English society. In theory, then, the power of the law was all-encompassing— but the reality was dramatically different. England had no police force or standing army through which judgments given in royal courts could be directly enforced. Even had such a force existed, its deployment would have presented insuperable problems, since messages could travel only as fast as a man on a horse could carry them—on average, perhaps forty miles in a day. Difficulties of communication and transport, in a world without telephones, radio communication, cars, trains, or planes, meant that, in practice, governments could govern effectively only if some means of enforcement were available rapidly, on the spot, wherever and whenever required.

For that reason, it had been decreed in 1285 that every Englishman should "have in his house arms for keeping the peace," ranging from a horse and full armour for the rich, down to scythes, knives, and bows and arrows for the peasantry.[7] If a crime had been committed, the sheriff of the county, a local man appointed each year by the king to take responsibility for the enforcement of law in the shire, had the right to raise a "hue and cry" summoning the county posse—that is, the king's loyal subjects, armed with their swords, scythes, and bows—to arrest the malefactor. But crime, like the rest of life, was not always clear-cut, and justice could all too easily lie in the eye of the beholder. If a dispute arose in which both sides considered themselves the wronged party, then the provision that all law-abiding subjects should bear arms to keep the peace might precipitate a violent brawl, with each side claiming that they were trying to restrain or arrest the other.

If the king were to keep control of local law enforcement, he therefore had to rely on the support of powerful local intermediaries: the nobility and gentry, whose estates gave them not only wealth and status but also authority over the peasants who lived and worked on their lands. This authority— which contemporaries described as "lordship"—was partly economic, since tenants owed rents and services to their lord in return for the land they cultivated; partly social, since deference to superiors was a religious as well as a cultural obligation; and partly jurisdictional, since the lord of each manor had the right to hold a court through which he regulated the land transactions, agricultural techniques, and personal quarrels in which his tenants were involved. This direct control over people meant that, in any given region, it was the leading landowners who could raise men quickly and effectively to enforce royal commands. If this solved one problem, it also raised another, since landowners could raise men quickly and effectively for other purposes too. It was an inescapable fact of medieval life that the nobility and gentry had the capacity to use force for their own private ends as well as for the public good.

The king's ability to rule therefore depended on his ability to harness the power of his landed subjects to serve his government, something that—despite the popular caricature of the medieval robber baron—was surprisingly easy to achieve under normal political circumstances. If power depended on the possession of land, then the king's law—as the unique authority that guaranteed the security of landholding—had an overriding power of its own. All landowners needed the law to justify their possession of their estates; all landowners had a great deal to lose if order were allowed to disintegrate into anarchy. As a result, their power was the king's to command, a relationship in which political pragmatism merged seamlessly with their accepted duty of obedience to the anointed monarch. So long as the nobility and gentry were confident that the king would protect their interests by defending the realm from external attack and upholding the framework of law within it, they could get on with the important business of competing with one another for position and influence. Landownership brought with it endless possibilities for conflict—over title to estates, rights of inheritance, contested boundaries, competing jurisdictions, and so on, ad infinitum—and landowners of all ranks did not hesitate to turn to the courts if they felt their rights were under threat. Even if, as was often the case, disputes were eventually settled out of court by mediation, negotiation, or arbitration, the law invariably played some part in the process. The courts could be used to pressure an opponent to come to terms, or to validate a settlement once agreement had been reached. In this profoundly law-minded and litigious society, lawyers would never be short of opportunities to make money.

That much was certain: but the political world in which the newly qualified William Paston embarked on his legal career was much less secure. True enough, it was not difficult for the king to command the services of the nobility and gentry under normal political circumstances—but by the end of the fourteenth century, circumstances had not been normal for some time. The fearless belief in his own majesty that had enabled the boy king Richard II to defuse the threat of the rebel hordes at Smithfield in 1381 had not served him well in his attempt to govern England as a grown man. Richard had an imperious temper, and an acute aesthetic sensibility, but he utterly lacked the instincts of a politician. He failed to see that the authority of his crown was at its most potent when it was exercised with the cooperation of the great nobles of the realm. Instead, he interpreted the leading role that his magnates had taken in government during the years of his adolescence as a derogation of his royal rights and an illegitimate encroachment on his power. His reign was scarred by a series of bitter political conflicts, culminating in 1397 in a coup led by the king himself within his own kingdom, intending to rid himself of those magnates whom he now considered his mortal enemies, and to create a form of government which he could bend more readily to his autocratic will.

For two years, England was subjected to a regime based on fear and intimidation: "nobody dared to stand for the truth, or to say openly what they believed, because of the tyranny and malice of the king," one chronicler reported.[8] But in 1399, Richard's failure to understand the basis of his own power exposed him to the ultimate sanction. When his uncle John of Gaunt, duke of Lancaster, died in February of that year, Richard thought he saw the chance to remove a thorn from the royal flesh by destroying the greatest magnate family in the land. He disinherited Gaunt's son, Henry Bolingbroke, and seized the duchy of Lancaster for himself. But he did so without any kind of legal justification. It was the king's responsibility to guarantee the rule of law over all his subjects, and Richard had now trampled it deliberately and ostentatiously underfoot. What security could any of his subjects expect from such a dangerously capricious king? It was no accident that, when Bolingbroke began to muster support to defend his rightful inheritance, Englishmen did not rally to Richard's side. In August 1399, the king was taken prisoner by Bolingbroke's forces; a month later, now a captive in the Tower, he was compelled to resign his throne.

On 30 September, Henry Bolingbroke walked in solemn procession through the doors of the great hall at Westminster, his jewelled sword carried before him by one of his closest friends, the Norfolk knight Sir Thomas Erpingham. The wooden bars marking out the courts of King's Bench and Common Pleas and the benches on which the judges sat had been cleared away, and in their place the hall had been prepared as if for a parliament.

The royal throne was bedecked with cloth of gold—a precious fabric of silk interwoven with the finest gold thread—and before it sat the peers of the realm: bishops, dukes, earls, and lords. Behind them the throng was so great that it spilled out of the hall and into the courtyard beyond. There, shortly after midday, with the sun at its height, it was declared that Richard II had forfeited his crown. Henry Bolingbroke was acclaimed king in his royal cousin's place and, as the new Henry IV, took his seat on the shining throne to the echoing cheers of his subjects.

Henry's accession gave England an unnerving start to the new century. Richard had been the architect of his own fall, his authority fatally undermined by his own arbitrary rule, but the process by which he had been replaced was born of political expediency rather than constitutional legality. Henry's claim to the crown was by no means watertight, and the new Lancastrian regime was shaken by repeated rebellions, which were not halted by Richard's suspiciously convenient death in custody, at Pontefract Castle in Yorkshire, in February 1400. Nevertheless, the driving force behind the dramatic events of 1399 had been essentially conservative, aiming to safeguard the law from a king intent on overruling it—and in southeastern England, away from the main centres of revolt in the north and west, the change of government came as a relief from the tension and menace of Richard's last years.

In fact, it rapidly became clear that early fifteenth-century Norfolk was a particularly opportune place for a young lawyer to be seeking his fortune. The duke of Lancaster—who was now, of course, also the king—was the greatest landowner in the shire, and some of the region's gentry emerged as leading figures in the Lancastrian government, King Henry's friend Sir Thomas Erpingham prominent among them. And proximity to powerful political contacts was not the only potential benefit of William Paston's Norfolk roots. The county was populous and wealthy, and patterns of landholding there complex and fragmented. What more could a lawyer want than a place in which endless occasions for dispute arose among a large population with plenty of money to spend on litigation? William was not the only one to spot the opportunity: a contemporary petition to parliament complained of the excessive number of attorneys touting for business in Norfolk fairs and markets, persuading the gullible to go to court on the slightest pretext in the hope of securing large damages. The only beneficiaries, the petition protested, were the lawyers themselves, who ruined their hapless clients with their demands for fees and costs before their spurious cases had even come to judgment. The proposed solution to this social menace was to limit the number of licensed attorneys to a maximum of six in Norfolk and a further eleven in the city of Norwich, all to be chosen by the chief justices of the realm on the basis of their expertise and sober bearing. The scheme never came close to being adopted, but even if it had been taken more seriously, it would have done little to hamper William Paston's chances. Even in such an overpopulated legal world, he proved to be a lawyer of uncommon calibre.

His career began to take wing as the fifteenth century moved into its second decade—years during which the Lancastrian dynasty settled into its place on the throne, first under the tenacious but increasingly weary leadership of Henry IV, a man aged before his time by debilitating illness, and then, from 1413, in the unflinching grip of his son Henry V. This second Lancastrian monarch seemed intent on demonstrating that he was, in every facet of his rule, an exemplar of kingship. After two years during which he set his house in order in England, stamping his personal command on all aspects of government from the provision of local justice to the accounting of royal revenues at Westminster, he set out to revive the claim of his great-grandfather, Edward III, to the throne of France—a claim that had lapsed almost into irrelevance during the dark decades of political implosion at the end of the fourteenth century. Edward III's great victories at Crécy and Poitiers had faded into distant memory, but England still clung to footholds on French soil at Calais in the north, and around the great city of Bordeaux in the southwest. Now, in only five years between 1415 and 1420, English armies under Henry's command seized control of a vast swathe of northern France, reaching eastward beyond Paris and southward to the Loire.

In May 1420, the irresistible force of the English military position was acknowledged in the Treaty of Troyes, by which Henry married the French princess Catherine de Valois, and was recognised as heir to the throne of France after her father, the mentally unstable Charles VI. The treaty did not end the war: its terms were unacceptable to many Frenchmen, not least Charles VI's son, the disinherited dauphin. But what Henry's campaign did achieve, without question, was the removal of any lingering doubt about the legitimacy of Lancastrian rule in England. His great victory at Agincourt in 1415—won against the odds by an English army hungry and exhausted from seventeen days of forced march, and outnumbered by three to one—seemed to his subjects to offer conclusive proof of God's support for his kingship and his cause. From that moment on, they rallied to his vision of their country's destiny. So much so that, when Henry died of dysentery in France in August 1422, at the age of only thirty-five, there was not a whisper of dissent at the accession of the baby boy to whom his new French queen had given birth nine months earlier—a son whom Henry himself had never seen. Instead, the great lords of the realm committed themselves unhesitatingly to the defence of Henry's legacy in both England and France in the name of the infant Henry VI.

Back in Norfolk, a few hundred miles and a whole world of experience away from the bloodstained fields on which his countrymen were risking their lives in pursuit of the king's military ambitions, William Paston had committed his own future to the practice of the king's law—and was finding it extremely profitable to do so. His intelligence, his shrewd judgment, and his capacity for hard work recommended him to a growing circle of influential clients as the 1410s went on. By 1420, he had been retained as legal counsel in various capacities by the powerful city corporation of Norwich; by the bishop of Norwich, Richard Courtenay, one of Henry V's closest friends until he succumbed to dysentery at the siege of Harfleur in 1415; by the duke of Norfolk, a magnate whose East Anglian lands, confusingly, lay mainly in the county of Suffolk; and by the duchy of Lancaster, the private estate of the Lancastrian crown and the leading landholder in Norfolk itself. All the while, the number of lesser landowners for whom he acted as lawyer and trustee (or feoffee, to use the contemporary term) steadily increased. The widow of one such gentleman later told William of "the great trust that my lord had in you, making you one of his feoffees and also one of his attorneys, as for one of his best trusted friends."[9]

But it was not only on home ground that his résumé was beginning to look exceptionally impressive; he also won recognition at a national level. In 1418, at the age of forty, he was raised to the ranks of the sergeants-at-law, a small group of elite lawyers practising in the central courts at Westminster. No longer a student observer scribbling notes in the crib, William now stood at the bar that marked out the dimensions of the court within the great expanse of Westminster Hall to plead his clients' cases, clad in the robes that distinguished the sergeants-at-law from their junior colleagues—a long gown of striped fabric, the shoulders covered by a short matching cape trimmed with white lamb's fleece, and on his head a neat white coif covering his hair and fastened under his chin. On this demanding stage, William shone. By 1423, it is obvious from the legal Year Book—a professional work of reference in which records were kept of the year's most significant cases—that he was one of the five most prominent and influential lawyers then active in the court of Common Pleas.

William's workload was diverse and intensely challenging. Lawsuits that reached a hearing at Westminster could be fiendishly complex; sergeants were required not only to master intricate legal arguments but also to negotiate the political hinterland that lay behind the bare bones of each case. William's success therefore depended on his rhetorical agility and an adroit sense of diplomacy as well as on his expertise in the interpretation of statute and case law. Pleading a suit was always in some sense a performance, even when the issues at stake turned on points of law too obscure for the layperson to grasp with any confidence. But one extraordinary case in which William was involved in the summer of 1423 became a piece of pure judicial theatre—and a reminder that the legal system within which he worked was rooted in a society where force might play an unexpectedly public role in the pursuit of justice.

In that year William agreed to represent a knight named Sir Peter Tilliol in a complaint against the powerful northern lord Henry Percy, earl of Northumberland. The suit—which alleged that the manor of Torpenhow in Cumberland, currently in the earl's hands, rightfully belonged to Tilliol— would normally have been resolved by summoning a jury of twelve local men to adjudicate between the two sides' claims on the basis of their local knowledge. For some reason, which, frustratingly, the surviving records do not explain, it was decided that the case should instead be determined by combat between two "champions," one representing each of the litigants. Trial by battle was an ancient practice, which entrusted the difficult task of deciding guilt to divine rather than human judgment. By the fifteenth century, however, it had almost entirely fallen out of use, certainly for cases of disputed land ownership such as this one. As a result, the imposing ceremonial that attended a judicial battle was already so antique and unfamiliar that the court found itself uncertain of some of the finer points of detail. Should the plain red staff, or "baston," which was carried with a red shield into the court behind each champion, have a knob at one end? One of the judges thought so, but when he commented to that effect, "there was no reply," and the question remained unresolved.[10]

Nevertheless, the main outline of the ritual was clear enough for the case to proceed. On the first day of the hearing, at the judges' command, each of the two champions placed five pennies into the fingers of a glove. Then, using their right hands with their arms uncovered to the elbow, they threw the gloves into the court. Once the challenge to combat had been laid by this symbolic throwing down of the gauntlet, the two men retired from the hall, but returned the next day, "bare-headed and ungirdled, well-hosed and without shoes."[11] They climbed over the bar at which the sergeants-at-law stood; one was directed to the western side of the court, the other to the east. William Paston and his opposite number, the earl of Northumberland's lawyer, were called upon to declare that the champions were ready to fight, and that there was no legal reason to delay the duel. Once they had done so, battle was awarded to take place three days later. The champions were not to meet or communicate in the meantime; one was sent westward to Westminster Abbey, the other east to St. Paul's Cathedral, to pray that God would give victory to the rightful claimant.

On the appointed day, William appeared in court with Tilliol's champion, who stood at the bar dressed, as was traditional, in red leather over his armour (in order that, according to a contemporary treatise, if he were to be injured, "his adversary shall not lightly espy his blood," and thereby gain an advantage by playing on the injury, "for in all other colours blood will lightly be seen").[12] Once they were ready, Northumberland's champion was summoned into the hall. The order was given three times, but neither the earl nor his man appeared. The court therefore judged that Northumberland had defaulted, and the disputed estate was awarded to Tilliol. A man of the earl's influence was unlikely simply to abandon his case, and his non-appearance seems certain to have been the result of a private settlement negotiated behind the scenes, although there is now no way of reconstructing the substance of the discussions. The judicial proceedings may well therefore have been an exercise in brinkmanship, with each side hoping to press the other into some form of capitulation. Behind the public front of William's serenely dignified performance in court, all his legal expertise and his political experience had been deployed in a race against time to secure the best possible deal for his client—and the formal confirmation of Tilliol's right to the land with which the case ended suggests that he succeeded.

The fact that William acted for the plaintiff in probably the last case of English land law ever tried by combat—even if the duel itself did not ultimately take place—is a curiosity among the many distinctions of what was fast becoming a remarkable legal career. In 1426, he was appointed a king's sergeant, one of a select group from among the sergeants-at-law who were retained by the crown to act in the Westminster courts for the king himself.

Those who received this professional distinction could confidently expect in due course to be raised to the bench (a phrase that had not yet lost its literal meaning, since the long form on which the judges sat was elevated on a platform from which they could survey the workings of the court). William was no exception to the rule. In 1429, at the age of fifty-one, he exchanged his sergeant's striped gown for a judge's red robe, covered with a miniver-trimmed red cloak pinned at the right shoulder. He was now one of the six justices who presided in Westminster Hall over the court of Common Pleas.

William had reached the top of his profession: the peasant's son from Paston village was now one of the king's most senior judicial representatives. Neither his parents nor his uncle had lived to see this triumph, but they had survived long enough to know that he was flourishing in the career on which they had made it possible for him to embark. Beatrice died in 1409, and her brother, Geoffrey, seven years later. Clement Paston had at least seen his son raised to the rank of sergeant-at-law before he died in his sixties—an old man, by contemporary standards—in 1419. William's only remaining relative was his paternal aunt, Clement's sister Martha; but in any case his professional success was distancing him further and further from the life that previous generations of his family had known in the villages of north Norfolk.

William was now a rich man, earning money on a scale that gave him a standard of living far removed from his father's experience, riding to mill "on the bare horseback with his corn under him." A labourer or peasant farmer working on the land in the favourable economic conditions of the fifteenth century might earn something of the order of three pounds a year. When Clement Paston died, he left charitable bequests—mainly to the church at Paston, where he was buried at Beatrice's side—which came to a total of not much more than one pound.[13] A minor member of the gentry, meanwhile, might find himself with a disposable income of perhaps twenty pounds a year. William, on the other hand, received an annual sum of more than seventy pounds for his work as a justice of Common Pleas, to replace the lucrative fees from the landowners, religious institutions, and town corporations by whom he had previously been retained as legal counsel. But wealth alone was not enough to establish him securely in the aristocratic circles in which he now moved: for that, he needed to use his money to buy himself an estate.

Landownership was the defining mark of a gentleman, but it was landownership of a particular kind that counted; simply accumulating farmland of the type that Clement Paston had held would not do. Aristocratic landholders owned whole manors—that is, estates that brought with them the jurisdictional rights of lordship. Such estates varied hugely in size and form: a manor might extend over one village or several, or a single village might be made up of several manors or parts of manors. Most of the land in each manor was allocated to peasant tenants in return for rents and services owed to the lord, but the rest—known as the demesne—was reserved for the lord's own use, whether to be cultivated directly by his servants and officials, or leased out for an annual cash sum. Often the lord maintained a residence—a manor house—on the estate, which might range from the modest to the grandiose; but sometimes the seigneurial buildings were no more than a rudimentary administrative centre. Whatever the nature of the manor's management and makeup, its defining characteristic was the authority that its lord exercised over the peasants who worked the land there.

The acquisition of estates of this kind would not be a straightforward business. Despite the massive population loss caused by the plague, competition for such properties remained fierce because of the status and influence they conferred on their owners. The increase in social mobility after the depredations of the Black Death meant that, for every gentry family that died out or mismanaged its affairs, there was a wealthy newcomer—or, more likely, several wealthy newcomers—waiting to snap up its lands. Even once a purchase had been secured, the new owner might still face further challenges. The political, social, and financial value of manorial land was such that no one would willingly relinquish any sort of a claim to its possession, and the heirs of whoever sold the property, or of those who had owned it in the past—even the distant past—might allege that they had been unlawfully deprived of their rights. Claims of this kind could embroil a purchaser for years in troublesome and costly litigation, and a particularly unwise or unlucky buyer, who failed to check the seller's title to the estate with sufficient care or who faced a particularly powerful challenger, might even lose the land altogether. The irony of the situation—that his professional success had now brought him to a point where he would have to confront the very difficulties that had been such a fruitful source of employment in his legal practice—cannot have been lost on a man as astute as William.

The residual power of lineage and inheritance, even in the face of lawful purchase, also presented rising professionals such as William with a further problem. Social mobility in late medieval England took place within a culture which publicly proclaimed that power, wealth, and status were inextricably linked with birth, however great the evidence to the contrary. In theory, gentlemen were born, not made, and land was handed down from generation to generation of irreproachably blue blood. In practice, of course, gentlemen were ever more frequently made rather than born. The trick was to cover the traces of such transactions as quickly and deftly as possible, in order that social appearances could be preserved by allowing new blood to be accepted as old. The Pastons themselves later took great pains to suppress the story of Clement Paston's labour on the land, not because it was inaccurate, but precisely because it was true. The single surviving account of his life, which makes his hard work sound so impressive to modern ears, was compiled in the middle of the fifteenth century by an anonymous enemy of the family to demonstrate that Clement's descendants had no right to the exalted social status they were attempting to claim. The document had a sarcastic title—"A Remembrance of the Worshipful Kin and Ancestry of Paston"—and a far from subtle theme: much of Clement's land, the author says, was "bond land"; his wife Beatrice was "a bond woman"; "and as for Geoffrey Somerton, he was bond also."[14] The word *bond* came from Old Norse, and had equivalents deriving from each of the other languages that had contributed to the formation of late medieval English—*serf* from Latin, *churl* from Old English, and *villein* from Old French. All four were equally unwelcome to Paston ears: a bondman, serf, churl, or villein was an unfree man, who could be regarded in some senses at least as the property of the lord of the manor on which he lived.

"Unfreedom" was an inherited, personal status that imposed onerous obligations, at least in theory. Unfree peasants were required to work on their lord's land as well as on their own holdings; they also had to pay for his permission to marry, to leave the manor, or even to send their sons to school. In practice, in a world changed forever by the plague, it was becoming much harder for lords to enforce their rights over their unfree tenants, who could now simply walk away from the manor of their birth to take advantage of the profusion of new opportunities elsewhere. In many cases, it was even becoming difficult to identify who was free and who was not. If Geoffrey Somerton, William's maternal uncle, was a bondman, for example, it did not stop him pursuing a career as a local attorney. Nevertheless, the allegation remained a serious threat to the Paston family's standing or "worship" (a term suffused with significance for contemporaries, meaning the qualities characteristic of gentility and the respect in which someone who displayed those qualities was held). It might also be a dangerous weapon in the hands of a resourceful opponent, since unfreedom brought with it specific and potentially devastating legal disabilities. Bondmen technically had no right of access as litigants to the king's courts, for example, and no right to exercise jurisdiction in a manor court. The charge that they had servile blood in their veins might therefore be used to challenge the Pastons' right to hold manorial land, and with it their right to count themselves gentlemen.

Despite these myriad complications, William Paston proved more than equal to the task he faced. He set about building up a landed estate with the same combination of perceptive intelligence and ruthless efficiency that had served him so well in his legal career. Most of the properties he bought over a twenty-year period from the late 1410s onward were concentrated in his home region of northern Norfolk, not far from the land he inherited from his father and his uncle. Paston itself was not a manor in its own right, but William began to buy up as much land as he could in and around the village, with the intention of creating a new manor there to serve as the ancestral home of his dynasty. The whispers that he came of villein stock might be silenced, after all, if he could assert his lordship over villeins of his own. It was an ambitious project, politically as well as practically, but by no means an unrealistic one. William had the contacts to help him find manors to buy, the expertise to see purchases safely through, and the influence to defend his new possessions. By the early 1440s, he had succeeded in accumulating estates that brought him a landed income of about £250 a year—a sum of which his father could scarcely have dreamed, and which propelled William into the ranks of the most substantial landholders in the county.

But success, as always, came at a price. Competition among the Norfolk gentry and would-be gentry—men like William himself—was intense, and he had to fight every inch of the way. Each step forward for William inevitably represented a reverse for someone else, whether a reluctant seller or a rival buyer. Land purchases could be acrimonious affairs, and it was easy to make enemies. Given the fundamental importance of landholding to a family's standing, and the prodigious memory required to keep track of hereditary claims through complex genealogical descents, such antagonisms could become feuds lasting for generations. It took William ten years, for example, to complete his purchase of the north Norfolk manor of East Beckham, and the hostilities provoked by the saga dogged his family for decades more. The surviving documents from William's extended campaign to buy the property give us only fleeting glimpses of the protagonists' personalities, and little sense of the debilitating strain to which they must have been subjected as the dispute dragged on. But even in unembellished outline, the battle for East Beckham shows how tortuous the ascent of a self-made man into the world of the landed gentry could prove to be, and how dubious the tactics to which he might be forced to resort.

The estate was offered for sale in 1434 by a widow named Joan Mariot. Her husband had made money in the fishing industry at Cromer on the north Norfolk coast, but his aspirations to gentility had not removed him from the dangers of his trade; he drowned "by tempest of the sea," and Joan was forced to sell off land in the attempt to clear his debts.[15] East Beckham was well placed for Paston interests—it lay a little more than ten miles to the west of Paston village, but only a mile from Gresham, a valuable manor that William had acquired seven years earlier—and he immediately made Joan Mariot an offer for the property. However, a rival bid came just as quickly from a gentleman named Edmund Winter, from whose family the Mariots had originally bought the manor twenty years before.

Edmund Winter's father, William, like William Paston a generation later, was a lawyer from a poor family who made himself a fortune and used his money to buy estates in northern Norfolk. After his death, East Beckham was sold to the Mariots to pay for religious bequests in Winter's will. Such sales were not uncommon: even the most ambitious and apparently worldly of characters might decide at the eleventh hour that the imminent fate of their souls in purgatory should take precedence over the financial security of the family they were about to leave behind. But the loss of the manor rankled with Winter's son, whose prospects were on the slide by the early 1430s. As Edmund struggled to defend his family's interests, he did not forget that the estate had once been (and, he felt, should still be) Winter property. At least, however, he had the consolation that East Beckham in the hands of a Cromer fisherman posed little threat to what remained of the Winters' local influence. The possibility that the manor might now be taken over by Judge William Paston—whose star was rising as rapidly as Winter's was falling—was an entirely different matter. Edmund became so desperate that, when it became clear at the end of 1434 that his bid to buy the property back had failed, he took it by force, installing some of his servants there to hold the manor in his name and instructing the peasantry to pay rent to no one but him.

Winter seized the estate before its sale to William Paston had been completed. It was Joan Mariot who would therefore have to sue for recovery of a manor that was still technically hers—but William offered to act for her in the courts, on the understanding that his costs would be offset against the purchase price he had already agreed to pay. The lawsuit was labyrinthine, and despite William's eminence and expertise, Edmund Winter scored some early successes. The Mariots' frustration with Winter—and perhaps William's too—spilled over in the course of proceedings in Chancery in 1436: "another so great a forswearer," they declared, "nor so damnable a slanderer, nor so shameless usual languager, visager and contriver of untrue, feigned and slanderous tales and matters as he is, was never in his days of his degree in that shire."[16]

The case was still not resolved when Joan Mariot died in 1441. Her son John rapidly realised that, even if the final verdict were to go his way, virtually all of the money his family desperately needed to raise by selling East Beckham would now be eaten up by William's costs for seven years of litigation. Mariot saw no alternative but to back out of the sale. It cannot have been an easy choice—but once the decision was taken, the battle lines were immediately redrawn. Mariot suddenly found that he had a new and, on the face of it, deeply unlikely ally in the person of his opponent, Edmund Winter. Despite his success in spinning out the lawsuit thus far, Winter knew that his claim to the manor was technically weak; his overriding priority all along had been to protect his wider interests by stopping William from taking possession of the estate, and he stood a much better chance of doing so if he now backed John Mariot's decision to keep it for himself. However, after seven years in court, William was not about to let go without a fight. His own claim was shaky to say the least, given that the purchase agreement had never taken legal effect. On the other hand, he did hold all the title deeds—which the Mariots had given to him when he agreed to represent them against Winter—and had no intention of returning them. He dug in his heels, and brought to bear all the political and judicial influence he could muster. He managed to secure custody of the manor in 1442, and finally, in July 1444, nearly ten years after his first attempt to buy it, William's title to the land was confirmed by the courts.

Edmund Winter and John Mariot must have thought, when they first joined forces, that the battle would be theirs. And it should have been, had technical points of law been the deciding factor. But they had reckoned without William Paston's determination and his blazing ambition. As an outstanding lawyer and now a royal judge, he knew that litigation was as much a political process as a legal one, and he was prepared to use all the means at his disposal—both inside and outside the courtroom—to achieve his goals. Other disputes in which he was involved are not as well documented as the fight for East Beckham, but the scraps of surviving evidence confirm that he was tough and totally uncompromising in defence of his own interests. A Norwich widow named Juliana Herberd alleged that, in order to get his hands on her property, William had her imprisoned for three years "in the pit within the castle of Norwich in great mischief, in so much that she had not but a pint of milk in ten days and ten nights and a farthing loaf."[17] Herberd clearly believed that William was pitiless; another opponent during the 1420s, a former soldier named Walter Aslak, also found him to be a relentless adversary, claiming that William reneged on an arbitration agreement and "broke his faith and his troth" by securing a court order for Aslak's imprisonment.[18]

Whatever the rights and wrongs of these cases, which are now impossible to recover, the ruthlessness of William's tactics is manifest. This unyielding approach was an essential element of his success, both in the courtroom and as a new player in the competitive world of the Norfolk gentry. But, by his own lights at least, his refusal to compromise did not mean that he lacked scruples or a sense of personal morality. Most of the information that has survived about the Herberd and Aslak cases comes from petitions submitted in the course of judicial hearings, complete with legal jargon and overheated rhetoric, but William also mentioned the disputes in a private letter written in the spring of 1426, when both cases were in full flood. His comments are little more than a brief aside, but even so they give pause for thought about the Machiavellian colours in which he was painted by his opponents. In his letter, William talked of his "three adversaries"—Herberd, Aslak, and a priest named John Wortes, who was harassing Bromholm Priory, the monastic foundation close to Paston village, by claiming to have been appointed prior there himself. "I have not trespassed against none of these three, God knows," William said, "and yet I am foully and noisingly vexed with them to my great unease, and all for my lords' and friends' matters and not for my own."[19]

In other words, he had become involved in all three cases not on his own account, but in his professional capacity as a lawyer. This was certainly true in the Wortes case: William was the priory's legal representative, and became personally embroiled as a result when Wortes, who was something of a loose cannon, not only began proceedings to have William excommunicated, but also claimed that his own real name was Paston and that he was William's cousin. ("God defend that any of my poor kin should be of such governance as he is of," William said feelingly.)[20] But the same was also true of Aslak and Herberd. Aslak's hostility was rooted in the fact that William represented Norwich Priory against him in a dispute over the right of appointment to a local benefice; and Juliana Herberd's lands were caught up in a lawsuit in which, again, William was acting on behalf of someone else. Not only that, but William clearly believed that he had done nothing wrong in the course of these disputes, either legally or morally. Of course, his healthy confidence in the rectitude of his own position did not necessarily mean that his conduct was beyond reproach, but the gulf between his perspective and that of his opponents is an indication of the complexities of a world where the personal, the professional, and the political could not easily be distinguished, let alone separated.

The fact that the William of the 1426 letter—weary at the harassment he felt he was enduring, and eloquent in his irritation—is so much more human than the villain of his enemies' petitions emphasises the difficulties of drawing conclusions from evidence that is fragmentary at best. The voices of later generations of Pastons speak clearly in their letters, but very little of William's correspondence has survived: only seven letters in all, six of them concerning his legal affairs, and one specifying the masonry he required for a mill he was building at Mundesley near Paston village.[21] His domestic life has left so few traces in the existing documents that it is touching to find, among his legal papers, a note in his own handwriting of a recipe for a "wholesome drink of ale" given to him by a Norfolk gentlewoman named Sybilla, Lady Boys. Aromatic herbs, including sage, rosemary, thyme, cloves, mace, and spikenard, should be placed in a bag inside each barrel of ale, Sybilla told him, together with "a new-laid hen's egg" which would "keep the ale from souring."[22] Sybilla Boys was a friend, but by the 1420s there was another, much more important woman in William's life: his wife, Agnes.

As a young man, William seems to have made no attempt to marry, preferring instead to dedicate himself to his career. Like everything else he did, that was a matter of calculation. Marriage negotiations among the landed classes were an elaborate ritual, a mating dance choreographed on the basis of intricate computations concerning the relative merits of money, land, influence, status, and sentiment. Amid the politics and the pitfalls, one conclusion was inescapable: a wealthy lawyer and landowner in his forties could secure an infinitely better marriage than a legal student from a poor background in his twenties. Perhaps, too, it was no accident that William remained a bachelor while his parents were still alive. However close he was to Clement and Beatrice, however grateful for their love and support, his own transformation into a gentleman could not embrace them retrospectively—at least, not to the extent of obliterating their past lives in the way that his education and his career had enabled him to do for himself—and the chasm between his peasant roots and his new identity would be mercilessly exposed by the inevitably public nature of a society wedding.

In the event, William waited so long that, when he did finally become a bridegroom, he was the same age as his new father-in-law and more than twice as old as his young bride. In 1420, at the age of forty-two—two years after his promotion to the rank of sergeant-at-law, and only twelve months or so after the death of his father—William finally felt ready to commit himself to family life. Now, at last, after two decades of single-minded devotion to his work, he had the wealth and connections to make an excellent match. His new wife was the elder daughter of a knight named Sir Edmund Barry. The family owned rich estates in the southeastern counties of Hertfordshire and Cambridgeshire as well as in Norfolk, and Barry had no male heirs to follow in his footsteps. Under the common law, an eldest son would inherit everything, unless his father took steps to put estates in trust for his younger siblings; but in the absence of sons, daughters had equal rights to a share of the inheritance. As co-heiress of her father's estates, Agnes therefore brought William three valuable manors; and at more than twenty years his junior, she could also be expected to produce the heirs who would secure the future of the Paston name. William was not disappointed: their first child, a son named John, was born at six in the morning on 10 October 1421.

Beyond these bare facts, we are left with no more than tantalising hints about the nature of William's relationship with his new bride. None of his letters to his wife has survived, and only one written by Agnes to William. That one, at least—so far as it is possible to tell from a single short note, scribbled in haste, years into their marriage—seems to confirm the impression Agnes gave in later life of being matter-of-fact, unromantic, and thoroughly practical. William was away in London, which gave Agnes the opportunity to ask him to do some shopping for her. In this case it was gold thread she wanted: "I pray you do buy for me two pipes of gold," she wrote, before adding news of her husband's fishponds ("Your stews do well").[23] Pragmatism rather than imagination in his young wife probably suited William well. There is no sign that any deep sentimental attachment developed between them, nor that either assumed that it should. Theirs was a functional bond founded on mutual respect and shared expectations—a practical partnership that proved enduring and fruitful. Over the next twenty years, Agnes gave birth to three more sons, Edmund, William, and Clement, and one daughter, Elizabeth. At least one more boy, Henry, died in childhood.

By the early 1440s, Judge William Paston—now in his sixties—had good reason to survey his achievements with satisfaction. While his father had "lived upon his land that he had in Paston, and kept thereon a plough all times in the year,"[24] William was building a manor house there, beside the flint church in which he had worshipped as a boy—a gracious residence fit for the new lord of the manor, complete with a spacious parlour and its own private chapel. In fact, it was William who now insisted that the road through the village should be diverted away from the church door, to afford this new home greater privacy. The one gamble this gifted, driven man had taken was the decision to wait until middle age before settling down to family life. His late marriage had brought him many advantages, but it also meant that his son and heir would still be a young man, without the weight of his father's hard-won experience, when he took his place as head of the family. It remained to be seen whether the gamble would pay off.

⅄

no will of them

in writing

ILLIAM PASTON'S DECISION to invest two decades in
his spectacularly successful career before marrying and
starting a family meant that his son was born into a different world from the one William himself had known in childhood. The villagers of Paston had limited horizons—literally so to the north, where the
fields gave way to sandy beaches stretching to the sea. But their experiences
were bounded just as clearly to the west and east by the markets at Cromer
and Winterton, and to the south by the metropolis of Norwich twenty miles
away. With the help of his parents and his uncle, William had been able to
reach beyond those limits; but his son John faced no such obstacles. The
Paston family estate, now supplemented by Agnes's share of the Barry
inheritance, included homes across northern Norfolk, a townhouse in
Norwich, and well-appointed rented accommodation in the capital, close to
the lawyers' Inns on Fleet Street between Westminster and the City. The
Paston children slept on featherbeds; they wore clothes of fine fabrics
trimmed with fur and lambskin; and they lived in a household staffed by
perhaps ten or fifteen servants, from estate manager to stable boy, chaplain
to cook.

John Paston had all the material advantages of birth that his father had
lacked, but William could not yet let go of his driving ambition: his own
father's life at the plough was still too fresh in the memory for the family's
position to be completely secure. He was determined that John's education

should mark him out as a gentleman, in his ease with courtly manners, the range of his learning, the refinement of his speech, and the dignity of his bearing. But John would also need other skills—a mixture of political savoir faire and familiarity with legal process—if he were to defend Paston interests against envious and acquisitive rivals. It was an arduous training that William devised for him.

Like his father—but without the financial struggles that dogged William's education—John was first taught at home in Norfolk, either at a local grammar school or by a tutor within the Paston household itself. In his mid-teens, however, he was sent to study at Cambridge, a small town in the fens sixty miles southwest of Norwich. The university there, like its counterpart in Oxford, was already more than two hundred years old. All the scholars who taught at the universities were members of the clergy, whether priests or monks, and almost all of those who undertook the four years of study required to graduate to the degree of Bachelor of Arts, or seven to become a Master of Arts, were also destined for a career in the church. However, by the early fifteenth century it was increasingly common for the sons of noblemen and gentlemen to further their education by spending a year or two sampling the courses on offer—which included grammar, logic, rhetoric, arithmetic, music, geometry, astronomy, and philosophy, and more advanced tuition in theology, canon law, civil law, and medicine—without proceeding to a degree. At the heart of their studies was an intensive programme of instruction in linguistic logic, which would serve John Paston well, his father hoped, should he ever be forced to defend the family's interests in the courts.

Most undergraduates lived in private lodgings and worked under the individual direction of one of the university's Masters of Arts, but by the later 1430s, when John Paston arrived in Cambridge, there were also six colleges in the town: Peterhouse, Clare, Pembroke, Gonville Hall, Trinity Hall, and Corpus Christi.[1] The colleges were religious foundations which provided a privileged academic environment for the scholars who made up their fellowships, but they also accommodated a limited number of undergraduates. Supporting a student at a college was a particularly costly business—perhaps six to eight pounds a year, although details are scarce—but Judge William's wealth meant that expense was no bar to his ambitions for his family. John was sent to Trinity Hall, a college in an exquisitely serene setting on the banks of the River Cam, which had Norfolk connections—its founder was William Bateman, bishop of

Norwich in the mid-fourteenth century—and which specialised in the study of civil and canon law. John and his fellow students attended lectures between six and nine in the morning, followed by "disputations" in which questions of natural and moral philosophy were debated.

However, these young men were not exclusively preoccupied with scholarly concerns. When a new college, King's, was founded in Cambridge a few years after John's arrival there, it was felt necessary to specify in the foundation statutes that its students should not wager money on "games of dice, hazard, or ball"; nor should they throw stones or balls or shoot arrows within the college, nor leap about, nor wrestle with one another, in case of damage to the windows and furnishings. They were not to spend their time hunting or fishing, "nor keep in King's College any monkey, bear, fox, stag, hind, doe, or badger, or any other wild animal or strange bird." And they were not to deck themselves in fashionable dress: parti-coloured clothes in bright hues were forbidden, as were red and green shoes, long hair and fancy hoods.[2] Clearly, not every Cambridge student was as serious-minded as the colleges might have wished.

John Paston, though, did not have much time to indulge in academic debate or youthful indiscretions. At seventeen, after a brief stay at Trinity Hall, he was sent to court to serve as a yeoman of the stable in the royal household. The stable was—exactly as it sounds—the division of the household establishment responsible for the care of the king's horses, a major enterprise given the number of animals needed to transport the court when it moved, as it frequently did, between the royal palaces. In the winter, when the roads turned to rutted mud, the king and his entourage might stay in a single residence for as much as two or three weeks, and spent much of their time in the palaces nearest to the capital: Westminster, the heart of the great government departments; Windsor, the glorious castle twenty miles westward along the Thames, which had been Edward III's favourite home; Eltham, a grandly moated palace little more than five miles southeast of London; and Sheen, less than ten miles southwest of the city. In the summer, however, the court braved the potholes and the dust of the highways much more often, moving from place to place every two or three days in a royal "progress" around the country.

Such relentless travelling required a large and well-equipped stable, full of thoroughbred horses on which the king, his family, and attendants could ride in suitable style. Sturdier animals were also needed to pull laden carts and wagons, since the household on the move might pack up beds and wall hangings, kitchen equipment and precious silverware as well as clothes, arms, and money. Just a few years after John Paston arrived at court, an ordinance of the royal household listed sixty horses within the king's stable proper, and a further 186 packhorses and mounts for his servants. The animals were tended by a sizeable staff, organised into the same kind of ceremonial hierarchy that characterised the rest of the court. The yeomen of the stable, John among them, answered to the overall command of the master of the horse, but worked under the immediate supervision of the avener, whose title derived from the Latin word for the oats with which the animals were fed. Looking after horses was too menial a job for John to have undertaken in his own family home, but menial jobs became honourable ones if they were performed in a noble household, or especially in the service of the king.

A placement in the stable did not give John the same degree of personal access to the monarch enjoyed by the yeomen and grooms of the chamber, who helped the esquires of the body to dress and undress the king at the beginning and end of each day. (They were also responsible for the preparation of the royal bed, jumping up and down on the feather-filled mattress to smooth out lumps, plumping up the pillows, and shaking out the fine linen sheets and elaborately worked coverlets of silk and velvet.) However, John did get a chance to observe at close hand the workings of political life at the very highest level, and to cultivate the polished manners of the aristocracy. The young gentlemen who took such service, whether in the chamber or the stable, were often the most ebullient element within the royal household—but, despite the fact that the king was a teenager, a couple of months younger than John himself, Henry VI's court was not a boisterous establishment. The king was a mild-mannered, unworldly adolescent. He was physically strong and capable—standing around five feet nine inches, and fond of hunting—but it was already becoming apparent how much less sure-footed he was in the field of politics than in the chase. As yet, he had done little to remind his subjects of his charismatic father, Henry V, who at seventeen had already commanded an army and survived an arrow wound in the face, sustained while fighting to defeat a rebellion against his own father, Henry IV, in 1403. Henry VI, by contrast, showed no inclination to join his soldiers in the occupation of northern France. His nobles and ministers continued to direct his government while he listened to their counsels with an abstracted air, preferring to immerse himself in religious devotions rather than diplomatic intrigue.

Even had the temper of Henry's court been more exuberant, it seems unlikely that John Paston would have found himself embroiled in questionable behaviour. Like the young king, he was not inclined to frivolity—and, unlike Henry, he was acutely focused on the pressing need to live up to his father's expectations. He had only a year to soak up the sophisticated culture and intricate politics of the royal household before it became clear that his education was not yet complete. William did not want his son to follow in his own footsteps: his ambitions for the future of the Paston dynasty depended on establishing John as a gentleman with an income accrued from a landed estate, not as a professional lawyer earning a living in the courts. But William also knew that a working knowledge of the law might prove to be an indispensable part of his son's preparation for his future responsibilities as head of the family. ". . . he said many times," Agnes later recalled, "that whosoever should dwell at Paston should need to know how to defend himself."[3] In the autumn of 1439, at the age of eighteen, John therefore went to Westminster, as his father had done forty years earlier, to study the common law. As he sat in the crib in the court of Common Pleas, and followed the moots held in the comfortable surroundings of his Inn, John knew that he was being prepared, not for a career as an attorney, but for life as a litigant. If ever he had to go to court to defend his family's lands, he would, at least, find himself on familiar territory.

Even for an eighteen-year-old of John's sober temperament, the Inns of Court were congenial surroundings, where students learned to dance and sing and "all games proper for nobles, as those brought up in the king's household are accustomed to practise," as the chief justice of the King's Bench later noted with nostalgic pride.[4] John certainly found like-minded companions there: "And when your leisure is, resort again unto your college the Inner Temple," a friend wrote warmly in November 1440, "for there be many which sore desire your presence."[5] But by then, John's whistle-stop educational tour had taken him back to Norfolk, and to greater responsibilities than had so far rested on his young shoulders. That autumn, at just turned nineteen, John became a married man.

Judge William, the son of a peasant, had waited twenty years to find himself a wife, until his professional success had transformed him into a fit match for a wealthy heiress. But William's self-reinvention as a landed gentleman also ensured that his own son would not have to wait nearly so long for a bride. As the heir to a rich estate, John had a great deal to offer as a prospective husband—not only his own personal charms, but the promise of an affluent future among the upper ranks of the Norfolk gentry. He also had a responsibility to his family to marry sooner rather than later, in order to secure the dynasty's future by providing a new generation of Paston heirs. William and Agnes lost no time in searching for a young woman of good birth whose prospects matched his own. Their choice fell on an heiress named Margaret Mautby.

Margaret was an only child, whose father had died when she was ten or eleven. Her mother had married again, and Margaret was now living at her stepfather's manor of Geldeston in southeastern Norfolk. Her own Mautby lands, however, lay in the north and east of the county, handily placed to complement the Paston estates, and they brought in the fine sum of £150 a year—a substantial addition to the annual landed income of £300 or so which William and Agnes between them now commanded. Calculated in the practical, hard-headed currency of wealth and status, it was a good match, and plans for the wedding had probably been under discussion for years, since William had known Margaret's father and grandfather well and was a trustee in the Mautby estates. But the young couple did not meet for the first time until April 1440, when they were eighteen years old. It was a crucial encounter, fraught with nerves on both sides. An arranged marriage, however profitable or prestigious, would serve dynastic interests only if it became a lasting partnership. A husband and wife who could not tolerate each other's presence stood little chance of managing their household and estates with dignified efficiency, still less of producing the children on whom the family's future would depend. The hope was always that affec-tion, or even love, would grow once the couple had spent some time together. In this case, the omens looked good. "And as for the first acquain-tance between John Paston and the said gentlewoman," Agnes reported to her husband, "she made him gentle cheer in gentle wise, and said he was verily your son. And so I hope there shall need no great treaty between them."[6]

Agnes's instincts could not be faulted. Neither John nor Margaret was prone to romantic fantasy; even as teenagers, they were sensible, pragmatic people who understood and appreciated their parents' reasons for bringing them together. Nevertheless, their union was no soulless contract born of political and financial expediency. They had much in common, in tempera-ment as well as values, and as a result their compatibility was obvious, their connection immediate. Within six months of meeting they were married.

After the wedding—at which Margaret perhaps wore the gown of "goodly blue, or else a bright sanguine red" that Agnes had suggested William should buy for her[7]—John returned to Cambridge to continue his education, this time at Peterhouse, the oldest college in the university. Margaret, meanwhile, remained at home in Norfolk. She was an intelligent young woman, strong-minded and robustly articulate, who had been educated as befitted an heiress who would one day be mistress of a wealthy estate. She had learned to read and to run a household, as well as receiving instruction in the articles of the Catholic faith and the feminine accomplishments of music and needlework. However, in a culture where oral traditions of learning still had deep roots, education did not necessarily imply literacy in its full modern sense. Like most gentlewomen, Margaret was not taught the technical business of writing with a quill pen; even the handwriting of her expensively educated husband was much cruder than that of a trained clerk for whom writing was a professional skill. While John usually dictated his letters and then corrected and signed them himself before they were sent, Margaret was wholly reliant on the few members of their household who could write if she wished to send messages to her husband while he was away. But the impossibility of completely private communication— something of which, of course, she had no expectation—did not deter Margaret from committing personal thoughts to paper in John's absence. Her hand may not have held the pen, but it was unquestionably her voice that spoke in the words on the page.

In December 1441, a little more than a year after their marriage, Margaret was staying with her mother-in-law, Agnes, at Oxnead, a manor nine miles north of Norwich that William had bought more than twenty years earlier, and which had become one of the family's principal residences. John had now finished his studies in Cambridge, but was yet again away from home, this time on family business in London with his father. Margaret was looking forward to his return, but his absence did at least raise the enticing prospect of the fine shopping that the capital had to offer. Judge William had promised her a new girdle—the long decorated belt with which ladies cinched their floor-length gowns at the waist or hips (gowns that were worn over a kirtle, or underdress, which in turn covered a linen shirt, and hose held up with garters). But the girdle had not arrived, and William was blaming his failure to produce it on John's forgetfulness, an explanation which Margaret was reluctant to believe: "I suppose that is not so," she wrote; "he said it but for a scusation." There was a connection, it transpired, between her eagerness to have John home and her impatience to have the new girdle: she was almost six months pregnant with their first child. She had grown so elegant, she reported wryly, that only one of the belts she already owned could still reach around her swollen form. A close family friend, John Damme, had paid the household a visit, and said it was the best news he had heard all year, Margaret told her husband, sounding both excited and self-conscious about her changing shape: "I may no longer live by my craft; I am discovered of all men that see me."[8]

Childbirth was a process managed exclusively by women—usually an experienced midwife with the help of the expectant mother's female relatives. Unnervingly, the local midwife, Elizabeth Peverel, had been incapacitated by a bad back for the best part of four months, but Margaret had been reassured to receive a message that she would nevertheless come when needed, "though she should be pushed in a barrow." Despite the fact that John himself would have no part to play at the birth, it was clear how glad Margaret would be to have him home for the later stages of her pregnancy. "I pray you," she asked, "that you will wear the ring with the image of St. Margaret that I sent you for a remembrance till you come home"—St. Margaret being the patron saint of pregnant women as well as her own namesake. She added a rueful afterthought: "You have left me such a remembrance that makes me to think upon you both day and night when I would sleep."[9]

St. Margaret's story might not, at first sight, seem to offer much comfort to women approaching their first labour. She was not even a mother herself, but a virgin martyr, beheaded on the orders of the Roman emperor Diocletian at Antioch around the turn of the fourth century. Her particular efficacy as an intercessor for women in childbirth sprang from a miracle said to have taken place before her martyrdom, when she was swallowed by the devil in the form of a dragon; the crucifix she held in her hand stuck in the dragon's throat, and the saint was disgorged from the beast's belly, alive and unharmed. In the same way, it was believed, women who called upon her in labour would be safely delivered of the babies they carried. Certainly, Margaret seemed to find her own identification with the saint a comfort, and the birth—probably attended by Margaret's mother, Margery, and mother-in-law, Agnes, as well as Elizabeth Peverel and other capable female servants—did in the end go as smoothly as she had hoped. The baby, born in the spring of 1442, was a healthy boy, named John like his father.

Like all gentle and noblewomen, Margaret remained at home for a month after the birth, a period of rest and recuperation known as "lying-in." Her reemergence into the world was marked with the ceremony of "churching," when a new mother presented herself publicly in the parish church for a service of ritual purification, and offered candles to the Virgin in thanksgiving for her infant's arrival. The rite was followed by feasting—a chance to celebrate with family and friends, and to demonstrate the magnificence and munificence of the dynasty into which the baby had been born. Once this ceremonial was complete, however, Margaret had to adjust quickly to her new role as mother as well as wife. Parenthood did not mean that John could spend all of his time at home, any more than William had been able to do so when John himself was growing up, and during his frequent absences Margaret had to take responsibility for the running of their household in Norfolk.

Officially, the couple's main home was now Gresham, a moated manor house built in the form of a quadrangle, with a round tower at each corner, set in valuable lands near the north Norfolk coast about ten miles east of Paston. William had bought the manor in 1427, and it would eventually form part of the estate he would pass on to his heirs, but in the meantime William had chosen to use it as part of the complex property negotiations that accompanied any marriage proposal among the landed classes, in which both sides would seek to maximise the benefits of the match to their own family, and to safeguard the future financial security of both bride and groom. Margaret was bringing a great deal to the marriage in the form of her rich inheritance, of which she and her new husband would take control when she was twenty-one, and the Pastons therefore had to make a good offer to secure her hand. She could expect, of course, to become the mistress of the Paston estates as a result of her marriage—but only after Judge William's death, and only for so long as John himself remained alive. Immediate provision had to be made to enable the young couple to establish a new household of their own after their wedding; and in the longer term, Margaret required assurance that her enhanced standard of living would be maintained if she were left a widow, when the bulk of the Paston estates would pass to a new heir. Gresham therefore became her jointure— Paston property which William settled on John and Margaret jointly when they married, to provide them with a home and an income until John came into his inheritance, and to ensure that Margaret would still have a home and an income from the Paston estates for her lifetime if John died before she did.

In practice, however, for the first few years after the wedding, Margaret and her baby son spent a good deal of time at her mother's home at Geldeston, and probably more still with her mother-in-law, Agnes, at Oxnead and Norwich. Margaret and Agnes got on well, despite the twenty-year age gap. They were alike in character—direct, straightforward, and down to earth—and also had babies very close in age, since Agnes gave birth to her fifth surviving child, a son named Clement, not long before the arrival of John and Margaret's little boy. Margaret's letters give the distinct impression that she and her "mother" (as married women described their mothers-in-law, since husband and wife were deemed to share their blood relationships through the sacrament of marriage) could be a formidable combination when they chose. "My mother greets you well and sends you God's blessing and hers, and she prays you, and I pray you also, that you be well dieted of meat and drink, for that is the greatest help that you may have now to your health," Margaret told John firmly in the autumn of 1443. He had been seriously ill, and she and Agnes had done everything they could think of to intercede for his recovery; Agnes promised a wax statue weighing as much as John himself to the famous shrine of the Virgin Mary at Walsingham in northwest Norfolk, and Margaret vowed to travel there on pilgrimage. ". . . by my troth," she told him, "my mother and I were not in heart's ease from the time that we knew of your sickness till we knew verily of your amending." At twenty-one, Margaret was still very young, and her affection for her husband was expressed in endearingly blunt fashion. "If I might have had my will I should have seen you before this time. I would you were at home," she said, ". . . rather than a new gown, though it were of scarlet."[10]

At least she had good news to cheer John during his convalescence. She was pregnant again, and in the spring of 1444 gave birth to another boy. Confusingly, this second son was also named John, like his brother and father. Christian names often ran in families, but they normally did so in succeeding generations, and to find three Johns in only two generations is extremely unusual. (Not unparalleled, however: the early fifteenth-century grave of one Surrey gentlewoman records her thirteen siblings by name, among them four Johns, two Williams, and two sisters named Agnes.) The most likely explanation for such repetition is the widespread custom of naming babies after their chief godparent. No information survives about the Paston boys' baptisms or the identity of their godparents (traditionally two men and one woman for a boy, two women and one man for a girl); but it is certainly possible that John and Margaret chose two godfathers who shared the same name as John. There are a number of plausible candidates in the Pastons' circle: Sir John Fastolf, for example, a wealthy relative of Margaret's, for whom William Paston acted as a legal adviser; her maternal uncle John Berney of Reedham near Yarmouth; or perhaps Judge William's friend John Damme, who had been so delighted to hear the news of Margaret's first pregnancy.

Whatever the reason for the repetition, the family themselves never seem to have had problems distinguishing between father and sons. Years later, Margaret saw no difficulty in writing a letter to John Paston to let him know that "I received a letter . . . from John Paston, in the which letter he wrote that you desired that I should have John Paston . . . look in the great standing chest in one of the great canvas bags which stand against the lock."[11] It was clear to her when she wrote the letter, and to her husband when he read it, that she had passed on instructions sent by her elder son, staying with his father in London, to her younger son, at home with her in Norwich. Even in the family's most informal correspondence, there is no sign of diminutives or nicknames; the boys usually signed themselves "John Paston the elder" and "John Paston the younger" or "the youngest," to distinguish themselves from their father, who was simply "John Paston, esquire." The younger son did once sign a letter to his mother as "John of Geldeston"—Margaret's mother's home after her remarriage, and the place where he was born. However, this was an isolated attempt in a time of political danger to identify himself in a way which Margaret alone would understand, lest his letter should fall into unfriendly hands, rather than a reflection of any need to differentiate himself from his brother.[12]

By the summer of 1444, Margaret, at twenty-two, was growing up fast. She had two young sons and increasing domestic responsibilities, including the often pressing need to manage the family budget, since their income from the manor of Gresham, like all estate revenues, was sporadic. Like most of the gentry and nobility, the Pastons leased out nearly all of their lands to tenant farmers rather than farming them directly themselves. In theory, leasing out estates had the benefit of generating a regular income that was not dependent on variable harvest yields or fluctuations in the market for agricultural produce. In practice, however, rents were paid seasonally, and—wealthy though the Pastons were—cash might run short as rent day approached, or even after that, if the harvest was bad or prices low and the tenants could not pay what they owed. "I suppose I must borrow money in short time unless you come soon home," Margaret told her husband that July. "So God help me, I have but four shillings, and I owe near as much money." She was confident enough of their finances to ask John to do some shopping for her in London, but she was clearly under strain; she could not suppress her irritation, for example, at his inability to remember that the boys might grow while he was away: "As for caps that you sent me for the children, they are too little for them. I pray you buy them finer caps and larger than those were."[13]

Such domestic worries were about to be swept aside, however, by the dramatic changes which engulfed her life, and that of her husband, only weeks later. Her father-in-law, Judge William, was now in his mid-sixties, and beginning to suffer from serious ill health—so much so that six months earlier he had been forced to take sick leave from his judicial duties, which included not only sitting to hear cases in the court of Common Pleas, but also serving on commissions of assize. Assize judges, appointed from among the justices and sergeants-at-law of the Westminster courts, travelled on circuits around the country twice a year to bring the king's justice directly to the people outside London and its suburbs. William was due to ride the southeastern circuit in the early spring of 1444, but had to with-draw from the commission because of his illness. Quite apart from the demands of hearing the cases themselves, the physical strain of moving between the towns where the sessions were to be held was too much to con-template. John stayed with him in Norfolk, helping to write his letters, while in London his legal clerk, James Gresham, conveyed his apologies to John Fortescue, the chief justice of the King's Bench. Fortescue was partic-ularly sympathetic since he, too, was unwell. "He has had a sciatica . . . , and dares not yet come on no horse's back," Gresham reported. "And therefore he has spoken to the lords of the council and informed them of your sickness, and his also." Gresham's own concern for his master's health was evident: "Almighty Jesu make you hale and strong," he wrote.[14] William did recover—he was back in court later in the spring—but the episode was serious enough to convince him that he should update his will. That summer, he was in London, staying with Agnes at his lodgings just outside the city walls, near St. Bride's Church in Fleet Street, when he again fell ill. This time, there was no escape. On Thursday, 13 August, not long before midnight, William died.

William's career had brought him a long way. Born in a cottage in Paston village, with animals in the yard outside and fields beyond, he died in an elegant townhouse in the capital, resting on a featherbed with linen sheets and finely embroidered hangings. His parents were buried together in a simple grave in the church where he had been baptised, but William's body was brought back from London to Norfolk and interred, as he had wanted, in the Lady Chapel behind the high altar of Norwich's great cathedral, beneath soaring pillars and richly stained glass. His father had made bequests in his will of a few shillings apiece, but William left one of the most substantial landed estates in northern Norfolk, and personal possessions, including a great deal of cash, with a total value of several thousand pounds.

Nonetheless, despite the extraordinary fortune he had amassed, his legacy was not a straightforward one. William's success had ensured that his son was a gentleman born, not a professional lawyer trying to clothe himself in the trappings of gentility, and William had done everything he could to give him a privileged training for the role he was about to take up. However, John was just twenty-two years old, and what he lacked was time: time to gain experience of the political world, and to develop his own standing within it. Fresh from his studies, in August 1444 he was left alone and exposed at the head of a family that had powerful enemies as well as powerful friends. Inexperienced though he was, he was not a fool, and he must have anticipated that the Pastons' local rivals would try to take advantage of his loss. But even if he was prepared for trouble, he could scarcely have imagined that his first challenge as head of the family would come from within the family itself, in the form of his father's will.

The quandary that had confronted Judge William as he lay struggling for breath on his sickbed that summer was how best to satisfy all the different demands on the estate he would leave when he died. He had to consider the needs of his five surviving children, ranging in age from John, now married to Margaret and with two boys of his own, to Clement, a toddler not much older than John and Margaret's first son. William's ambitions for the future of the Paston name dictated that he should hand the bulk of his estates over to his eldest son, to secure the position of the senior line of the family. As a father, however, he was also determined to provide generously for all of his children. Here the concerns of a loving parent merged with the preoccupations of the ambitious dynast: if the junior Pastons were not given the means to sustain themselves among the ranks of the gentry, not only would their own lives be a struggle, but they might drag the Paston name down with them—a risk to which a family whose status was so recently acquired would be peculiarly vulnerable. William also had to provide for his wife, Agnes, in her widowhood, which might well be lengthy given that she was still only in her early forties. Once all of these claims had been accounted for, he also had to consider the needs of his own soul. He was a devout man, within the conventional limits of his time and adopted class, but he had dedicated his life above all to the worldly pursuit of wealth and power. Now, in his final illness, the message of the Three Dead— leering from the walls of the parish church at Paston as a reminder of the purgatorial torment that awaited all sinful souls—began to weigh on his mind more heavily. His last chance had come to shorten his stay in this antechamber of hell by setting aside money for penitential works of piety and charity, and for prayers to be said and masses to be sung for the good of his soul after his death.

William had drafted his will a couple of years earlier, in late 1441 or 1442. The division of the Paston estates on which he had settled was characteristically careful. To Agnes, he left a large share of the Paston lands, reflecting the benefit that her name and her inheritance had brought to the family. She of course retained possession of her own three manors, as well as the Pastons' home at Oxnead, which she had received as her jointure when she married; but William also gave her his estates in and around Paston on the northeast Norfolk coast, including the land that his father, Clement, had left him, and other properties bought in the 1420s as William's career gathered pace. All in all, Agnes would have an annual income of around one hundred pounds; if not a merry widow, she would at least be a rich one.

To his eighteen-year-old son Edmund, William left the manor of Snailwell in Cambridgeshire, worth a little more than twenty-six pounds a year, a sum that would allow him to sustain a comfortable, if modest, living. William intended that Edmund should have the means to supplement this income, if he chose, by practising as a lawyer; he would receive his inheritance when he was twenty-one, and until then, William directed, he was to study law—dialectics for six months, civil law for a year, and the common law after that. His third son, seven-year-old William, was to have lands in mid-Norfolk, west of Norwich, worth about sixteen pounds a year; and the baby of the family, Clement, would receive lands in eastern Norfolk, just north of Yarmouth, also valued at around sixteen pounds a year. Both sons were to be educated well enough to allow them to embark on professional careers. To his only daughter, twelve-year-old Elizabeth, William left a dowry of two hundred pounds in cash. Unlike Agnes or Margaret, Elizabeth would bring her future husband no land, but two hundred pounds was a good sum—certainly enough to secure the hand of a prosperous gentleman. William was, as always, determined to drive a hard bargain, even from beyond the grave: the dowry should be paid if Elizabeth married with her mother's consent, he said, so long as the match provided her with a landed income of at least forty pounds a year.

John, his eldest son, was to have what was left. The only property specifically allocated to him in the will was Gresham in north Norfolk, which he and Margaret already held by the terms of their marriage agreement as Margaret's jointure. By law, however, anything not specifically bequeathed elsewhere in William's will would automatically pass to his heir. By that token, John would receive three more manors: East Beckham, a couple of miles from Gresham, which William finally succeeded in wresting from Edmund Winter and John Mariot only a month before his death; Sporle, in western Norfolk; and Swainsthorpe, just south of Norwich. The last remaining issue was that of William's own spiritual needs: he specified that masses should be celebrated for his soul for seven years after his death—a modest bequest, by contemporary standards, when those who could afford it often sought to spare their souls from the horrors of purgatory by commissioning prayers to be said in perpetuity.

William had pulled off a complex balancing act. The settlement could not be said to be overgenerous to his eldest son, who would need all the resources he could muster for the difficult task of protecting William's legacy, particularly given that there was every chance that Agnes might hold her share of the estates for another twenty years at least; but then again, as William was well aware, John did also have the benefit of Margaret's Mautby inheritance. Prompted by his first bout of serious illness, William confirmed and dated the will in January 1444.

Seven months later, with death this time close at hand, he seems to have had second thoughts. It was Agnes who claimed to have been privy to her husband's thinking as he lay dying. He was gripped with fear, she said, for the future of the youngest Paston boys, telling her repeatedly that "the livelihood which he had assigned to his two youngest, William and Clement, by his will in writing was so little that they might not live thereupon without they should hold the plough by the tail."[15] That his sons might go straight back to the life his own father had lived on the land was a possibility which Judge William could not easily endure, having worked so hard to ensure that they were born into the ruling classes rather than the world of the labouring peasantry. He was also, understandably, more deeply preoccupied than he had previously been with the imminent sufferings of his soul. At the eleventh hour, Agnes said, he decided to use the three manors he had not mentioned in his written will to buy himself some peace of mind, castigating himself as he did so for his sloth "that his will was not made up."[16] It is, on the face of it, surprising that a lawyer of William's talents and experience had not made sure that every last item among his affairs was in perfect order well before his final illness—but perhaps the reality of death had been at once too unnerving and too remote a prospect to contemplate for such an energetic man.[17] Now, Agnes claimed, he instructed that East Beckham, Sporle, and Swainsthorpe should be divided between their two youngest sons, and that the revenues of Swainsthorpe should also pay for masses for his soul, not for the limited term of seven years specified in his will, but instead as a perpetual bequest. These arrangements—if they were allowed to stand—would leave John with his home at Gresham, and little else.

Agnes's version of the events leading up to her husband's death was written two decades later. It is by no means an impartial account; Agnes, the proud heiress, took care to report William's concern that she herself deserved a larger share of the estate—although he could spare her nothing more, since "he had more to care for which were mine as well as his."[18] Her story was also confusing, if not confused: she described her husband on his sickbed telling John of his intentions—"asking him the question whether he held him not content, so saying to him in these terms, 'Sir, if thou do not, I do, for I will not give so much to one that the remnant shall have too little to live on'"[19]—but later said that she herself had "opened and declared" the new will to their eldest son after William's death. Elizabeth Paston, asked to testify to the facts many years later, confirmed that she had been at the St. Bride's house in London during her father's final days, but that her older brother had not.

What is not in doubt is John's reaction. On Friday, 21 August, a week after William's death, his four executors gathered to read his will: his wife, Agnes; his son John; his cousin William Bacton, the son of Clement Paston's sister Martha; and his friend John Damme. "I let them see it," Agnes wrote, "and John Damme read it. And when he had read it, John Paston walked up and down in the chamber; John Damme and I kneeled at the bed's feet."[20] The difficulty was that the properties about which Judge William had allegedly changed his mind were not mentioned in the written will in the first place. When Agnes explained what she claimed were William's last wishes, John reacted with fury, utterly refusing to countenance the suggestion that his inheritance should be so drastically reduced. "And the said John Paston would in no wise agree thereto," she reported, "saying that by the law the said manors should be his, in as much as my husband made no will of them in writing."[21]

John's uncompromising response compounded the grief of Judge William's death by threatening to divide the family against itself. But his reaction was at least understandable, since—if Agnes was right about her husband's final intentions—William had placed his eldest son in an extraordinarily difficult position. It had always been clear that John would face many challenges on his father's death, but William now proposed that he should be sent to meet them with both hands tied behind his back. If he had to defend Paston interests not only without the benefit of his father's experience, reputation, and connections, but also without most of his lands, his chances of maintaining the family's standing were slender indeed.

It was the first test John had to face as head of the family, and he responded with more than a hint of his father's toughness. He took urgent steps to make sure that it was the written will which was put into effect, securing the title deeds to the estates and initiating the legal process by which he would take possession of the lands from William's trustees. He also retrieved the store of valuables that his father had deposited for safekeeping with the monks at Norwich Priory—said to be the immense sum of nearly one thousand pounds in cash, as well as expensive jewellery and silver plate—without consulting Agnes or the other executors. His prompt action saved him: despite his mother's vehement protests, probate was awarded on William's written will, without modification, on 24 November 1444.

But the cost, in personal terms, was high. His unequivocal rejection of Agnes's account of his father's last wishes caused a bitter breach between them. "After that my son John Paston had never right kind words to me," Agnes wrote years later.[22] That was not quite true: she and John found a way to paper over their differences, and her relationship with Margaret remained close. Equally, the issue did not disappear. Agnes would not forget about it—something which might come back to haunt John, given that she held such a substantial part of his inheritance—and his younger brothers, with encouragement from their mother, might well feel hard done by in years to come. But his intransigence was not purely, or even mainly, rooted in selfishness. Generosity to his siblings, his mother, even his father's soul, would benefit no one if the social and financial position of the entire family was so compromised that they all sank back to the ranks of the peasantry as a result. John had confronted the reality of what he believed to be necessary to safeguard the interests of the Paston dynasty, and had shown that he was willing to face the consequences, however personally unpleasant. It was not the last time in his life that he would be required to do so.

Hard-headed as he was prepared to be within the family, however, to the wider world he was young, and inexperienced in the political and legal manoeuvreing at which his father had excelled. How serious the consequences of the loss of Judge William might be on this broader political stage was all too soon apparent. William's long battle for the manor of East Beckham against Edmund Winter and John Mariot had finally ended with a judgment in his favour only a month before he died. His opponents were resourceful and resolute, but the combination of William's legal expertise and his powerful connections in the end proved too much for them to overcome. But in the autumn of 1444, only a matter of weeks after William's death, Mariot initiated new litigation in the court of Common Pleas, attempting to overturn that judgment and retrieve the manor. It took a year, but he won his case. East Beckham was one of the estates for the sake of which John had endured such bitter confrontation with his mother, and he had managed to hold on to it for only a matter of months. And—as John must have realised as he surveyed the lands for which his father had fought so long and so hard—this was only the beginning.

a perilous dwelling

O N 17 MAY 1448, Margaret and her mother-in-law, Agnes, went to hear mass in their parish church in Norwich. It was their choice to join a public act of worship that day, since, like most wealthy families, the Pastons employed their own priest to officiate in the private chapels at their various residences. In fact, a new chaplain—a young man named James Gloys—had recently joined the Paston household, and was staying with Margaret and her children at Agnes's home in the city while John was away in London. But, while private devotions had their own exclusive social cachet, very few gentlefolk abandoned their local churches entirely. In spiritual terms, it was essential to remain part of the community of the faithful, to be in "charity"—united in a state of Christian love—with one's neighbours. And participation in that spiritual community had other, more worldly benefits. Gracing a local congregation with their presence enabled the leading families of a parish to put their power and prestige on public display by appearing at mass bedecked in finery, and by embellishing the church with lavish additions to the fabric of the building: luminous stained glass, wall paintings in vibrant colours, delicately carved masonry, even a new chapel or bell tower—all, more often than not, emblazoned with their own heraldic devices. When John and Margaret later rented a house of their own in the centre of Norwich near the great castle mound, for example, they marked their arrival by paying for the rebuilding of their new parish church, St. Peter Hungate, with an elegantly austere façade of black flint. But Margaret and Agnes's destination on this particular Friday morning was probably St. Mary Coslany, a much-extended building with a distinctively round Norman tower near Agnes's home in the northeast of the city.

His employers' decision to go out to mass left James Gloys (known to the family as "Sir James," using the respectful title reserved for priests as well as knights) at loose ends. He wandered into town for a couple of hours—perhaps to run some errands, call on an acquaintance or two, or simply to amuse himself in Norwich's markets and shops—and then walked alone back toward the Paston residence. He was not far from home when his route took him past the door of a town house belonging to a gentleman named John Wyndham.

Like so many Norfolk gentlemen, Wyndham was a self-made man. His background was so obscure that his family had no firmly established sur-name, and he had experimented with a number of aliases, including John Day and John Branch, before finally settling on Wyndham as the name he would leave to posterity. Despite his lowly beginnings, he had made a for-tune in trade, and like William Paston before him, he was rapidly convert-ing his substantial reserves of cash into land and the status that came with it. Relations between Wyndham and the Pastons were not warm. Their ambitions to tread the path of social advancement at the same time in the same place were always likely to cause friction, and their rivalry had found a flash point during the previous summer in a petty wrangle over their respec-tive rights to employ a particular shepherd to tend their sheep. As a result of the squabble, Wyndham had brought a prosecution against two of the Pastons' tenants, which was still pending in the courts.

It became clear on this May morning that Wyndham's tireless campaign of self-promotion could be pursued in town just as well as in the country or a court of law. A servant at his side, he stood at the gate of his half-timbered house, in the shadow of the jettied upper storey that overhung the street. Another of his men, Thomas Hawes, had taken up position beyond the open drain that ran down the middle of the road. The approaching figure of James Gloys rapidly realised that he was left with no option but to run the gauntlet between them. This was provocation—unspoken, but unmistak-able all the same. The young chaplain, however, had robustly competitive instincts of his own, and he accepted the challenge without a flicker of hesi-tation.

It was customary for gentlemen to demonstrate their good breeding and impeccable manners by acknowledging one another with a courteously doffed cap, but Gloys walked brazenly on, making no move to tip the brim of his hat as he strode toward them. The slight could not be ignored. Riled by his insolence, Wyndham resorted to withering sarcasm—"Cover thy head!"—using the insultingly familiar "thy" instead of the respectful "your." Gloys's retort—"So I shall for thee!"—threw the insult back. He had taken only three or four more steps when Wyndham cried, "Shall thou so, knave?" and drew his dagger—a tempered steel blade more than a foot long, which all gentlemen carried for self-defence, but which also therefore came to hand with dangerous ease when the owner's pride, rather than his person, was under threat.

Gloys turned, his own blade in his hand, but a barrage of stones flung by Wyndham and Hawes forced him to run for shelter up the street to Agnes's house. Hawes dashed after him "and cast a stone as much as a farthing loaf into the hall after Gloys, and then ran out of the place again." Gloys gave chase as far as the gate, "and then Wyndham called Gloys thief and said he should die, and Gloys said he lied and called him churl, and bade him come himself or else the best man he had, and Gloys would answer him one for one."[1] It was fighting talk, and Wyndham, who could not contemplate losing face by failing to answer this dare, sent Hawes running to fetch his sword and spear.

Margaret and Agnes heard the shouting from inside the church. Whether they recognised the raised voices, or were simply anxious that a violent fracas had erupted so close to their home, they slipped away from the service to investigate. They were confronted with an alarming spectacle: their fiery young chaplain, at bay in the gateway to Agnes's house, hurling taunts at their enraged neighbour and enemy. But Margaret was not easily daunted. She had an acute sense of responsibility, and a resolute bravery so deeply ingrained that she did not pause even for a moment to consider whether she might be in any personal danger. She stepped between the two men, peremptorily dispatching Gloys back into the house and away from the confrontation. She managed to stop the fight, but succeeded also in drawing Wyndham's abuse onto herself and her mother-in-law: "then Wyndham called my mother and me strong whores, and said the Pastons and all their kin were churls of Gimingham, and we said he lied, knave and churl that he was." There was more, which Margaret did not have time or inclination to commit to paper: "And he had much large language, as you shall know hereafter by mouth."[2]

Wyndham might trade venomous insults with women, but he remembered himself enough not to risk his reputation as a gentleman by threatening them with physical harm. There was no doubt that Margaret could hold her own when it came to defending the Pastons' honour, but she was much less confident of her hot-headed chaplain's good sense and therefore of his safety. She was right to be uneasy. That afternoon she and Agnes went to seek help from the prior of Norwich, who, as a powerful man of the church, might offer a means of conciliation between the two families. The prior summoned Wyndham to explain his disorderly conduct—but while Wyndham was closeted at the cathedral, violence flared again between Gloys and Thomas Hawes.

Gloys, it was rapidly becoming clear, was as proud as he was obstinate. Although he had accepted Margaret's intervention in the quarrel without demur, he could not bear to concede defeat in public. He was standing in the street at Agnes's gate, ostentatiously occupying his territory in full view of Wyndham's servants, whose determination not to forfeit an iota of the respect they believed to be their due matched Gloys's own. Hawes burst out of Wyndham's house, this time armed with a sword so heavy it could only be wielded with two hands. There was a scuffle: Gloys himself escaped without injury, but another of Agnes's servants suffered a graze to his palm as he tried to fend Hawes off. Hawes could surely have inflicted more than a scratch with his great sword had he been serious about the business of bloodshed; ultimately, it seemed, this was a show of intimidation in which neither side wanted to risk the penalties of a murder charge. But as tempers frayed amid the bluster and bravado, there was always a danger that macho posturing might run violently out of control.

It was a chance that Margaret was no longer prepared to take: ". . . by the advice of my mother and others I send you Gloys to attend upon you for a season, for ease of my own heart," she wrote to her husband in London, "for in good faith I would not for £40 have such another trouble." But removing Gloys from the streets of Norwich was not necessarily the end of her worries. She had heard that Wyndham, too, would soon be travelling to the capital, and feared that he would seek the opportunity to ambush John himself. "I pray you beware how you walk if he be there," she warned her husband, "for he is full cursed-hearted and lumish" (an evocative dialect word meaning malicious or spiteful). "I know well he will not set upon you manly, but I believe he will start upon you, or on some of your men, like a thief."[3]

The incident was intensely unsettling. Private though the substance of the quarrel was, it was played out in public, on a city street in broad daylight. Even if the violence was more rhetorical than real, reputations were nevertheless at risk, and the stakes were high. Gentlemen were men to be reckoned with, who could command respect and defend themselves, their families, and their honour—and for John Paston and John Wyndham, the need to demonstrate that they were indeed gentlemen was at the heart of the argument. Both Wyndham and the Pastons lived in glass houses when it came to their families' origins, and on this occasion both started throwing stones. One word, churl, was repeated over and over as gibes were traded: "Gloys said he lied and called him churl," "the Pastons and all their kin were churls of Gimingham," "we said he lied, knave and churl that he was." This insulting claim—that the would-be gentleman was in fact a peasant, and an unfree peasant at that—was fraught with threatening implications. An unfree man could not legally become the lord of a manor, precisely the kind of authority that allowed upwardly mobile men to claim gentility. The Pastons were so sensitive to the charge that, at some point after Margaret's account of the confrontation was written, the words with which Wyndham had struck so close to the bone were excised from the letter, leaving a hole in the paper where "churls of Gimingham" had been.[4] The irony was that both Margaret and Agnes, the targets of this vituperative tirade, were better born than either their husbands or Wyndham himself, even if they had little choice but to accept that their status was now defined by the family into which they had married.

What was disquieting above all was that few people would have dared to insult the Pastons so openly when Judge William was alive. The loss of his influence was everywhere apparent in the family's new vulnerability to attack, of which the street fight with Wyndham was only the most spectacularly public manifestation. Agnes was finding that being William Paston's widow was not at all the same as being his wife. For example, William's plans to divert the road at Paston village around the churchyard and away from their new home there had been agreed upon with the vicar in the spring of 1444; but after William's death a few months later, the priest reneged on the deal, plunging Agnes into a vitriolic dispute that poisoned her relations with the villagers for years. ("All the devils of hell draw her soul to hell for the way that she has made!" a woman cried in the churchyard after mass one Sunday.)[5] Meanwhile, a couple of miles away, at the neighbouring village of Trunch, a man named Palmer who had leased some land from the family for almost a decade suddenly refused to pay eight shillings of what he owed, claiming it was rent due to the feudal overlord of the land—and when asked why this objection had not been lodged before, Palmer explained that no one had dared mention it because William "was a great man, and a wise man of the law." His authority, it now seemed, could not bind his tenants from beyond the grave. Six months after her husband's death, it was with feeling that a beleaguered Agnes told their son Edmund, a student in London, "to think once of the day of your father's counsel to learn the law," and recalled William's maxim that "whosoever should dwell at Paston should have need to know how to defend himself."[6]

The family's inescapable problem was the fact that their estates had been bought so recently. However legally sound a purchase agreement might be—even if its every clause was contractually unimpeachable—the new owner of an estate was not safe against challenge from the family to which the land had previously belonged. The commercial market in land, booming though it was, sat uneasily within a culture steeped in the concept of inheritance, and the heirs of those who had put estates up for sale often acted as though such transactions were an illegitimate interruption of their rightful possession—such rights being conceived more in terms of visceral attachment than legal technicality. And the tension between these nebulous dynastic claims and property rights acquired by purchase was not always resolved according to the letter of the law. All too often, litigation was a skirmish within a wider battle in which strict legal form might be overwhelmed by the superior forces of political influence and powerful connections. John Mariot and Edmund Winter had discovered as much when they failed, after ten rancorous years in the courts, to retrieve the manor of East Beckham from Judge William's well-connected grasp. But William's death left the Pastons suddenly bereft of both allies and ammunition—and within months East Beckham was back in Mariot's hands, without hope of recovery.

The resuscitation of existing disputes was not the only difficulty with which John Paston now had to contend. His father's death also gave opportunists the chance to come forward with fresh claims that, however spurious, might cause the family problems in their newly exposed state. The valuable lands and delightful manor house at Oxnead had been settled on Agnes as her jointure when she married, and now formed her principal country residence when she was not staying in town at her Norwich home. But a chancer named John Hauteyn now came forward to allege that the manor was rightfully his, on the grounds that his ancestors had owned it in the time of Edward III, a century earlier. Hauteyn made little headway—he lacked sufficiently powerful backing to make a specious case stick—but he was persistent in his efforts. It was an irritant which the family could well have done without, particularly given that her sons were concerned that Agnes was not reliably discreet about her legal affairs. John should remind their mother as a matter of urgency, his younger brother Edmund requested with barely suppressed exasperation in 1447, that she should speak to no one about her private business, "for she will tell many persons of her counsel this day, and tomorrow she will say by God's fast that the same men be false."[7]

Hauteyn was a nuisance, but John Paston's greatest enemy, a friend of John Wyndham's named John Heydon, was a much more dangerous adversary. Had Judge William still been alive, he would have recognised Heydon as a rival cast in his own image: a gifted young lawyer from a poor background, driven by a consuming ambition to establish his family among the Norfolk gentry. Heydon, like Wyndham, had changed his name during his professional rise, swapping the tradesman's surname of Baxter (meaning "baker") for the more genteel place name of Heydon, the village where his father had laboured on the land. It was as John Heydon, lawyer and gentleman, that he bought the manor of Baconsthorpe in northern Norfolk, only three miles away from the Pastons' estate at Gresham, and embarked on building himself an elegant new home there, a moated manor house to reflect his newly elevated status.

Heydon's career was spectacularly successful, but his personal life was an unedifying mess. His marriage broke down in 1444 when his wife, Eleanor, gave birth to a child by another man—a scandal that became the talk of Norfolk society. Heydon's anger was ferocious, his response brutal: ". . . he said, if she comes in his presence to make her excuse, that he should cut off her nose to make her to be known what she is, and if her child comes in his presence he said he would kill it," Margaret reported to John that summer. "He will not be entreated to have her again in no wise, as I heard say."[8] We have no way of gauging the emotional wounds that provoked this rebarbative reaction; we know nothing of the personal history between John and Eleanor Heydon, nor of the circumstances of her adultery. The violence of Heydon's rage speaks of injured pride at such a public betrayal, but the potential damage wrought on his family and his name went far beyond individual hurt: the future of the lineage that Heydon had worked so hard to establish was at risk. Dynastic landholding depended on female sexual fidelity, and Eleanor's wantonness cast retrospective doubt on the parentage of the child she had already borne Heydon, as well as the infant whose birth had precipitated this crisis. Whatever the dynamics of their personal relationship, then, Heydon was the wronged party in the eyes of the wider community. Eleanor was expelled from her home and ostracised by her family, who nevertheless remained close to her estranged husband. Eleanor's father cut her out of his will completely, but showed his continuing appreciation of his son-in-law by leaving Heydon a bequest of a precious book of chronicles, and entrusting him with the sensitive task of overseeing the execution of his will after his death. It was the identity of Heydon's friendly father-in-law that was so disastrous from the Pastons' point of view: he was Edmund Winter, their opponent in the bitter fight for East Beckham.

If Heydon's relationship with Winter was one reason for him to be hostile to the Pastons, the location of his own lands was another. He was buying up properties around his new home at Baconsthorpe to create an estate that would make him a landowner of substance in northern Norfolk—exactly the same area where William Paston had concentrated his own acquisitions. John and Margaret's home at Gresham, together with the disputed manor of East Beckham and two of Margaret's Mautby estates, all lay within a radius of three miles from Baconsthorpe. Trying to expand their holdings in the same small area was always likely to set Heydon and the Pastons on a collision course, but Heydon—as a mere attorney, however up and coming—stood little chance of denting the regional standing of a man of Judge William's influence. William's son John, however, was a different matter. William's death could not have coincided more neatly with the blossoming of John Heydon's political career, and John Paston, fresh out of university at the age of twenty-two, could not hope to compete. In the year after Judge William died, it was almost certainly Heydon who used his legal expertise to mastermind the campaign to snatch East Beckham from John's inexperienced hands. That loss was bad enough; but three years later it became terrifyingly clear that Heydon's assault on Paston interests had only just begun.

This time the conflict moved closer to home. John and Margaret had started their married life at Gresham in north Norfolk, and despite John's frequent absences in London and Margaret's liking for the company and shopping available in Norwich, it was still their young family's main residence. Until the end of the fourteenth century, the manor had belonged to an aristocratic family named Moleyns, whose main estates lay in the county of Buckinghamshire, northwest of London. The circumstances that brought the manor on to the open market were convoluted in the extreme, but—unlike the case of East Beckham—William Paston's purchase of the property in 1427 was incontrovertibly legal. In theory, John Paston should have encountered no difficulties there. But, lacking his father's consummate political skills and friends in high places, John found that a watertight legal title was worth little more than the parchment on which it had been so carefully inscribed.

By the 1440s, the Moleyns inheritance, of which Gresham had once been a part, had passed to a nobleman named Robert Hungerford, heir to a large estate in the county of Wiltshire, west of London. His wife, Eleanor, was the Moleyns heiress, and Hungerford had adopted the title of Lord Moleyns, to which his marriage now gave him a claim. There was good reason why the young lord might want to make the most of his wife's birthright: his own father and grandfather were still alive, and it might well be years—decades, even—before he succeeded to the Hungerford title and lands. But trying to recover parts of the Moleyns inheritance that had been lost as long ago and as comprehensively as Gresham should have been no more than wild speculation. After all, northern Norfolk was a long way from either Wiltshire or Buckinghamshire, and it would be difficult for any lord to make a dubious claim stick at such a distance from his own "country."

Difficult, that is, unless he had local help. Moleyns was making a political career for himself at court, where he met the canny Norfolk lawyer John Heydon. Moleyns had birth and status on his side; Heydon had a sharp legal brain, and personal and professional connections that reached, tendril-like, throughout the claustrophobic hothouse of Norfolk society. The combination proved lethal for the Pastons. On 17 February 1448, Lord Moleyns—"by the excitation and procuring of John Heydon," as John Paston later claimed[9]—sent a posse of armed men riding more than 150 miles from Wiltshire to north Norfolk, to seize Gresham for himself. John and Margaret were not there and, with no warning of Moleyns's plans, had no chance to organise any attempt at defence. The manor was overrun, their home invaded, and the doors barred against them. Gresham was gone before they knew what had happened.

It was calamitous news. There was, of course, no police force on whom the Pastons could call to expel the intruders from their property. They would have to take their complaint to the courts—and even there the awful reality was that Moleyns's powerful family, with their atavistic attachment to Gresham, might outweigh the Pastons' legitimate title. As soon as he started legal proceedings to retrieve the estate, John discovered quite how heavily the cards were stacked against him.

It was not only the Pastons' place in the political world that had changed out of all recognition since Judge William's death four years earlier. In that time, the government of England had undergone a subtle but far-reaching metamorphosis, the reverberations of which were now beginning to be insistently felt even in this corner of northern Norfolk. Now in his twenties, King Henry VI was still the naïve and artless figure he had been as a teenager, smiling at his advisers with mild benevolence and uttering a reproof only at any hint of immodesty in his courtiers' manners or morals. No panegyrist could now conceal the fact that the king had inherited none of the military acumen, political judgement, or magnetic charisma that had made his father, Henry V, a legend. Instead, he bore a much closer and much more unfortunate resemblance to his maternal grandfather, King Charles VI of France, who did not enjoy robust mental health even between the bouts of insanity by which he was repeatedly incapacitated (at one time insisting that he was fashioned out of glass and would shatter into a thousand fragments at the slightest touch). Henry VI had not yet shown any symptoms of serious mental illness, but neither was he any more capable of directing his own government than he had been as an infant. It gradually became apparent that the great nobility would have to continue to manage his authority for him, just as they had done during his childhood, but this time behind a public veneer of "normal" monarchical rule.

By the mid-1440s, England was governed by just such a regime. Henry VI was its figurehead, but the power behind the throne was William de la Pole, duke of Suffolk (great-grandson of the merchant of the same name whose commercial genius had set the family on the road to greatness). At a distance of six hundred years, Suffolk is an enigmatic character. Whether he was motivated by ambition, greed, or a sense of responsibility to his country, it is impossible to know: perhaps, inevitably, it was a combination of all three. He was an experienced soldier, who had served in France for fifteen years in a war that cost his father and three of his brothers their lives. When he finally returned to England, he threw himself into the political arena with an intensity that soon brought him the stewardship of the royal household and a leading place on the king's council. He also acquired a brilliant and wealthy wife, Alice Chaucer, granddaughter of the poet

Geoffrey Chaucer, and widow of the earl of Salisbury, Suffolk's commander at the siege of Orléans until he was killed there by a rogue artillery blast.

Now in his early fifties, Suffolk was, as his ducal title suggests, one of the greatest landowners in East Anglia as well as the king's chief minister. This combination of local influence with national authority meant that Suffolk undoubtedly had the power to help John Paston resist Lord Moleyns's aggression. But John's chances of enlisting his support were vanishingly slender. The duke was so preoccupied with the business of government that he scarcely had a moment even to set foot in the twin counties of Norfolk and Suffolk, making his home instead at his wife's Oxfordshire estate of Ewelme in the Thames Valley, from where the royal palaces of Westminster and Windsor were more easily accessible. Dispiritingly, while John Paston had no ready means of petitioning this absent but apparently all-powerful duke, the same was not true of his opponents. Lord Moleyns could find opportunities to lobby Suffolk almost daily at court, and John Heydon had been employed in the duke's service for more than ten years.

If there was no prospect of rescue by the hand of the duke of Suffolk, John needed to look for another powerful patron to press his case—and there were precious few on the horizon. Norfolk had its own duke, John Mowbray (whose estates, confusingly, lay mostly in the neighbouring county of Suffolk). But the duke of Norfolk had a mere fraction of the gravitas, judgment, or—crucially—power of the duke of Suffolk. As a teenager, Norfolk had been so delinquent that he was summoned before the royal council to answer for his disorderly behaviour; his closest friends were dismissed from his service as a corrupting influence, and he was subjected to a daily regime that prescribed even the times he should get up in the morning and retire to bed at night. Now in his early thirties, he was struggling to leave his misspent youth behind and prove himself as a serious political contender, but found himself thwarted at every turn. The crushing dominance of the duke of Suffolk would always have been hard to escape, but in truth, Norfolk's ambitious efforts to assert himself in local politics had so far proved almost laughably incompetent. He spent most of the 1440s preoccupied by a festering dispute with a disgruntled former servant, staging an armed assault on the unfortunate gentleman's Suffolk home, as a result of which the duke was subjected to costly and humiliating fines and even spent a few days imprisoned in the Tower of London.

It was all too apparent, therefore, that the duke of Norfolk was not the answer to John Paston's prayers. What he desperately needed was access to the very top of the political hierarchy, if he were to have any hope at all of standing up to enemies who could call on the towering figure of the duke of Suffolk as their patron. Given the peculiarities of Henry VI's government, that meant finding a patron of his own at court, someone who had direct access to the impressionable king but owed nothing to Suffolk, and might therefore be able to circumvent the duke's stranglehold on royal authority. Luckily for John, he already knew the man he believed he needed: an esquire of the royal household named Thomas Daniel.

Daniel, who was originally from the northwest of England, arrived in East Anglia in the autumn of 1446 through one of the most outrageous acts of fraud perpetrated even in this increasingly flexible political world. The victim of his chicanery was a gentleman named Henry Woodhouse, whose estates lay around his home at Roydon, near the port of King's Lynn in western Norfolk. Woodhouse was the son of one of Henry V's closest aides—so close that the great king himself had stood godfather to his young namesake. But a royal blessing at birth could not make up for the fact that Henry Woodhouse had inherited none of his father's political skills, and he had made little name for himself in the wider world by the time his thoughts turned to marriage in the mid 1440s.

The bride on whom he set his sights was Thomas Daniel's sister Elizabeth. Woodhouse was naïvely desperate to secure an alliance with this urbane and well-connected courtier, and as a result agreed to an unusually generous marriage contract, by which all of his estates would be settled jointly on himself and his new bride once they were man and wife. The legal disposition of the lands had to be put into effect through the offices of a trustee, who would first take possession of the estates from Woodhouse and then grant them back to the happy couple after the wedding. When Thomas Daniel himself volunteered his services as the trustee to whom legal title to the lands should be made over, Woodhouse accepted eagerly, so keen was he to expedite his courtship. But as soon as Daniel's name was on the deeds, he broke the news to the guileless and unsuspecting Woodhouse that Elizabeth was already married to someone else. And Daniel himself, it now transpired, had no intention whatsoever of giving back the lands.

Henry Woodhouse was distraught. He had been the dupe of an elaborate con practised by a pair of accomplished actors; Elizabeth Daniel had played along with her brother's ruse to such an extent that Woodhouse had spent a romantic evening wooing her, funded by twenty pence that Daniel had sent his prospective brother-in-law "to make the said Elizabeth good cheer withal."[10] Now the sting had been revealed, but there was little that the woebegone Woodhouse could do to redeem this humiliation and rescue his family's fortunes. Technically, he had handed over the estates of his own free will, and Daniel lost no time in exploiting his influence at court to reinforce his new East Anglian power base. In November 1446, he secured his own appointment as sheriff for Norfolk and Suffolk—an office for which, as a landholder in the region, he was now well qualified—and five months later obtained royal permission to fortify "his" manor house at Roydon.

Daniel had succeeded in defrauding a gentleman out of his entire inheritance, but his boundless ambition was not yet satisfied. He decided, with breathtaking chutzpah, to use the Woodhouse estates as a base from which to establish himself as a major player in local politics, even if that meant throwing existing power structures into disarray—in effect, challenging the overwhelming dominance of the duke of Suffolk in his own backyard. For the Pastons, battered and bruised by the loss of Gresham in the spring of 1448, Daniel's plans exercised a magnetic attraction. His unsavoury methods should perhaps have repelled them—they, too, after all, were victims of an unscrupulous courtier helping himself to a Norfolk estate—but the prospect of a court insider who might allow them to bypass the duke of Suffolk in their campaign to mobilise royal support against their enemies proved irresistible. John Paston showed no qualms about hitching himself to Daniel's star, and by April 1448, Margaret was asking her husband to convey respectful greetings to "my lord Daniel" in London.[11]

It was not yet clear how successful their new patron would be in chipping away at Suffolk's regional supremacy, and the flurries of rumour and counter-rumour that were carried on the wind between Norfolk and the capital were making Margaret apprehensive. "It is said in this country that Daniel is out of the king's good grace," she reported anxiously, "and he shall down, and all his men and all that be his well-willers. There shall no man be so hardy to do nor say against my lord of Suffolk, nor none that belong to him; and all that have done and said against him, they shall sore repent them."[12] But it was not so simple for the duke, at the head of a sprawling regime beset by problems at home and abroad, to see off Daniel's persistent and focused ambition in one small corner of his empire. By the summer of 1448, Daniel's success in thumbing his nose at Suffolk was causing much local comment, and the Pastons were doing what they could to encourage others to follow their lead in joining him.

Despite all their hopes, however, it gradually became apparent that the Pastons' alliance with Daniel was producing very little in the way of practical benefit in their battle to retrieve their home at Gresham from the hands of Lord Moleyns and John Heydon. It was perhaps always likely that an opportunist as ruthlessly self-serving as Daniel would have little energy to spare for other people's troubles. The further problem was that, however unrewarding Daniel's patronage was turning out to be, it also came at a price. By identifying themselves with Daniel and supporting his disreputable behaviour, the Pastons had involved themselves in a much wider web of rivalries and hostilities than simply their own fight with Heydon and Moleyns. They already knew that Heydon had friends who could help to make their lives unpleasant—the recent incident with John Wyndham in the street in Norwich had made that all too clear—but through their association with Thomas Daniel they invited even more hostile attention.

Daniel had probably seen the inept Henry Woodhouse as an easy target, but Woodhouse was not without allies of his own. His brother-in-law Sir Thomas Tuddenham was an influential man who held powerful offices both at court and in Norfolk, a trusted adviser of the duke of Suffolk, and a close friend of John Heydon. It was a matter of extraordinary coincidence that Tuddenham's marriage had broken down in a very similar way to Heydon's own, when his wife, Henry Woodhouse's sister Alice, gave birth to a son as a result of a liaison with her father's chamberlain. Here the parallels diverged: Tuddenham responded with none of his friend's fury at being cuckolded so publicly. He allowed his wife to retreat to a nunnery, and a decade passed before he initiated proceedings to annul the marriage in a church court. During the divorce hearing, Thomas and Alice both testified that their relationship had not been consummated during the seven years they had lived together, and Alice confessed that the father of her baby was a Woodhouse servant named Richard Stapleton, with whom, she said, she had had sex only once. The infant died soon after birth; Alice remained cloistered in her convent, and Tuddenham himself never remarried, thereby eschewing the possibility of fathering an heir to carry on his name and inherit his estates. A modern observer might suspect that Tuddenham was struggling with latent (because socially unacceptable) homosexuality, or perhaps a physical or psychological problem with sexual intimacy.

Whatever the cause of the rift in his marriage, Tuddenham—like his friend Heydon—remained on good terms with his estranged wife's family. Despite his closeness to Heydon, Tuddenham had not previously concerned himself with the Pastons, but once they had associated themselves with Daniel's appalling treatment of his brother-in-law Henry Woodhouse, Tuddenham joined the snowballing campaign of harassment that the family now faced. "It is told me that he that keeps your sheep was outlawed on Monday at the suit of Sir Thomas Tuddenham," Margaret reported to her husband in April 1448, "and if it be so you are not like to keep him long."[13] Outlawry was the legal process by which individuals could be placed outside the protection of the law, and their possessions declared forfeit to the crown. Often imposed on those who repeatedly failed to appear in court to answer an indictment, it was now so routinely invoked that it had become a standard means of enforcing the court's authority rather than a penalty from which the "outlaw" could not easily recover; but it remained a judicial manoeuvre that could be exploited to exert pressure on political opponents, either in person, or indirectly (as in the case of the Pastons' shepherd) via their servants and tenants.

John was becoming profoundly frustrated. Lord Moleyns's men were living in his home at Gresham and collecting rents from the tenants there, and Daniel had so far failed to do anything at all to help. In June, John turned instead to the possibility of a negotiated settlement through the good offices of the church, in the person of William Wainfleet—a scholarly and conscientious man, formerly the headmaster of the school that the king had recently founded at Eton, and newly promoted to the bishopric of Winchester. In public, Moleyns declared himself amenable to such an arbitration, but in private he made no move to cooperate. On every front, John's desperate efforts to retrieve his property were running into the sand.

It was increasingly obvious that procrastination was entirely in Moleyns's interests. He was in command at Gresham, and the status quo therefore suited him down to the ground. Given the weakness of his title to the estate, he had no interest in bringing the case to speedy judgment in the courts. The longer he could take the profits of the manor and postpone formal hearings into its ownership, the better. John Paston was a stubborn man who believed in the process of law, but even he was beginning to realise that he could not depend on the authority of a court in which he simply could not force his adversary to appear. Direct negotiation was working no better: sixteen separate meetings took place between lawyers representing the two sides, and John believed he had answered every claim Moleyns's advisers raised. When opposing counsel admitted "they could no further in the matter," John rode eighty miles from London to Wiltshire to petition Moleyns in person, and "none answer had but delays."[14] By the autumn, he had decided that more assertive action was needed to resist Moleyns's annexation of Gresham—but John himself, of course, could not leave their legal business in the capital for long. So, on 6 October 1448, it was Margaret and their two young sons, now aged six and four, who went to take up residence at a house in Gresham village almost on the doorstep of the men who had taken over their home.

The presence at Gresham of Margaret and her two boys with their handful of servants—twelve souls, all told—served as a physical embodiment of the Pastons' claim to the manor: she had reentered the property, even if not their own house, and was demanding rent payments from the tenants in recognition of her husband's rights. From her position on the front line, she was also able to send John detailed information about what Moleyns's servants were doing there. Their house was held by a small company from Wiltshire led by one John Partridge, with help from a few local men including the Pastons' old enemy John Mariot, to whom they had lost East Beckham three years earlier. And Margaret's arrival had spurred this occupying force into a frenzy of activity: ". . . they have made great ordinance within the house, as it is told me," she reported sombrely to her husband. "They have made bars to bar the doors crosswise, and they have made wickets on every quarter of the house to shoot out at, both with bows and with handguns; and the holes that are made for handguns they are scarce knee high from the floor, and of such holes are made five."[15]

Confronted with these alarming preparations, Margaret felt that she, too, needed to ready her defences. Crossbows were first on the list she sent John in London, "for your houses here are so low that there may no man shoot out with no longbow, though we had never so much need." The longbow was the classic English weapon—the scourge of the French at Crécy, Poitiers, and Agincourt, unleashing ten or twelve arrows a minute in the strong hands of a skilled archer, and capable of piercing plate armour at a hundred yards or chain mail at twice that distance. Every loyal Englishman was required by law to reach a basic level of proficiency by practising in the local butts on Sundays—but a fine yew bow was useless inside a house where the ceilings were too low to allow its six-foot length to be drawn at a man's shoulder. A much better prospect, Margaret knew, was the crossbow, shooting two deadly bolts a minute from its horizontal mechanism—ideal for use in a confined space and less risky to operate than the slowly evolving technology of the handgun, which might, on unpredictable occasion, prove

lethal to the shooter as well as the target. Two or three short-handled combat axes would also be valuable, she added, in case she and her entourage
were forced to defend the doors against assailants trying to rush the building, and "as many jacks"—armoured jackets, made of quilted fabric or
leather into which metal plates were sewn to deflect glancing blows or
missiles—"as you may." However frightening her situation, Margaret was
practical and resourceful, and she was not panicking. Together with the
weapons and body armour, she asked John to send her a pound of almonds
and a pound of sugar, and material to make gowns for the children, as well
as "a yard of broad cloth of black for a hood for me of 44d or 4s a yard, for
there is neither good cloth nor good frieze [a sturdy woollen fabric] in this
town."[16]

Others were not so sanguine. On 5 November, Margaret's uncle Philip
Berney paid her a visit at Gresham and blenched with shock when he saw
her servants wearing their helmets and leather jacks. He left as soon as he
decently could after lunch, promising Margaret that he would come again
soon, but a week later sent his servant Davy instead with a tale of woe. Her
uncle's horse had gone lame; he had ordered Davy to saddle another
mount, and "he stood by and made water while he saddled him"—but,
while Berney was relieving himself, disaster struck. Without warning, the
horse "slinked round and took his master on the hip such a stroke that
never man may trust him after, and broke his hip." Margaret was full of
sympathy at this unfortunate accident, but her chaplain James Gloys—now
back in Norfolk after his Wyndham-inspired exile—was incensed at
Berney's cowardice. "I know well that it was not so," he told John angrily;
he had heard in Norwich the very next day that Berney was "hale and
merry." He wanted to warn his master of such feeble friendship, but could
not bear to tell Margaret of her uncle's duplicity: "if my mistress knew that I
sent you such a letter I were never able to look upon her, nor to abide in her
eyesight."[17]

However, Margaret was not completely bereft of support. John
Damme, their good friend whose home at Sustead lay only a mile away
from Gresham, kept in close touch with her and spoke to Partridge and
Mariot on her behalf, even if the conversation all too easily turned into a
pantomime of threats: ". . . he said, if you put them out, you should be put
out soon after again," Damme reported later to John in London. "And I
said, if it happens so, they should not long rest there." Damme still hoped
that their arrogance would be misplaced—"Partridge and his fellow bear

great visage and keep great junkets and dinners, and say that my Lord Moleyns has written plainly to them that he is lord there and will be and shall be, and you not to have it; but I trust to God's righteousness of better purveyance"—but he was fearful, particularly of what John Heydon might do, "being of my lord's counsel and not your good friend nor well-willer." He left it to a postscript to suggest that now might be a good time for John to order an elegant "jack defensible" for himself.[18]

It was not John, however, but Margaret who would need that kind of protection. In the early morning of Tuesday, 28 January 1449, the small Paston household heard the muffled drumbeat of hooves on icy ground, and saw, in the distance, the dull gleam of metal—breastplates, visors, bits and bridles—in the bleak winter light. An army had come to drive the Pastons from Gresham. Margaret's defensive instincts had been right; but a handful of crossbows and a couple of axes in the hands of her loyal servants were pitifully inadequate protection against the scores of well-armed men Lord Moleyns had sent to harry them. In an outraged complaint to parliament, John Paston later described Margaret's attackers as a thousand strong and fully equipped for a military assault. Even allowing for the poetic licence that every petitioner permitted himself, it was clearly a terrifying onslaught. Still, Margaret could not bring herself to surrender; she would not give her enemy the satisfaction of seeing her abandon an estate that was rightfully hers. Moleyns's men "mined down the wall of the chamber wherein the wife of your said beseecher was," John wrote, "and bore her out at the gates, and cut asunder the posts of the houses and let them fall, and broke up all the chambers and coffers within the said mansion, and rifled and in manner of robbery bore away all the stuff, array and money that your said beseecher and his servants had there."[19] Margaret, her two boys, and the family servants were mercifully unhurt amid the looting, and were treated respectfully enough once they had been removed without ceremony from the house. But it was abundantly clear that Moleyns was no longer prepared to tolerate their presence at Gresham. The beleaguered Paston household fled a mile southeast to Sustead to seek shelter with their friends John and Elizabeth Damme.

John's strategy of using physical confrontation to force Moleyns to show his hand had worked a little too well. The Pastons could at least now claim—with substantial justification—that Moleyns was guilty of a violent breach of the peace, and John lost no time in pursuing the charge. Another nobleman, the earl of Oxford, had a home at Winch in western Norfolk, and John rode there as soon as news came of the sack at Gresham, to ask the earl to act in his capacity as a justice of the peace—one of a panel of local landowners appointed to sit as judges in minor cases in the county—to challenge Moleyns's occupation of the manor. Oxford had promised John Damme a couple of months earlier that he would come to Gresham if he were needed ("if it were fair weather he would not tarry, and if it rained he would not spare"), and now he was as good as his word.[20] The earl arrived in the village the day after the assault, but Moleyns's men barred the gates of the manor house against him, declaring that neither he nor anyone else should enter except by the explicit permission of their lord. Oxford's sympathies translated into little direct action: he did nothing more than inspect the scene, claiming that he had no time because of his imminent departure to attend parliament, but he did at least send a written report into the court of King's Bench detailing John's allegations and certifying that the doors of the house at Gresham had been closed against him by Moleyns's servants.

It was better than nothing, but not much. Accompanied by the stalwart John Damme, John Paston returned, downhearted, to London to pursue his complaints against Moleyns at the new parliament, which opened on 12 February. Margaret and the boys meanwhile remained at Sustead with Damme's wife, Elizabeth. The few tenants at Gresham who continued to support the Pastons were harassed with physical threats and lawsuits; for many, it was easier simply to pay Moleyns's agents the rent they demanded. At Sustead, Margaret was still close enough at least to try to protect the villagers who had backed her, and to exert pressure—moral, political, or practical—on Moleyns's supporters and servants in whatever way she could.

An esquire from Wiltshire named Walter Barrow had now taken over John Partridge's command at Gresham, and on John Paston's instructions Margaret sent him a message to complain about the intimidating behaviour of his men. She dispatched her own servant Katherine to speak to him, "for I could get no man to do it." There were at least some benefits of being a woman in this menacing situation: where the conversation between John Damme and John Partridge two months earlier had descended rapidly into a competitive show of swaggering bravado, communication from Margaret via a female servant allowed Barrow to be gracious. He received Katherine with "great cheer," and told her courteously that he would like to speak to her mistress, suggesting that he should pass by the house at Sustead on a hunting trip later in the day. When Barrow and his servants duly arrived that afternoon, they waited at the roadside and sent, again politely, to ask if Margaret would receive them.

Their courtesy did nothing to persuade her of their good intentions. She refused to invite them into the Dammes' home—"inasmuch as they were not well-willing to the good man of the place, I would not take it upon me to bring them in to the gentlewoman"—but went out to the gate to hear what Barrow had to say for himself. He was all charm, responding to Margaret's message with "such an answer as they hoped should please me," and giving his word that none of her servants or tenants would be harmed. Rumours she had heard that she was vulnerable even at Sustead—"that I should not long dwell so near them as I do"—were also vehemently denied. Barrow and his man "spoke to me in the most pleasant wise," Margaret reported, and "said they would do me service and pleasure, if it lay in their powers to do anything for me."[21] But his blandishments left her cold. "I trust not to their promise," she told her husband, "inasmuch as I find them untrue in other things." Before they parted, she took care to let Barrow know that she was well aware of the role John Heydon was playing behind the scenes of Lord Moleyns's manoeuvres. "I told him I knew well he set never thereupon by no title of right that he had to the manor of Gresham," she said stoutly, "but only by the information of a false shrew. I rehearsed no name, but methought by them that they knew who I meant."[22]

Margaret was holding her own with extraordinary courage and dignity, but she was now genuinely frightened, especially—and amazingly, given that it was she who had faced an armed attack—for her husband's safety. "I hear say that you and John Damme are sore threatened always," she wrote in some agitation, ". . . and therefore I pray you heartily beware how you walk there and have a good fellowship with you when you shall walk out." Moleyns's men were nothing but "a company of brothel"—worthless degenerates—"that reck not what they do, and such are most for to dread. They that are at Gresham say that they have not done so much hurt to you as they were commanded to do." Under the circumstances, she was finding it increasingly difficult to cope with their enforced separation. "I pray you heartily that you will send me word how you do and how you speed in your matters," she wrote, "for by my troth I cannot be well at ease in my heart, nor not shall be, till I hear tidings how you do."[23]

Two weeks later, at the end of February, her fears finally became too much to bear. Word reached her that Moleyns's men were planning to kidnap her from Sustead and hold her captive at Gresham, whether as a tactical move to force John into confrontation, or simply for their own enter-tainment ("they said it should be but a little heart-burning to you," she told her husband). Either way, their motives hardly mattered: Margaret was intensely unnerved. She gathered her possessions and left Sustead for Norwich, telling no one of her departure except Elizabeth Damme, and pretending even to her that she would be away for only two or three weeks while she had some clothes made for herself and the children. She was wor-ried that John would be angry that she had left—"beseeching you that you be not displeased," she begged—but too anxious to stay so near Gresham any longer. She sounded, for once, shaken and very scared. "After that I heard these tidings I could no rest have in my heart till I was here," she wrote from Norwich. On her way to the city she had stopped at Oxnead to see Agnes, who offered her town house to Margaret and the children for as long as they needed, a suggestion that was accepted with relief and grati-tude. At least now they were physically safe, although Margaret continued to worry about John's vulnerability in London. "At the reverence of God," she told him, "beware of the Lord Moleyns and his men, though they speak never so fair to you, trust them not, nor eat nor drink with them, for they are so false it is not for to trust in them."[24]

It was a measure of the strain they were under that their letters made no mention of happier news. At some point in 1448 or 1449 Margaret gave birth again, to a girl named Margery, after her own mother. The new baby may have arrived even before the Paston household took up residence at Gresham in October 1448, or Margaret may have been pregnant during some or all of the upheavals there. Either way, it is clear that Margaret, now twenty-six, was an astonishingly brave and resourceful woman—and also that she and her husband had almost no time to enjoy their growing family. From March 1449, while Margaret and the children remained in Norwich, John did what he could to press their case in London, but—in the absence of any assistance from influential men—it was not much. He submitted a petition to parliament describing the assault on Gresham and detailing their losses there, but to depressingly small effect. One infuriating problem he faced in trying to bring charges in the courts was that, by law, indict-ments required the name, status, and place of residence of each man accused—and because Moleyns's men came from Wiltshire, no one in Norfolk knew who they were. As he pointed out in his petition, "your said beseecher can have none action by your law against the said riotous people for the goods and chattels by them so riotously and wrongfully taken and borne away, because the said people be unknown, as well their names as their persons, unto him."[25]

While John struggled with legal technicalities, Lord Moleyns himself, who had not once set foot in Norfolk since the conflict began, sent an expansively authoritative letter designed to reassure his supporters and intimidate those who were still daring to defy him, which John Heydon was showing around polite society in Norwich. "The Lord Moleyns wrote in his foresaid letter that he would mightily with his body and with his goods stand by all those that had been his friends and his well-willers in the matter touching Gresham," Margaret heard.[26] Walter Barrow too had been irritatingly complacent when she talked to him last before leaving Sustead, telling her that no one in England held better evidence than his master did to justify his claim to Gresham. Margaret did what she could to puncture his self-assurance—she knew exactly what kind of documents Moleyns had, she told him, and "the seals of them were not yet cold"—but without much success. Barrow was still all public smiles, offering to buy John a drink next time he was in London "for any anger that was between you," Margaret told her husband. Nevertheless, disturbing rumours were circulating in Norfolk that "you have had one shot, and unless you beware you shall have more before Easter": now that Gresham had gone, word had it that the manors of Sporle and Swainsthorpe would be next, on what grounds Margaret had no idea, although on past experience, she knew that grounds of any kind were hardly needed.[27] And of course, now that the Pastons had been forced onto the back foot, the blows might come from more directions than one. Their old adversary John Hauteyn thought he saw an opportunity to revive his campaign to wrest Oxnead from Agnes, and began to issue renewed threats. "There was a person warned my mother within these two days that she should beware," Margaret told her husband on 2 April, "for they said plainly she was like to be served as you were served at Gresham within right short time."[28]

One deeply distressing blow had already fallen by the time Margaret wrote with this news. John's brother Edmund was taken ill suddenly at London and died on 21 March, at the age of only twenty-five. The will he dictated hours before his death was short—he had no wish to occupy his mind with the things of this world, he said, now that he had so little time to prepare himself for the next—and simply left everything he had to his elder brother. John took pains to make sure that Edmund's gravestone should be finely made—"it is told me that the man at St. Bride's is no cleanly por-

trayer, wherefore I would fain it might be portrayed by some other man"—
but had almost no time to mourn.[29] He was having to spend time and
energy on the Hauteyn claim to Oxnead when he could ill afford to divert
any of his attention from Moleyns and Gresham, and he had no effective
support on which to call in either case. He tried to impress a lawyer at the
papal court in Rome, whose advice he wanted, by claiming that he could
call on the good will of "my lord of Winchester, and Daniel,"[30] but the
truth was that the bishop of Winchester had not been able even to persuade
Lord Moleyns to the negotiating table, and Thomas Daniel was an
unscrupulous chancer who looked after no one but himself.

Margaret felt the time had come for a change of strategy, even if her
uncharacteristically convoluted way of saying so indicated how hesitant she
was about suggesting it: "folks that be your right well-willers have counselled me that I should counsel you to make other means than you have
made, to other folks that would speed your matters better than they have
done that you have spoken to thereof before this time." Her husband was
both stubborn and proud, and the implication that his efforts over the last
year had had no appreciable effect could hardly be welcome, particularly
given that Margaret wanted to propose that it was the duke of Suffolk—the
patron of their enemy Heydon—to whom they should be suing for help.
"Sundry folks have said to me that they think verily, unless you have my
lord of Suffolk's good lordship while the world is as it is, you can never live
in peace . . ." Once she had summoned up the courage to broach the subject, her usual fluency returned as she tried to persuade John of the urgent
need to follow this course: "therefore I pray you with all my heart that you
will do your part to have his good lordship and his love, in ease of all the
matters that you have to do, and in easing of my heart also."[31] As a reading
of their experiences over the last year, Margaret's analysis of the urgent
need somehow to enlist the duke of Suffolk's support had a lot to recommend it—even if, given Heydon's closeness to Suffolk, their chances of persuading the duke to intervene seemed hopelessly remote.

Margaret's conclusions could not be faulted, but the timing of her suggestion could scarcely have been worse. One of the reasons why her husband had struggled so much to interest anyone of influence in their
problems at Gresham was that much greater troubles were threatening to
engulf the very highest levels of Henry VI's government. For almost thirty
years, the most pressing issue that the great nobles had faced was how to
defend Henry V's conquests in France in the name of a king who could not

lead his own army, at first because he was a child, and then because his engagement with the world was so vague that his presence on a battlefield would have been nothing but a liability. Henry VI set foot on French soil only once, at the age of nine, when he travelled to Paris for his coronation as king of France in 1431. Six months earlier, Joan of Arc had been burned as a witch and a heretic by the English at Rouen, but her death came too late to stop the French military resurgence that she had inspired by driving the English from the gates of Orléans in 1429. The English commanders in France succeeded in holding the line for a few more years against the armies of the French dauphin, now crowned as Charles VII, but by the 1440s the last remaining question was how best to protect English interests in retreat.

Peace was the only realistic option. In 1444, the duke of Suffolk led an embassy to France that agreed to a temporary cease-fire and a marriage alliance between King Henry, now twenty-two, and the French king's fifteen-year-old niece, Margaret, daughter of the duke of Anjou. Given the strength of the French position, English chances of securing a lasting settlement now depended on combining resolute defence of those French territories that were still in English hands with a willingness to put something concrete on the table that might persuade the French to come to terms. The attempt failed on both counts. A secret deal was made during 1445 whereby England agreed to cede the county of Maine to the French in return for an extended truce, an agreement that in theory should have allowed the English forces in Normandy time to establish themselves on a soundly defensive footing, and provided France with a reason to settle for peace. In practice, the difficulty of enforcing a single, clear policy in the name of a vacuous king ensured that neither happened. No advantage was taken of the breathing space afforded by the truce to regroup in Normandy, while at the same time, the surrender of Maine did not take place as the treaty had promised, giving Charles VII legitimate reason to consider the agreement broken and himself absolved of the need to abide by its terms. In August 1449, he sent his armies into Normandy, and the result was a rout. Rouen fell to the French at the end of October, and by the beginning of 1450 almost all of Normandy had been overrun. In only four months, Henry V's spectacular conquests had been lost forever.

Recriminations in England began even while the disaster in France was still unfolding. When parliament convened in November 1449, the House of Commons could not contain its outrage that a war which had cost thousands upon thousands of pounds in taxation was ending in such devastation and ignominy. It was clear that, for once, the Lower House was speaking not only for the gentlemen and rich merchants who made up its members but also for the mass of the king's subjects in blaming those closest to the king for the catastrophe. Inside parliament, leading courtiers were subjected to lacerating criticism; outside, the hostility they met could take much more brutal form. One leading minister, the bishop of Chichester, was fatally unlucky to find himself in the wrong place at the wrong time at Portsmouth on 9 January 1450, when he was hacked to death by a howling mob of mutinous soldiers. A month later, however, the consensus in both country and parliament was that principal responsibility for the cataclysmic failure of English policy in France lay squarely with William de la Pole, duke of Suffolk. Treason was the only possible explanation for what had happened, and the only person whose treason could have led to such terrible consequences was the man at the king's right hand.

On 7 February, articles of impeachment were presented against Suffolk by the Commons in parliament who claimed—with righteous anger and total indifference to the lack of either evidence or plausibility—not only that the duke had plotted the destruction of English interests in France, but also that he had sought to depose King Henry in favour of his own son. Fundamentally, the charges added up to the fact that a scapegoat was needed for the loss of France, and Suffolk's preeminence in government made him the only possible candidate. His fall was now both inevitable and necessary in order to defuse the political crisis—and yet his fellow magnates were acutely uneasy at the prospect of handing him to a lynch mob for a policy in which they had all been involved, a shared responsibility that Suffolk would expose as publicly as he could if the treason charges were pursued against him. The accusations could not be ignored completely, but Suffolk's trial was postponed for several weeks, a delay that gave rise to rumours in Norfolk that "the duke of Suffolk is pardoned, and has his men again waiting upon him, and is right well at ease and merry, and is in the king's good grace and in the good conceit of all the lords as well as ever he was."[32]

The Commons used this interval to come up with a further slew of allegations against the duke, this time concerning domestic misgovernment and financial improprieties. But rather than compounding the pressure on Suffolk as the Commons must have hoped, these additional charges offered the lords a way out of the public process of impeachment. On 17 March, a

declaration was made in King Henry's name dismissing the charges of treason, but accepting the second set of articles against the duke that the
Commons had produced, those "touching misprisions which are not criminal."[33] There would be no formal judicial hearing; instead, Suffolk was sentenced to banishment for a term of five years.

It seemed as though the worst of the political storm was over. On
Thursday, 30 April, the duke of Suffolk left England. His two ships took up
position in the Channel while he sent ahead to Calais—the wealthy fortified
port on the northern French coast that remained the principal English gateway to the Continent—to see what reception awaited him there. At some
point during the day he wrote a touching letter to his only child, his seven-
year-old son John, charging him to be true and faithful to God, the king,
and his mother; "and last of all, as heartily and as lovingly as ever father
blessed his child on earth, I give you the blessing of our Lord and of me,
which of his infinite mercy increase you in all virtue and good living. . . .
Written of my hand, the day of my departing from this land. Your true and
loving father, Suffolk."[34] The duke was still waiting for an answer from
Calais when his ship was approached by another, the *Nicholas of the Tower*.
At the insistence of the master of the *Nicholas*, Suffolk came aboard the
ship to speak with him. He was greeted with a cry of "Welcome, traitor."[35]

Suddenly, shockingly, it was clear that neither the charges of treason
that had been levelled at the duke in parliament, nor the violent anger that
had precipitated them, could be sidestepped quite so easily. The sailors on
Suffolk's own ship disowned him, and when the duke asked the name of the
craft on which he was now being held prisoner he fell into despair. A
prophecy had been made before he left England that "if he might escape
the danger of the Tower, he should be safe." On board his own ship en
route for Calais, the Tower of London had seemed comfortingly far away,
but the *Nicholas of the Tower* had been close at hand to intercept him, "and
then his heart failed him, for he thought he was deceived."[36] Two days later,
on Saturday, 2 May, the crew of the *Nicholas* used their ship as a makeshift
court to try Suffolk for treason, declaring that, "as the king did not wish to
punish these traitors of his own will, nor to govern the aforesaid realm better, they themselves would do it."[37]

The verdict was never in doubt. In full view of Suffolk's men, the duke
was taken from the *Nicholas* into its small launch, where a stock and an axe
had been laid out. One of the sailors, "one of the lewdest of the ship,"
ordered the duke to "lay down his head, and he should be fair fared with

and die on a sword"—it being a nobleman's prerogative to choose a chivalric blade rather than a plebeian axe for his execution. The sword was rusty, and it took half a dozen sickening strokes to sever Suffolk's head from his body. The shipmen "took away his gown of russet and his doublet of velvet mailed, and laid his body on the sands of Dover." As news spread that Suffolk's mutilated corpse lay on Dover Beach, the political world was temporarily paralysed with shock. "The sheriff of Kent does watch the body," it was reported three days later, "and sent his undersheriff to the judges to wit what to do."[38]

At Norwich, the Pastons received word of what had happened from their friend William Lomnor. "I recommend me to you and am right sorry of that I shall say," he wrote, "and have so washed this little bill with sorrowful tears that scarcely you shall read it."[39] John and Margaret themselves had little cause to weep for Suffolk. The regime over which he had presided, battered from without by the French advance and eroded from within by the strain of Henry VI's incompetence, had utterly failed to bring Lord Moleyns to heel or to offer them justice at Gresham. And yet the duke's power had seemed so unassailable that their only hope, Margaret had believed, lay in securing his favour—at least "while the world is as it is."[40] In May 1450 the world, it seemed, had changed.

↲

the world

is changed greatly

*T*HE DUKE OF SUFFOLK'S MURDER unleashed chaos across the country. Little more than two weeks after his headless body was thrown onto the Kent shore, popular revolt erupted in the shire under the leadership of a man of humble birth and undeniable charisma named Jack Cade. As disturbances spread across southern England, Cade's followers marched on London in their thousands. Margaret Paston's seventy-year-old kinsman Sir John Fastolf, an old soldier who had made a fortune in the French wars, found himself caught in the eye of the storm. He was living in retirement in the capital less than a mile downriver from London Bridge, in a grandly moated riverfront residence on the edge of the bustling streets of Southwark, the suburb where the motley band of pilgrims in Chaucer's *Canterbury Tales* gathered at the Tabard Inn. But on 1 July 1450, Southwark found itself playing host to much less welcome visitors when the rebel horde set up camp there as a prelude to their final surge into the city.

Many of the specific grievances of the Kentish contingent were local ones—particularly their hatred of a courtier named Lord Saye, whom they accused of oppression and extortion in their county—but what made them so dangerous was that they also gave voice to much more widespread anger at a regime which had expended thousands of English lives and thousands of English pounds on a war that ended in abject failure. As the rebels were approaching Southwark, Fastolf sent a servant out to see if he could secure a copy of their manifesto. The poor man barely escaped with his life, but the document he brought back encapsulated the popular perception of the past few months' events in stark terms. King Henry, the rebels declared, "has had false counsel, for his lands are lost, his merchandise is lost, his commons destroyed, the sea is lost, France is lost, himself so poor that he may not pay for his meat nor drink." And they were in no doubt where the blame should fall: the insatiable greed and extravagance of his courtiers— "his traitors that are about him"—were bleeding the realm dry.[1] Fastolf was no friend of Henry VI's household men, but neither was he prepared to give the rebels the benefit of the doubt; he ordered his servants to pack up his valuables, and found a wherryman to row him across the foul-smelling waters of the Thames to take refuge within the colossal fortifications of the Tower of London.

With the government in disarray, the king was dispatched northward to the Midlands for safety, leaving the rebels to storm across London Bridge and into the city itself. Cade was determined to demonstrate that his pro-gramme of reform was legitimate, and convened quasi-judicial hearings at the Guildhall (the splendid new building just east of St. Paul's Cathedral where, in calmer times, the mayor presided over the city council), at which twenty leading courtiers were formally indicted for treason. Violence could not be restrained for long, however. Lord Saye and his equally reviled son-in-law, the sheriff of Kent, were executed, and their heads paraded on pikes through the streets, from time to time being made to kiss one another in gruesome pantomime as the crowds jeered.

But the bloodshed and looting proved the rebels' undoing. Many Londoners were sympathetic to their complaints, but the mayor and lead-ing citizens would not simply stand by and watch their city being destroyed. On the night of 5 July, they decided to seize control of London Bridge, intending to leave Cade and his men shut out of the city, marooned in the lodgings they had commandeered for themselves among the inns of Southwark, on the south bank of the river. Hundreds were killed in a bloody battle that raged all night, but when light came and the smoke cleared, the city gates had finally been locked against the insurgents. Negotiations followed, during which the rebels were allowed a formal opportunity to present their complaints, and many took up the offer of a pardon for those who would return to their homes. Cade himself, knowing by now that a pardon would not save him, retreated first to his native county of Kent and then westward along the south coast, to Sussex. He was wounded and captured on 12 July, and died shortly afterward of his injuries. The mere fact of his death, however, did not spare him the penalties of treason. His naked body was brought back to London for formal identification, and on 16 July his corpse was publicly beheaded outside the prison at Newgate on the western edge of the city; his head was then placed on a spike on London Bridge, and his body dragged through the streets before being cut into pieces to be displayed in towns around the country as a dreadful reminder of the fate of traitors.

Cade's part in the revolt was over, but unrest continued across the southeast, fuelled by the anger of the soldiers and settlers who were straggling home as the last outposts of English rule in northern France fell to the French. News reached London on 19 August that "Cherbourg is gone, and we have not now a foot of land in Normandy";[2] the great port of Calais and the beleaguered remains of the duchy of Aquitaine around the southwestern city of Bordeaux were all that was now left of the English empire in France. The loss of naval control in the Channel made southern England, already staggering under the impact of revolt, a yet more dangerous place. That much had been frighteningly clear in Norfolk as early as the spring, when French ships were raiding the coast from Yarmouth to Cromer, stealing English boats and kidnapping anybody, man or woman, who was foolish enough to walk on the beaches. "The said enemies are so bold that they come up to the land and play them on Caister sands and in other places as homelily as they were Englishmen," Margaret told her husband.[3]

And yet, despite the terror of these upheavals, the disintegration of the duke of Suffolk's regime also represented an unprecedented opportunity for anyone who had suffered under his rule. Political structures that had seemed immovable and invulnerable were suddenly in flux. The situation was dangerous and chaotic, but the sweeping away of old certainties meant that those who had been excluded from power might now have a real chance to assert themselves. John Paston, a small fish in a small pond, certainly thought so, but it was equally true for much greater men. For the duke of Norfolk, smarting at his failure to achieve the political recognition he felt was his due, the way was now open to step out of Suffolk's shadow and claim the place he believed was rightfully his, at the centre of East Anglian politics. Sir John Fastolf, too, harboured an acute sense of grievance against Suffolk's regime. The valuable lands in France that the old knight had acquired during his long years as a soldier had now been lost, along with the rest of the English conquests there, in the disaster that

Suffolk's peace policy had become. And Fastolf felt just as much of a victim at home, believing that his interests in Norfolk—where he had built up a massive estate with the proceeds of his lucrative military career—had suffered at the hands of the duke's allies, especially John Heydon and his friend Sir Thomas Tuddenham. Now, Fastolf thought, the time had come for restitution and revenge.

For others, such as Thomas Daniel, the situation was more complicated. As a prominent member of the royal court, Daniel had been a target of fierce hostility in the wake of Suffolk's fall, but he was no friend of the duke's, and in the summer of 1450, he saw the possibility of manoeuvring for his own advantage as well as the need for self-defence. He had been friendly with the duke of Norfolk for a couple of years already, and now began to cultivate an acquaintance with the earl of Oxford, whose Norfolk home at Winch was only a few miles from Daniel's fraudulently acquired house at Roydon. All in all, these developments could scarcely have seemed more positive for John Paston. His connections with Thomas Daniel had been little use before this point, but the alliance of Daniel with Oxford, who had at least been sympathetic when he visited Gresham in the previous year, and the association of both men with the duke of Norfolk and Margaret's cousin Fastolf, seemed a great deal more promising, especially given that Suffolk's death had left the Pastons' enemies Heydon and Lord Moleyns suddenly vulnerable. After two years of struggle, whatever the chaos that surrounded him, it finally seemed possible that John might find a way to expel Moleyns's men from his property.

It was a summer of frantic activity on all fronts. Sir John Fastolf set to work within days of Suffolk's death to compile an exhaustive list of all the wrongs he felt he had suffered over the previous twelve years. His temporary displacement from his Southwark mansion at the hands of the rebels did nothing to deflect him from his purpose, although it did encourage him to stock up on weaponry, so long as it could be done economically and discreetly: "purvey me at the least five dozen longbows, with shot belonging thereto," he told his chaplain in Norfolk, "and purvey also quarrel heads"—bolts for crossbows—"to be made there, for the price is dearer here than there; and let no language be had of ordinances making."[4] John Paston, meanwhile, presented a petition to the chancellor—one of the highest-ranking ministers in royal government, with a particular responsibility for the provision of equitable justice—asking that a special judicial commission be appointed specifically to investigate Moleyns's seizure of Gresham. He proposed that Lord Moleyns be compelled to remove his men from Gresham immediately, and that the profits of the estate go to a neutral party until the commission could sit and the matter be decided.

The chancellor was not unsympathetic to the suggestion, and wrote to Moleyns accordingly, but the very circumstances that were finally giving John this access to the heart of government also told heavily against him. With the country engulfed in chaos, powerful men had more important things to think about than injustices done in a small corner of northern Norfolk. Rumours were sweeping the south of more risings to follow Cade's revolt, and word came to London that nine or ten thousand rebels were massing to the west, in Wiltshire. The rumour subsided as rapidly as it had developed, but by then it had already served Lord Moleyns's purpose. The Pastons' attorney, James Gresham, wrote in the middle of August to report Moleyns's response to the chancellor's letter. Of course, Moleyns said, "if he might attend to be in Norfolk and leave the necessary service that he did to the king now in Wiltshire," he would be "well pleased" for John's plan to be put into action; but, he explained in tones of the utmost sincerity, he simply could not leave Wiltshire, since he was needed there "to peace and still the people there to restrain them from rising, and so he was daily laboured thereabout in the king's service."[5] James Gresham's advice was that—given the ongoing unrest, and Moleyns's obvious determination to continue stonewalling for as long as he could—John should abandon his campaign for a special investigation into his own case, and rely instead on the fact that general judicial commissions were being appointed to deal with disorder across the south of England. When the justices sat in Norfolk, John could present his complaints against Moleyns to them.

In the circumstances, it was a hardy man who would argue with that; but John was, if nothing else, hardy. He had heard all Moleyns's fine words before, and he was angry. In John's mind, the situation was clear: he had a right to Gresham that he could establish in law, and he wanted his day in court to prove it. Not for the last time, his conviction that right as he saw it should prevail made him incapable of negotiating the complex politics of the situation. He could not accept that he might have to take the pragmatic route and cede some ground to a man who had less right but more power than he. Moleyns had indicated that he would consider the possibility of arbitration, but the two sides could not even agree on what that should mean. In John's eyes, arbitration was a chance to put his case to impartial referees for judgement, "so they would determine by our evidences the right." For Moleyns, however, it represented an opportunity to bargain from a position of strength with all the leverage he could muster; he wanted the arbiters to broker a compromise deal "by offer and proffer, to my conceit as men buy horses," John explained heatedly to his attorney. He was so infuriated, and so impatient with the sprawling mess of his affairs, that he urged James Gresham to press the chancellor for a decision one way or the other on the question of the special judicial commission, even if to do so was to risk a negative response: "I pray you heartily labour you so to my lord Chancellor," he wrote, "that either he will grant me my desire or else that he will deny it."[6]

In the end, as James Gresham had foreseen, the answer was no. All John's hopes now rested on the general commission of oyer et terminer, which would convene at Norwich in September 1450. Oyer et terminer literally meant "to hear and to determine," and this law-French phrase meant that the judges would sit at Norwich with the full power of the Westminster courts at their disposal, not only to hear indictments but to pass verdicts on them as well. This was an attempt by a profoundly shaken government to clamp down on continuing unrest, and at the same time to defuse the simmering volatility of southern England by enabling all those who believed themselves to have been victims of crime or injustice to bring their grievances directly before the king's judges. There was no shortage of complainants eager to point the finger at alleged malefactors, and leading the charge—albeit by proxy, given that he was still living in his Southwark townhouse 120 miles away from Norwich—was the Pastons' kinsman Sir John Fastolf, who believed that he had been subjected to a criminal vendetta by Heydon, Tuddenham, and other associates of the duke of Suffolk for more than a decade. For John Paston himself, the hearings represented the opportunity—finally, after almost three years of strain and anguish—to hold Lord Moleyns and John Heydon to account for the theft of his home at Gresham.

After so many years when Heydon's closeness to the duke of Suffolk had made him all but impervious to legal challenge, his aura of invulnerability was now faltering in the wake of his patron's death—and the location of the judicial hearings also seemed to bode well for his enemies. Norwich itself had been a focus of seething hostility to Heydon for more than a decade, ever since he had served as a judge in the city in 1437 and became embroiled in two interminably bitter political disputes, one between rival factions within the city government, and the other between the city corporation and the cathedral priory. Now, when the king's justices held preliminary hearings there to which all comers were free to present complaints, that hostility came flooding out in a deluge of allegations against Heydon that smacked more of pent-up antagonism than any kind of factual accuracy.

Heydon and his friend Tuddenham, it was said, were the ringleaders of a criminal conspiracy to pervert justice and extort money from the good people of Norfolk and Suffolk, a malevolent compact that dated back to 1439 (or 1441, or 1434, or 1435, or perhaps 1436, depending on which of the mass of contradictory indictments one consulted). It was further—and even less credibly—alleged that Heydon had added treason to his list of crimes in the spring of 1450 by expressing the view that the king had never had any right to rule the lost territories of northern France, and that it might be a good idea to get rid of Calais, too, given that its defence was costing ten thousand pounds a year (although privately there was anxiety that the witness who had purportedly heard Heydon utter these treasonable words was proving difficult to produce in court). The catalogue of his supposed offences was brought right up to date with the allegation that on 6 September, less than a fortnight before the start of the hearings, Heydon had ridden into Norwich with sixty armed men and tried to incite the townspeople to revolt. It was further claimed that, ten days later, on the very night before the sessions began, he had stealthily removed the mangled fragment of Jack Cade's dismembered body that had been strung up on Norwich's main gate, in the hope that the city's inhabitants would be suspected of sympathising with the failed rebellion and incur the displeasure of the king's chief ministers as a result.

This macabre accusation was made by the Pastons' friend John Damme; other cases were brought by Sir John Fastolf's chaplain, Thomas Howes— who was acting as Sir John's agent in Norfolk while the old man himself directed the legal campaign from the comfort of his London residence— complaining of the wrongs that Fastolf believed he had suffered at the hands of Heydon and Tuddenham over a decade and more. While this array of charges was being presented in Norwich itself, another hearing took place at Swaffham, a wealthy market town twenty-five miles west of the city, where John Paston's complaints were finally put before the court. At long last, Moleyns's men—including the supercilious Walter Barrow and the pugnacious John Partridge, as well as the Pastons' old enemy John Mariot of East Beckham—were formally charged with the forcible seizure of the manor of Gresham on the orders, the indictment alleged, of both John Heydon himself and Robert, Lord Moleyns.

Once the commissioners were satisfied that all those who wished to petition for justice in the county had been given a chance to speak, the first substantive hearings were held at Norwich on Tuesday, 22 September. This was the beginning of a protracted legal process. It was the sheriff's responsibility to assemble juries of local men to pronounce a verdict on each of the hundreds of indictments that had so far been enrolled, but the task of compelling the attendance of both jurors and defendants in court on the appointed day was complex in political as well as logistical terms, given that the sheriff had no professional administrators or police officers at his disposal. To enforce the court's summonses, he could rely only on the respect due his office, and whatever manpower he could raise in his private capacity as a local landowner—and, as a result, it could take months of postponement, even under less politically tense circumstances than these, before cases came to final judgment.

Nevertheless, even in this febrile atmosphere, there were encouraging signs for the Pastons and their friends. The royal commissioners sitting as judges to hear the charges in Norwich were the duke of Norfolk, the earl of Oxford, and Justice William Yelverton, a Norfolk-born judge in the court of King's Bench who was a friend and counsellor to Sir John Fastolf. None of the three had any reason to be sympathetic to John Heydon and his former colleagues in the duke of Suffolk's service. On the other hand, Suffolk's death had not left the Pastons' enemies defenceless. Far from it: Lord Moleyns still had his place at court from which to gain access to the almost infinitely malleable king, and procured a royal letter commanding that legal process against himself and his servants be halted until Moleyns could be present in person at the Norfolk hearings—which would not be for some time, the king's letter declared, since "our right trusty and wellbeloved Lord Moleyns is by our special desire and commandment waiting upon us."[7] There seemed little that John Paston could do but wait to see how the indictments would proceed.

Meanwhile, the perspective of the unpredictable courtier Thomas Daniel was almost entirely different. John and the patron he had once hoped might help him could hardly have been more temperamentally mismatched. All John's instincts reinforced his belief that due process of law would eventually vindicate the rightfulness of his position, whereas the law seemed at best an irrelevance to Daniel's policy of anarchic self-interest. He was not concerned with justice, but with identifying new targets for his grasping ambition—and it soon became apparent that, despite John's former optimism, Paston interests had barely registered on Daniel's political radar. That much was clear from the next move he made to expand his property portfolio in Norfolk: he set his sights on the manor of Bradeston in eastern Norfolk, halfway between Norwich and the port of Yarmouth, an estate that belonged to the Berneys of Reedham, the family of Margaret Paston's mother, Margery.

The head of the family, Margaret's oldest Berney uncle, Thomas, had died nine years earlier, leaving a young son as his heir. Thomas's widow Elizabeth remarried, and her new husband, a Norfolk gentleman named Osbert Mundford, took over the guardianship of Bradeston and the other Berney lands. Daniel had as much of a claim to Bradeston as he did to Henry Woodhouse's home at Roydon—that is, none whatsoever—and this time he did not even bother to cloak his predatory intentions in a veil of quasi-legal subterfuge. Unabashed by the scathing criticism of avaricious courtiers in parliament in the spring of 1450, Daniel took a leaf out of Lord Moleyns's book and simply sent his men to occupy Bradeston by force.

This time, however, Daniel did not succeed in holding on to his booty for long. Unlike the ineffectual Woodhouse, Osbert Mundford was a battle-hardened soldier with long years of experience in the French wars, and he was not about to stand aside while Daniel trampled his family's rights underfoot. He resolved to fight fire with fire, and on 6 September—with the help of John Heydon, who was no friend of Daniel's—he sent an armed force to repossess Bradeston for himself. (In fact, it was this expedition that resulted in Heydon being charged with insurrection when the torrent of allegations against him inundated the judicial commission that autumn. As Heydon himself explained later in court, far from leading an army into Norwich in the attempt to incite a rebellion, he had gathered twenty-six armed men—defensibly armed, he pointed out—to help Mundford recover his own property, and had simply ridden through the city on his way eastward to Bradeston.) For John Paston, these were confusing times. John Heydon was his bitterest enemy, but Osbert Mundford and the Berneys were the Pastons' old friends and relations—so much so that Margaret Paston was godmother to Mundford's daughter Mary—and if Heydon had helped to expel Daniel from their property, then that, at least, had to be a mark in his favour to set against the long list of Paston complaints.

There was another reason, apart from events at Bradeston, why John

Paston's former adherence to Thomas Daniel was under strain. Survivor extraordinaire though Daniel was, the swirling political currents were at last threatening to drag him under. His nemesis, it seemed, had appeared in the person of Richard Plantagenet, duke of York, one of the greatest magnates in the realm and a close relative of the king: while Henry VI was descended in the male line from the third son of his royal forebear Edward III, the duke of York was descended in the male line from the fourth son of the same monarch. King Henry had not yet been presented with a son of his own by his young queen Margaret of Anjou (the French bride chosen for him during the failed peace negotiations of the 1440s), and for as long as the royal couple remained childless, the duke of York was the heir presumptive to the throne. Through his mother, Anne Mortimer, the duke could also trace his ancestry back to the second son of Edward III—a line of royal descent senior to that of the king himself. There could be no serious suggestion that this claim through the female line might supersede the authority of the anointed king, but the concentration of royal blood in his veins gave York confidence that he could speak for the realm more authoritatively than any other nobleman.

In 1450, there was much to speak about. York had spent years fighting to defend the English conquests in France, until, in 1447, he was appointed the king's lieutenant in Ireland (a turbulent land over which the English crown claimed lordship, although in practice English authority extended little farther than an area around the city of Dublin known as the Pale). In the summer of 1449, the duke finally made the journey across the Irish Sea to take up his lieutenancy there in person, and his absence from both England and France at this specific point in 1449–1450—during the catastrophic losses in France and the subsequent terrors of Cade's rebellion— allowed him to claim that his hands were clean in the aftermath of the disasters, as few other noblemen could. When he returned to England in early September, he aligned himself immediately with the House of Commons in denouncing leading members of the court for their destructive greed and evil counsel, and presented himself as the champion of reform in the interests of the common good: ". . . my said lord has put a bill to the king and desired much thing, which is much after the Commons' desire," Justice Yelverton's clerk, William Wayte, told John on 6 October; "and all is upon justice." With parliament in session, the extent to which York could call on vociferous support from the gentry and leading townsmen was plain, and under his influence a number of the most hated members of the royal household, including Thomas Daniel, were formally charged with treason. The implications were not lost on John Paston and his friends: "there is none other remedy but death for Daniel and for all those that are indicted," Wayte warned John urgently.[8]

The scramble for position around York was frantic. It was reported that John Heydon and Thomas Tuddenham were ready to pay the staggering sum of two thousand pounds—more than the annual income of all but the richest noblemen—to win the favour of the duke's right-hand man, Sir William Oldhall, and gossip had it that they had earmarked another one thousand pounds to secure a sympathetic sheriff. Neither rumour was financially plausible, but it was certainly true that Heydon was having to work hard in his own defence for the first time in years. In London he visited one of the judges of the King's Bench, hoping to solicit some legal support, and instead received an unexpected moral lecture—"how that he lived ungoodly in putting away of his wife and kept another, etc." Heydon was taken aback but defended himself stoutly ("he turned pale colour, and said he lived not but as God was pleased with, nor did no wrong to no person"), and was equally robust in his repudiation of the Pastons' version of events at Gresham. He had had nothing to do with what happened there, he said, but would not give an inch, all the same, on the justice of Moleyns's claim: "he enforced greatly and said his title was better than yours," John was told.[9]

Despite Heydon's bravado, the news of Lord Moleyns seemed more heartening now that the duke of York was dictating the political agenda. William Wayte reported that Moleyns was "sore out of grace, and that my lord of York loves him not"—or, as Judge Yelverton himself more laconically put it, "some men suppose that my lord of York cherishes not much the said Lord Moleyns."[10] Moleyns was exactly the kind of acquisitive courtier against whom York had publicly set his face—but the duke's antipathy to their enemy could not in itself guarantee victory for the Pastons. Moleyns had still not appeared in Norfolk in person at any stage in the two and a half years of the contest over Gresham; instead, he continued to issue violent threats from a distance. Some of his men had been taken into custody at Norwich as a result of the charges laid against them, and Moleyns was furious, swearing that he would have his revenge on those who had dared attack him. He was reported to be on his way to Norfolk with more than a hundred men, and "if he comes to Norwich, look there be ready to wait upon the mayor a good fellowship," William Wayte told John, "for it is said here that they are but beasts."[11] The Pastons' friends were taking the threats seriously. Wayte and his master, Judge Yelverton, both warned John to be careful, particularly of Heydon's influence behind the scenes: "Sir, beware of Heydon," Wayte wrote on 6 October, "for he would destroy you, by my faith."[12] On the other hand, Moleyns had so far gone to great lengths to avoid setting foot in Norfolk and therefore having to face any judicial process against him, and the hearings were after all continuing, with the next sessions scheduled for November.

Sure enough, Moleyns and his "great people" failed to appear in the county to back up his bluster. The manoeuvring around the duke of York intensified, however, as news came that the duke was on his way to visit Norfolk. Even the great and the good were feeling the pressure in the frenetic activity that preceded his arrival: "Sir, it were wisdom that my lord of Oxford wait on my lord of York," Wayte told John.[13] "Spend somewhat of your goods now, and get you lordship and friendship there," Judge Yelverton advised sagely, "for thereupon depends all law and profit."[14] Such feverish anticipation, however, could only meet with disappointment. The roots of the political crisis were too deep to be susceptible of a quick fix, even had the duke been the saviour some wished to paint him. In practice, York's self-promotion as the champion of popular grievance meant that he was regarded with increasing suspicion by many of his fellow magnates—and without broad support among the nobility, the duke would find it difficult either to create a viable regime or to establish the legitimacy of his own leadership. It was perhaps not surprising, therefore, that his eagerly awaited visit to East Anglia produced no decisive political result.

So much was now happening at once that it was hard to know where to be. The judicial hearings in Norfolk were scheduled to reopen on Monday, 16 November, but one could not be in Norwich and at parliament, which opened at Westminster on 6 November, at the same time. John Damme and James Gresham wished that John were there in person to defend himself when "the Lord Moleyns had language of you in the king's presence"— "your absence does no ease here," they wrote anxiously on 11 November— and as a result John hurried to join them in the capital.[15] On the other hand, absenting himself from the legal sessions in Norwich was equally problematic, and Justice Yelverton sent an urgent letter to London on the eve of the hearings to ask "that my cousin Paston be so hastily helped in his matters that he may soon come hither again."[16] The judges themselves faced the same dilemma. The duke of Norfolk rode with an imposing entourage to Westminster to attend parliament, but the earl of Oxford was given royal permission to miss the parliamentary session in order to preside over the hearings at Norwich when the court reconvened.

Judge Yelverton's position, meanwhile, hung in the balance. Heydon and Tuddenham tried to exploit their access to powerful men at the royal court in order to argue that he should be removed from the bench for the hearings against them, and it was not hard to see why. As a Norfolk landowner as well as a royal judge, Yelverton had deep roots in the society over which he was now called to sit in judgment; and as a close friend of Sir John Fastolf—so close that Fastolf called him "my brother"[17]—he was as partisan a presence as anyone in this intensely politicised legal process, sending a constant stream of information and advice to those who were seeking to bring Heydon and Tuddenham down. From his Southwark home, Fastolf lobbied frantically behind the scenes to make sure that Yelverton should in the end be allowed to sit, and once the decision had been confirmed, he sent a manservant and horses to convey the judge safely to Norwich. Yet Yelverton's worries were not over: he was as apprehensive as anyone else about the opportunities his departure from London would give to his enemies in this agitated political atmosphere, and he asked his old friend Fastolf to "be my shield and my defence against all false noises and slanders moved against me by their means in my absence." On the other hand, he was also convinced that, now the commissions had begun their work, there was a real opportunity to strike a lethal blow against their enemies. "Here is a marvellous disposed country," he reported from Norfolk with grim satisfaction, "and many evil-willed people to Sir Thomas Tuddenham and Heydon."[18]

When Yelverton finally took his seat in court at Norwich on 16 November, the earl of Oxford at his side, he did so with high hopes that they were about to preside over the judicial humiliation of Heydon, Tuddenham, and all those whose service to the dead duke of Suffolk had allowed them to lord it over their enemies for the last ten years—gentlemen including Heydon's friend John Wyndham, who stood charged with assaulting the Pastons' chaplain, James Gloys, as a result of their affray in a Norwich street two years earlier. (The assault had been so brutal, the indict-ment reported in pious tones, that Gloys had "despaired of his life"—a reminder that legal language was deployed to maximise the gravity of the charges in relation to relevant statute law, not to provide an accurate description of events, since, by Margaret's account of the fracas, Gloys was not so much in fear of his life as having to be held back from the fight.)[19] But it did not take long for Yelverton's hopes to be utterly dashed. So many legal technicalities could be cited as grounds for delay, and so much pressure brought to bear to obstruct the officers of the court in the laborious business of producing both the accused and the jury in court on the appointed day, that very little was resolved. In the event, legal process was postponed yet again to further hearings to be held at the port of King's Lynn, in western Norfolk, after Christmas.

The court's new location was matched by a change in personnel: Justice Yelverton and the earl of Oxford would be joined as judges at Lynn by a nobleman named Thomas, Lord Scales, whose Norfolk home at Middleton lay only a couple of miles away from the port. It was not easy to know what to make of Lord Scales's sudden intrusion onto the bench. Now about fifty years old, he had returned to England only in 1449 after spending the best part of three decades fighting in France. During his military career he had become so close to Sir John Fastolf, with whom he commanded the campaign in Maine after the English victory at the Battle of Verneuil in 1424, that he addressed him respectfully as "father."[20] He had also developed a strong relationship with the duke of York, and stood godfather to York's eldest son, Edward, when he was born at Rouen in Normandy in 1442. Scales's commitment to the war, including a decade spent as lieutenant-general of western Normandy, meant that he cannot have been sanguine about the humiliating collapse of English policy there at the end of the 1440s. But that in itself did not mean that he would blame the duke of Suffolk for the disaster. Suffolk himself had fought in France for fifteen years—he had lost his father and three brothers in the war, and was captured briefly in 1429—and Scales might well view him as his brother-in-arms just as much as Fastolf or York. Would Scales support Suffolk's men Heydon and Tuddenham against the grievances of their neighbours? Or would he throw his weight behind the chorus of complaint led by his old friend John Fastolf? Both sides had much to hope for, and neither could be sure—on this, Scales's first real foray into the snake pit that Norfolk politics had become—which way he would jump.

It was nerve-wracking to have this new element introduced into the already complex political equation at such a late stage in proceedings, but John Fastolf at least was hoping that the presence of Judge Yelverton and the earl of Oxford would be enough to secure a favourable outcome, whatever Lord Scales chose to do or say. Indeed, fresh charges against Heydon and Tuddenham were still coming in—enthusiastically encouraged, of course, by John Fastolf and his allies, among them John Paston—including a bill of complaints from the market town of Swaffham, in western Norfolk, where Tuddenham had held office as the king's steward for the past sixteen years. A petition detailing the Swaffham allegations was even submitted to parliament; "the said Sir Thomas is a common extortioner," the townspeople trenchantly declared, and demanded that, because he "would never appear in his person, nor by his attorney" at the commission's hearings in Norfolk, he should be arrested and held in prison until the sessions at Lynn took place.[21] The prospect of a man as well connected as Thomas Tuddenham awaiting the verdict of a Norfolk court under lock and key was never a realistic one, but it was striking that those in the town who had grievances against him now felt bold enough to request it.

Meanwhile, Heydon and Tuddenham were trying everything they could think of to extricate themselves from the charges. Crucial to the campaign on both sides was political spin—the attempt to control the two-way flow of information, rumour, and innuendo along the rutted, icy roads between Norfolk and London. For John Fastolf, John Paston, and their friends, it was imperative that the lords around the king at Westminster be convinced that the county was convulsed with popular anger at their opponents. Their hope was that, in the aftermath of the terrifying revolts of the previous summer, the fall of Tuddenham and Heydon would seem a small price to pay to avoid further unrest. Tuddenham and Heydon themselves, on the other hand, knew that every report which reached Norfolk of the powerful backing on which they could call at court made it less likely that any local jury would dare to convict them. In the meantime, most of the region's gentry—who had no personal stake in the grievances between the two sides, and whose overriding concern in these chaotic months was political survival—were simply waiting to see what the political landscape looked like once the dust finally settled.

At the beginning of January 1451, it was impossible to tell who had the upper hand. The Pastons' hopes received a sudden boost from Simon Blake, a courtier who had held office for the past six months as bailiff of Swaffham, where feeling against Thomas Tuddenham was running so high. Blake arrived in the capital just after Christmas and launched into a public relations offensive, telling the chancellor that, if the trials of Tuddenham and Heydon did not proceed as planned, "London should have as much for to do as they had for to keep London Bridge when the Captain"—the rebel leader Jack Cade—"came thither," since five thousand Norfolk men stood poised on the brink of revolt. Blake had arrived just in time, it seemed: Tuddenham and Heydon had been on the verge of securing a pardon, on the grounds that they had been victims of a vendetta inspired by "great malice" against them.[22]

The newly appointed judge Lord Scales, meanwhile, had not yet shown his hand in public, but Justice Yelverton's clerk, William Wayte, feared that he would throw his weight behind Heydon and Tuddenham. Scales was also seeking to resolve the bitter acrimony between Tuddenham and the townspeople of Swaffham—the risk being that, if he succeeded, other complaints might fall by the wayside. To counter this threat, Yelverton and John Paston did what they could to mobilise support from the strongly anti-Heydon faction at Norwich, canvassing the city's mayor and aldermen to recruit crowds of protesters willing to travel the forty miles to Lynn—a whole day in the saddle—to make "a great noise upon the Lord Scales" against Tuddenham and Heydon and "all those that are of that sect."[23] But this attempt to muster an angry mob outside the court was a dangerous game that could be exploited by their enemies. Just as Heydon's role in helping to retrieve the manor of Bradeston from Thomas Daniel was parlayed into an armed riot in the indictments that John Paston helped frame, so John's own efforts to ensure that Norwich's grievances should be clamorously represented at the Lynn hearings were seized on by his old rival John Wyndham. "And sir, at the reverence of God, labour your matters wisely and secretly," Wayte—who was now sending Paston weekly bulletins from Yelverton's side—urged him, "for Wyndham noised you sore before my lord of Oxford and my lord Scales that you should raise much people with great array out of Norwich; and therefore, sir, let the people be wisely and manly guided in their speaking and demeaning."[24]

In public, John Heydon was all confidence. "It seems by their countenance that they trust of a good year," Wayte reported gloomily. By 9 January he had also heard that two of Heydon's most trusted servants, Thomas Bridge and William Prentice, were "at home with the Lord Scales"—a figure of speech of apparently innocuous domesticity, but one with threatening implications: if Scales was now prepared to find room in his own household for Heydon's men, it was bad news indeed. On the other hand, Scales's attempt to settle the allegations of extortion laid against Thomas Tuddenham by the townspeople of Swaffham had collapsed amid a welter of recriminations, so that the town's representatives would, after all, be in court "in their best array" to press their complaints. After months of raised hopes and interminable delays, the wait for judgment was becoming acutely frustrating. "Sir, I would there were a thousand of good manly men to cry out on Tuddenham, Heydon, Prentice, and Bridge for their false extortions," Wayte wrote in a rare moment of departure from measured analysis of the latest developments. In the meantime, there was still much to fear. "I beseech you beware to whom you show your letters. Let them be burned," he added—not that John, an inveterate filer of correspondence, complied.[25]

The sessions at Lynn finally opened on Tuesday, 13 January, but yet again all hopes that the charges might at last come to judgment were dashed almost immediately. Once again, Heydon and Tuddenham failed to appear at the hearings, and the process was adjourned, this time for three whole months, to Norwich in Easter week. If there was a silver lining to be found, it was that this postponement did at least allow more time to regroup and plan for the next round of what was becoming a marathon struggle. For John Paston, that meant focusing on Gresham. He had considered the possibility of trying to repossess what had once been his home there four months earlier, but decided against it, discouraged both by the intimidating noises Moleyns was making and by his own determination to settle for nothing less than full judicial restitution for all the wrongs he had suffered. By the end of January 1451, however, the situation looked a little different. Despite all Moleyns's sound and fury, it was becoming clear that his repeated threats to arrive in Norfolk armed to the teeth were not about to materialise, something which left his men holding out at Gresham in an increasingly precarious position. At the same time, judicial restitution had not proved as easy to secure as John had once hoped, and direct action seemed correspondingly more appealing. In February, John Paston equipped his servants with the most intimidating weapons he could assemble, and dispatched them to the manor. At last, after three long years, Gresham was back in Paston hands.

Moleyns's response was prompt and utterly predictable: he sent word that he would "come down himself and enter in the said manor within a short time." To this belligerent declaration he added a magnanimous rider—a well-worn stratagem in the battle for hearts and minds among the villagers—that, when he reclaimed "his" property, he would not harass the tenants for any rent paid to John Paston in the meantime. And his continued posturing meant that John could not rest easy in his recaptured home.

After Margaret's distressing experiences under attack at Gresham two years earlier, there was no suggestion that she and the children should move back to the manor house, but no tenant could be found who was prepared to live there either. The villagers remained jittery, and one at least was refusing to pay his rent unless he was forced to do so by the Pastons' bailiffs—something that would indicate his resistance to Paston authority if he later had to deal again with Moleyns. The Pastons' chaplain, James Gloys, who was managing the estate for John, tried to seize some of the man's goods but was routed by his formidable mother. ("I dared not for her cursing," he explained sheepishly.)[26]

Meanwhile, there were worrying signs that the campaign against their enemies was beginning to fray around the edges. News arrived in Norwich at the beginning of March of their opponents' latest tactic in this judicial war: a time-honoured device, of bringing indictments in a completely different county from the main arena of conflict. Even if the allegations were essentially spurious, this could be a debilitating form of legal harassment. It might take weeks even to find out about accusations made so far away from home, let alone to muster any kind of defence, and a gentleman might find himself outlawed for failing to appear in court before he was even aware that he was under indictment. Word had it that proceedings had been brought in the county of Kent, southeast of London, against John Paston, his friend John Damme, Judge William Yelverton, and even the earl of Oxford himself, on a charge of "maintenance"—that is, improper attempts to influence the outcome of other people's litigation—at the Norfolk hearings. Margaret was deeply uneasy about what this all meant: ". . . the people that are against Sir Thomas Tuddenham and Heydon are sore afeared," she told John anxiously, "because of this noise and of other language that is had, both in this town and in the country, that these said Tuddenham and Heydon should be as well at ease and have as great rule as ever they had."[27] There was even a rumour that Heydon was about to receive the honour of a knighthood, "and much other language there is which causes men to be afeared, thinking that he should have a rule again."[28]

The crippling uncertainty continued throughout March. Margaret at least had some domestic issues to occupy her time—finding a Norwich draper to supply suitable cloth for their servants' new livery, for example. The Paston household would be decked out in red that year, but the wares of local shopkeepers did not live up to Margaret's exacting standards when it came to new wardrobes for her growing children: "I pray you that you will buy two good hats for your sons," she asked John sternly, "for I can none get in this town." But the Norwich streets were full of disquieting whispers that both Heydon and Tuddenham, and Lord Moleyns, had secured their positions and would shortly be back in Norfolk in full force. John was in London, staying in his familiar lodgings at the Inner Temple, where Margaret sent him the latest news from home: ". . . it is said they shall have as great rule in this country as ever they had," she wrote on Monday, 15 March, "and many more folks are sorry therefor than merry. Sir Thomas Tuddenham's men and Heydon's sow this seed all about the country, that their masters shall come home in haste in their prosperity and be as well at ease as ever they were." The propaganda battle would play a vital part in determining what happened when the court finally came to judgment. So many people were waiting to gauge the political climate before committing themselves to one side or the other that being perceived to be confident of success might go more than halfway toward achieving it. Dispiritingly, it was a battle the Pastons' enemies seemed to be winning. The tenants at Gresham, Margaret reported, were terrified, "the language is so great on the other party."[29] By the end of the month, the manor was awash with rumours that Moleyns himself would be there very soon. "Other tidings have we none," Margaret reported wearily, "but that Tuddenham and Heydon should have again the rule in this country as much as ever they had, or more."[30]

Easter week, the new date set for the hearings, fell in the last week in April. By the middle of the month, Sir John Fastolf—still nursing his grievances in his Southwark mansion—heard that Heydon and Tuddenham would definitely ride to Norwich to appear in court; good news in itself, in that it offered a chance of proceeding with the indictments at long last, but only so long as all those who had brought allegations forward could be kept steadfast when the time finally came for the charges to be heard. There was bad news, too, however. Neither the duke of Norfolk nor the earl of Oxford would be present at the long-delayed sessions, and their place on the bench would now be taken by John Prisot, chief justice in the court of Common Pleas, an old friend of both Heydon and Tuddenham. It was a blow, but not necessarily a decisive one. Prisot would, after all, be sitting with William Yelverton, the staunch ally of John Fastolf, John Paston, and their supporters. Whatever happened, it was clear that this, at last, would be the final showdown.

The court convened in the council's assembly room in the Norwich

Guildhall—a grandly imposing flint building on the north side of the market square—on Thursday, 29 April. Counsel for the city of Norwich spoke first, followed by the lawyers for the town of Swaffham. Sir John Fastolf's cases were put forward, then John Paston's, and many others. But it rapidly became apparent that Justice Yelverton's determination to see these cases through was more than matched by Justice Prisot's determination to head them off. Despite Yelverton's best efforts to interject, Prisot "would suffer no man that was learned to speak for the plaintiffs, but took it as a venom, and took them by the nose at every third word, which might well be known for open partiality."[31]

The worst news of all was Prisot's decision that the hearings should not, after all, go ahead at Norwich as planned, but should be adjourned for a few days and then reconvene at Walsingham, a small market town twenty-five miles northwest of the city. Fastolf's chaplain, Thomas Howes, who was in court to report back to his master in London, saw this as a blatantly partisan move. Walsingham was famous for its celebrated shrine to the Virgin Mary, and thousands of pilgrims visited the town each year to pay their respects at the Holy House (a replica of the Nazareth home where the archangel Gabriel first appeared to Mary), and to venerate relics, including a phial of the Virgin's milk. Politically, however, Walsingham was deep in the heartlands of the duchy of Lancaster estates in northern Norfolk, where Thomas Tuddenham and John Heydon had been powerful for years—or, as Howes put it, "where they have greatest rule."[32] But if Prisot's decision to shift the hearings to Walsingham appeared to Fastolf and the Pastons to be a corrupt manoeuvre by a biased judge, the trouble was that Tuddenham and Heydon could easily make the same claim about Yelverton's unsuccessful attempts to keep the court in Norwich, a city where the two men faced more hostility than anywhere else in the county. Either way, the end game had begun with a shattering setback for the Pastons and their friends. Justice Prisot's decision stood: the hearings would reopen the following week, on Tuesday, 4 May, at Walsingham.

Some of the duke of Norfolk's men arrived in Walsingham over the weekend and sent disheartening news back to John Paston in Norwich. Now that it was clear that the court would give its judgment on territory dominated by Heydon and Tuddenham, the drift of support away from the Pastons and their allies was reaching a critical mass: "there is great press of people," Norfolk's men reported, "and few friends as far as we can feel yet."[33] They would do their best, they said, but John ought to think carefully about whether or not he should be there himself. The information they had already gathered about his own case was devastating. Lord Moleyns's connections in the royal household had finally come to his rescue: the sheriff had received a letter from the king instructing him to enlist a panel of jurors who would acquit Moleyns on all charges. Victory through this court now seemed an impossibility.

When the sessions finally reopened on Tuesday morning, any last remaining embers of hope were extinguished. The Pastons had been so full of excited optimism when the hearings began at Norwich more than seven months earlier, with the sympathetic figures of the duke of Norfolk, the earl of Oxford, and Justice Yelverton on the bench. Now, at Walsingham, the judges were Justice Prisot and Lord Scales, both of whom had already made plain their support for the Pastons' opponents. Sir John Fastolf's chaplain, Thomas Howes, wrote to the elderly knight in despair at the wrecking of all their hopes: ". . . it was the most partial place of all the shire," he reported despondently. Tuddenham and Heydon and "other oppressors of their sect" had gathered a menacing crowd of supporters outside the courthouse, "and, considering how their well-willers were there assembled at their instance, it had been right jeopardous and fearful for any of the plaintiffs to have been present," Howes went on, "for there was not one of the plaintiffs nor complainants there, but your right faithful and trusty well-willer John Paston."[34]

The scene he met when he arrived at Walsingham can only have been a bitter blow for John. But even he, hardy soul that he was, had not dared to attend at the start of the sessions. By the time he arrived, Moleyns had already been acquitted on the charge of commanding his servants to enter Gresham illegally. On this, Moleyns's first, belated visit to Norfolk, he had had to push hard before the verdict had gone his way. No local jury, however bold, could easily reject the word of one of the king's courtiers, and this, in the end, was what the case came down to: not John Paston's title deeds, but Moleyns's solemn oath, made with a hand laid on a Bible: ". . . the Lord Moleyns should not have been acquitted of his commandment had he not sworn on a book, such evidence was against him," John was told.[35] Even after his arrival, John's lone, if sturdy, presence was no help to his cause or those of his allies. Thomas Howes was disgusted at what he saw as the perfidy of the "faint friends" from whom Fastolf had hoped for so much in the heady days after the duke of Suffolk's death: gentlemen such as Sir John Heveningham, a local landowner who "might not find it in his heart to go four furlongs"—half a mile—"from his dwelling place to the shirehouse" while the court was sitting at Norwich, "but now he could ride from Norwich to Walsingham"—a distance of twenty-five miles—"to sit as one of the commissioners." Fastolf's cases, like John Paston's, had ended in disappointment: jurors and judges alike, Howes wrote, had "found none obstacle nor impediment in their conscience in all your matter."[36]

The problem was that the situation had never really been as simple as the moral outrage of Fastolf and his servants made it sound. Fastolf's military career in France meant that he had not lived in Norfolk for years, and if the rights and wrongs of the disputes in which he had now become embroiled looked black and white from the comfort of his Southwark home, more than a hundred miles from Norwich, not all of them appeared so clear-cut from other perspectives. Lord Scales, whose friendship with Fastolf did not long survive his own return from the war in 1449, clearly felt that right was not entirely on one side. "Father, if you had been to me as faithful and kind since I came into England as you were in France," Scales told him in January 1452, "by my troth there had been no man of your estate that so much I would do for."[37] Fastolf, like John Paston, had undoubtedly suffered in the later 1440s at the hands of unscrupulous and conniving courtiers, and both men blamed John Heydon and Thomas Tuddenham for the reverses to which they had been subjected. But some of their friends and neighbours had good reason to value Tuddenham and Heydon's support in the face of exactly the same sort of attack. Osbert Mundford, for example, would not have been able to defend himself against the outrageous belligerence of Thomas Daniel—a subject on which Fastolf and John Paston remained strangely silent—had it not been for John Heydon's help. It was hardly surprising, then, that Mundford was prepared to serve at the Walsingham sessions on the jury that acquitted Heydon of the charges brought against him by Fastolf.

The reality was that disputes—even bitter and violent disputes, mobilising scores of armed men in defence of contested property rights—were a fact of life in such an intensely competitive and mobile society. What was increasingly apparent, however, was that conflict could not be resolved, nor even kept within manageable limits, under the rule of a king who had the unchallenged authority to maintain order and dispense justice but was incapable of exercising it. In those circumstances, judicial process became as susceptible to political control as the king himself. And by the spring of

1451, it was clear that, after a year of chaos, political control was back with the court. The person of the king—totally ineffective though Henry was—remained the only source of legitimate authority. The duke of York had ridden a wave of popular support in the autumn of 1450, but in the long run his attempt to seize control of government from the lords closest to the king could not succeed, given that they, not he, were the ones who could plausibly claim to speak for King Henry himself. It was another of Henry's cousins—Edmund Beaufort, duke of Somerset—who emerged to take the duke of Suffolk's place at the king's right hand, and with it his ability to demand the cooperation of the great nobles in government. The reemergence of the power of the royal household meant a return to the structure of power that had sustained Suffolk's rule in the 1440s. In Norfolk, the acquittal of Suffolk's men at Walsingham in May 1451 was the inexorable result.

However inescapable the wider political realities, the outcome of the Walsingham hearings was devastating for the Pastons. Stubborn and dogged as ever, John did not stop trying to impose the sanctions of the law on his opponents. By the end of the month his servant John Osbern was making renewed overtures to the sheriff to try to hold him to his promise that he would help prosecute the Paston case against Moleyns's men, even if their lord had escaped punishment. It was no longer possible, however, to cling to the belief that the world was now a different place. The sheriff "said he would do for you that he may," Osbern wrote on 27 May, "except for the acquittal of the Lord Moleyns's men, in so much as the king has written to him for to show favour to the Lord Moleyns and his men. And, as he says, the indictment belongs to the king and not to you, and the Lord Moleyns a great lord."[38] A more brutal summing-up of the situation could hardly be imagined.

John had to face the fact that his campaign was over. In the summer months that followed, he attempted to negotiate terms with Moleyns over the Paston belongings which had been looted from Gresham, but it was clear now that Moleyns and Heydon were successfully blocking further legal process against them. However bruised Heydon and Thomas Tuddenham had been by the events of the previous eighteen months, they and their former colleagues in the duke of Suffolk's service were now finding their feet again as a political force in the region under the new leadership of Lord Scales, whose support had been so vital to their victory at Walsingham. Suffolk's men could also call upon the backing of the duke's widow, Alice Chaucer. The duchess's grandfather was the author of the *Canterbury Tales*, and her father had risen to a position of great wealth and influence in the service of the Lancastrian crown. Alice herself had inherited a keen intelligence and a shrewd political brain along with the Chaucer family fortune, and finding herself a widow at the age of forty-six, she applied her formidable talents to the defence of her husband's legacy on behalf of their young son. She was more than a match for the duke of Norfolk, whose ambition vastly outstripped his abilities, and who was discovering that he could not, as he had hoped, simply step into Suffolk's shoes as the dominant force in East Anglian society. With Norfolk still shadowboxing the ghost of a dead rival, and Sir John Fastolf at Southwark doggedly pursuing the lawsuits he still had in train, John Paston was left to find his place as best he could in a world that turned out to have changed very little.

ᵗ

a squire of worship

1451, WHICH HAD STARTED WITH SUCH PROMISE, had turned into a year of bitter disappointment for John and Margaret. John remained in London, staying at the Inner Temple, for much of June and July, and Margaret tried to cheer him with news of good wishes from Norwich. At a lunch party she attended at the end of June, the other ladies present "desired to have had you there," she told her husband; "they said they should all have been the merrier if you had been there."[1]

The idea that John would be a cheerful presence at the dining table seemed implausible given the circumstances, but the inhabitants of Norwich had worries of their own from which any distraction might be welcome. There was sickness in the city, and Margaret and their daughter, Margery, now a toddler, had both been ill. In the absence of antiseptics, antibiotics, or a reliably clean water supply, disease was a painful fact of fifteenth-century life. Gastroenteritis, dysentery, typhus, and measles were endemic, and those who sustained open wounds through injury or surgery all too easily succumbed to septicaemia or gangrene. As always, it was the poor who suffered most, especially those crammed into filthy tenements on polluted urban streets—although at least, in the wake of the Black Death's ravages, malnutrition now claimed many fewer victims among a savagely reduced population.

The rich, meanwhile, could use their wealth to secure the fullest range of treatment: the esoteric attentions of university-educated physicians, whose extortionate fees put their skills beyond the reach of all but blue-blooded patients; the agonising ministrations of surgeons, who learned their trade in a seven-year practical apprenticeship under the aegis of a professional guild; the advice of apothecaries, who often dispensed medical diagnoses along with their potions, unguents, and elixirs; the services of barbers, who performed rudimentary surgery such as blood-letting, bone-setting and tooth-drawing; the care of herbalists and other empirical practitioners, many of them women, whose skills derived from generations of traditional lore; and the healing power of prayer and pilgrimage. Some of these therapies were remarkably sophisticated. King Henry V, for example, survived a terrifying injury sustained in battle at the age of sixteen—a barbed arrow embedded six inches deep in his face, just to the left of his nose—thanks to an expert surgeon who used specially designed tongs to extract the bolt. Other remedies, however, were at best useless, and at worst actively harmful, even lethal. An inexperienced or inept phlebotomist might kill rather than cure if he punctured an artery by mistake; and a miscalculated dose of opium or hemlock to dull the excruciating pain of surgery could rapidly prove fatal.

Disconcertingly, to modern eyes, there was no straightforward correlation between expense and efficacy. That much was clear from the treatment in which Margaret placed her trust: an alarmingly expensive medicinal paste known as theriac, or more colloquially as "treacle." Made to an ancient recipe handed down through classical and Arabic texts, treacle was widely revered as an almost miraculous panacea; one contemporary text declared with utter conviction that it could cure fevers, epilepsy, palsy, and insomnia, clear the intestines and the skin, repair wounds, promote cardiac and gynaecological health, restore the power of speech to those who had lost it, counteract poison, and ward off the plague. Its celebrated reputation and fearsome cost derived from its long history, its exotic provenance (it was usually imported from Italy, often from Genoa), and the rarity of its ingredients—more than sixty of them, including the flesh of roasted viper, which were prepared over forty days and left to mature for up to twelve years. Its benefits, either as a restorative or a prophylactic, can only have been those of a placebo; but in its usual prescription—a twice-daily dose mixed into wine, ale, or rosewater—it does not seem to have been unsafe, given the frequency with which Margaret asked John to send supplies from London.

And Margaret would need her health, if she were to cope with the relentless demands on her time and energy. At least the acute strain of the

Pastons' legal battle had finally been lifted, however frustrating the outcome; and the estate at Gresham, with the rents it produced, was back in
Paston hands, even if Lord Moleyns had neither been convicted nor forced
to pay any kind of compensation. Meanwhile, Margaret had found herself
pregnant for a fourth time, and they now had a new baby, Edmund, named
after John's dead brother. One all-too-pressing question was where their
growing family was going to live. After the events of the past three years,
their former home at Gresham was too dilapidated, and still too insecure,
to be a realistic option. Margaret's estate at Mautby, near the port of
Yarmouth, on Norfolk's eastern coast, would be a possibility in the future,
but not until building work had been completed on the manor house
there—a great hall with a thatched roof, private chambers for the family,
and its own chapel. Margaret supervised operations during John's absences,
and as a result was a more realistic judge of progress—which was inevitably
slow, given the perennial difficulties of bad weather and unreliable workmen—
than her husband. "As for your work at Mautby," she wrote in November,
"it is not likely that there shall more be made thereof this year but the
gables of the chamber and the chapel windows. . . . The masons failed till
more than a fortnight after I came thence."[2]

What they really wanted was a home of their own in Norwich. There,
Margaret would have congenial company when John was away; a town
house would also give them firsthand access to all the news, rumour, and
speculation for which the region's capital acted as a conduit, and ensure
that letters could be delivered to and from London as swiftly as possible,
carried in saddlebags along the main road between England's first and second cities. They were actively looking for a place to buy, and in the meantime Margaret and the children could find lodgings with friends in the city,
but it was not a long-term solution. "I shall abide in Talvas's place till you
come home," she told John, "but, as for your being there when you come
home, the houses are too small for your men and your horses, and therefore
you had need to come home the sooner to purvey you of another place."[3]

As the year dragged on, the old heavyweights of the Norfolk political
scene were not only finding their feet again, but reemerging in new
alliances. Thomas Daniel was engaged in a bravura display of political
escapology, for which he turned out to have a remarkable talent. In the
spring of 1451 he was acquitted of the charges of treason laid against him
the previous autumn. Not only had he survived the tidal wave of public
hostility that engulfed the court in 1450, but he came up clutching the hand

of a powerful new patron, the duke of Somerset, Suffolk's successor as the leading figure in King Henry's government. When Daniel's formerly close relationship with the duke of Norfolk became strained in the autumn of 1451, Somerset persuaded Norfolk's mother—the redoubtable Catherine Neville, one of twenty-two siblings and half-siblings of the most powerful noble family in northern England—to intervene. The dowager duchess was so successful in effecting a reconciliation that, shortly afterward, Daniel married Norfolk's cousin, a gentlewoman named Margaret Howard, in a lavish ceremony at Framlingham, the great twelfth-century castle thirty miles south of Norwich that was the duke's ancestral home.

More startling were reports that Lord Scales had taken Daniel under his wing at the end of 1451. Given the long-standing enmity between Daniel and the duke of Suffolk's men, whose patron Scales now was, this development was both unexpected and perplexing. It may have been an indication that the political dislocation caused by the upheavals of 1450 was taking time to play itself out; or it may just have been the latest surprise in a career that was full of them. Thomas Daniel consistently embarked on—and got away with—exploits which other people would not even have thought of, let alone attempted. Perhaps he was extremely able, as well as unpredictable and unreliable; perhaps he had enormous personal charm; or perhaps he simply dared to do what other people did not, and had the nerve to brazen out the consequences. Whatever the explanation, there seemed to be a real prospect that Daniel's hostility to Suffolk's supporters, and his barefaced defrauding of Henry Woodhouse at Roydon, might now be swept under the carpet, and a rapprochement brokered between Daniel, Tuddenham, and Heydon. If that did happen, it was rumoured that Daniel "shall be suffered to enter into Bradeston"—the manor that he had temporarily seized from the Pastons' friend Osbert Mundford in 1450—"and keep it."[4]

Speculation that such a reconfiguration of local politics was imminent proved to be little more than hot air, but the threat to Bradeston was real enough. Daniel's aggression had survived the crisis of 1450–1451 disturbingly intact, and on 8 February 1452 he dispatched a company of armed men to capture the estate for the second time. Osbert Mundford—a distinguished soldier who was currently serving in the garrison at Calais, the last remaining English foothold in the hostile territory of northern France—was incensed, but unable to leave his post to organise any kind of retaliation. "I may not come, nor I will not come, though I should lose all

Bradeston," he wrote angrily, ". . . considering that the enemies draw daily hitherward." It was doubly outrageous, he felt, that Daniel should choose to take advantage of the fact that he could not defend himself in Norfolk because he was busy defending his country. He petitioned King Henry for help—although, given that Daniel had inveigled himself into the good books of the duke of Somerset, the king's new chief minister, that seemed unlikely to produce immediate results. Mundford therefore also wrote to his friend John Paston to ask advice on how best to bring legal action against Daniel, promising, touchingly, to buy him a drink for his pains if ever he came to Calais ("you shall have a stoop of beer to comfort you after your travail of the sea").[5] It soon became clear, however, that Daniel's hold on the manor could not be shaken off so easily.

Like Lord Moleyns before him, Daniel did not come to Norfolk in person, but installed a gentleman named Charles Nowell, from the neighbouring county of Suffolk, at Bradeston as his deputy. Nowell and his supporters—principally his younger brothers Otwell and Arthur, and a lawyer named Robert Ledham from the nearby village of Witton—lost no time in establishing themselves as a menacingly intimidating presence in the surrounding area. This was the usual bullying attempt to deter local people from daring to support Mundford's right to the estate, just as Moleyns's servants had done at Gresham. Being Daniel's men, however, Ledham and the Nowells engaged in the campaign of threats with unusual vigour and enthusiasm. Their principal objective was to follow Daniel's orders in protecting Bradeston, but that mission also afforded them a chance to pursue their own vendettas. Ledham, for example, had fallen out several years earlier with a neighbour named John Wilton, whom he had accused of assaulting him in the summer of 1447; Wilton's account of events, by contrast, was that a fight had broken out after he had "peacefully and modestly" asked Ledham's men to stop trampling his crops.[6] When the opportunity to reopen hostilities presented itself five years later, Ledham took it with gusto, brawling with Wilton in a local churchyard, knocking his heavily pregnant wife to the ground, and seizing his cattle and sheep in lieu of what Ledham claimed were rent arrears. To add insult to injury, not only did Ledham take the animals but he "killed them and laid them in salt, and afterwards ate them."[7]

The surviving accounts of the alleged crimes of Ledham and the Nowells are not, of course, neutral or impartial documents. Accusations were presented with no explanation of context but plenty of circumstantial detail designed to provoke horror and outrage. During a late-night assault on the house of John Coke, another tenant at Witton, for example, they allegedly "gave him seven great wounds," and then hit his eighty-year-old mother on the crown of her head with a sword, "which wound was never whole to the day of her death." One poor soul, Thomas Baret of the nearby village of Burlingham, was said to have been beaten so badly "that he kept his bed a month," and when he had the temerity to complain about the beating, Ledham's men lay in wait for him and "beat him again."[8]

Some of the charges were patently weak, little more than an attempt to pin anything bad that happened in the area on the people who had become the local bogeymen. An unsolved murder, for instance, was included among the complaints despite the rider that "whether any of the said fellowship were there or not, men cannot say, there are of them so many, of which many be unknown people."[9] But whether or not Nowell's men had anything to do with this killing, and however much other charges may have been embellished in the telling, such an influx of violent strangers into these close-knit communities cannot have been less than terrifying—and maddening, too, since men who could not be officially identified by name, place of residence, and status or occupation could not be formally charged with a crime. Some of the villagers targeted by Nowell and Ledham were too afraid of ambush to move about with confidence on public roads, and in some cases they felt vulnerable even in their own homes. "And so, for salvation of their lives and in eschewing of such inordinate costs as never was seen in that country before," a petition to parliament later alleged, "many of them forsook and left their own habitation, wife and child, and withdrew to fortresses and good towns as for that time," John Wilton and Thomas Baret among them, the former to the city of Norwich and the latter to the port of Yarmouth.[10]

John Paston, who had once hoped for so much from Thomas Daniel, had supported his friend Osbert Mundford from the beginning in the fight with Daniel over Bradeston. In the spring of 1452, however, the issue suddenly became intensely personal. On Monday, 3 April, outside the great door of Norwich Cathedral, John came face to face with Charles Nowell and five of his men. It was a confrontation of which few details were afterward committed to paper—it is not clear, for example, whether words were exchanged or provocation given on either side—but John's account made it clear that violence was frighteningly quick to erupt, with Nowell "smiting at me while one of his fellows held my arms at my back."[11] Thankfully, John suffered no serious injury, but later the same day Osbert Mundford's brother-in-law Philip Berney—Margaret's timorous uncle, who had told her his hip was broken in order to avoid having to brave a return visit to Gresham—was ambushed near his home by Nowell and his men. They shot and injured Berney's horse, allowing them to ride him down, and then "broke a bow on the said Philip's head," before taking him and his two servants prisoner with the words "traitors, you shall die!" It became apparent soon enough that they intended to bully Berney rather than injure him: he was under arrest, they declared, before forcing him to provide security that he would keep the peace—a laughably implausible ruse, given Berney's temperamental aversion to any hint of trouble. At that point, they let him go. Berney did not dare to return to his home at Reedham, eight miles or so from Bradeston, but took refuge instead in the greater safety of Sir John Fastolf's imposing castle at Caister near Yarmouth.[12]

The campaign of intimidation was as frightening as it was unsubtle. The message that no one—former allies included—should dare question Daniel's possession of Bradeston was underscored with violence at every possible opportunity. Even the activities of Lord Moleyns's men at Gresham had been more recognisably within the bounds of "normal" behaviour than this, in that Moleyns had some sort of claim to Gresham—however far-fetched and atavistic—which he chose, as many people did, to pursue by direct action, even if the ejection of Margaret and her household from the estate was direct action of a particularly forceful kind. What Daniel's men were engaged in was much more like a reign of terror, in both its nature and its intensity: what Moleyns had only threatened, Daniel was putting into practice.

And the peculiarly alarming thing from John Paston's point of view was that there was nowhere to turn for help. Daniel himself had been John's major hope for support when it came to his battle with Heydon and Moleyns, even if it was hope that was ultimately disappointed. Even worse, the duke of Norfolk—whose ambition to become the most powerful lord in the region still burned fiercely, however erratic and inept his progress so far—was also implicated in what was now happening. The willingness of Daniel's men to involve themselves in violently disruptive tactics had come in handy for the duke in 1450, when they joined some of Norfolk's own retainers in launching an aggressive campaign of harassment against the duke of Suffolk's estates and servants in the aftermath of Suffolk's death. The association between Daniel and Norfolk was already a couple of years old by this point, and both men stood to gain from the attempt to over-throw the local power of Suffolk's men. Although they fell out briefly in 1451, by the beginning of 1452 Daniel's marriage to Norfolk's cousin had cemented their alliance. Only weeks later, Daniel sent his men—who were now also part of Norfolk's entourage—into Bradeston, and the brutal reprisals against anyone who opposed them began.

John Paston had had reason enough before this to be sceptical about Daniel's reliability as a patron, but he was baffled by the duke of Norfolk's apparent willingness to condone the victimisation of gentlemen such as himself who had been willing to offer the duke their service in his struggle against Suffolk's overpowering local dominance. Quite apart from the breach of the bond of mutual loyalty that was supposed to underpin the relationship between a lord and his supporters, it seemed ludicrous that Norfolk would be prepared simply to throw away gentry backing when it had been so hard for him to attract any in the first place. The only possible explanation, John thought, was that the duke was unaware of what was happening—and the perfect opportunity to seek redress seemed to be about to present itself, since Norfolk would shortly be arriving at Framlingham Castle, his dynastic home in Suffolk.

At least, that was what John had been told. By 23 April, having waited for ten days for the duke's coming, and being assured each day that his arrival was imminent, John was becoming frantic. He wrote to the sheriff to explain his predicament, drafting the letter over and over again in the attempt to convey his desperation with sufficient urgency. He described the attack he had suffered at Charles Nowell's hands outside Norwich Cathedral, and tried, respectfully, to point out why it might be a matter of concern to the duke. It "was to me strange case," he wrote, "thinking in my conceit that I was my lord's man and his homager"—his sworn liegeman—"before Charles knew his lordship, and that my lord was my good lord." He was all the more confused, he explained, since he had seen the duke in person in London only two months earlier, when Nowell had already forced his way into Bradeston, and even then Norfolk had "granted me his good lordship so largely that it must cause me ever to be his true servant to my power."[13] The rest of the letter maintained this tone of genteel bewilderment rather than anger. Either the constraints of courtesy and policy were keeping John's pen under iron discipline, or he truly believed that Norfolk would clear up the whole sorry mess as soon as he realised what had happened. If his faith in the duke was genuine, he was about to be grievously disappointed.

At the end of the month, Norfolk finally arrived at Framlingham, riding at the head of his richly caparisoned household through the massive gate in the castle's eight-feet-thick curtain wall. But before John and the other gentlemen who had suffered at the hands of Ledham and the Nowells had a chance to present any of their complaints, it became clear that Daniel's men had laid plans for just this eventuality, and now they set their scheme in motion. Three months earlier—before Nowell had even set foot in Bradeston on Daniel's behalf—an underling of his named Roger Church had convened a secret meeting of fifteen local men in a wood at Postwick, a couple of miles from Ledham's home at Witton. It was a motley gathering, and the villagers later claimed they "knew not why they assembled, but only by the excitation of the said Church and his men."[14] At the time, it must have seemed an essentially inconsequential, if somewhat eccentric, encounter. Now, however, at the end of April, with the duke of Norfolk newly arrived at Framlingham and John Paston and his friends waiting to tell him of Nowell and Ledham's thuggery, Roger Church allowed himself to be arrested by his own associates—Nowell and Ledham themselves— and brought before the duke.

There, in Norfolk's presence, Church launched into an extraordinary "confession." The assembly in Postwick wood had been part of a treasonable plot, he declared, to raise a revolt against King Henry's government. He himself had been the captain of the would-be insurgents—under the alias "John Amend-All," one of the pseudonyms formerly used by the rebel leader Jack Cade in 1450—but his co-conspirators numbered three hundred men more, he said, than the fifteen unfortunates who had gathered with him in the forest back in January. It was at this point, when Church embarked on a roll call of his supposed partners in crime, that it became clear why he had so cheerfully exposed himself to charges of treason: this was an elaborate plot to frame as traitors all those who had opposed Daniel's annexation of Bradeston. Church would be in no personal danger, since, whatever happened, Daniel had promised to use his influence at court to secure him a pardon; and the apparently aimless gathering in the wood had been staged to lend credibility to the supposed "rising." Church now implicated "many notable and thrifty men" as rebels-in-waiting (among them John Paston, still waiting to see the duke in blissful ignorance of the Machiavellian scheme that was now unfolding), so that "the substantial men of the country should be, by that means, so troubled and endangered" that they should "not be of power" to offer further resistance to the belligerence of Nowell, Ledham, and their master Daniel.[15]

It was a tortuous plan, but an ingenious one. An accusation of treason, however spurious, could do a lot of damage in these uncertain times. At the very least, John and his friends would be deflected from pursuing their catalogue of complaints against Daniel's men by the need to defend themselves against the charges. All Nowell and Ledham now needed was for the duke of Norfolk to take the story seriously—and, right on cue, he ordered that formal indictments be drawn up on the basis of Church's allegations. It was the sheriff who smelled a rat. He summoned the fifteen villagers who had been enticed to the baffling woodland assembly in January and then coerced into corroborating Church's fantastical story when they were hustled into the duke of Norfolk's presence by Daniel's lackeys. In their relief at finally being able to speak freely, the truth came tumbling out. "The substance of the tale told by the said Roger Church was untrue and feigned and imagined by the same Church," one asserted vehemently.[16] Church himself had instigated the gathering in the forest at Postwick—possibly by promising some kind of campaign to tackle popular grievances in the shire—and John Paston and his allies had not been present, nor even spoken of, at that damp squib of a meeting. With the threat of sedition now exposed in the cold light of day as a convoluted hoax, the sheriff sent an account of his investigation to the royal council at Westminster, and John saddled his horse yet again for the long ride to the capital, ready to rebut the story of the rebellion in case of any sign that it might be taken seriously.

The duke of Norfolk, around whom Daniel's men would have run rings had it not been for the sheriff's shrewdness, had demonstrated yet again that his grandiose pretensions to "have the principal rule and governance through all this shire of which we bear our name" were fatally undermined by his lack of political acuity.[17] Realising at last that it would be futile to petition the duke further, John instead sent a trusted servant named John Osbern to lobby the bishop of Norwich, a consummate politician named Walter Lyhert. The bishop had taken a leading role in royal government under the duke of Suffolk's ill-fated regime during the 1440s, and was now waiting for the storm whipped up by Suffolk's fall to blow itself out, keeping his head down away from London in the safety of his own diocese, where his personal badge—a punning device of a deer at rest amid the gentle eddies of a stream ("Wa'ter Lie-hart")—can still be seen carved into the corbels that support the soaring vaulted roof of the great cathedral.

John had made no previous appeal to Lyhert because the bishop's closeness to the duke of Suffolk would have made him an unlikely source of assistance in normal circumstances; but the circumstances he now faced were far from normal. In supporting his friend Osbert Mundford at Bradeston, John Paston had found himself in a disconcertingly improbable alliance with Suffolk's men, including his archenemy, John Heydon. In this context, Bishop Lyhert provided an astute and sympathetic ear. "I had great cheer," Osbern reported after the meeting, clearly impressed by the quality of episcopal hospitality, with "wine and ale both." The bishop promised his support in the campaign to bring Nowell and Ledham to justice and to retrieve Bradeston from their clutches, and told Osbern that John could also count on the backing of Lord Scales, the old soldier who had emerged as the new noble patron of Suffolk's local supporters after the duke's murder. Scales "is well disposed to you and in the best wise, and will do for you what he can," Osbern reported. The sole condition of Scales's goodwill was "that you would forsake Daniel"—a stipulation with which John was now only too happy to comply.[18]

Yet four days later, despite this encouraging news, the rot seemed to have spread even further. Charles Nowell's dubious methods had apparently rubbed off on another of his associates in the duke of Norfolk's service, an old acquaintance of the Pastons named Richard Southwell, who seized a valuable manor—Holme Hale, near the market town of Swaffham, in western Norfolk—from Sybilla Boys, the gentlewoman who had sent Judge William her recipe for ale many years earlier. Southwell was holding the estate "with strength, with such another fellowship as has been at Bradeston," Margaret reported, "and wastes and despoils all that there is. . . . It seems it was not for naught that he held with Charles and his fellowship," she added tartly.[19]

A harrowingly traumatic story lay behind Southwell's aggression. He had wooed and won the hand of Lady Boys's widowed daughter-in-law, Jane, but in the summer of 1451 their engagement had been violently interrupted. Jane had been staying at her parents' home when a neighbour named Robert Langstrother—a gentleman by birth, if not by demeanour—burst into the house at the head of a band of armed men. Whether he was driven by love for Jane or lust for her riches, Langstrother knew that he had missed his chance as a suitor, but could not bring himself to take no for an answer. He kidnapped her at swordpoint, tying her into the saddle behind one of his men as she wept and begged and swore "that, whatsoever befell of her, she should never be wedded to that knave, to die for it. . . ." Her mother ran after the horses for as long as she could, but fell at the roadside as her daughter's voice faded into the distance, still pleading piteously for help. But rescue did not come soon enough. During a bruising ride eighty miles northwestward into Lincolnshire—and knowing full well that it could take weeks for her family to find her—Jane Boys's spirit was broken. By the time Langstrother was formally charged with kidnapping, she had married her abductor. Despite her parents' frantic attempts to pursue Langstrother in the courts, the indictment was blocked when Jane herself—left with no choice but to salvage what she could of her dignity and reputation— testified that she had consented to the wedding. Southwell had lost his bride, and with her a share of the Boys estates; and it was presumably in desperate frustration at this injustice that he decided to force his way into Holme Hale.[20]

The Pastons had done what they could to help Jane and her parents during the previous summer—John working tirelessly behind the scenes to gather evidence of "the great horrible deed" for the aborted court case— but a year on, Margaret was concerned about what the spreading disorder might mean for their own family. "As for tidings," she wrote, "we have none good in this country; I pray God send us good." But, resourceful as ever, she was not worried enough to let the immediate practicalities of domestic life slip her mind. She reminded John of the shopping she needed from London, including a new girdle for their small daughter, Margery, and added the nearest she ever came these days to a sentimental word: "I hope you shall be at home so soon that I will write no more tidings to you. . . ."[21]

In London, John was busy preparing a petition detailing all of Nowell and Ledham's crimes, and appealing for a special inquiry into the faked rebellion orchestrated by Roger Church ("such a misruled and uncredible man," as John bitterly described him). Despite all of John's efforts to make clear that he had had no part in the fictional "revolt," rumours that he was "one of the captains of the risers in Norfolk" reached Cambridge, where his brother William was a student, by the middle of June. On 3 July, Bishop Lyhert arrested Roger Church and imprisoned him in Norwich Castle, but Church stood by his story with insolent defiance. "Men think that have spoken with him that he hopes to have good help," Margaret told her husband; "I pray God that the truth may be known." It seemed hardly surprising that John had still not remembered Margery's girdle.[22]

Nor was there any immediate relief from the pressure. Only two years earlier, immersed in the labyrinthine process of trying to secure convictions against Heydon and Moleyns in the autumn of 1450, it must have seemed to John scarcely imaginable that the political world in which he lived could become any more tortuous and complex. But that was exactly what had happened. The blazing hostility between John and his allies and Heydon and his associates had been stifled, not extinguished, by the outcome of the judicial inquiries of 1450–1451; the smouldering embers were starved of oxygen for the time being, but might prove dangerously combustible the moment they were raked over. And now more sparks were flying because of Daniel's anarchic opportunism and the duke of Norfolk's misjudgments. Norfolk's retainers had been stampeding across the late duke of Suffolk's estates in Suffolk, vandalising his parks and threatening his servants, in a provočative effort to intimidate the widowed duchess and demonstrate what Norfolk hoped was his new supremacy in local affairs. Meanwhile, Daniel and his men, with the duke's support or at least his acquiescence, were causing chaos in Norfolk.

What was needed was a king who would stamp his authority on this mess by bringing the chief protagonists sharply to heel, while at the same time brokering a settlement of all outstanding grievances between the warring parties to prevent the violence from recurring. But a king of that kind was exactly what the country lacked. The duke of Somerset had been able to establish his hold on King Henry's government, but his regime was more fragile than his predecessor Suffolk's had been. The crisis of 1450—defeat abroad, revolt at home, and Suffolk's disgrace and murder—had begun to expose to public view the fact that the king was an insubstantial puppet rather than the mainspring of royal rule. As a result, the task of governing in his name had become all the more difficult, especially now that the duke of York had made himself an ostentatiously outspoken mouthpiece for criticisms of the court. Norfolk was not the only shire disintegrating into serious disorder, and it was apparent that decisive action would be needed if the threat of anarchy were to be averted.

On 8 January 1453, a huge judicial commission was appointed to punish crime and suppress disorder across the southeast of England. This should have been a powerful statement of royal intent, but the duke of Somerset's hands were tied by the need to sustain noble support for his regime across the political spectrum, even if members of the aristocracy were themselves implicated in the trouble that the commission was supposed to be investigating. The noblemen named among the commissioners therefore included the duke of Norfolk, the earl of Oxford, Lord Scales, and even Lord Moleyns. It hardly seemed likely that a tribunal in which Norfolk could claim an official role would be able to take a robust lead in dealing with violence for which his own men were responsible—but at least the commission's hearings opened the way for formal charges to be presented, whatever might or might not happen thereafter.

If any doubt remained about the need for some kind of royal intervention to deal with the increasingly unruly state of local politics, it was dispelled on 12 February, when Thomas Daniel, at the head of an ominously large group of the duke of Norfolk's retainers and servants, attended the meeting in the neighbouring county of Suffolk where the shire's representatives for the forthcoming parliament were to be elected. Their plan—that Daniel himself should be nominated as one of the prospective members of parliament—did not get very far. The sheriff reported back to Westminster that he had been unable to hold a valid election "because of menaces and threats," and pointed out that Daniel was in any case not qualified to represent the county in parliament because he held no lands there; it was in Norfolk, not Suffolk, that he had managed, however fraudulently, to acquire some estates.[23] Nevertheless, it was precisely this kind of casual assumption on Daniel's part that he could get what he wanted by bullying and intimidation that had caused such problems for more than a year, and when the king's judges arrived in the region three days later, they were inundated with complaints against the servants of both Daniel himself and the duke of Norfolk, who was now looking more like Daniel's stooge than his patron.

It took the royal justices two weeks to hear all the indictments that the gentlemen of Norfolk and Suffolk were clamouring to present to them. Charles Nowell and Robert Ledham were charged with a string of offences committed in and around Bradeston, including their assault on Margaret's faint-hearted uncle Philip Berney; and the story of Roger Church's elaborate conspiracy to frame Daniel's opponents was also told in court. In Suffolk, meanwhile, the duke of Norfolk's men, with Nowell and his brothers among their number, were accused of violent attacks on the duchess of Suffolk's estates and servants going back as far as February 1450. For good measure—presumably on the principle that a treason charge was always a useful weapon, however unsubstantiated or implausible it might be—several of Norfolk's leading retainers, including Charles Nowell, were accused of planning to kill the king and make the duke of York "king and governor" of the realm. There could be no better demonstration of the political convulsions which Daniel and Norfolk had precipitated in only twelve months than the fact that, during the course of these hearings, John Paston found himself serving on a jury shoulder to shoulder with his old enemies Sir Thomas Tuddenham and John Wyndham.[24]

Nevertheless, the duke of Somerset, as the power behind King Henry's throne, could not afford to alienate Norfolk and risk driving him into the arms of the duke of York, who had been forced for the time being to retreat to the safety of his own estates but would surely seize any opportunity to reassert himself in government. Norfolk was therefore able to secure letters in the name of King Henry himself (drafted, of course, on Somerset's instructions) ordering that legal process against Norfolk's leading retainers be halted—a decision justified, with magnificent vagueness, by "certain causes and considerations moving us."[25] However, even if there was no prospect that any of the accused would actually be convicted, the very fact that so many of the duke's men had been hauled into court represented a slap on his wrist. Not only that, but the extent to which he was under pressure from his peers was apparent in the manoeuvring that surrounded the court hearings. All the main protagonists demanded that their opponents bind themselves over to keep the peace, on pain of financial penalties ranging from a couple of hundred to a couple of thousand pounds, but Norfolk was the only one required to bind himself in the cripplingly and humiliatingly large sum of ten thousand pounds (a figure more than three times his annual income). As a result, the February inquiries meant that the freedom of action that Daniel and Norfolk had previously enjoyed was at last curtailed. Daniel's men were still in occupation at Bradeston, but their reign of terror was over. Finally, after years of subordinating family life to the pressing demands of self-defence, the Pastons had a chance to catch their breath.

Two months later, they experienced the excitement—along with all the other inhabitants of Norwich—of a royal visit to the city. Margaret of Anjou, Henry's twenty-three-year-old French queen, was pregnant at last after eight barren years of marriage, and favoured the region's capital with her presence for two days on her way to Walsingham to give thanks at the Virgin's shrine for the child she was carrying. For once, the arrival of the queen's entourage brought Margaret Paston worries that were sartorial rather than political. She was anxious not to look like the poor relation among the great and the good who assembled for the royal reception, and in the end had to borrow a necklace from her close friend Elizabeth Clere, "for I dared not for shame go with my beads among so many fresh gentle-

women as here were at that time." It was a difficulty she was determined
would not be repeated, telling her husband firmly that he must find the
money to buy "something for my neck" before the spring was out.[26]

In the summer she finally found the family a home in Norwich, even if
the house was to rent rather than buy and a little more expensive than they
had hoped, despite Margaret's best efforts at negotiation over the price. But
her pleasure in their new home was tempered by sad family news. "As for
the chamber that you assigned to my uncle," she told John on 6 July, "God
has purveyed for him as his will is."[27] Philip Berney had died four days earlier, "with the greatest pain that ever I saw man," Agnes reported—a loss
that was immediately counted among Charles Nowell's crimes, on the
grounds that Philip had never been the same since Daniel's men had
ambushed him at the roadside fifteen months earlier. Margaret herself had
been ill again, and she was not the only one. The day after Philip Berney's
death, Sir John Heveningham—their neighbour and "faint friend," who
had failed to support their cause in the judicial proceedings of
1450–1451—"went to his church and heard three masses, and came home
again never merrier, and said to his wife that he would go say a little devotion in his garden and then he would dine; and forthwith he felt a fainting
in his leg and sank down. This was at nine of the clock, and he was dead
before noon."[28]

However, the rest of that autumn passed peacefully enough. Margaret
and John had a small falling-out, about what is not clear from their letters,
but it was enough for an unusual and contrite apology from Margaret
("beseeching you that you be not displeased with me, though my simple-
ness caused you for to be displeased with me. By my troth it is not my will
neither to do nor say that should cause you for to be displeased, and if I
have done I am sorry thereof and will amend it; wherefore I beseech you to
forgive me, and that you bear no heaviness in your heart against me, for
your displeasure should be too heavy to me to endure with").[29] Otherwise
she was busy stocking up provisions for their new household. By
November, frustrated at the lack of choice she found in Norwich, she was
delegating purchases to John in London. Some were expensive delicacies:
sugar, for example, sold in solid loaves imported from the Mediterranean
island of Cyprus by Venetian and Genoese merchants, and used to make
medicinal syrups as well as puddings and dainties (thus bearing responsibility for the blackened, rotting teeth from which so many wealthy men and
women suffered); or cinnamon, shipped from India and southeast Asia

through the Persian Gulf and the Red Sea, prized, like sugar, both for its pharmaceutical properties—mixed into thick, cloying cordials to improve the digestion—and as a delicate seasoning for spiced wine, sweetmeats, and custards. But it was not only in their stock of such exotica that Norwich's shopkeepers fell short of Margaret's high standards; even the local special- ity, woollen fabric, failed to please. "As for cloth for my gown," she told John indignantly, "I can none get in this town better than that is that I send you an example of, which methinks too simple both of colour and of cloth; wherefore I pray you that you will vouchsafe to buy for me three yards and a quarter of such as it pleases you that I should have, and what colour that pleases you, for in good faith I have sought all the drapers' shops in this town and here is right feeble choice."[30]

Meanwhile, building work continued at Mautby, although Margaret was still having trouble with supplies; "I can neither be purveyed of joists nor of board not yet," she wrote in some frustration in January.[31] By then, she knew she was pregnant for the fifth time. She was already thinking ahead about names for the new baby; "I pray you if you have another son," she asked John a few days later, "that you will let it be named Henry in remembrance of your brother Henry," William and Agnes's son who had died in childhood. Margaret, at thirty-one, was not having the easiest time in this pregnancy—she signed herself "your groaning wife, M.P."[32]—and at times her letters to her absent husband now struck an uncharacteristically wistful note. "I pray you that you be not strange of writing of letters to me between this and that you come home," she wrote. "If I might, I would have every day one from you."[33]

One particular reason for wishing John in Norwich was Margaret's growing anxiety about the predicament of his sister, Elizabeth, still not mar- ried at the advanced age of twenty-four and trapped at home with her increasingly irascible mother, Agnes. "It seems by my mother's language that she would never so fain to have been delivered of her as she will now," Margaret told her husband in January 1454.[34] It had been a long time since any warmth had been apparent in the relationship between Agnes and her only daughter. Five years earlier, Margaret's friend Elizabeth Clere had implored John to pay some attention to his sister's plight, "for she was never in so great sorrow as she is nowadays." Agnes, like most of her con- temporaries, believed that disobedient children should be physically chas- tised by their parents, but the occasions on which Elizabeth incurred her displeasure were becoming worryingly frequent. "She has since Easter the most part been beaten once in the week or twice," Elizabeth Clere reported, "and sometimes twice on one day, and her head broken in two or three places." She was apprehensive about the effect her own intervention might have on a valued friendship—"I pray you burn this letter," she asked John anxiously, "for if my cousin your mother knew that I had sent you this letter she should never love me"—but she was increasingly fearful that his sister would accept an unsuitable match simply to escape from Agnes: ". . . sorrow often times causes women to beset them otherwise than they should do," she wrote, "and if she were in that case I know well you would be sorry."[35]

As Elizabeth Clere had suspected, Elizabeth Paston proved willing to countenance any of the suitors suggested for her, however ostensibly unappealing. She had even been prepared, at not quite twenty, to contemplate marriage to Sir John Fastolf's stepson Stephen Scrope, a pox-scarred widower more than twice her age, whose estates were still in the hands of his elderly but tenacious stepfather. Not that these potential objections made the match unacceptable, in Elizabeth Clere's judgment: "methinks he were good for my cousin your sister," she told John, "without that you might get her a better."[36] The difficulty was that, absorbed first by his struggle with Moleyns over Gresham and then by the outrages of Daniel and his men, John had neither the time to give any thought to his sister's misery, nor the inclination to set aside the money she would need as a dowry. Several more matches were proposed over the next few years, but nothing concrete had come of any of the discussions by the autumn of 1454, when Scrope's name was put forward for a second time. John's younger brother William was not convinced that the suggestion was a good one, but he, too, urged John to rescue their sister one way or another: "at the reverence of God draw to some conclusion, it is time."[37]

By then, however, political events were once again engrossing John's attention. At the beginning of August 1453, King Henry suddenly suffered a devastating mental collapse, so severe that it could not be kept hidden. Although he could still walk and eat, he did not speak, and showed no flicker of recognition or understanding. Two months later, Queen Margaret gave birth to a son and heir, named Edward in honour of King Edward the Confessor, the Anglo-Saxon royal saint on whose feast day he was born; but even the sight of his first child failed to penetrate Henry's catatonic state. Bells pealed and services of thanksgiving were celebrated in churches across the country, but when the young queen presented the longed-for infant to her husband, the king remained mute, his gaze vacant and impassive, "saving only that once he looked on the prince and cast down his eyes again, without any more."[38]

With Henry so utterly incapacitated, it could no longer be claimed with any vestige of plausibility that he was a functional part of his own government. His breakdown proved to be a fatal blow for a regime that was already teetering under debilitating pressure because of yet more military catastrophe. In northern France, the lone English port of Calais was safe behind its massive fortifications, but the last remaining English territories around the city of Bordeaux, in the southwest of the country—tattered fragments of the once-great duchy of Aquitaine—were under sustained attack by superior French forces. The Battle of Castillon, in July 1453, proved to be the final engagement of what would come to be known as the Hundred Years' War: the sixty-six-year-old earl of Shrewsbury, the "English Achilles" in command of King Henry's army, was defeated and killed, and Bordeaux was lost to the French after three hundred years of English rule.

This was not only a national disaster—the ultimate destruction of an empire that had once stretched as far south as the Pyrénées—but also a personal one for the duke of Somerset. Three years earlier, he had been in command of the English army when Normandy was overrun by the French, a military calamity for which his archenemy, the duke of York, held him personally responsible. Now, when Aquitaine had gone the same way, Somerset was once again in charge, this time as a statesman rather than a soldier. And, at a stroke, the king's collapse cut the foundations of the duke's power from under him. If Henry was ill, then—just as had been the case when he was a child—his rule would have to be delegated formally to a noble council. Under those circumstances, the claims of the duke of York to a leading role in government could no longer be dismissed. By November, York was back in London, and this time he found a new ally in his campaign to bring his adversary down. Somerset's attempt to make the duke of Norfolk toe the line in East Anglia without alienating him completely had failed. Norfolk now accused Somerset of taking to himself "over-great authority in this realm," and publicly denounced him as a traitor on the grounds of his failure to defend Normandy as the king's lieutenant there in 1450. With all the melodrama he could muster, Norfolk petitioned his fellow magnates to take action against Somerset—a cry for justice, he said, "which you have not yet done to me, whereof I am so heavy that I may no longer bear it, specially since the matter by me pursued is so worshipful for all the realm, and for you, and so agreeable to God, and to all the subjects of this realm, that it may be no greater."[39] On 23 November, with York now dominating the royal council, Somerset was charged with treason and imprisoned in the Tower of London.

The mid-winter months were tense and uncertain. The atmosphere was so jumpy that many of the lords were arming themselves; the powerful duke of Buckingham, for example, was said to have had made two thousand livery badges—lead pins in the form of a nobleman's heraldic device (a knot, in Buckingham's case), to be worn by members of his household or those retained to fight for him—"to what intent men may construe as their wits will give them." York had succeeded in removing his rival from power, but it was much less clear that the rest of the nobility would allow him to take formal control of government during the king's illness; and although Somerset was in custody, he had not completely lost the means to make his influence felt. His men were encamped in all the available lodgings in the streets around the Tower, where their lord was being held captive, and he was reported to have "spies going in every lord's house of this land." The duke of Norfolk was warned to be careful of his own security: "the duke of Somerset makes him ready to be as strong as he can make him, wherefore it is necessary that my lord look well to himself, and keep him among his household, and depart not from them, for it is to dread lest ambushments be made for him." Thomas Daniel and some of his colleagues in the royal household sought to safeguard their position by requesting funds for a garrison to guard the king and his baby son—a garrison that would, of course, be under their own command. Meanwhile, the young queen began to show her mettle, realising that her new role as the mother of the heir to the throne might enable her to claim the right to govern in her son's name, and she did so in January 1454, in what would turn out to be characteristically resolute and unsubtle fashion: ". . . she desires to have the whole rule of this land," it was said, along with the authority to name all the officers of state, all sheriffs, and all bishops.[40] The alarming prospect of the French-born queen taking unfettered rule for herself went a long way to persuade the nobility that the duke of York's claim to lead the council of the lords was in fact the best available option, and on 27 March 1454, York was named protector of the realm, with the powers of a regent to govern in King Henry's name.

York's influence in government was good news for John Paston, just as it had been in the autumn of 1450. The duke's ascendancy meant the retreat of the power of the royal household, something that was apparent as early as the beginning of November 1453, when Osbert Mundford at last succeeded in expelling Daniel's men from his manor of Bradeston. Daniel himself, installed with the prostrate king at Windsor Castle, was now preoccupied with the more pressing matter of his own survival, and his patron Somerset could offer little support from his prison quarters overlooking the Thames. Once York became protector, John therefore lost no time in drafting a petition that detailed yet again all of Nowell and Ledham's iniquitous activities. Robert Ledham's household was a disorderly establishment full of criminals, John said—"six or seven of the said Ledham's men daily, both workday and holiday, used to go about in the country with bows and arrows, shooting and playing in men's closes among men's cattle, going from alehouse to alehouse and menacing such as they hated."[41] Meanwhile, Daniel's alliance with the duke of Norfolk, which had caused so much havoc in East Anglia, had been stretched to the breaking point by their polarised reactions to York's protectorate. Unimpressed by Somerset's attempt to discipline him, Norfolk was one of York's most vociferous supporters in the autumn of 1453. Daniel, on the other hand, derived all of his influence from his position in the royal household, and therefore had an immovable interest in supporting Somerset. However much damage they were each capable of causing on their own, they would never again join forces as they had done to such disruptive effect in 1452.

The enforced retreat of Daniel's men from Bradeston was not the only benefit of York's rule from the Paston point of view. The end of Somerset's household-based regime also meant that John Paston's old enemy John Heydon was now more politically vulnerable than at any point since 1450, and some of the indictments that Heydon and his friend Thomas Tuddenham had faced in that year—and thought they had seen off for good at the Walsingham sessions in 1451—were revived early in 1454. By that stage, John Paston had also received welcome news of Lord Moleyns. Moleyns had neither given up his claim to Gresham, nor paid any compensation for the damage his men had done there, but at least he was no longer in a position to trouble the Pastons further. He went to France in 1453 to take part in the last-ditch defence of Aquitaine, and was captured by the French during the devastating defeat at Castillon. He remained a prisoner there for six years, until his family had sold and mortgaged enough of their estates to raise the exorbitant ransom—the huge sum of eight thousand pounds—demanded for his release.

By the summer of 1454, John had good reason to feel more optimistic than he had for years. Since 1448, when Moleyns had first seized Gresham, John had been almost constantly on the defensive, desperately trying to protect both his family, and the estates that his father had so painstakingly assembled, from predatory rivals and the terrifying effects of political chaos. Now, at thirty-two, he had a chance at last to emerge from his father's shadow as a man of influence in his own right. His new standing was the subject of a gratifying conversation which his brother William reported from London in July. Thomas Billing, a member of the elite legal caste of the sergeants-at-law, had spoken sharply to Daniel's man Robert Ledham on the subject of his feud with John. "It is the guise of your countrymen," Billing told Ledham, "to spend all the goods they have on men and livery gowns and horse and harness, and so bear it out for a while, and at the last they are but beggars; and so will you do. . . . As for Paston," Billing went on, "he is a squire of worship, and of great livelihood, and I know he will not spend all his goods at once. . . . He may do his enemy a shrewd turn and never fare the worse in his household, nor the less men about him."[42]

It made a pleasing change for John to be spoken of with such respect. Just as welcome was the imminent arrival in Norfolk of Margaret's kinsman Sir John Fastolf. His magnificent new home at Caister, less than two miles from John and Margaret's manor of Mautby, near the east Norfolk coast, was finally finished and ready for his occupation, and Fastolf was preparing to move his household there permanently from his London mansion at Southwark. The events of the past few years, and particularly their joint enterprise in trying to bring down the duke of Suffolk's men in 1450–1451, had made Fastolf appreciative of John's loyalty and tenacity. "He says you are the heartiest kinsman and friend that he knows," John's brother William told him in the summer of 1454. "He would have you at Mautby dwelling."[43] John's experiences at the hands of the duke of Norfolk and Thomas Daniel had given him little cause before this to feel that the friendship of great men was worth having. In Fastolf, however, he had at last found a mentor whose influence on his career, and his life, would be profound.

the heartiest kinsman

and friend

OHN PASTON had lost his father when he was still a young man. For more than a decade, he had struggled to defend his family from powerful enemies without the benefit of paternal advice or support. But in Sir John Fastolf, he now found a surrogate father who would have a defining influence—perhaps *the* defining influence—on his life. They had known each other for years, of course; Judge William had known Fastolf well, and Margaret was a distant relative. But it had always been a relationship conducted at arm's length, with Fastolf ensconced in retirement in his grand Southwark town house, and John commuting wearily between Norwich and the Westminster courts. All that was to change in 1454, when the old knight finally came home to Norfolk, the shire of his birth.

Sir John Fastolf was later immortalised by Shakespeare as Prince Hal's disreputable friend Sir John Falstaff, but the bard took outrageous liberties with the life story of his model. The debauched and cowardly old knight dying in Mistress Quickly's care on the eve of the battle of Agincourt bears little relation to a man whose career as a soldier brought him a dazzling fortune, and who fought at Agincourt at the age of just thirty-five. The Fastolfs were yet another of Norfolk's parvenu gentry families: Sir John's grandfather Alexander was a shipowner at the port of Yarmouth, who accumulated enough profit from the lucrative trade off Norfolk's eastern coast for his son John, Fastolf's father, to establish the family as lords of the nearby manor of

Caister. Fastolf himself was born at Caister in 1380, and when his father died three years later he inherited the family's modest estate there, with an income of a little less than fifty pounds a year.

It was not fabulous wealth by any means—enough, at least, to put the Fastolfs solidly among the ranks of the respectable gentlemen of the county, but still unimaginable riches from the point of view of the young William Paston, just two years older than Fastolf, growing up in a two-room cottage almost twenty miles away at Paston village. But however great the social gulf between them, John and William shared a stubborn determination to better themselves. While William applied himself to his books, Fastolf's talents proved to be practical rather than intellectual, and his status as a gentleman gave him the chance of a military career in noble service. In 1401, at the age of twenty-one, he enlisted under the command of Henry IV's second son, Thomas, duke of Clarence, and travelled with him to Ireland when the duke took up his appointment as his father's lieutenant in Dublin. After fourteen years serving in Clarence's household, Fastolf joined the army with which the duke's elder brother, Henry V, invaded northern France in 1415. A series of overwhelming victories followed as the English swept through Normandy, and Fastolf was rewarded with the honour of a knighthood for his part in the conquest.

But by the time he turned forty, in 1420, Fastolf's career had proved much less spectacular than the campaigns in which he had served. The most notable social or financial advance he had so far achieved had come through his marriage in 1409 to Millicent Scrope, a wealthy widow twelve years his senior, whose lands were five times more valuable than his own. It was not until 1422, at the age of forty-two, that his hitherto unexceptional fortunes began to change out of all recognition. The duke of Clarence was killed in battle at Baugé, in the Loire Valley, in 1421, and after his death Fastolf moved into the entourage of John, duke of Bedford, the king's next oldest brother. This seemed, on the face of it, to be a sideways move rather than a sudden promotion—but it was only a matter of months before the significance of Fastolf's position in charge of Bedford's household establishment was utterly transformed.

On 31 August 1422, King Henry—a dynamic leader in the prime of his life—succumbed to dysentery at Vincennes, near Paris. Amid the shock and confusion caused by his unexpected death, a minority government was hurriedly assembled to rule in the name of the infant Henry VI, and the duke of Bedford—the baby king's oldest surviving uncle—was appointed regent of the French lands now held by the English crown. Under Bedford's command, Fastolf quickly rose to an eminence far beyond anything he had experienced before. He was appointed to the ruling council in France over which Bedford presided, and in 1423 he became governor of the territories of Anjou and Maine, to the south of Normandy. In August 1424, at the Battle of Verneuil, on Normandy's eastern border, he was created a knight banneret, a mark of distinction awarded for valour in combat; two years later, he was elected a knight of the chivalric Order of the Garter, an exceptional honour bestowed on only twenty-five men at any one time, most of them members of the nobility. And in 1429, he made a heroic name for himself in a skirmish at Rouvray, twenty-five miles north of Orléans, when he drove off a surprise attack on an English supply train—an engagement known as the Battle of the Herrings, after the contents of the wagons Fastolf saved from the French marauders.

But his military commands brought him more than simply glory. Through a combination of wages, rewards, ransoms, and plunder, he amassed an extraordinary fortune. In recognition of his service to the crown he was granted lands in northern France, including the barony of Sillé-le-Guillaume, with an annual income of four hundred pounds, but he was also able to dispatch vast amounts of cash back to England via the secure hands of English and Italian financiers. There the trusted servants who managed his affairs in his absence invested the money, on his instructions, in the acquisition of a huge landed estate.

Fastolf spent nearly fourteen thousand pounds buying properties in his native East Anglia and around his London base in Southwark, and thousands more building houses in both places of a size and grandeur befitting his new status. Given that most Englishmen supported their families on an income of perhaps three or four pounds a year, and lived in timber-framed houses that cost about the same amount to erect, this was astonishing wealth and breathtaking expenditure. The construction of his moated townhouse at Southwark alone cost 1,100 pounds, but his spending there was dwarfed by the money that he lavished on his birthplace at Caister. Over three decades, he spent more than six thousand pounds on a new castle that combined defensive fortification with all the modern comforts money could buy.

Built largely in brick, Caister Castle had two halls (one for summer, one for winter) among its fifty rooms and, at one corner of the rectangular design, a tall and slender tower overlooking the moat. The house was furnished with an opulence to match the elegance of its architecture. The bedrooms contained featherbeds with woven or embroidered hangings which, in Fastolf's own room, were "white and green with maple leaves." He also kept an astrolabe in his chamber and, in the room he used for bathing, part of his collection of books, including a Bible and works by Livy, Julius Caesar, and Aristotle, as well as a "book of King Arthur" and the Roman de la Rose, a thirteenth-century allegorical poem exploring themes of courtly love. Glass stained with oxides of cobalt, iron, and manganese flooded the interior of the halls with intensely coloured light; and the walls—some painted with compounds of red lead, vermilion, and oil—were covered with fine tapestries, many of them in a richly woven fabric known as arras, after the town in northeastern France from which it originated. One, behind the dais in the Winter Hall, depicted a wild man of the woods carrying a child in his arms, while on the west wall hung a scene of the town of Falaise in Normandy besieged by Henry V's forces in 1418. There were more than forty wall hangings in all, of which two alone—"a rich cloth of arras of imagery work of Justice administering, with another cloth of arras, containing every of the said cloths about sixteen yards long and five yards in breadth"—cost Fastolf more than £220.[1]

He also invested heavily in silver plate and fine jewels, acquiring three particularly exquisite pieces in pledge from the duke of York as part of a loan agreement in 1452: "a brooch of gold with a great pointed diamond set upon a rose enamelled white; a brooch of gold in fashion of a ragged staff, with two images of man and woman garnished with a ruby, a diamond and a great pearl; and a flower of gold, garnished with two rubies, a diamond, and three hanging pearls."[2] The spear-pointed diamond set in an enamelled white rose of York had cost the duke more than £2,500 and was one of the most valuable jewels known to have existed in fifteenth-century England outside royal hands—but even the crucifix that Fastolf wore around his neck every day, supposedly containing a fragment of the true cross, was worth two hundred pounds, four times the sum that had once been his annual income from his father's estates.

These sumptuous trappings of aristocratic living were not merely display for display's sake. Gems in elaborate settings and finely worked plate did not lose value over the years, and in times of need—which came even to noblemen as great as the duke of York—they could be pledged out to raise ready cash. Fastolf had an astute financial brain, and his spending, however apparently ostentatious, was planned with care and meticulously supervised. His business interests included not only the profits of arable farming on his estates, but the wool that his flock of almost eight thousand sheep produced for the English and continental cloth markets, and a fleet of between eight and fourteen ships that, in the Fastolf family tradition, traded out of Yarmouth harbour. Even after Fastolf's French estates were lost in the military disasters of 1450, his English lands brought him a net income of more than one thousand pounds a year, and by the later 1450s, his stock of cash and plate, not including his jewels, was worth more than five thousand pounds, most of it deposited for safekeeping within the walls of the monastery of St. Benet of Hulme, eight miles northwest of Caister. There was a small handful of noblemen whose wealth far outstripped even these riches, but very few men without a noble title could afford to live in such style.

The price that Fastolf paid for his fortune was a personal one. His marriage to Millicent Scrope was financially advantageous, but her age—she was forty-one when they married—meant that it was always unlikely they would have children, even had Fastolf himself not spent most of the next thirty years abroad on campaign. When he finally retired from the war in 1439, his wife was already seventy-one, and she died seven years later. Fastolf was stepfather to her son from her first marriage, Stephen Scrope, but the two men were never close, and their relationship deteriorated after Millicent's death because of Fastolf's implacable determination to hold on to her estates rather than allowing Scrope, who was already approaching fifty, to take possession of his inheritance.

By the early 1450s, Fastolf—now a widower in his seventies—was an isolated figure. He was living in his Southwark mansion while building work continued on his new house at Caister, but it was hard to say that either place was really his home. Most of his adult life had been spent away from England, first in Ireland and then in France. Without question, he thought of himself as a Norfolk man, but he had left East Anglia a long time ago, and in reality he was not, and had never been, an active participant in political life there. Back in London after his long years as a soldier, he found himself bewilderingly out of his element. The men in charge of government were a generation or more younger, and they were not listening as Fastolf thought they should to his voice of experience. The whole course of politics in the 1440s, culminating in the loss of the French lands that he had spent his life defending, was anathema to him. His sense of grievance was palpable, about the defeats in France, the personal losses he had sustained as a result, and the fact that, despite the wealth he had amassed, he was convinced that he had not yet been paid all of what was due to him for half a century of service to the crown.

What made all this still worse in Fastolf's eyes was that the man who had presided over the ill-fated regime of the 1440s, the duke of Suffolk, had proved to be his nemesis in England as well as in France. Fastolf had embarked on an astoundingly ambitious attempt to turn his wealth into landed power in East Anglia, where many of the duke's estates also lay—and, as the Pastons had discovered to their cost, lands that were bought rather than handed down through many generations often embroiled their buyers in vicious disputes over ownership. Initially at least, Fastolf was lucky; his properties remained relatively untroubled when his spending on land was at its height, during the 1430s and early 1440s, and his dealings with the duke of Suffolk were civil during those years. Suffolk—who was short of money in the 1430s because he had been captured in France in 1429 and had to find a large ransom to secure his release—even sold Fastolf one of his own manors in his quest to raise the cash he needed.

As the 1440s went on, however, the relationship between the two men began to sour, whether because Fastolf opposed Suffolk's policy of seeking to negotiate a peace with France, or because tensions at a local level brought their interests into conflict in East Anglia—or perhaps a destructive combination of the two. Discord first erupted in 1447, when Suffolk sent a posse of men to seize Fastolf's manor of Dedham in Essex, northeast of London, which had belonged to the duke's family three-quarters of a century earlier. In the same year, a niggling legal dispute also began between Fastolf and Suffolk's ally John Heydon, over an old debt in a will of which Heydon was executor. At the same time, two courtiers, Sir Philip Wentworth and Sir Edward Hull, took the opportunity to challenge Fastolf's possession of three of his Norfolk estates. In 1448 Hull was able to secure a legal judgment to deprive Fastolf of the manor of Titchwell on the northwest Norfolk coast on the grounds that his wife was the rightful heir to the property; Wentworth meanwhile claimed Beighton and Bradwell, both near Caister, in the name of Thomas Fastolf of Cowhaugh, the young son of the distant relative from whom Fastolf had bought the manors.

It was never likely that Fastolf would be able to avoid having to fight—legally or literally—for at least some of the estates he had bought. The scale of his newly acquired wealth made him a conspicuous target for atavistic or opportunistic claims, and his East Anglian estates were all the more vulnerable because he was not a powerful political presence there—or, in fact, a presence at all—to supervise and protect them. But as the disputes over his lands multiplied in the increasingly volatile political atmosphere of the later 1440s, Fastolf himself had no hesitation in interpreting his troubles as a concerted campaign of harassment inspired by the malice of the duke of Suffolk and his men. Always prone to see things in black and white rather than the murky shades of grey in which the political world operated, he nursed a growing conviction that he was the victim of a vendetta pursued by criminal means.

His sense of persecution compounded his isolation: those who were not for him were against him, he believed, and some old friendships foundered as a result. A lengthy and fruitless dispute with the priory of Hickling, ten miles northwest of Caister, over an annual rent of little more than fifteen pounds—a significant sum of money to most of Fastolf's contemporaries, but small change to a man of his riches—cost him his friendship with his fellow soldier Lord Scales, who as lord of the manor of Hickling was the priory's patron. Scales expressed heartfelt regret about this rift with the man he had once addressed as "father," but Fastolf himself seems simply to have discounted any possibility of compromise. Even the entire city corporation of Norwich could be cast from grace for being insufficiently supportive in one of his disputes; ". . . there was no city in England that I loved and trusted more upon, till they did so unkindly to me and against truth," the old knight wrote bitterly.[3]

Fastolf was not an easy man. He took good fortune for granted, but could not accept its opposite with any kind of equanimity. Every grievance, every perceived slight, was not only carefully noted but taken to heart, nourishing a sense of injustice and ill-treatment that expressed itself in the vehemence with which he spoke of those he believed had wronged him. William Dalling, the official responsible for the verdict that deprived him of the manor Titchwell, for example, was a "false harlot," "that old shrew Dalling"; "he is sore at my stomach," Fastolf wrote resentfully in January 1451.[4] Nevertheless, this difficult, demanding character did not find himself completely alone. Without close family, he relied instead, in both practical and (though he would not have admitted it) emotional terms, on a tightly knit circle of loyal servants. His chief representative at Caister in the years before he moved there himself was his chaplain, Thomas Howes. Howes had his limitations—he could be garrulous to the point of indiscretion, and was not the most sophisticated political operator—but he was devoted to his master and tolerated a heavy and disparate workload without demur. His family also played a pivotal role in Fastolf's household: his sister Agnes was married to another of Sir John's servants, William Barker, and his niece Margaret was the wife of Fastolf's secretary William Worcester (or, when he chose to use his mother's maiden name, William Botoner).

Worcester was a remarkable man, and a complex one. Well educated and acutely intelligent, with a deep intellectual curiosity, he immersed himself in the study of astronomy, medicine, geography, natural history, philosophy, rhetoric, and history. He compiled antiquarian and topographical collections, read widely in Latin and French, and was himself a prolific writer, although few of his works now survive. Somehow, he pursued these scholarly interests at the same time as serving a master who left him almost no time to himself. From the moment Worcester entered Fastolf's employment in the late 1430s as a young man not long out of Oxford University, he became indispensable to the old knight, not only as his amanuensis but as the servant to whom Fastolf could entrust the detailed archival research necessitated by his increasingly convoluted legal affairs. Worcester travelled widely on Fastolf's business, in Normandy in the early 1440s (where, Worcester later noted, he was captured by the French on the coast at Dieppe, and managed to escape only by bribing some sailors), and across England, from Yorkshire in the north to Devon in the southwest, in the attempt to elucidate the descents of the properties his master had bought.

His relationship with Fastolf was extremely close—he was probably a more constant companion to his elderly master than anyone else in the last two decades of Fastolf's life—but also extremely complicated. Worcester knew his limits as a man of business, and was particularly aware of his lack of legal expertise ("I have said no word, for I cannot meddle in high matters that pass my wit," he wrote on one occasion),[5] but this self-effacement was a little disingenuous. He also, with good reason, took himself seriously, and sometimes felt that he was both unappreciated and underpaid. In the early stages of their acquaintance, John Paston addressed him respectfully as "Master Worcester," but soon after the household moved to Caister in the summer of 1454, Worcester asked John pointedly to drop this courtesy title, which, he said, brought him not a farthing (the smallest coin in circulation, worth a quarter of a penny) in income; whereas, he explained, as plain "Worcester or Botoner," servant of Sir John Fastolf, "I have five shillings yearly, all costs borne, to help pay for bonnets that I lose." The point that he had neither independent means nor a decent salary was directed at Fastolf rather than at John, but when Worcester raised the matter with his employer, Fastolf said "he wished me to have been a priest" so that the Church could have provided him with an income and spared Fastolf the expense. "And so I endure," Worcester went on, slipping briefly and discreetly into Latin, "among the needy, as a serf at the plough." He tried to make light of it—"forgive me, I write to make you laugh," he told John—but it was clear that it was not, for him, a joking matter.[6] Yet, difficult and tightfisted though Fastolf was, Worcester's commitment to him was absolute. One of the projects on which he embarked in what little spare time he had was an attempt to write his master's life story, and although no manuscript survives, it is clear that this was a labour not just of duty but of love.

Worcester and Howes were the heart of the large household, but there were others—servants, friends, and associates—on whom Fastolf relied heavily, among them his auditor, Watkin Shipdam; his servant John Bocking; his legal advisers, William and John Jenney and Judge William Yelverton; and a Franciscan friar named John Brackley, an aggressively opinionated and decidedly unlovely man who was, nevertheless, as loyal to Fastolf as the rest of his inner circle. It was among this close-knit group that John Paston began to make his mark once Fastolf finally arrived in Norfolk in 1454, leaving only a skeleton staff in his London residence and bringing cartloads of bedhangings, chairs, tapestries, and cushions over the rutted roads to Caister.

Fastolf and the Pastons were already steadfast allies by that point: they had stood shoulder to shoulder in their attempt to bring their mutual enemies, Heydon and Tuddenham, to justice in 1450, and had suffered the crushing disappointment of failure together. John saw the old knight regularly during the late 1440s and early 1450s, when Fastolf was living at Southwark and John was in London for long periods dealing with his legal affairs. But Fastolf's move to his elegant new home at Caister, coinciding as it did with John's emergence from the worst of his struggles with Lord Moleyns and Thomas Daniel, offered an opportunity for their relationship to develop under less stressful circumstances, for John at least.

Fastolf himself still had legal battles to fight, principally his dispute with Philip Wentworth over the wardship of his young kinsman Thomas Fastolf of Cowhaugh. Not only that, but Sir John's chaplain, Thomas Howes, was in serious trouble as a result of the failed prosecutions of 1450–1451. Howes had been his master's representative in Norfolk throughout the hearings, but he was out of his depth in the fight against Heydon and

Tuddenham, and his role in the legal proceedings, acting as a litigant on Fastolf's behalf, gave his enemies the opportunity to charge him with conspiracy and malicious indictment. Fastolf was annoyed at the prospect that his own good name might be dragged into a case which he saw as entirely Howes's responsibility ("I commanded you not for to labour nor do thing that should be against the law, neither unlawfully against right and truth"), and point blank refused to pay any damages for which his chaplain might be found liable.[7] Nevertheless, he did agree, however grudgingly, to fund Howes's defence, and entrusted the management of the case not only to his lawyer William Jenney but also to his friend John Paston, who had both a basic legal training and, by now, a good deal of experience in handling complex and politically charged lawsuits. By November 1454, Fastolf had also asked John to help him in his own struggle with Philip Wentworth: "I pray you heartily to take this matter tenderly to heart," he wrote, "and . . . to guide this matter in such wise as my intent might be sped."[8]

By the spring of 1455, after a few months during which John became increasingly busy in Fastolf's service, Howes reported that his master now valued his counsel more than that of either William Jenney or Judge Yelverton. "I know verily," he wrote, "your advice shall weigh deeper in my master's conceit than both theirs shall do." This might have been flattery on Howes's part—he was certainly desperate for John's continuing support in his own case ("You have daily great labour for me, God reward you, and my poor prayer you shall have")[9]—but his judgment was borne out by the growing extent to which Fastolf was relying on John's guidance. By May, Fastolf was prepared to trust John not only to carry out his wishes in pursuing his lawsuits, but also to make strategic decisions on his behalf. His cases, he said, were "so strange and divers for me to understand, or to make any answer by me, that in good faith it lies not in my discretion. But if you might be at London yourself this term, if you tarried but three days there, it should speed much better than any writing from me."[10] A month later Fastolf was taking it increasingly for granted that he could direct the activities of a man who clearly now played a central part in the management of his affairs. "I desire that you will haste you to London," he told John on 11 June, "for there is great labour against our intent." If John was now at Fastolf's beck and call, at least it was apparent that this was a result of Sir John's high opinion of him. "I had rather you were at London two days too soon than two days too late," he wrote, "for I trust no man's wit so well as your own."[11]

In a matter of little more than six months, John Paston had overtaken all of Fastolf's other advisers in his closeness to the old man and the confidence that Fastolf placed in him. It was becoming clear that John now occupied a unique role in the inner circle at Caister. He had a legal training, but he was not, like William and John Jenney or William Yelverton, a professional lawyer with other clients to take care of or a judicial career to pursue. Nor was he, like Thomas Howes or William Worcester, an employee on Fastolf's staff; he was a "squire of worship," a landowner of substance with political experience and contacts of his own. His willingness to devote an increasing amount of his time to Fastolf's concerns was therefore both striking and extraordinarily valuable. Howes and Worcester were not resentful of John's influence, but grateful for his help with an employer who was always demanding, and sometimes unreasonably so. There was never a question of Fastolf being in any man's pocket—he was too tough-minded and fiercely independent for that; but he liked John and trusted him, and was convinced by his loyalty and commitment. The two men were temperamentally very similar, in their tendency to see the world in absolute terms of right and wrong, and in their certainty of the justice of their own cause, a conviction verging on self-righteousness. If that meant they were often disappointed, it also brought them closer together. Fastolf's letters make it clear that his reliance on John was founded not only on respect for his abilities but also on genuine affection, perhaps almost for the son he never had. "I feel well that I was never beholden so much to any kinsman of mine as I am to you, who tenders so much my worship and my profit," he wrote warmly at the end of 1455.[12] And after all the difficulties he had faced over the previous decade, John had found an ally and a mentor—almost exactly the same age as his dead father—who valued his service and needed his help.

John was now thirty-four, and his life was more comfortable than it had been for a long time. He was still embroiled in complex and protracted lawsuits, but the all-important difference now was that they were not his own. For the first time in years, despite his trips to London on Fastolf's business, he was able to live mainly at home with his wife and family in Norwich. The baby, their fifth, to whom Margaret gave birth in 1454, turned out to be not a son named Henry but a daughter named Anne, and she was followed before the end of the decade by two more boys, Walter and William. And in the autumn of 1454, John suggested to Fastolf that one of his daughters—Margery, now five or six, or Anne, the new baby—should in time marry Sir

John's young cousin Thomas Fastolf of Cowhaugh, if Fastolf's suit for the boy's wardship was successful. Fastolf was delighted at the suggestion: "which motion I was right glad to hear of," he wrote, "and will be right well-willing and helping that your blood and mine might increase in alliance."[13]

The match did not come off, but John's sister Elizabeth, for one, might have been forgiven for expressing surprise at her brother's sudden interest in things matrimonial. She was still waiting for John and Agnes to find her a suitable marriage, but neither showed any sign of treating her need for a husband as an urgent priority—perhaps because they were less than eager to find the large lump sum (two hundred pounds, roughly a year of John's landed income) that Judge William had bequeathed to Elizabeth as a dowry. She was left stranded in the miserable limbo of spinsterhood until 1458. By that time she had at least escaped from under her mother's roof to board in the household of a family acquaintance, where, Agnes told her brusquely, "she must use herself to work readily as other gentlewomen do, and somewhat to help herself therewith."[14] An arrangement that would have been entirely normal as part of the education of a teenage girl from a good family was rather less dignified for an unhappily unmarried woman of twenty-eight, and it cannot have been anything but a huge relief when a husband was finally found for her by the end of that year in the person of Robert Poynings, one of the twin younger sons of the Sussex landowner Robert, Lord Poynings.

It was not a love match, by the sound of a letter Elizabeth sent to her mother shortly after the wedding, even if she was hopeful that affection might grow between herself and her new husband—"my master, my best beloved that you call, and I must needs call him so now, for I find no other cause and as I trust to Jesu never shall, for he is full kind to me." Nor had Agnes lost her reluctance to part with her daughter's dowry. "I beseech you, good mother," Elizabeth wrote anxiously, "as our most singular trust is in your good motherhood, that my master, my best beloved, fail not of the 100 marks at the beginning of this term the which you promised him to his marriage, with the remnant of the money of my father's will."[15] Nevertheless, Elizabeth was at long last free to begin an independent life as a married woman—something for which she owed a debt of thanks to Fastolf's secretary, William Worcester, who had travelled back and forth on John's behalf to negotiate the details of the agreement.

While John and Margaret were enjoying their newly regained domesticity, however, the political world was again growing darker and more turbulent. After seventeen months during which he "knew not what was said to him, nor knew not where he had been while he has been sick," King Henry finally woke from his catatonic state at Christmas 1454. The king was overjoyed to see his baby son, now more than a year old, and declared himself to be "in charity with all the world, and so he would all the lords were."[16] However unwittingly, in those few words he revealed exactly what had always been wrong with his kingship: vague benevolence was no substitute for the assertive leadership that would have commanded the compliance of his nobles. The duke of York had done his best during Henry's illness to impose impartial rule on the festering disorder in the country, but he was not the king, and he could not sustain his fellow magnates' support for his role as protector now that Henry was well enough, at least in theory, to take charge of his own government. The duke of Somerset was still in prison—York had tried and failed in the summer of 1454 to persuade the rest of the nobility to try him for treason on the grounds of his role in the loss of France—but as soon as the king recovered his health it became clear that Somerset, too, would recover his position of influence. When York's protectorate formally ended, early in February 1455, Somerset was released from custody, and York had no choice but to withdraw from the court.

With his enemy Somerset back in power at the king's side, York's situation was now extremely perilous. However, he was no longer quite the isolated figure he had been during the previous period of Somerset's rule in the early 1450s. Violent conflict within the ranks of the nobility, unresolved after years of royal inertia, had deep roots by now in some parts of the country, and neither York nor Somerset had been able to put an end to the disorder. The great northern family of the Nevilles, led by York's brother-in-law Richard Neville, earl of Salisbury, and his eldest son Richard, earl of Warwick, had become convinced that the rule of Somerset and the court gave them no chance of securing justice in their vicious feud with their regional rivals the Percys. As a result, they were now prepared to join York in opposition to Somerset's reconstituted regime. Bolstered by the Nevilles' support, and fearing that Somerset would seek to destroy him, York decided that attack was the best form of defence. He and the Nevilles mustered their forces in the north in the spring of 1455 and moved to intercept Henry on his way from London to a great council that Somerset had summoned to meet at Leicester—a midland city that, ominously for York and his allies, lay at the heart of the king's private powerbase, the estates of the duchy of Lancaster.

But Somerset and the court did not move fast enough to reach this Lancastrian stronghold. The two sides met at the town of St. Albans, twenty miles northwest of the capital—a confrontation that demonstrated just how disastrously intractable political division among the nobility had become. For the majority of the lords, the sight of three great magnates marching at the head of an army against their anointed sovereign was a terrifying one which convinced them, whatever their attitude toward Somerset, that King Henry must be defended. York, Salisbury, and Warwick, meanwhile, believed that they would never be safe while Somerset remained at the king's right hand; their call to arms was a last resort, designed to enforce the removal of "our enemies of approved experience, such as abide and keep themselves under the wing of your Majesty Royal."17

The attempt at negotiation that took place at St. Albans did nothing to reassure them, since Henry himself took no part in the discussions, and there were suspicions in York's camp that the letters which the duke had sent to explain his grievances had not even reached the king's hands. Fighting began when York's forces entered St. Albans at around ten in the morning on Thursday, 22 May, and continued for several hours through the streets and houses of the town. York and the Nevilles rapidly secured the advantage, and there were probably fewer than a hundred casualties in all by the time their victory was apparent. Among the dead—almost certainly deliberately hunted down and killed—were the Nevilles' chief enemy, Henry Percy, earl of Northumberland, and the duke of Somerset himself.

King Henry had been wounded in the neck by an arrow as he sat under his banner in the market square while his nobles fought in the streets around him. He was not seriously hurt, however, and if any further demonstration were needed that he would endorse the views of whoever had most immediate access to him, it came later that day when York and the Nevilles formally submitted to his authority "and besought him of his Highness to take them as his true liegemen, saying that they never intended hurt to his own person." In response, it was reported, Henry "took them to grace, and so desired them to cease their people, and that there should no more harm be done."18 The duke and his allies took the king back to London in ceremonial procession, amid tight security. This public display of unity was underlined by a service held at St. Paul's Cathedral on Sunday, 25 May, during which York himself presented King Henry with his crown. That day a friend of John Paston's wrote from London to tell him what had happened at St. Albans; "and as for what rule we shall have," he said, "yet I know never."[19]

Whatever the wider significance of the battle, Sir John Fastolf certainly believed that York's victory would help him in his lawsuit against the courtier Philip Wentworth, especially since Wentworth himself was in disgrace. He had carried the royal standard at St. Albans, but once the fighting began to turn against the king's forces, he "cast it down and fled. My lord Norfolk says he shall be hanged therefor, and so is he worthy," Fastolf's servant William Barker reported tartly to William Worcester. "He is in Suffolk now. He dares not come about the king."[20] John Paston shared Fastolf's optimism, and put feelers out about the prospects of getting himself elected as one of the representatives of the county of Norfolk for the parliament that was called to meet early in July. Fastolf's lawyer John Jenney thought this ill advised, given the enormity of the events of the last month—"Some men hold it right strange to be in this parliament," he told John, "and methinks they be wise men that so do"[21]—but John's plans were in any case thwarted by the duke of Norfolk's determination to have his own choice of candidates returned.

Norfolk had arrived at St. Albans a day too late to take part in the fighting, whether by accident or design was not clear. But he was generally thought to be sympathetic to York's cause—or, at least, known to share the duke's hostility to Somerset—and was therefore well placed to get his own way in the parliamentary election. However, he made an elementary mistake in putting forward the name of his cousin Sir John Howard, a Suffolk landowner who held no estates in Norfolk itself. As John Jenney pointed out, "it is an evil precedent for the shire that a strange man should be chosen, and no worship to my lord of York nor to my lord of Norfolk to write for him." Once the duke had been made aware of his misjudgment, he was willing to agree that "the shire should have free election," so long as "Sir Thomas Tuddenham were not, nor none that was towards the duke of Suffolk"[22]—an understandable stipulation, but one that revealed how much he was still struggling against the influence of a rival who had by now been dead for five years. Nevertheless, his authority in the wake of York's victory was such that Howard (who was said to have been "mad as a wild bullock" that his nomination had been challenged) was in the end elected, despite the misgivings of many gentlemen in the county.[23]

When parliament opened on 9 July, Fastolf took the opportunity to submit a petition outlining yet again in exhaustive detail his losses in France, the vast amounts of money he claimed he was owed by the crown, and his grievances against the late duke of Suffolk's men. Another petitioner was Henry Woodhouse, the victim of Thomas Daniel's trickery over his engagement to Daniel's already-married sister, who at last secured restitution of his title to his own estates at Roydon. The judgment came too late to save his home there, however; ten months earlier, desperate at his inability to defend himself more effectively, Woodhouse had arranged for the manor house to be demolished, rather than let it fall into Daniel's hands for good. Tension pervaded the parliamentary proceedings: ". . . the king our sovereign lord and all his true lords stand in health of their bodies," it was reported, "but not all at heart's ease." On 18 July, in a bold attempt to draw a line under the conflict, a bill was passed placing the blame for the fighting at St. Albans on the dead duke of Somerset, "and nothing done there never after this time to be spoken of."[24] Despite the optimistic rhetoric, however, it hardly seemed likely that the battle could simply be expunged from public memory, and York, Salisbury, and Warwick were taking no chances; London was heaving with heavily armed men wearing their colours. It took several more months of fraught negotiation, during which violent disorder continued unchecked in Wales and the southwest, before York was once again installed as protector, with authority to rule in King Henry's name, in November.

In some respects, it seemed that York's task of trying to restore unity in government under his own leadership would be easier now that his bitter personal rivalry with Somerset was at an end. On the other hand, the shocking fact of Somerset's death also brought a traumatic new dimension to the conflict. After years of fighting in France, the nobility were accustomed to war, but war fought overseas, in which it usually suited their enemies far better to capture the wealthy and powerful than to kill them; large ransoms could not, after all, be demanded for dead bodies. Now the blood of English noblemen had been shed on English soil by the hands of their fellow magnates, something which the heirs of those who had died would find it difficult either to forget or to forgive.

And if the prospect that the most powerful aristocratic families in the country might be riven by blood feuds were not threatening enough, it was also clear that York's role as protector was much less easy to justify, and therefore more vulnerable, than it had been a year earlier. Then the king had been ill, and explicitly unable to rule. Now he was no less fit to govern than he had been for most of his reign. If that was not saying much, it still did not mean that it was a simple matter for York to claim the right to rule in his place. The duke's position became all the more difficult to defend once it became apparent that Queen Margaret, a powerful and fiercely partisan presence at King Henry's side, would not accept the protectorate but intended to lead her husband's government herself. ("The queen is a great and strong laboured woman," John Bocking reported to Fastolf, "for she spares no pain to sue her things to an intent and conclusion to her power.")[25]

York clung to power for three months, but by February 1456 he was left with no choice but to bow to the inevitable. He resigned as protector, and six months later Margaret moved her husband and his court a hundred miles northwest of the capital to Coventry, a midland city that was, like Leicester, surrounded by the king's own duchy of Lancaster estates, some of which Margaret herself had been granted after her marriage. With the queen entrenched in the Midlands, and York and the Nevilles still powerful in London, with backing both from their northern lands and from the garrison at Calais, where the earl of Warwick was now captain, the nobles who made up the royal council were left desperately searching for enough common ground to build some semblance of a workable government. The result, for the time being at least, was an uneasy impasse.

After a lifetime of involvement in war and politics, Sir John Fastolf heard of these disquieting events at second or third hand. At home in the luxurious calm of Caister, his mind was still sharp, but the rude health that had sustained him through a lifetime of arduous campaigning was not as robust as it had once been. His world was narrowing; he could no longer travel, and his interest even in the tumultuous course of politics was increasingly refracted through his obsessive quest for justice in his own legal battles. Even that, however, could be too much to cope with when he felt unwell. John Paston received an unusually abrupt response when he requested Fastolf's instructions on some business matters during one such period of illness: "you know how that I have put my trust in you both for my soul's health and also for the pursuit and defence of all worldly matters touching my person . . . ," the old man wrote, with an unfamiliarly bleak weariness. "For you know well I am so visited by the hand of God that I may not deal with such troublous matters without it should be too great hurt to my bodily welfare, which I trust you will not desire, etc."[26]

That even John Paston, of whom Fastolf was normally so appreciative, could be told to get on with his job in such relatively direct terms is an indication of how onerous the demands were that the old knight was now making on his closest household servants. "At reverence of God, be as soon as you may with my master, to ease his spirits," the long-suffering William Worcester asked John some time later. "He questions and disputes with his servants here, and will not be answered nor satisfied some time but after his wilfulness, for it suffices not our simple wits to appease his soul. But when he speaks with Master Yelverton, you, or with William Jenney, . . . he is content and holds him pleased with your answers and motions, as reason is that he be. So would Jesus one of you three, or some such other in your stead," Worcester added with feeling, "might hang at his girdle daily to answer his matters."[27]

By the spring of 1457, Worcester felt that Fastolf's control of his finances was beginning to slip, and he appealed to John as an ally in the campaign to ensure that the household at least kept proper accounts. "My master cannot know whether he goes backward or forward till this be done," he told John on 20 April, and returned to the subject again ten days later: "my master was wont to lay up money yearly at London and Caister," he said, "and now the contrary, from bad to worse."[28] Worcester was writing in confidence ("I pray you and require you keep this matter to yourself"), because he believed the problem stemmed from the failure of others in the household to do their jobs properly, while his own role as a mere secretary did not allow him to take command of the situation.[29] As Fastolf became less reliable and more irascible, his closest servants were all under increasing strain. The old man was so quick to criticise that some of his household responded to the pressure by rounding on each other. Any expression of disapproval from their master was now viewed with suspicion lest he had been unduly influenced by other members of his staff, Worcester told John on one occasion, when questions were raised about accounts that William Barker had drawn up; "and so it is imagined of me when I write letters to London to Bocking or Barker, that, in such matters as please them not, then it is my doing; if it take well to their intent, then it is their doing." Characteristically, having written heatedly, he tried to make light of his words. "I am eased of my spirits now that I have expressed my lewd meaning"—*lewd* here used self-deprecatingly to mean "foolish"—"because of my fellow Barker, as of such other barkers against the moon, to make wise men laugh at their folly . . . ," he wrote with unconvincing brightness. "Forgive me of my lewd letter writing, and I pray you laugh at it."[30]

But Worcester could not so easily sweep away the fact that his master's previously iron grip on his affairs was beginning to loosen. It was no coincidence that, by the end of 1457, the part John Paston played in Fastolf's business had expanded to include the supervision of his estate management. John travelled with Worcester around some of Sir John's Suffolk manors in January 1458, and in May he rode much farther afield, undertaking a round trip of almost three hundred miles with the chaplain Thomas Howes to check on properties Fastolf owned in the northern county of Yorkshire, which he found in a state of some neglect.[31] John had become indispensable, in personal terms to the old knight himself, and in practical terms to his household, a fact that did not go unnoticed in the world beyond Caister's walls. "My master can do nothing the which shall come in open audience at these days but it shall be called your deed," one correspondent told him.[32]

Fastolf was now in his late seventies. It was clear to everyone, including the old man himself, that he did not have much time left, and he was increasingly preoccupied with the question of what should happen to his spectacular wealth after he was gone. Whereas Judge William Paston, in the same situation, had had to weigh up the competing claims of his heir, his younger children, and the spiritual needs of his soul, the task confronting Fastolf was ostensibly much simpler, and certainly much lonelier. He had founded no dynasty; all he could hope for from his riches was to ensure some aid for his soul on its agonising way through the terrors of purgatory, and to create some fitting earthly memorial to his name and family. That much was clear—but it was a great deal less obvious how it should be achieved, and in any case the contemplation of his own approaching death was not an agreeable pastime. Worcester was worried that his master was simply putting off matters that were too important and too complex to be left hanging: "a great lack is in him," he told John in 1456, "he tarries so long to put all things of charge in a sure way."[33]

Worcester was an acute judge of character, and his concerns were well founded. Landowners could never be sure that their last wishes would be carried out promptly and to the letter; even the most dutiful heirs were liable to prioritise their own worldly interests over the timely fulfilment of religious bequests, often waiting until they lay on their own deathbeds to stipulate that their parents' wills should be performed as well as their own. Fastolf himself, despite the lavish scale of his disposable income and his undoubted concern to honour his lineage, had still not arranged for memo-

rial stones to be placed on his own parents' tombs. But Fastolf's childlessness made his situation yet more difficult. Without a son and heir, he would
have to entrust the administration of his will to a group of executors. Some
at least would need to be powerful men, if they were to have the influence
to carry through whatever Fastolf's plans for his fortune might be; but powerful men were busy men, and the time they would be able to devote to the
well-being of Fastolf's soul would be strictly limited. On the other hand,
men such as Howes and Worcester, whose commitment to his interests was
unquestionable, lacked the political weight necessary to turn ambitious
schemes of commemoration and intercession into reality.

And Fastolf knew all too well from personal experience what the consequences might be. He was one of the executors of his former lord the duke
of Bedford, who had died without direct heirs in 1435, leaving a will that
was nuncupative—that is, dictated on his deathbed rather than formally
drafted—and unhelpfully vague. More than twenty years later, its terms had
still not been completely fulfilled, and Fastolf, who was by now the only one
of the duke's seven original executors still alive, was struggling to locate the
remainder of his dead master's possessions. Worcester was unhappily aware
of the potential parallels, as he told John after Christmas 1456, when Fastolf
refused him leave to visit Bristol, his home town, on the grounds that he
was needed to help Sir John draft his will. "God give him grace of wholesome counsel and of a good disposition," he wrote gloomily. "It is not the
work of a single day nor a single week. My lord Bedford's will was made in
so brief and general terms that unto this day by the space of twenty years
can never have end, but always new to construe and opineable; so a general-
ity shall nor may be so good as a particular declaration. I write bluntly."[34]

The idea on which Fastolf eventually settled was the foundation of a
religious college at Caister, to be dedicated to St. John the Baptist. Fastolf's
reverence for the saint was such that, at great expense, he had acquired one
of his fingers—a costly relic that was kept in the castle's chapel. The college
would be made up of seven monks or priests and seven poor men, to form
an institution that would simultaneously provide perpetual prayers for his
soul and those of his family, and keep the Fastolf name alive for posterity. It
would be a complex project, requiring a licence from the king to allow the
endowment of the college with a substantial part of Fastolf's estates. Sir
John himself was, as usual, so convinced of the merits of his case that he
saw no reason why he should not be granted the necessary licence "without
any great fine, in recompense of my long service continued and done unto

the king and to his noble father, whom God absolve, and never yet rewarded." Warming to his theme, he added that, since he intended that his priests and poor men should also pray for the king himself, "methinks I should not be denied of my desire, but the rather to be remembered and sped."[35]

As so often, the finer points of the political circumstances had escaped him. Henry VI's government was not only profoundly unstable but chronically short of money, and it was not plausible that a man as wealthy as Fastolf would be allowed to pour his riches into a new religious foundation without the crown taking a cut of some sort. Sure enough, word came back in the summer of 1457 that "it is too great a good"—too much money, possibly even the immense sum of one thousand pounds—"that is asked of you for your licence."[36] The prospects of a more favourable response seemed limited in the extreme, given that the Lord Treasurer was John Talbot, earl of Shrewsbury, whose father had fought in France with Fastolf thirty years earlier and had charged Sir John with cowardice after he made a tactical retreat during the English defeat at the Battle of Patay in 1429. Fastolf had succeeded in clearing his name after a formal investigation, but relations between the two men never recovered, and there seemed little point in hoping that Shrewsbury's son might now be sympathetic to Fastolf's claims to a preferential rate for his licence on the grounds of his record in royal service. Fastolf himself was constitutionally incapable of agreeing to pay a sum he believed to be extortionate and unfair; he simply could not bring himself to do it, even if the needs of his immortal soul were at stake. As a result, he was unable to secure formal permission to endow his college—something that could only have compounded his more general reluctance to commit his wishes to paper in any final form.

The other problem with Fastolf's plan was that his home at Caister was so conspicuously desirable. For Fastolf himself it was crucial that his lasting memorial be at Caister itself, his birthplace, on which he had lavished so much money and care. But it was already abundantly clear quite how many covetous eyes were focused on a valuable house which was large, luxurious, and defensible, and which would not, of course, pass in uninterrupted succession from father to son, thus rendering it vulnerable to opportunistic manoeuvres by the greedy and powerful. In the early 1450s, Thomas Daniel—never one to miss an underhand trick—sought to lay the groundwork for a potential claim by declaring that he had been named Fastolf's heir, a "slander" that the old knight complained was a "great vexation" to him.[37] Not to be outdone, the duke of Norfolk let it be known in 1451 that "Sir John Fastolf has given him Caister, and he will have it plainly."[38] The duke's own ancestral home was a chilly and forbidding three-hundred-year-old castle in Suffolk, and the possibility of acquiring a comfortable and fashionable new house, strategically placed on the Norfolk coast, was too tempting to ignore.

Others were a little more subtle in approach. Cecily Neville, duchess of York, whose husband had estates in East Anglia but no residence there, visited Fastolf in the autumn of 1456 and "sore moved me for the purchase of Caister," he reported to John Paston once she and her entourage had gone.[39] Rumour had it that other magnates interested in buying the property included the duchess's nephew Richard, earl of Warwick, as well as John, Viscount Beaumont, and, before his death, the duke of Somerset. Fastolf did not entertain the offers for a moment, but they did make him all the more anxious about how to ensure that his wishes would be carried out. He needed, first of all, to find a way of guaranteeing that his college would be founded at Caister, as he wanted, and then to make sure that it could be protected from the acquisitive hands of the great and the not so good.

Fastolf made a new trust for his estates in 1457, but he did not finally draft his will until the summer of 1459.[40] The long delay reflected his deep ambivalence, even at the age of seventy-nine, about setting down his last wishes. The text itself, however, was suffused with his desperate desire to bind the future, and his fear that he might not succeed in doing so. It was a lengthy and minutely detailed document, in the course of which, with characteristic stubbornness, he required his executors to take over the disputes in which he was still engaged, and also warned them to beware of "divers persons of divers descents" who "pretend . . . at this day to be next inheritor to me after my decease," when in fact, he said, "no creature has title or right to inherit" anything he owned. But the main business of the will was the foundation of the college at Caister, which his executors were to establish with an endowment of two hundred pounds a year. If a licence for this new foundation could not be obtained, then the endowment was to be given to the nearby Abbey of St. Benet of Hulme, where Fastolf intended to be buried, to support his monks and poor men there instead—although it was manifestly clear that this option was an unhappy second best, raising questions in his mind about whether his wishes would be adequately fulfilled within an institution over which he could have little hold from beyond the grave. The rest of his lands were to be sold and the money disposed of for the good of his soul. Here his anxiety broke through the formality of the legal language; his executors, he said, "shall so dispose my goods in effect faithfully that my soul, vexed in painful anguishes, with holy Job be not compelled to say, with great lamentation and mourning, 'Have mercy on me, have mercy on me, namely you that my friends should be, for the hand of God's punishing has grievously touched me.' "[41]

It was not hard to see why he was so uneasy. His difficulty in securing royal authorisation for the foundation had already brought into question the viability of his scheme. Even if the licence could be secured, the responsibilities which he proposed to entrust to his executors were so overwhelmingly complex and wide ranging that he could not be certain that they would have the time or the commitment to see them through with any urgency, or perhaps at all. It cannot have been lost on either Sir John himself or those closest to him that what he really needed was a man of political standing who would be prepared to devote himself totally to the realisation of Fastolf's designs. And an alternative proposal, along just those lines, did emerge in the last months of the old knight's life.

The exact course of events remains shrouded in uncertainty, not least because, after Fastolf's death, the other main protagonists spent years arguing about what precisely had happened. John Paston later claimed that Fastolf had been set on the new plan since the summer of 1457, but if that was the case, it was not reflected in the draft will of 14 June 1459. An oblique reference in the surviving correspondence suggests both that the new proposition came directly from John himself, and that it was not raised until a few days after the will of June 1459 had been written. In a letter of 24 June 1459, William Barker told John that "your matter that you have moved of to Sir Thomas"—the chaplain, Thomas Howes—"for the purchase, etc., my master is well agreed thereto, but first it was taken strangely, etc."[42] The proposal—if this was indeed the "matter" to which Barker alluded, with such tantalisingly elliptical et ceteras—was a radical one. John suggested that he alone should take personal responsibility for the foundation of Fastolf's college at Caister. In return (and this, it seems safe to assume, was the part that might well be "taken strangely"), he should be named sole heir to all Fastolf's estates in Norfolk and Suffolk, for which he would pay a sum of 4,000 marks—that is, 2,666 pounds, a small fraction of their market value—to Sir John's executors for the performance of his will.[43]

This was a daring move. If John succeeded in persuading Fastolf to accept him as his heir, he might effect a second transformation in his family's fortunes as astonishing as the one his father had achieved before him. On the other hand, the risk he ran by raising the issue at all was that he might taint himself in Fastolf's eyes by association with Daniel, Norfolk, and all the others who had been circling acquisitively around the inheritance, and thereby destroy the relationship of trust between himself and his patron. The hard fact of the matter was that John was both practical and unsentimental, and it must have occurred to him almost from the beginning that he might one day be a beneficiary of Fastolf's will in some form or other. Fastolf's childlessness meant that there had been speculation for years about what would happen to his estates. Agnes Paston thought she had seen an opportunity for her sons to profit from the family's association with him, and from Margaret's blood relationship as his distant cousin, as early as 1451, when Fastolf was rumoured to be selling some of his Norfolk properties. "I pray you, as you will have my love and my blessing," she told John that November, "that you will help and do your duty that something were purchased for your two brothers. I suppose that Sir John Fastolf, if he were spoken to, would be gladder to let his kinsmen have part than strange men."[44]

But a moment's reflection would have told Fastolf that, practical and unsentimental though John might be, he was not a cynical man, and his sustained commitment to Fastolf's concerns was too deep and full-hearted to be written off now as a mercenary act of self-interest. There were also potent reasons why Fastolf might conclude that the proposal would work to his advantage. He had trusted John implicitly in the handling of his affairs for a number of years, and had not been disappointed. If there was any gentleman of his acquaintance to whom he could confide responsibility for the welfare of his soul, it was surely John—and John would have an extraordinarily good reason, in the shape of Fastolf's estates, to do his utmost to carry out his patron's wishes. Once the college was safely established, Fastolf would be able to rest easy in his grave knowing that John would be on hand, living at Caister with his family, to make sure that the priests were fulfilling their spiritual duty of care for their founder's soul, and to protect the castle from the predatory interest of other landowners.

All the signs are that Fastolf did come round to John's suggestion. "My master is well agreed thereto," William Barker said in June 1459, and a revised draft of the 14 June will exists in which the complex instructions to the executors about the founding of the college, and the frantic language that accompanied them, are replaced by the streamlined simplicity, expressed in cool legal prose, of John's scheme.[45] But if this revision was carried out on Fastolf's instructions, the old man did not formally endorse the result; if he did indeed agree to make John Paston his heir, he never said so in writing. The absence of a sealed written will in John's favour cannot be taken as proof that Fastolf had rejected the idea of naming him his heir. He had taken years to come round to drafting one version of his will, and it was never likely that he might be prevailed upon to write another almost immediately. Apart from anything else, the very idea of settling once and for all on his final intentions came, for Fastolf, too uncomfortably close to acknowledging the proximity of death.[46] On top of this general unpredictability, Fastolf was also aware of the hold that the prospect of future reward gave him over his long-suffering servants, a hold that would remain useful only so long as they remained uncertain of what their reward would ultimately be. Over the years, he had made promises to many, perhaps all of them, but the will of June 1459 made no specific bequests to any members of his household.[47] John Paston was not a servant to be kept dangling on a string, but the reward he hoped to receive was almost all of what Fastolf had to give, and the old man was never likely to give the decision official form either quickly or straightforwardly, however convinced he might be of the merits of the idea itself.

John's difficulty was that there was so little time left. Fastolf had been in remarkably good health in the early summer of 1459—"my master is as fresh as ever he was these two years, thanked be God," William Barker reported to John in London[48]—but by the autumn he was gravely ill, and Friar Brackley sent an urgent message summoning John to his bedside. "It is high time," he wrote. "He draws fast homeward, and is right low brought and sore weaked and feebled, etc." The question of the inheritance was clearly now urgent, but John was no nearer securing a written statement of his patron's wishes. Brackley was as oblique as Barker had been in mentioning John's proposal; neither he nor Howes, he said, had "no more touched of the matter, etc., to my master, etc." At least it was clear that Fastolf's high opinion of John had not faltered. "Every day these five days he says, 'God send me soon my good cousin Paston, for I hold him a faithful man,'" Brackley reported.[49]

By the beginning of November, with John now maintaining a vigil at his side, Fastolf was sinking fast. He was confined to his bed, "so short in his breath, and so overcome with the pain of his sickness, that a man might not hear him speak but he laid his ear to his mouth."[50] For the second time, John Paston was about to lose a father. And for the second time, John's claims on the estate that the old man would leave would be the subject of fierce controversy. His hopes now rested on the last whisperings of a frail and feverish invalid—and John, who had rejected his own father's dying requests so angrily on the grounds that he "made no will of them in writing," was about to find that the issue looked dramatically different from beside a second deathbed.

CHAPTER 7

ᡐ

neither in trust

nor favour

O N 3 NOVEMBER 1459, the great house at Caister was full of bustling activity. It was a Saturday, the day when the household's weekly provisions arrived from the teeming markets of Yarmouth: cuts of beef, veal, and pork, and fine capons—cockerels that had been castrated and fattened for the table; oysters, mussels, whelks, and the port's speciality, barrels of white and red herring—that is, fish which had been salted (white) or smoked (red) to preserve them through the winter months. In charge of purchasing supplies, and transporting them the three miles or so to Caister, was John Russe, a Yarmouth merchant and shipowner who had served Fastolf for years. As always, mass was celebrated in the castle's chapel that morning, and Fastolf's servants gathered in the hall at eight for a breakfast of bread, cheese, and ale.

But in the chamber where their master lay, it was clear that this was not a normal day. Fastolf was now close to death. Attendants came and went as the old man lay unmoving in his bed: Nicholas Newman, the most senior of his chamber servants, brought him spiced wine to sip; his barber, Harry Wynstall, came to shave his beard; his doctor, John Barnard, looked in from time to time to check on his condition; and his devoted chaplain, Thomas Howes, said mass at his bedside. Among them all, John Paston was a constant presence. He was there still the following afternoon, when Robert Inglose, the son of an old friend of Fastolf's, arrived at the house, intending to discuss some financial matters. John stepped in to protect his patron:

Inglose could see Fastolf, he said, only on condition that he promised not to talk business. When Inglose was brought in to the bedchamber, he understood why. Sir John was "right weak and full feeble in his spirits," he later recalled, "as a man ready to die."[1] The old knight held on for twenty-four hours more, but on Monday, 5 November, at around six o'clock in the evening—with John Paston still at his side—Fastolf died.

For John, it was a huge personal loss. The gruff and petulant old man had not been easy to deal with, particularly toward the end of his life, but he was capable of inspiring fierce loyalty in those around him. John had been his closest confidant and friend for five years, and Fastolf's trust and esteem had been supremely important to him, especially given how bereft of political support he had been in the aftermath of his own father's death. But whatever the emotional consequences, it was also clear that this was the pivotal moment of John's life.

Before him lay two choices. The first was simple and uncontroversial. If the will to which Fastolf had put his seal four months earlier were allowed to stand, John would go on being what he had always been—a safe pair of hands, not quite on the political inside track, but a determined champion of his family's interests and his father's legacy. There was nothing simple about the other choice. John could try to enforce what he believed to be his mentor's last wishes, despite the fact that the old knight had left no formal written statement of his intention to make John his heir. The scale of Fastolf's wealth, and the fact that he left no son of his own to inherit, meant that it was always likely that others would come forward to challenge for a share of the estate, even had John possessed incontrovertible evidence to support his claim. Because John could not produce such evidence, it was virtually certain that he would face a protracted and costly fight to secure the inheritance. If he succeeded, he would utterly transform his own position and that of his family: possession of Fastolf's lands would give him riches and influence on a scale far beyond even his father's remarkable achievements. If he failed, the cost would be counted not only in the strain that years of struggle would inflict on himself and his family, but also in putting everything his father had achieved at risk.

John did not hesitate. He announced that, on the Saturday morning before his death, Fastolf had dictated a new will, in which he spoke of his "very trust and love to his cousin John Paston"—his "best friend and helper and supporter"—and at last put into formal effect the scheme that John had mooted in the final months of the old knight's life. The foundation of the college at Caister was to be entrusted to John alone, "for which, and for other charges and labours that the said John Paston has done and taken upon him, to the ease and profit of the said Sir John Fastolf," John should have all his lands in Norfolk and Suffolk for the sum of 4,000 marks, or £2,666, to be paid in instalments over the next decade. Ten executors were named—headed by William Wainfleet, the bishop of Winchester, and including John himself, Judge William Yelverton, Fastolf's secretary William Worcester, his spiritual adviser Friar John Brackley, and his chaplain Thomas Howes—but the administration of the will was to be committed to John Paston and Thomas Howes alone. Fastolf's fear that Caister might fall victim to the greed of great men was reflected in a contingency plan more drastic than anything he had previously specified: if John were prevented from founding the college there "by force or might of any other desiring to have the said mansion," the document said, ". . . that then the said John Paston should pull down the said mansion and every stone and stick thereof," and support the seven priests or monks at religious institutions elsewhere instead. There was one more afterthought, apparently added when the whole text was read over to Fastolf during that last weekend of his life: if John succeeded in founding the college as he had directed, then "the said John Paston should be discharged of the payment of the said 4,000 marks, and naught pay thereof."[2]

It is impossible to know whether Fastolf really did dictate this document word for word as John claimed, or whether John allowed himself some creative latitude in interpreting his patron's final, laboured attempts to make himself understood. Either way, it is certain both that this proposal had indeed been under discussion in the months before Sir John's death, and that John himself genuinely believed that the new will represented the old man's last instructions. His conviction that right was on his side was a constant in his life; in John's mind, there was nothing fraudulent about his claim to be Fastolf's heir. The question was whether others would agree—both Fastolf's friends and servants who would be involved in the execution of the will, and his enemies who would hope to find a way to get their own hands on the estates. All John could do now was stake his claim, and wait to confront whatever challenges lay ahead.

The first signs were encouraging. There was no immediate outcry from anyone in the household at Caister; no shocked protest that this was not what Fastolf had intended; no outraged denunciation of the new will as a forgery. When John's younger brother William left for London on the day after Fastolf's death to take the first practical steps on his brother's behalf toward claiming the inheritance, William Worcester rode with him. By the following Monday, they had positive news to report. Bishop Wainfleet, the most senior of Fastolf's executors, and currently the chancellor of England, was "well disposed in all things." William Paston had also spoken to John Stokes, another of the executors and a judge in the archbishop of Canterbury's court where the will would have to be proved, as well as to the archbishop himself, "and I find them right well disposed both," he reported.[3] Some of Fastolf's valuables that had been left for safekeeping in London had been discreetly secured, and William had also retained a specialist in ecclesiastical law to represent the family at the probate hearing.

This was progress; but the two men also encountered the first stirrings of trouble. As soon as they reached London, rumours reached them that a predatory interest in Fastolf's elegant town house at Southwark had already been shown by the duke of Exeter, Henry Holland, one of the most powerful noblemen in the country—married off as a teenager to the daughter of the duke of York, but now one of York's most vociferous opponents, riding high in the favour of Queen Margaret and her court. Before Exeter could attempt to seize the mansion by force, Paston and Worcester quickly arranged to meet his legal advisers, and managed to persuade them instead to "move my lord to sue by means of the law." The duke's claim was no more than an opportunistic attempt to acquire a desirable London residence by strong-arm tactics, and he retreated rapidly once it became clear that John would not be intimidated so easily. However, other possibilities were potentially more threatening. "My lord Treasurer speaks fair," William told his brother, "but yet many advise me to put no trust in him." As the most senior financial officer of a regime with unremitting financial problems, the earl of Wiltshire, who had succeeded the earl of Shrewsbury as treasurer a year earlier, was only too well aware of the value of Fastolf's estate, and was trying to find a way to argue that the old knight's properties should be sequestered by the crown: "there is laboured many means to entitle the king in his goods," William reported darkly.[4]

It also transpired that speculative claims on the inheritance might emerge from less grand sources. One such, although the details remain obscure, was an attempt to stake a claim to Caister itself by Elizabeth Heveningham, widow of the Pastons' Norfolk acquaintance Sir John Heveningham—a project in which she was egged on by her newly acquired second husband, the Pastons' old enemy John Wyndham. Elizabeth's son had been deeply unhappy at the prospect of his mother's remarriage ("he has said as much thereagainst as he dares do to have her good mother-ship"), and Margaret had tried to help him dissuade her from the match, offering to show her a copy of Wyndham's less-than-blue-blooded pedigree to demonstrate that he was not the honourable gentleman he claimed to be.[5] Nevertheless, Wyndham had both the formidable support of the dowa-ger duchess of Suffolk, and enough cash to pay off the Heveninghams' out-standing debts—and as a result, the marriage went ahead despite all objections. Elizabeth's claim to Caister, wherever it came from, was clearly a nonstarter, and was dispatched within weeks, if not days. Wyndham, as usual, was full of "noiseful language," but his bluster had no effect other than to confirm that "my lord Chancellor is right good and tender lord in all your matters," John Paston was told early in December.[6] Nevertheless, it was a reminder that nothing could be taken for granted in a process that would be as much a matter of complex and unpredictable politics as it was of legal technicalities.

In the meantime, Fastolf's burial had still to be organised. It took place, as he had instructed, in the monastery of St. Benet of Hulme, eight miles northwest of Caister. His body was interred with elaborate ceremony next to that of his wife, Millicent, beneath the towering arches of the abbey church, on the south side of the chancel in a new aisle which had been built by Fastolf himself at a cost of more than six hundred pounds. William Worcester worked tirelessly on the arrangements for the lavish funeral; he commissioned craftsmen in London to paint eighteen banners and more than fifty pennants displaying Fastolf's arms and those of his parents, as well as images of the Holy Trinity, the Virgin Mary, and Saints George and Nicholas. Hundreds of pounds were spent on fine black gowns for the mourners, including Judge William Yelverton, accompanied by his wife and thirteen servants, and John Paston, who—in his concern to demon-strate his respect for his patron, and his own standing as Fastolf's heir—attended with an even larger entourage. Once the funeral was over, Worcester continued to devote himself to his dead master's affairs, com-piling detailed inventories of Fastolf's possessions and distributing alms for the good of his soul, while John left Caister for London to push ahead with preparations for the probate hearing in the archbishop of Canterbury's court. Pressure of business meant that, for the first time in years, he was unable to come home to spend Christmas with his family. "I pray you that you will come as soon as you may," Margaret wrote wistfully on Christmas Eve. "I shall think myself half a widow because you shall not be at home."[7]

Neither Margaret nor John yet realised that a Christmas apart would be the very least of their worries in the months to come. However, there were already disturbing indications that progress might not be as smooth as they had hoped. Fastolf's servants at Caister had been under increasing strain during the last years of their master's life as the old man became ever more cantankerous and demanding, but it had not been clear until now quite how deep the rifts within his household had grown. Friar Brackley, for example, loathed William Worcester with a passion, and missed no opportunity to warn John against him in letters full of poisonous invective. "For God's sake," he wrote within weeks of Fastolf's death, "beware of trusting in that black Irishman"—Worcester's home town of Bristol, the wealthiest port in southwestern England, apparently being near enough to Ireland for the purposes of an abusive tirade. Worcester, he said, was "half-blind and shifty-eyed; would that he were not still more shifty in heart, word and deed." Brackley was not simply letting off steam, but accusing Worcester of a serious breach of trust: he was conspiring, Brackley alleged, with Fastolf's valet, Nicholas Newman (known in the household as Colin, and disparagingly christened "Colin the Frenchman" by Brackley), to undermine John Paston's claim to their master's estate. ". . . they shit out of the same arse," he wrote, with characteristic elegance, in the colloquial Latin he habitually used in correspondence.[8] His hostility to Worcester must have been simmering for years to have reached such a pitch, but now that the restraining influence of his master's authority had disappeared, he was free to express his feelings with a new degree of vituperation and malice.

There is no evidence that Brackley's specific accusations against Worcester and Newman had any foundation, and his obnoxiousness might have remained an irritation and nothing more, had it not been for the fact that trust—or the lack of it—was fast emerging as the most difficult and dangerous issue John Paston had to face in his quest for acceptance as Fastolf's heir. From Fastolf's point of view, the idea of bequeathing his estate to John made sense in terms of trying to ensure that one man had both the means and the commitment to carry out his wishes. However, the fact that he did not give this decision unchallengeable legal form before his death meant that John had to rely on others in Fastolf's circle to trust his word that the new will did indeed represent Sir John's final intentions. At the same time, neither the original will of June 1459 nor the new one of 3

November made any specific bequests to anyone else among Fastolf's servants and advisers. If they were to receive the reward they felt they deserved for years of dedicated and often badly paid service—reward that many of them had been promised over the years by Fastolf himself—they in turn would now have to rely on John to give them their due. Their support for John's claim to the estate might therefore go hand in hand with an expectation that John would give their own claims similar recognition.

William Worcester, for example, had been away from Caister during the weekend when the new will had allegedly been dictated, and did not get back in time to see his master before he died. As a result, he was not in a position either to confirm or to deny John's story, although the fact that this conscientious man made no protest in the tense weeks immediately after Fastolf's death suggests both that the idea of John as Fastolf's heir did not come as a surprise to him, and that he saw nothing inherently improbable in John's account of his master's last days. Despite the fact that he could not testify to Sir John's final wishes, Worcester's closeness to Fastolf over the previous twenty years, and his detailed knowledge of the old knight's affairs, meant that he would be an invaluable ally in John's campaign to secure the inheritance. William Paston seized the opportunity of their journey to London together to sound him out on his brother's behalf, and reported back that Worcester would be loyal to John if he were confident that John would be loyal to him: ". . . he trusts verily you should do for him and for his avail in reason," William wrote, "and I doubt not, if he may verily and faithfully understand you so disposed toward him, you shall find him faithful to you in like wise." Worcester had steadfastly tolerated years of high-handed treatment from an increasingly irascible old man, and what he now looked for was a financial settlement from Fastolf's will that would allow him to live independently in a modicum of comfort, without having to seek new employment elsewhere. William Paston believed his claims should be taken seriously. "I understand by him he will never have other master but his old master," he told his brother—a stance that William clearly felt was justified, ". . . considering how my master trusted him and the long years that he has been with him, and many shrewd [that is, dangerous or unpleasant] journeys for his sake."9

The very fact that William felt it necessary to point out to his brother that Worcester would be a deserving beneficiary suggests that there was some hesitation in his mind, only days after Fastolf's death, about whether John would recognise the urgent need to acknowledge other claims on the estate. Like Fastolf himself, John was not a natural politician; he had little instinctive understanding of other people's emotional reactions or of the motivations that drove their behaviour. His perception of the world was rooted in concepts of right and wrong that he understood as absolute values, making little allowance for the nuances and complexities of human interaction. Rather than seeing that a policy of trust and open-handedness might be the best way of sustaining a relationship of mutual support with his colleagues in Fastolf's service, John's overriding concern from the very beginning was to establish his own rights as Sir John's heir, and the uncertainty of his position made him immediately suspicious that others might try to challenge his claim to inherit. While he kept watch for signs of disaffection or disloyalty in those around him, they interpreted his behaviour as an indication that what they considered their rightful share in the will and its administration might be withheld. The result was a vicious circle of mistrust that spiralled out of control with disturbing speed.

Its corrosive effects were already apparent by the new year. In January 1460, William Paston and William Worcester were again in London, but this time neither travelling nor working together. Paston—this time accompanied by Thomas Playter, one of Fastolf's lawyers—was trying to find out whether Worcester was actively pursuing his own agenda in relation to the will, "but we cannot espy openly that he makes any labour," William reported, "nor privily neither, by no manner of hearkening nor by no manner of talking." When Playter spoke to him face to face, Worcester flatly denied that he had been engaged in any private lobbying or manoeuvring—but he did so in terms that made clear that he would not be fobbed off: "he says right not, saving that he will be rewarded for his long true service . . . like as my master promised him in his life." Worcester was now presenting his demand for a share of the inheritance in such bald terms because his confidence that he would receive satisfaction from John Paston had been badly eroded—and his willingness to support John's claim to be Fastolf's heir was proportionately diminished.

The difficulty for John was that he still needed Worcester, even if he was no longer sure he could trust him. Worcester's intimate knowledge of Fastolf's finances meant that his participation in the administration of the estate might make a vast difference to its final value—perhaps even the huge sum of one thousand pounds or more, Worcester told Playter. Playter did not know whether or not to believe him, "and to feel whether he lied or said truth, I asked him whether he would take what might not be saved without his help for his reward, and he said yes, with good will," a response that went a long way toward convincing him that Worcester was telling the truth.[10] It did not apparently occur to Playter, or to John, that it might be a political mistake to hint at this financial offer without any intention of seeing it through. From Worcester's point of view, it was a welcome suggestion that disappeared like smoke—a disappointment which could only reinforce his conviction that he was not being treated fairly and honestly.

A week later, Worcester wrote a letter justifying his actions to another of Fastolf's servants with whom he was still on good terms, asking his friend to show the letter to those in Norfolk who were speaking ill of him—an instruction that was clearly carried out, since Margaret asked Richard Calle, the Pastons' estate manager, to make a copy of it to send to her husband. Worcester's grievances were now multiplying rapidly, as the pervasive atmosphere of mistrust compounded his alienation from John. He had heard that his departure from Norfolk for London had been seen as deeply suspicious—"that I should, by crafty counsel of some men, suddenly have departed into these parts, etc., and that I estranged me from certain persons too much, etc."—a charge against which he indignantly defended himself. Far from being suborned by the Pastons' enemies, he had worked unstintingly over the previous three months to do his part in the execution of the will, committing himself in the process to payments of more than a hundred pounds for the funeral and other expenses. He now needed to repay these burdensome debts, which were way beyond the capacity of his own purse; but John had not made it a priority to see that he was reimbursed from Fastolf's estate, with the result that he was now facing crippling financial difficulties. Moreover, he had been deeply hurt and angered to find that, despite his closeness to Fastolf, he was not empowered as an executor to distribute money directly from the estate in charitable donations to help speed his master's soul through the horrors of purgatory: "I was not put in trust among the said attorneys there to give one penny for my master's soul unless I paid it of my own purse before; neither in trust nor favour to give an alms gown but that I prayed for it as a stranger should do, albeit my authority is as great as theirs, and rather more.... And these precedents considered," he added heatedly, "would discourage any man to abide but a little amongst them that so estranged themselves from me and mistrusted me without any cause."[11]

If Worcester felt that he had not been treated with proper confidence, he also believed that he had a specific claim on the inheritance which John

Peasant farmers at the plough. No portrait survives of any member of the Paston family, but this manuscript illumination shows how Clement Paston must have looked as he tilled the Norfolk soil in the late fourteenth century. His unstinting labour on the land enabled him to send his only son, William, to London to train as a lawyer.

The court of Common Pleas, one of the four great central law courts in medieval England, which William Paston attended first as a student, then as a successful attorney (his colleagues are shown here in blue striped gowns, standing to plead their cases), and finally as one of the judges of Common Pleas, seen here sitting on the bench in their red miniver-trimmed robes.

Fifteenth-century London, a cosmopolitan city that was home
to forty thousand inhabitants, where William Paston, his son,
and grandsons spent much of their time. In the foreground
is London's royal palace, the Tower, which had already kept
guard over the capital for more than three hundred years. In the
background is London Bridge, at this point the city's only bridge
over the River Thames. The river was a teeming thoroughfare
for passengers and cargoes ferried in skiffs, lighters, and barges.

Caister Castle, built near the Norfolk coast by the Pastons'
patron, Sir John Fastolf (the model for Shakespeare's Falstaff).
The Pastons' controversial claim to inherit the castle after the old
knight's death plunged them into seventeen bitter years of legal and
political struggle. Caister was a luxurious home, lavishly furnished,
with two great halls, one for summer and one for winter, among its
fifty rooms. Now it stands in ruins, its elegant tower giving only a
hint of its former magnificence.

A family portrait of the Nevilles, one of the greatest noble houses in fifteenth-century England. Kneeling at the head of this formidable clan is Richard Neville, earl of Warwick, known as the "'Kingmaker" because of his leading role in the tumultuous events of the Wars of the Roses. Wearing a jewelled mitre, behind his many siblings, is George Neville, archbishop of York, who, like his elder brother, was a flamboyant character driven by boundless ambition and the healthiest of egos. In return for a large loan from the already depleted Paston coffers, a sum which was never repaid, the archbishop offered his help to the family in their quest to inherit the Fastolf estates.

Opposite: Letter to Margaret Paston from her eldest son, John Paston II, 20 November 1474. Unlike Margaret—who, like most medieval gentlewomen, could read but not write, and therefore dictated her correspondence to trusted servants—John II wrote his letters himself. The modern editor of the correspondence describes his handwriting as "dashingly careless but fluent," a description which applies equally well to his character. The letter is signed, in the bottom right-hand corner, "Yowre sone J Paston K [knight]."

The Battle of Mortimer's Cross, 2 February 1461—a key Yorkist victory in the first phase of the Wars of the Roses. On the morning of the battle three suns were seen in the sky, an eerie phenomenon claimed as a portent of his triumph by eighteen-year-old Edward, earl of March, who took the throne only a month later as King Edward IV. In this manuscript of scenes from Edward's life, crowns descend towards him with the suns' rays. Edward later adopted the "sun in splendour" as his personal badge, an emblem to which Shakespeare makes punning allusion at the opening of *Richard III*: "Now is the winter of our discontent/Made glorious summer by this sun of York."

Elizabeth Woodville, Edward IV's queen, whom Edward married in secret in 1464. It was an impetuous and politically inappropriate match—Elizabeth was a twenty-seven-year-old widow with two young sons whose husband had been killed fighting for the defeated Lancastrian dynasty—but the king was apparently unable to resist her exquisite beauty. John Paston II sought to make political capital out of the Woodville family's meteoric rise by proposing marriage to the queen's cousin, a gentlewoman named Anne Haute.

The figure on the left is the kingmaking earl of Warwick, Richard Neville. Warwick had no sons, and his dynastic ambitions therefore rested on the slender shoulders of his two daughters, the elder of whom, Isabel, stands beside him. On the right is her husband, George, duke of Clarence, an unstable and vainglorious character who followed his father-in-law Warwick into rebellion against his own brother, Edward IV, in 1469.

The Battle of Barnet, 14 April 1471, at which John Paston II and his brother, John Paston III, fought in the Lancastrian army. Warwick the Kingmaker was killed in this terrifyingly chaotic encounter, fought in semi-darkness amid densely swirling fog. The Paston brothers survived, although John III was wounded, "hurt with an arrow on his right arm beneath the elbow."

Edward IV and his fleet arriving at the English-controlled port of Calais in preparation for his planned invasion of France in 1475. John Paston II, John III, and their younger brother, Edmund, joined what one contemporary described as the "finest, largest and best appointed force that has ever left England." Much to the chagrin of the English taxpayers who had funded this imposing expedition, the invasion proved to be a damp squib. Failed by key allies at the eleventh hour, Edward pragmatically allowed himself to be bought off by Louis XI, the "Spider King" of France, without a single shot being fired.

RICARDVS · III · ANG · REX ·

Richard III, whose usurpation of the throne in 1483 after his brother Edward IV's sudden death threw the Pastons' world once again into turmoil and violence. Despite pleading letters from the duke of Norfolk, no Paston turned out on the battlefield at Bosworth in 1485 to defend Richard against the challenge of Henry Tudor.

Henry VII, who—despite a profoundly tenuous claim to the throne—vanquished Richard III and founded the Tudor dynasty. Under his rule, John Paston III rose high in royal favour, and in 1500 was summoned, as the king's "trusty and wellbeloved knight," to attend the Spanish princess Catherine of Aragon when she arrived in England to marry Henry's eldest son, Arthur.

and his co-executor, Thomas Howes—Worcester's uncle by marriage—were trying to withhold from him. Fastolf, he said, had granted him a modest amount of land in return for his years of loyal service—"a livelihood according to my degree, that I, my wife and my children should have cause to pray for him." Howes had even been there when the promise was made; "this is truth, by the blessed sacrament," Worcester protested in some agitation. "And because I demanded my right and duty of my Master Paston, he is not pleased." For Worcester, the security of his family's future was at stake; but this was about more than money. It was also about respect, and proper acknowledgment of the role he had played in Fastolf's life. "It is not universally known that I was one of the chief that kept both my Master Paston and my uncle in my master's favour and trust," he wrote with bitter dignity; "and if I had laboured the contrary, by my soul—that is the greatest oath that I may swear of myself—they would never have been near my master." However much John felt Worcester could not be trusted, in Worcester's eyes it was he who had been needlessly alienated and excluded by John. His was the righteous anger of a man who felt himself victimised and deceived: "I would be to them as loving and as well-willing as I can," he declared defiantly, "so I find cause." [12]

If it had been only Worcester who moved in a matter of weeks from supporting John's cause to a position of, at best, suspicion and, at worst, outright hostility, it might be tempting to give a little more credence to Friar Brackley's intemperate description of his duplicity—but it was not just Worcester. Another relationship that disintegrated with equally astonishing rapidity, and even more toxic consequences, was John's friendship with Judge William Yelverton. John and Yelverton went back a long way; they had worked closely together in the frenetic campaign against Heydon and Tuddenham in the chaotic days of 1450, and since then had been in constant contact as the two most senior figures in Fastolf's inner circle. Yelverton's backing would be crucial if the business of the will were to be settled quickly and peacefully. He was an intensely ambitious man, and perhaps it would never have been easy for him to accept the idea that John should be the main beneficiary of Fastolf's estate. What seems more certain is that John himself anticipated and feared Yelverton's resentment, since the breach was precipitated only weeks after Fastolf's death, when John accused the judge of betraying him.

The quarrel between the two men took place at St. Benet's Abbey, probably on the day of Fastolf's funeral. So quickly had relationships within the old knight's circle deteriorated that decorum could not, it seems, be maintained even until his obsequies had been completed. The only surviving details come from a letter written by Friar Brackley, who walked into the room when the argument was already in full spate—not in time to hear John's accusation, but just at the point when Yelverton exclaimed in response, "Whosoever says that of me, he lies falsely in his head!"[13] Being the fiercely partisan man that he was, Brackley did not stop to investigate what the row was about, instead backing John to the hilt without further question. But it later emerged that John suspected Yelverton of having instigated the speculative claim to Caister made by Elizabeth Heveningham and her new husband, John Wyndham. When the charge was put to Yelverton in person by the lawyer Thomas Playter, the judge denied it vehemently: "as touching to the provoking that my lady Heveningham should sue forth for Caister, he says he never thought it." It was Playter's belief, on the basis of this fraught conversation, that Yelverton was not yet completely alienated, nor irretrievably hostile to John's claim to the inheritance—but that his continued support and cooperation would depend on John's willingness to offer him trust and friendship: "he will not hurt you in your bargain if you could be friendlily disposed toward him as you have been . . . ," Playter wrote earnestly. "He lives somewhat aloof, and not utterly malicious against you."[14]

Playter's advice, however, was too little, too late. By the time he commended this course of action to John, he had already accompanied William Paston on a visit to John Stokes, the judge in the archbishop's court who was advising them on their application for probate of the will, to relay details of what John Paston saw as Yelverton's culpable misconduct as an executor. Yelverton was responsible, they said, for the "needless wasting" of Fastolf's goods; he was undermining those whom Fastolf had "most earthly trusted," John Paston principal among them; he had prompted Lady Heveningham into harassing John with her vexatious claim on the estate; and—the greatest fear, it seemed, at the heart of John's increasing paranoia about his former friend's intentions—Yelverton's "desire was singularly to have had the keeping of Caister and all stuff within it, and there to have lodged himself." These were very serious allegations, and John was proposing very serious consequences: to remove Yelverton altogether from the will and its execution. Could it be done, Paston and Playter asked Judge Stokes? "And he said, if he be false to the dead, it is a cause reasonable, and perjury is another cause."[15] On this evidence, the chances of John trusting

Yelverton enough to reestablish friendly relations with him were infinitesi-
mally slight. Meanwhile, should Yelverton hear a word about this consulta-
tion with Stokes, he would take it as no less than a declaration of war.

Any lingering doubts about the bitterness of the breach were dispelled
when Friar Brackley encountered Judge Yelverton on a visit to the
Augustinian priory at Walsingham, near the northwest Norfolk coast, in the
early spring of 1460. After a lavish lunch and plenty of good wine, the judge
began to talk more unguardedly than usual, "and held on so sore he could
not cease . . . ," Brackley reported to William Paston, "and there was not
forgotten none unkindness of my master J.P. your brother." Yelverton's
acute sense of betrayal—"my great grief," as he called it—emerges powerfully despite the hostility of Brackley's account, and it was a sense compounded by what he felt was the blank indifference of his peers. When the
prior told him how shocked and how sorry he was that two such close
friends should have argued in this way, Yelverton's bald retort was that
"there is no man busy to bring us together."[16] If the breach with William
Worcester was a disastrous loss in terms of his comprehensive knowledge of
Fastolf's affairs, the rift with Yelverton was even more so, in terms of John's
chances of making his claim good in the wider world. Yelverton was a judge
in the court of King's Bench, with political clout and influential connections, and he could make life very difficult for John if he chose. The damaging consequences of these disintegrating friendships were already beginning
to manifest themselves by the end of January 1460. When William Paston
and Thomas Playter visited Judge Stokes to warn him against Yelverton,
Stokes had already been informed—allegedly "by one which he could not
remember"—that what was now being put forward as Fastolf's will was a
forgery.[17]

Failing relationships with former friends were not the only problems
John Paston faced by the spring of 1460: his enemies were never likely to
stand quietly by while he took possession of such a rich inheritance. Their
first move was made on Tuesday, 29 April, not quite five months after
Fastolf's death, when an inquiry into Sir John's lands—officially known as
an inquisition post mortem, designed to establish whether the king had any
legal rights over the estate—was held at Buckenham in eastern Norfolk, ten
miles inland from Caister. The jurors declared, confidently but incorrectly,
that Fastolf's rightful heir was his distant relative Thomas Fastolf of
Cowhaugh, the boy over whose wardship the old knight had fought such an
acrimonious battle with Philip Wentworth. There was much that was amiss

with this inquisition—the jurors were so poorly informed, for example, that they gave the wrong date for Fastolf's death—but the principal error was that it had taken place at all: no royal commission had been granted to authorise it. The men who convened the hearing were closely associated with John Heydon, the Pastons' chief enemy for many years now, and Philip Wentworth himself. The inquiry was not legal, and they could not hope to make its conclusions stand up in the long run, but it nevertheless served as a preemptive strike, designed to throw obstacles into the path of John Paston's claim to be Fastolf's heir by producing evidence that he would have to work hard to set aside.

This was worrying enough, but what made it worse was the possibility that some of John's former friends might now ally themselves with his opponents, a spectre that raised its head only three days after the bogus inquisition was held. On 2 May, William Paston told his brother that he had spoken with Fastolf's servant John Bocking, and the news was not good. "He had but few words," William wrote, "but I felt by him he was right evil disposed to the parson"—Thomas Howes—"and you; but covert language he had. I think he is assented to the finding of this office taken at Buckenham." It had come to something if, knowing the depth of his late master's loathing for Wentworth and Heydon, Bocking was now prepared to fall in with their schemes—an unnerving development that was all the more threatening given Bocking's friendship with others in Fastolf's household: "it is he that makes William Worcester so forward as he is," William Paston reported anxiously to his brother.[18] Friar Brackley, meanwhile, was convinced that Judge Yelverton and his servants were, "with their heady and fumous language," fanning the flames of opposition to John by smearing his good name at every opportunity.[19]

In a terse postscript, William Paston made it clear what he believed lay behind the reverses they were now beginning to suffer. "Omnia pro pecunia facta sunt," he said: "everything is done for money." In one sense, of course, he was right; but this reductive view of the motivation of those within Fastolf's circle who now opposed them took no account of the fact that the issue of money was inseparable from that of recognition for service given. "Bocking told me this day that he stood as well in conceit with my master Fastolf four days before he died as any man in England," William reported. It did John no good to dismiss such talk as window dressing for unjustified claims on his patron's estate; it did not seem to cross his mind that greed might also appear, from the outside at least, to be the driving force behind his own actions. Whatever the rights and wrongs of the situation, its gravity was now alarmingly clear to William Paston. "It is full necessary to make you strong by lordship and other means," he warned his brother.[20]

The difficulty was that there could scarcely have been a worse time to be looking for help from powerful men. Political conflict at the highest levels of government was now sliding inexorably toward the battlefield. The standoff between Queen Margaret and the duke of York—now enmeshed in a poisonous personal rivalry—had persisted until the autumn of 1458, when the queen brought her vacuous husband back to London from her midland estates and seized control of government in his name. In the face of this aggressive self-assertion—and an attempt by members of the royal household to murder the earl of Warwick—the Yorkist lords had little choice but to withdraw from the capital for their own safety. Queen Margaret sought to press home her advantage in the summer of 1459 by summoning the rest of the nobility to a great council at Coventry, the wealthy town at the heart of her own lands that she had made a citadel of her rule. Her intentions were clear: if she could persuade the rest of the nobility that she offered the only legitimate and viable incarnation of royal authority, she might succeed in isolating the Yorkists comprehensively enough to destroy them.

In response, just as they had done four years earlier when the duke of Somerset summoned a similarly ominous assembly, York, his brother-in-law Salisbury, and his nephew Warwick mustered their forces and set out to defend themselves. In September, at Blore Heath, in the midland county of Staffordshire, Salisbury succeeded in fending off an attempt to intercept him on his way westward to meet York at the duke's castle of Ludlow, a massive eleventh-century fortress that dominated the border between England and the rugged, mist-shrouded mountains of Wales. It was a brutal skirmish that cost a couple of thousand men their lives. Three weeks later, the main contingent of Queen Margaret's troops arrived to confront York and his allies at Ludford Bridge, just below the looming hill on which the castle and town of Ludlow stood. This time the outcome was much less bloody, but much more profoundly damaging to the Yorkist cause. Marching under the earl of Warwick's command was a detachment from the garrison of Calais, the English stronghold in northern France that was home to the only permanent standing army maintained by the English crown. Warwick was their captain, but it soon became clear that the Calais soldiers were not willing to fight against an army under the command—nominal though it was—of their king. They defected to the ranks massing beneath the royal standard, undermining York's military position so severely that he was forced to flee under cover of darkness. He escaped westward across the water to Ireland, accompanied by his sixteen-year-old son, Edmund, earl of Rutland, while his eldest son, seventeen-year-old Edward, earl of March, took ship for Calais with the earls of Salisbury and Warwick.

The queen was determined to finish what she had started. A parliament was summoned to meet at her city of Coventry, and in late November 1459—a few weeks after Sir John Fastolf's death—a bill of attainder declared that the Yorkist lords were guilty of treason, and their lands forfeit to the crown. All hope of conciliation was gone. Faced with an enemy as implacable as Queen Margaret had now shown herself to be, York and the Nevilles would have to fight not only for control of government, but for their very survival. In June 1460, after Warwick had made a brief spring voyage to Dublin to agree upon an invasion strategy with his uncle of York, the earls of Warwick, Salisbury, and March set sail from Calais across the narrow waters of the Channel, heading for the southeastern coast of England. They landed at the sheltered harbour of the great port of Sandwich on 26 June, and a week later the citizens of London—who were deeply uneasy about the queen's decision to base her government in the Midlands and the north—opened the city gates to let their troops into the capital.

On 5 July, a Yorkist army led by Warwick and his young cousin, the earl of March, left London to advance against Queen Margaret and her allies. While the queen herself and her six-year-old son, Prince Edward, remained safely ensconced behind the city walls at Coventry, her forces in turn marched south under the command of the duke of Buckingham and the earl of Shrewsbury, taking King Henry with them. This time, the king's insubstantial presence did nothing to rally his own troops or deter his opponents. On 10 July, in pouring rain, the two armies met just outside the town of Northampton, sixty miles northwest of the capital, where the Yorkists overran the field in little more than an hour as their enemies' guns sank into the enveloping mud. Buckingham and Shrewsbury, two of the queen's staunchest supporters among the great peers of the realm, were hacked down in the fighting. Meanwhile, King Henry was captured, sitting docile in his tent as the battle raged around him.

With the king in their custody, Warwick and March returned to join the earl of Salisbury in London, where forces loyal to the queen were still holding out in the Tower under the command of Lord Scales and Lord Moleyns, John Paston's old adversaries from the dispute over Gresham ten years earlier. With the capital now under Yorkist control, Scales and Moleyns turned the Tower's cannons on the city it had been built to defend, bringing death and destruction to London's streets. But the terrors of the bombardment persuaded the mayor and aldermen to lend their support to a full-scale Yorkist siege of the fortress, and soon the city's own guns were firing at the Tower's colossal walls from the south bank of the Thames. With their small garrison running low on food and water, and realising that their beleaguered position was now hopeless, Scales and Moleyns tried to reach the safety of sanctuary at Westminster Abbey, a couple of miles upriver, during the night of 19 July. Moleyns escaped, but Scales—the veteran soldier who had once called Sir John Fastolf "father"—was recognised by boatmen on the Thames. He was lynched and murdered, and his naked body dumped without ceremony in the churchyard of St. Mary Overy in Southwark. It fell to the earl of March—to whom Scales had stood godfather in happier days—to give him an honourable burial.

Nine months on from the rout at Ludford Bridge, the Yorkists' reversal of their political fortunes was complete. The duke of York made preparations to return from Dublin to England, and a parliament was called to meet at Westminster in October. The problem confronting him was what to do next. Publicly, York still maintained that he was a loyal subject of King Henry, seeking reform of government in the interests of the common good. In practice, however, there could be no lasting security for him while Henry remained on the throne, now that Queen Margaret had made plain her determination to destroy him and all those who stood with him. With the king a prisoner, York was safe for the time being, but keeping the king in captivity would not in the long run enable the duke either to reunite the political community under his own leadership or to establish a legitimate basis for his government.

Meanwhile—with York and the rest of the nobility now playing for such terrifyingly high stakes—the normal cut and thrust of politics at a local level had been all but suspended. The fact that the entire framework of government was under threat meant that it was too dangerous for the gentry of Norfolk, or any other county, to indulge their competitive instincts to the full: it was in no one's interests to rock the boat when the waters around them were so treacherous. Even for a prize as valuable as the Fastolf inheritance, it was not worth taking risks that, in the absence of any effective royal authority, might precipitate the region into a state of unfettered anarchy. John Heydon and Philip Wentworth were not about to let John Paston's claim to be Fastolf's heir go unchallenged, and they had placed a stumbling block in his way by staging a fraudulent inquiry into Fastolf's lands—but neither they nor anyone else simply helped themselves to any of the old man's estates as Lord Moleyns had done at Gresham a decade earlier.

Queen Margaret had retreated westward into Wales with her surviving noble allies after their shattering defeat at Northampton. That encounter would evidently not be the last confrontation of what was now, more clearly than ever before, all-out war. Nevertheless, for the time being at least, the Yorkist resurgence did seem to be good news for John Paston, a doughty campaigner engaged in his own private battles. His opponents' close connections with the royal household meant that it was always unlikely that he would find support from a regime under the leadership of the queen. By the same token, Heydon and Wentworth could hope for little favour from the duke of York—whose attainder Heydon had helped to draft at the Coventry parliament in November 1459—whereas John was well placed to benefit from his restoration to power. By the autumn, John had been elected as a representative for the shire of Norfolk in the forthcoming parliament, and Friar Brackley was describing the earl of Warwick in straightforward, if typically apocalyptic, terms as their saviour: ". . . if aught come to my lord Warwick but good," he wrote, "farewell you, farewell I, and all our friends, for by the way of my soul this land were utterly undone, as God forbid."[21] John also took the opportunity to offer the duke a particular service: York's wife, Cecily Neville, and their three youngest children, fourteen-year-old Margaret, George, who was ten, and Richard, seven, came to stay at Fastolf's town house in Southwark in September, to await the duke's return from Ireland. The duchess left after a few days to travel to meet her husband, but the children stayed on, cheered every day by a visit from the earl of March, their eldest brother.

If the political world seemed to be turning in John's favour, there was also reason to feel a little more positive about the practical business of Fastolf's will. Legitimate inquisitions post mortem into Sir John's estates were finally held in Norfolk and Suffolk in late October, and "the matter is well sped after your intent, blessed be God, as you shall have knowledge of in haste," Margaret reported with relief to her husband after the Norfolk hearing.[22] What this meant, it transpired when Thomas Playter wrote with more detailed news, was that the jurors had confirmed what lands Fastolf had held, but had not committed themselves on the thorny question of who should inherit them. While this gave no positive support to John's case, at least it left the issue open and did not present him with further obstacles by registering another potential claimant.

On the other hand, no progress had been made toward repairing the disastrously ruptured relationships within Fastolf's household. By the beginning of December, it was apparent that William Worcester was avoiding further contact with the Pastons; "his wife says always that he is out when I send for him," Margaret told John in some frustration.[23] Worcester's antagonism had, of course, been apparent for some time already, but there were alarming signs that Thomas Howes might now be developing worryingly similar grudges. Howes had a critical role to play as the only one of Fastolf's executors appointed to share the administration of the estate with John under the terms of the new will. It had been clear from the outset, however, that John was the senior partner; Howes was politically a little naïve, and certainly not the most independent thinker among Fastolf's servants. All the more reason, perhaps, to have taken particular care to keep him on side—but John seems simply to have taken his support for granted. By January 1461, when the prior of Bromholm applied to Howes for a grant of alms from Fastolf's estate, the chaplain told him to speak to John instead, saying that he had recently given money to another monastery "whereof, as he said to me," the prior told John, "you grudged and were in manner displeased." It was John, Howes explained, who made the decisions, "for he said to me you had much goods of the dead to dispose, what of your father, God bless that soul, . . . and what now of his good master Fastolf."[24] This was uncomfortably reminiscent of Friar Brackley's account of Worcester's complaints about John's tightfisted approach to his duties as an executor ("he says that, whereas your father was a very rich judge, you did almost nothing for him in distributing alms for his soul, and since you did nothing for your own father, why should you do anything for Master Fastolf?").[25]

If John even noticed the potential implications of Howes's words, he had little time to contemplate their significance. Political events were now moving at frightening speed. By the time the duke of York arrived in

London on 10 October 1460, he had decided that the only way out of the intractable and increasingly virulent conflict was to cut through the whole question of who should rule in the name of the hapless King Henry by claiming the throne for himself. Heralded by blaring trumpets, and attended by an imposing retinue decked out in his own blue-and-white livery, he rode into the capital under banners boldly displaying the royal arms of England rather than the ducal ones of York. On his arrival at Westminster Hall, where the lords of the realm had gathered for the parliament, he strode immediately to the marble throne as if to take up his rightful place as king. He turned to the assembled peers, waiting for a shout of acclamation that never came.

Instead, he was met with consternation and confusion. York's position as the next in line to the throne after King Henry and his son was undeniable, but his claim to supersede them—based on his mother's descent from Lionel of Clarence, the second son of Edward III—was controversial in the extreme. Even had it been unequivocally established that the crown could pass through the female line, which it was not, the legitimacy of the Lancastrian dynasty had been put beyond question almost half a century earlier by Henry V's extraordinary victories in France—triumphs which demonstrated, to contemporary minds, that his kingship was sanctioned by God. Since then, of course, Henry VI's glaring personal inadequacies had gone a long way toward undermining the security of his crown, but it was not a simple matter to argue that he had forfeited his right to rule. Two fourteenth-century kings, Edward II and Richard II, had been overthrown as a result of their tyrannical behaviour, but the grounds that were used to justify their depositions could not easily be applied to Henry VI: he had not actively threatened the interests of his realm and his subjects, even if only because he had not actively done anything at all.

For York, his claim to the throne seemed to offer a means of establishing his own rule on a foundation that would give Queen Margaret no foothold from which to regain power. But, for his peers, the idea of York as king compounded the problem rather than solved it. They desperately needed to find some way to reunite the political community as a whole under a workable government—and after a decade of conflict, York was too profoundly divisive a figure to achieve that goal. After all, in the eyes of his enemies he had just vindicated the charges of treason that the queen had laid against him almost a year earlier. On 31 October, after three weeks of urgent negotiation between York and the assembled lords, a formal settlement was announced: King Henry would remain on the throne, but the duke of York was named as his heir—a compromise that served the immediate purpose of acknowledging York's claims while allowing his regime to retain the support of the wider political community by functioning in King Henry's name. It also meant that a renewal of war was inevitable, since the formidable and vengeful figure of Queen Margaret would never accept the disinheritance of her son.

By December the queen had travelled north to seek support for her cause at the royal court of the neighbouring kingdom of Scotland, leaving her forces in Wales under the command of Jasper Tudor, earl of Pembroke. Pembroke's allegiance to the Lancastrian dynasty was absolute and unquestionable; he and his brother, Edmund, earl of Richmond, were King Henry's half-brothers, born to Henry V's queen, Catherine de Valois, by her second husband Owen Tudor, a Welsh esquire who had grown up in the royal household. Other nobles loyal to the queen, including the heirs of the duke of Somerset and the earl of Northumberland who had been killed at St. Albans five years earlier, were mustering men in the north of England. York dispatched his eldest son, the earl of March, to head off the Lancastrian threat in Wales, and marched north himself with his brother-in-law, the earl of Salisbury.

The resistance he met was much greater than he had foreseen. York had hoped to see out the Christmas season peacefully at his castle of Sandal, perched on a lofty mound near Wakefield, in Yorkshire. But on 30 December 1460, his men were surprised outside the castle walls by the main contingent of the Lancastrian army. In an engagement of brutal ferocity, the duke of York was defeated and killed. This enigmatic man, in whose career personal ambition and political principle were so inextricably intertwined, lay dead at the age of forty-nine, the throne still tantalisingly just out of reach. His seventeen-year-old son, Edmund, earl of Rutland, perished at his side; so, too, did Salisbury's son Thomas Neville. Salisbury himself was captured and put to death once the fighting was over. A few days later, the severed heads of the four men—the duke's festooned with a paper crown in mockery of his pretensions of majesty— were impaled on spikes on the gates of the city of York by their jubilant enemies.

As soon as she heard the news, an exultant Queen Margaret left Scotland to rejoin her army, and immediately pushed southward toward London, where Salisbury's eldest son, the earl of Warwick, had been left in command. There was already deep suspicion in the city, and more widely in the south of the country, about the queen's intentions, and it was compounded by the fact that she allowed her troops—who included French and Scottish mercenaries—to loot the towns through which they marched. "In this country every man is willing to go with my lords here," John Paston was told by his youngest brother, Clement, a student in the Yorkist-held capital, on 23 January; "and I hope God shall help them, for the people in the north rob and steal and are appointed to pillage all this country, and give away men's goods and livelihoods in the south country, and that will ask a mischief."[26] Warwick gathered his forces and moved twenty miles north to the town of St. Albans, taking the captive King Henry with him. Despite having several days to prepare his defences, the earl misjudged his enemies' movements and was taken by surprise when the Lancastrian army attacked on 17 February. For the second time in six years, a running battle was fought through the streets of the town; this time, it was the Yorkists who lost both the battle and the person of the king to the Lancastrians. Henry was found sitting quietly under a tree, and taken to St. Albans Abbey to be reunited with his wife and son. Warwick was forced to retreat northward from the scene of his first military defeat, leaving the way clear for the queen to advance on London.

Only five months after York's return from Ireland, appearing at Westminster with such pomp and circumstance to declare his right to rule, the duke was dead and his cause seemed utterly lost. The last remaining hopes of his supporters rested on the youthful shoulders of his son and heir, Edward, earl of March, who, at eighteen, was now duke of York in his father's place. Edward's sortie into Wales had provided the only good news in two miserable months for York's allies: on 2 February, at Mortimer's Cross, near Ludlow in the Welsh borderlands, he inflicted a crushing defeat on the Lancastrian contingent in the west under the command of Jasper Tudor, earl of Pembroke. Pembroke himself escaped, but his father, Owen Tudor, the widower of Queen Catherine, was executed on Edward's orders after the battle. Even in death, the charms of the man who had won the heart of a queen could not be extinguished: when Tudor's head was put on public display in the market square of the county town of Hereford, "a mad woman combed his hair and washed away the blood from his face, and she got candles and set about him burning more than a hundred," one chronicler reported.[27]

Edward had little time to savour his triumph. When he learned what had happened at St. Albans, he turned his troops eastward as quickly as he could, joining forces with the retreating army of the earl of Warwick in the Cotswolds on 22 February. Their only hope, it seemed, was to race south in an attempt to take the capital before the queen could do so—although it scarcely seemed possible that this was a race they could win, given that London was at least four days' march away, and the Lancastrian army had already reached the town of Barnet, only ten miles north of the city. But it was a chance they had to take. As they drew nearer to London, the extraordinary news reached them that Queen Margaret had not advanced into the city, but instead retreated twenty miles to the northwest. She was now paying the price for identifying herself too closely with a regional interest rather than a national one, and for failing to keep her troops on a tight leash: the Londoners—fearing the devastation of their city by a northern rabble—had closed the gates against her. As she hesitated, word came of the Yorkist advance. Margaret turned away northward, her men still looting as they went, leaving Edward and Warwick to sweep into the capital on Thursday, 26 February.

Edward now had no choice but to show his hand. The attempt to construct a Yorkist regime under the nominal authority of King Henry had ceased to be an option once the king himself was recaptured by Lancastrian forces. In any case, it was striking that Henry's presence at the queen's side had not made his subjects in London any more inclined to admit her army to their city. With the authority of the Lancastrian crown now so profoundly compromised, the way was finally open for Edward to claim the throne for himself. It was, of course, only five months since his father's attempt to do the same thing had been rebuffed by his peers—but Edward's position in the spring of 1461 was dramatically different from his father's in the autumn of 1460. For what it was worth, Edward could argue that his claim was technically justified by the terms of the formal settlement that had named the duke of York as King Henry's heir. In theory at least, the king had endorsed the agreement; he could therefore be said—through his "decision" to rejoin his wife at St. Albans—to have reneged on his oath and, in effect, resigned his crown. Much more importantly, Edward himself was a young, magnetically charismatic and imperiously commanding leader who offered the political community the chance of a fresh start—something which his father, tainted by his central role in ten years of bitter and bloody conflict, could never have provided. On Wednesday, 4 March, lavishly arrayed in royal robes, Edward processed in state from St. Paul's Cathedral to the Great Hall at Westminster, where he took his seat on the marble throne to be formally acclaimed as King Edward IV.

The cautious welcome that the new king received in London was echoed by many of the East Anglian gentry, including the Pastons, whose interests clearly now lay with the restoration of effective government under a Yorkist crown. For one member of the family, however, Edward's accession had already come at too great a price. John Paston's sister, Elizabeth, had endured a long and unhappy wait before her mother and brother had found her a suitable marriage. Just two years after her wedding, and only three months after giving birth to her first baby—a son named Edward— she was left a widow when her husband, Robert Poynings, was killed fighting for the earl of Warwick at St. Albans. John himself was already well aware of the dangers of the battlefield: his friend Osbert Mundford had died in the summer of 1460, executed for his part in the unsuccessful Lancastrian defence of the port of Sandwich against the invasion of the Yorkist earls.

As a result, however relieved he was at the accession of a Yorkist king, John was deeply reluctant to commit either himself or his teenage sons to take up arms on Edward's behalf—and with the queen's forces regrouping in the north, it was clear that more fighting was inevitable if the new regime were ever to be securely established. In January, before the battle at St. Albans, his brother Clement had suggested that John should respond to Warwick's call to arms in London, "for it lies more upon your worship and touches you more near than other men of that country, and also you are more had in favour with my lords here"[28]—advice that John must have been heartily glad he chose to ignore when news came of the earl's defeat. But the fledgling Yorkist regime—should it survive—would require military support for months, if not years, to come. Service was not compulsory, but a matter of fine calculation between the certainty of risk and the possibility of reward. John had evidently decided that the former outweighed the latter. By March—in a letter so cagily drafted that he referred to himself in the third person—he was protesting that the situation was too dangerous to allow him to leave Norfolk, "for he would have his own men about him if need were here," although he was prepared to send one of his household men to join King Edward if it became clear that "other men of worship of this country" were doing the same.[29]

And it was not only the obvious hazards of combat against which he was trying to protect himself. Just as John was hoping for the final defeat of the queen and her allies by the new Yorkist government, his old enemy John Heydon was banking on the reverse, and had laid plans "to bring you to the presence of such a lord in the north as shall not be for your ease," Margaret warned her husband anxiously, "but to jeopardy of your life, or great and importable loss of your goods." The world was so unnervingly uncertain that Margaret did not dare refer to Heydon by name in case her letter fell into the wrong hands; the threat came, she told John carefully, "by the means of the son of William Baxter that lies buried in the Grey Friars."[30]

King Edward left London on 13 March—without John Paston in his company—to advance against the queen's army, which was massing in the north under the command of the duke of Somerset and the earl of Northumberland. The earl of Warwick had gone ahead a week earlier to muster his men in the Midlands. There he and Edward joined forces before pressing on to the town of Pontefract in Yorkshire, less than ten miles from Wakefield, the site of the Yorkists' most devastating defeat only three months earlier. On Palm Sunday, 29 March 1461, Edward and Warwick took up position just outside the nearby village of Towton, and readied themselves for one final assault on their enemies.

Both sides ordered their troops that quarter should be neither asked nor given once battle was joined. In atrocious conditions—limbs numbed by the biting cold, eyes stung and ears muffled by relentlessly driving snow—Englishmen fought Englishmen hand to hand for more than eight hours. The slaughter was so great that the two sides had to draw back from time to time while the heaped bodies of the dead were dragged out of their way. In the middle of the afternoon, the sudden arrival of the duke of Norfolk with reinforcements for the Yorkist army gave Edward's men fresh impetus; even then, it was another couple of hours before the Lancastrian line finally broke. The Yorkist surge became a rout in which thousands more died, cut down as they tried to flee, or drowned in the attempt to cross the freezing waters of the river that blocked their retreat. The melting snow was stained with blood, and a dark stream of clotted red was said to have snaked along the rutted roads all the way to the walls of York itself, from where the rotting head of Edward's father gazed down, hollow-eyed, on the evidence of his son's retribution.

Within the city, Queen Margaret was waiting intently for news, her husband and son at her side. When the appalling scale of the Lancastrian defeat began to emerge, the king, queen, and prince fled northward, and slipped across the border to seek refuge in Scotland. For Edward and his cousin Warwick—after years of conflict in which each had lost a beloved father and brother as well as thousands of their men—it was an overwhelming, awe-inspiring victory. Edward of March was now, in fact as well as in name, king of England.

the infinite process

*E*DWARD IV WAS ANOINTED and crowned in Westminster Abbey, amid the glittering shrines of venerable saints and the gilded monuments of his illustrious forebears, on Sunday, 28 June 1461. After the ceremony, he walked under a canopy of shining cloth of gold, borne on four silver poles above his head, to Westminster Hall for a coronation feast of rich meats and fragrant custards; swans, pheasants, and peacocks served re-plumed with their iridescent tails proudly displayed at their backs; and punctuating the many courses, elaborate "subtleties"— intricate confections of sugar, flowers, coloured glazes, and silver and gold leaf, shaped into edible sculptures with mythical and heraldic themes. To his cheering subjects, toasting their new monarch in the wine that ran from the city's fountains, the contrast between the gorgeous young king and the shabby and distracted figure of his predecessor could not have been more arresting. At nineteen, Edward was unusually tall, standing almost six feet four, broad shouldered and athletic in build, and jaw-droppingly handsome. His beauty was as regularly noted by men as it was irresistibly noticed by women: "I cannot remember ever having seen a finer-looking man," Philippe de Commines, a Burgundian diplomat who met him several times, later wrote.[1]

But neither the lavish ceremonial nor Edward's magnetic glamour could disguise the fact that his authority remained precarious in many parts of the country, especially the north, where there was still deep-rooted support for the Lancastrian cause. The Lancastrian royal family remained at large in Scotland, and there were already worrying signs that the Scots and the French would make the most of this enticing opportunity to destabilise the new government in England by offering Margaret men and money to revive her husband's cause. Nevertheless, it was also clear that the young king intended to impose his rule throughout his kingdom as quickly and decisively as possible; the date of the coronation itself had been brought forward by two weeks to allow him the option of leaving London all the sooner in order to deal with the threats he faced. For the first time in years, a framework of government was in place in which the landed classes could feel genuine confidence.

As a result, Edward's accession to the throne broke the spell that had held Norfolk affairs frozen in a state of suspended animation. Landowners were once again free to pursue their own interests as aggressively as they could without fearing that conflict might escalate into uncontainable disorder. And they had every incentive to do so, in the attempt to secure their position to the best possible advantage while the new regime was still in the process of taking shape. Of course, the turbulent and terrifying events of the past months had not prevented gentlemen such as John Paston from continuing to worry about their private concerns. Even in January 1461, with Queen Margaret's army advancing menacingly on the capital, John was still sending instructions for the prosecution of his own business to his brother Clement in London, but Clement—who had a wise head on his young shoulders—reminded him that it was a complicated time to be asking lords for favours: ". . . if you do well," he wrote, "remember these lords have many matters to think on, and if it be forgotten the harm is yours."[2] Now that King Edward's victory was clear, John had a fresh opportunity to press his claim to the Fastolf inheritance while his enemy Heydon was otherwise occupied trying to scramble clear of the network of connections that bound him to Queen Margaret's sinking ship, and were now threatening to drag him under.

However, John was not the only one who saw the chance to profit from the change of government. The nobility as well as the gentry had everything to play for in the establishment of a new local order—and amid the frantic jostling for position, it was not John's search for support that caught the attention of great lords, but the conspicuous charms of the Fastolf estates themselves. John's old unreliable patron the duke of Norfolk was one of the few magnates who had been prepared to associate himself with the Yorkist cause at a relatively early stage, and he could claim a critical role in Edward's victory through his timely arrival on the battlefield at Towton. After years of ineffectual struggle against the influence of his local rival the duke of Suffolk, it seemed that Norfolk at last had a chance to emerge as the dominant power in East Anglia under the new Yorkist regime. Unfortunately for John, the duke had also had an acquisitive eye on the castle at Caister for a very long time, attracted not only by its financial value—although that was interest enough, given that a third of the duke's estates lay in the powerful hands of his mother, the earl of Warwick's aunt Catherine Neville, as the jointure agreed upon when she married—but also by its strategic location between Norwich and the coast, not to mention its luxurious comforts. He had tried to persuade Fastolf to sell it to him on a number of occasions, most recently only two months before the old man's death. Now the combination of the duke's newfound influence with the uncertainty of John's claim to be Fastolf's heir gave Norfolk the perfect opportunity to meddle in the matter of the inheritance—and it was no longer the case that direct action was too risky a strategy for landowners keen to assert their rights to disputed properties. By the beginning of June, the duke had sent armed men to seize Caister for himself.

The new king's government was only two months old, and already John's hopes that he would find it easier to secure his position in this new Yorkist world than in the old Lancastrian one had been shattered. By the time of Norfolk's opportunistic raid on Caister, Edward had not yet even returned to the capital to be crowned; he had moved north from Towton to impress his personal authority on the northeast with visits to the towns of Durham and Newcastle, and was now making his way slowly back to London for the coronation, via Queen Margaret's former strongholds in the northwest and the Midlands. John immediately set out northward to petition the king for help, and sent his estate manager, Richard Calle, to Framlingham to make representations to the duke himself. The response was not encouraging. Norfolk had no intention of ordering his men to leave the castle; "he trusts to God to show such evidence to the king and to the lords that he should have best right and title thereto," Calle reported. It was a bluff, but one plausible enough to preempt any immediate royal intervention, given that the uncertainty over Fastolf's will was not yet resolved, and that Edward's attention was engrossed by infinitely more pressing problems on the national stage. With the utmost circumspection, Calle let John know that more direct steps could be taken to reclaim the castle, if he felt it necessary: "there are but two or three men within the place, and if you think it best to etc., send word and I suppose a remedy should be had."[3] However, attempting to eject a duke from a valuable house by force would not necessarily be either wise or easy. Norfolk's men were still in control there by 21 June, when John arrived home.

The loss of Caister was devastating. It was the heart of the inheritance, the place where Fastolf was born and where he died, and the site of the college that John was to found in the old knight's name and for the good of his soul. But it was not the only property to be snatched from John's hands during the summer of 1461. The valuable manor of Dedham lay just to the south of the Suffolk border, in the county of Essex, and had been the subject of an ill-tempered wrangle between Fastolf and the late duke of Suffolk, who had seized the estate in 1447. The duke's fall from power in 1450 ended the dispute in Fastolf's favour, but Suffolk's widow had not forgotten her husband's claim in the decade since his death. Alice Chaucer, now dowager duchess of Suffolk, could scarcely have been more closely associated with the Lancastrian court, and it therefore seemed highly unlikely that she would be in any position to benefit from the Yorkist victory. It was not for nothing, however, that her husband had appointed her sole executor of his will, declaring "above all the earth, my singular trust is in her."[4] With characteristic foresight, she took the opportunity before the autumn of 1460 to arrange a marriage alliance between her son John, the young duke of Suffolk, and the duke of York's daughter Elizabeth. Her political agility was such that in October of that year, with the conflict almost at its height, she managed the extraordinary feat of appearing to be in favour with both sides. When she wanted to lobby for her own choice of sheriff in Norfolk and Suffolk, she was able to send her son to petition his new father-in-law York; at the same time, Friar Brackley was telling John Paston that the duchess was among the "greatest supporters of the queen and prince," and suggesting pointedly that the loyalty of her son to the Yorkist cause should be tried in battle.[5]

Four months later, the eighteen-year-old duke passed Brackley's test with flying colours, and impeccable timing. He fought in the Yorkist army alongside the earl of Warwick during the defeat at St. Albans in February, and then commanded the vanguard of his brother-in-law Edward's forces on the advance toward Towton. As a result, in the spring of 1461 he was basking in the warm sunshine of the new king's trust and favour. The duke himself had three more years to wait before taking formal possession of his inheritance at the age of twenty-one, but in any case his formidable mother had a controlling interest in his estates for her lifetime, since they had all been settled on her as her jointure when she married. It seems likely, therefore, that it was Duchess Alice who was behind the decision to seize the manor of Dedham again that summer, fourteen years after her husband had first taken it from John Fastolf. This was bad enough for John Paston, already nursing his bruises from the loss of Caister, but the risk was that it might be only the beginning of the duchess's ambitions where the Fastolf estates were concerned. Her husband had also challenged Sir John's possession of Drayton and Hellesdon, two adjoining manors near Norwich which lay on the doorstep of Suffolk's own property at Costessey, only a mile away. Also potentially vulnerable was the manor of Cotton in Suffolk—the late duke's birthplace—which he had sold to Fastolf in 1434 when he was in desperate need of funds to pay the ransom demanded by his French captors. The duchess might well come to the conclusion that an enforced sale of this kind should not override her son's birthright, and that Cotton, too, should be restored to the de la Pole inheritance. Mustering some kind of resistance to the loss of Dedham was therefore all the more urgent to deter any further attacks.

In August, John sent his eldest son, John Paston II, who was now nineteen, to travel with the royal household in the hope that he would find some opportunity to lobby King Edward for redress. It took time, but when John II did finally succeed in getting a message to the king, Edward said only that "he would be your good lord therein as he would be to the poorest man in England"—in other words, that John could expect no special help from the crown. The new king's priority in his public pronouncements was to establish himself unequivocally as a credible and impartial lawgiver; "as for favour," John II was told, "he will not be understood that he shall show favour more to one man than to another, not to one in England."[6] But it was much less clear what that should mean in the specific context of the Fastolf estates; after all, John's right to the inheritance had yet to be formally confirmed. In the meantime, the king's attention was preoccupied by the campaign to suppress continued rumblings of unrest in the south and to defeat the Lancastrian loyalists doggedly holding out in Wales and the north, a process in which he needed the enthusiastic assistance of the dukes of Suffolk and Norfolk a great deal more than the gratitude of a mere gentleman who had so far refused to take up arms in support of the Yorkist cause. In John Paston's mind, it was obvious that he was the victim rather than the perpetrator of injustice, but from the king's perspective his troubles appeared to be one of many messy disputes that would take time to sort out once the turbulence that Edward's accession had precipitated at a local level had begun to subside.

The frenzied atmosphere in which Norfolk politics were still operating was all too evident from the attempt to select the county's two representatives for the parliament that was called to meet in July. Parliamentary elections were organised by the sheriff—this year the duke of Norfolk's cousin Sir John Howard—and all local landholders with an annual income from their estates of the modest sum of two pounds or more were qualified to participate by raising their voices at the election meeting. It was usually possible, sometimes with a nudge in a particular direction from an influential magnate, to find a consensus in support of two politically appropriate names. On this occasion, however, there was "much to-do," according to the deputy sheriff William Price, who conducted the election on his master's behalf. Price's interpretation of the wishes of the assembled electors was that John Paston and another gentleman named Henry Grey had been chosen as the shire's representatives, but the third-placed candidate, a distant relative of Margaret's named John Berney of Witchingham, challenged his decision. When news of the altercation was relayed to the sheriff, Howard refused to confirm the nomination of Paston and Grey, instead returning a report alleging that Berney and his supporters had intimidated the meeting with their riotous behaviour.

There clearly had been trouble, but John was adamant that he at least had been duly elected. With the airy confidence of the first-placed candidate, and his usual failure to appreciate that what seemed to him to be logically correct might not be politically acceptable, John pointed out that the solution was simple: Berney and Grey should each produce the names of those who had voted for them at the election, "which of them that had fewest to give it up as reason would."[7] But neither Berney nor Grey showed any inclination to fall on his sword, and the political temperature continued to run very high: ". . . the world is right wild," an alarmed friend told John on 6 July, and three days later Margaret, who was staying at the Fastolf manor of Hellesdon, just outside Norwich, warned her husband in London to "beware how you ride or go, for naughty and evil disposed fellowships. I am put in fear daily for abiding here, and counselled by my mother and by other good friends that I should not abide here unless the world were in more quiet than it is."[8] Amid all the pushing and shoving, the controversy over the disputed election would not go away, and by the end of July—with the parliament postponed until November because of continuing Lancastrian resistance in the north and west—a new election had been called for 10 August.

Margaret was right to fear that John faced real danger, both political and personal. John himself sounded sanguine about the prospect of the reconvened election when he wrote home from London at the beginning of the month; his main concern was the reliability of Price, the sheriff's deputy, who had initially seemed keen to confirm the result of the original meeting: ". . . the undersheriff was somewhat flickering while he was here," he told Margaret, "for he informed the king that the last election was not peaceable, but the people were . . . riotously disposed, and put him in fear of his life."[9] But it was John's life that proved to be at risk when the new election was held, and Sir John Howard, the sheriff, about whom he should have been worrying. Howard had multiple reasons for hostility to Paston interests: he was a leading supporter of his cousin the duke of Norfolk, who had seized Caister Castle only weeks earlier; his sister was married to Thomas Daniel, John's patron-turned-antagonist of the early 1450s; and his wife, Catherine, was the aunt of Lord Moleyns's wife, Eleanor, through whom Moleyns had acquired his claim to Gresham. When the gentlemen of the shire gathered at Norwich on 10 August, tempers were frayed, as they had been all summer. John and Howard argued; the quarrel got out of hand, and one of Howard's men lashed out at John with his dagger. A thickly padded doublet saved him from serious injury, but the incident left his family and friends deeply shaken.

What made it worse was that the repercussions of the confrontation seemed likely to play out against him. By early October, King Edward was back at his palace of Greenwich, pleasantly situated on the Thames just east of London. He was attended by both John Howard, who was a member of the new royal household, and the duke of Norfolk. Clement Paston wrote urgently from the capital to warn his brother that the duke "has made a great complaint of you to the king"—probably because by this stage John had made a move to eject Norfolk's men from Caister by force, although information on these manoeuvres is frustratingly scarce. Howard added his voice to Norfolk's accusations, and the duke of Suffolk too was helping to "call upon the king against you." Inspired by this hostile chorus, royal letters were dispatched to summon John to answer the charges laid against him, but John—preoccupied, it seems likely, with events at Caister—did not respond. The king was incensed by this apparent defiance. For Edward, the most important thing at this early stage in his reign—more important than the rights and wrongs of any individual dispute—was that he should be obeyed without question. His ability to master his kingdom depended on convincing his subjects that his authority was incontestable—not an easy task when an alternative king was still at large, with a number of English nobles and foreign powers willing to offer him their support. In those circumstances, John's failure to comply with a direct royal command was making Edward dangerously angry, and doing no good at all to the Paston cause. The king was sending another summons, Clement reported anxiously, and had declared furiously that, "by God's mercy, if he comes not then, he shall die for it. We will make all other men beware by him how they shall disobey our writing." Clement had been told in no uncertain terms that Edward meant what he said, and that John should show his face at court as soon as was humanly possible, even if it might seem a risky prospect for other reasons. ". . . if you do well, come right strong," Clement advised, since Howard's wife was boasting that John's life would not be worth a penny if he dared to come within a sword's length of her husband's men.[10]

The hopeful prospect of a new Yorkist regime had turned into a chaotic nightmare for John Paston. Dedham was lost to the duke of Suffolk; Caister was under continuing threat from the duke of Norfolk; and John's quarrel with John Howard had involved him first in a life-threatening fight and now in serious trouble with the king. He left for London as soon as he could, and on his arrival, he found himself committed immediately to prison. It was adding insult to injury to learn that he had managed to offend his brother as well. William had hired two horses, ready to ride south at John's side, Margaret wrote at the beginning of November, but was under the impression that John had not wanted his company: "because you spoke not to him to ride with you, he said that he thought you would not have had him with you."[11]

It came as an overwhelming relief to discover that good luck could arrive as unexpectedly as bad in this volatile new world. John was held under lock and key for only a few days. King Edward would not tolerate disobedience, but he also knew that the credibility of his justice would play an important part in his ability to maintain order in the longer term. Having brought John to heel, he therefore took the trouble to investigate the substance of the allegations against him, and as a result, John was released by royal command. Not only that, but to the Pastons' great satisfaction, John Howard was arrested instead, "for divers great complaints that were made to the king of him," Margaret was told on Monday, 2 November.[12] And four days later, without warning, the duke of Norfolk died at the age of only forty-six—a brutally sudden end to an unpredictable and largely unfulfilled career. His son and heir had just turned seventeen, still four years away from his majority, and any ambitions he had to pursue his father's claim to Caister would have to wait until he was in charge of his inheritance and could flex the political muscle it represented. If there seemed little that could be done about the loss of Dedham to the duchess of Suffolk and her son, at least John now had breathing space in which to consolidate his hold on Caister and the rest of the Fastolf lands.

It was crucial that John use the opportunity well. The summer's events were a warning that Fastolf's fears about the vulnerability of his estates had been well founded. Even though the change of regime meant that John's old nemesis John Heydon, the mastermind behind his troubles at Gresham, was unlikely to be in any position to harass him for some time to come, there would clearly be no shortage of new opponents keen to take advantage of the insecurity of his hold on the inheritance. John therefore urgently needed to obtain a grant of probate on the revised will—that is, formal confirmation of its validity, and of his own right to execute it—in order to give him a firm legal base from which any further attacks could be repelled. He stayed on in London, lodging in the congenial surroundings of the Inner Temple, where he had once been a student, and Margaret had no choice but to accept that yet again he would not be at home for Christmas.

This time she responded not with affectionate reproaches but with real apprehension about what his absence might mean. "I fear me that it is not well with you that you are from home at this good time," she wrote on 29 December.[13] By the end of the first week in January she was deeply uneasy at his failure even to write or send news. "I had no tidings nor letter of you since the week before Christmas, whereof I marvel sore," she told him. ". . . I pray you heartily that you will vouchsafe to send me word how you do as hastily as you may, for my heart shall never be in ease till I have tidings from you." The disorder in Norfolk seemed to be getting worse rather than better. Many who had hoped that King Edward would act swiftly to address their grievances were becoming frustrated by the lack of response from a government which was still occupied in defending its very existence. Others were exploiting the political uncertainty in the region to take matters into their own hands. Margaret was not easily unnerved, but even she was becoming frightened. "People of this country begin to grow wild," she wrote on 7 January. ". . . God for his holy mercy give grace that there may be set a good rule . . . in this country in haste, for I heard never say of so much robbery and manslaughter in this country as is now within a little time."[14]

John's protracted absence from home at such an uncertain time reflected the desperate urgency of the legal matters with which he was dealing, but he showed little sign of recognising that his chances of securing his possession of Fastolf's estates depended just as much on the personal politics of his situation. John's mishandling of his colleagues in Fastolf's service in the wake of the old man's death meant that he was facing opposition from within Fastolf's circle as well as outside it, and in the months since the establishment of the new government he had made no progress in repairing his fractured relationships with former friends such as William Yelverton and William Worcester. Judge Yelverton's local influence had been much bolstered by the change of regime; he had even hoped that King Edward might promote him to the rank of chief justice in the court of King's Bench, but had to settle for the honour of a knighthood instead. Yet his increasing political clout did not inspire John to make any more concerted effort to heal the rift between them. "Yelverton is a good threadbare friend for you and for others in this country, as it is told me," Margaret wrote bleakly from Norfolk in January 1462.[15]

A month earlier, it had seemed that the news of William Worcester might be a little more positive. With encouragement from Thomas Howes, Worcester spoke to John several times in London during the autumn, and paid a visit to Margaret at Hellesdon that Christmas: ". . . he told me that he hoped you would be his good master," she reported to her husband. "I hope," she added firmly, ". . . that he will do well enough, so that he be fair fared with."[16] What exactly "fair treatment" might mean, however, remained an insuperable sticking point. Worcester was still holding out for the lands he believed Fastolf had promised him before his death, and whatever other compromises he might be persuaded to countenance, he would not budge from that demand: "I feel by him utterly that he will not appoint in other form," Thomas Howes told John in February.[17] By that stage, doubts were again beginning to surface about the reliability of Howes himself. Since coming home from a trip to London he had neither spoken to Margaret nor sent any word to her, she reported at the end of January, but he had found the time for two meetings with Judge Yelverton, and "what they have talked I cannot say," Thomas Playter told John.[18]

The possibility that Howes might now be wavering in his support for John's claim was all the more disquieting given the first indications that there was yet another name to be added to the list of those with grievances about John's handling of the estate since Fastolf's death. In January, Fastolf's lawyer William Jenney appeared at his old master's manor of Nacton, near the market town of Ipswich, in Suffolk, declaring that he was owed money from Fastolf's estate and that the tenants should deliver their rents to him until the outstanding sum was repaid in full. As a result, when Richard Calle arrived to collect revenues on John's behalf at the end of the month, he was forced to leave empty-handed. "I can get no money of them until the time they have knowledge how it stands between your mastership and Master Jenney," he told John; ". . . wherefore that it please your mastership to remember to speak to Master Jenney."[19] Yet again, this was an apparently minor issue that became a major problem because, despite Calle's advice, John did not address its root cause soon or carefully enough to prevent it from escalating. The surviving correspondence from 1462 is patchy, but there is no sign whatsoever that John made any effort to stay in direct or even indirect touch with Jenney, a colleague with whom he had worked closely throughout the 1450s. Instead, by the end of the summer, Jenney had formed a powerful coalition with William Yelverton to launch an overt challenge to John's claim to the inheritance.

On Friday, 3 September 1462, Yelverton and Jenney rode, with an intimidating entourage, to Fastolf's manor of Cotton in central Suffolk, where they instructed the tenants to withhold their rents from John Paston and to pay them instead to Judge Yelverton. If they refused to comply, the villagers were told, they would be subject to distraint: in other words, their property—usually farm animals, which were both valuable and easy to move—would be seized in lieu of payment. The following day Yelverton and Jenney moved on to Nacton, where they made the same claims and issued the same threats. John dispatched a Paston servant, John Pamping, to find out exactly what had happened, but the news he sent back was alarming. Pamping tracked down Yelverton and Jenney at church in Ipswich on Sunday morning, "and there I spoke to them," he reported later that day, "and told them you marvelled that they would take any distraint or warn any of your tenants that they should pay you no money." Judge Yelverton's response was aggressively hostile: ". . . he said that he would do in like wise in all manors that were Sir John Fastolf's in Norfolk as they have begun, and other language as I shall tell you." On Yelverton's orders, Pamping was then unceremoniously arrested and clapped in leg irons like a common felon. "And so I am with the gaoler, with a clog upon my heel," he wrote disconsolately—adding, with remarkable forbearance, ". . . wherefore please your mastership to send me your advice."[20]

Yelverton and Jenney had made their intentions plain, and they had done so in disturbing company. They were accompanied on their visit to Cotton by a gentleman named John Andrew, a close friend of John Heydon and servant of the duchess of Suffolk, who had taken a leading role in the prosecution by which Thomas Howes had been so harassed in the years after 1450. Then, in the church at Ipswich two days later, Pamping saw them talking to John Wyndham, who had been the Pastons' implacable adversary ever since his street brawl with James Gloys more than a decade earlier, and also to Gilbert Debenham, a gentleman in the duke of Norfolk's household who had repeatedly challenged Fastolf's ownership of the manor of Caldecott Hall, less than ten miles south of Caister, a dispute that he was now threatening to resuscitate. There could be no clearer demonstration than this of John's failure to sustain Fastolf's circle as a group bound together by mutual interests and shared loyalties. If Jenney and Yelverton—whom Fastolf had called "brother"—were now prepared to ally themselves with their patron's enemies, then the battle over his will was no longer a dispute about the exact form of the old man's last wishes: it had become a fight to prevent John Paston from inheriting the estate, to be pursued by any means necessary.

Word of the weekend's damaging events spread quickly. Three weeks later the Pastons' chaplain, James Gloys, warned John that "there is great noise of this revel that was done in Suffolk by Yelverton and Jenney."[21] Under increasing pressure in London, John decided to strike back before they had a chance to extend their activities further. He sent instructions that his second son, eighteen-year-old John Paston III, should go with Richard Calle and as many men as they could muster to stamp his authority on the manor of Cotton by holding a court there and collecting rent from the tenants. The Paston contingent arrived in the village on Friday, 8 October; the next day, John III rode on with thirty men toward William Jenney's home at Leiston, twenty-five miles east. At six o'clock on Sunday morning, in the mist of an autumn dawn, he raided Jenney's estate, seizing three dozen of his cattle in retaliation for the beasts taken from the tenants at Cotton. Meanwhile Calle, whom John III had left at Cotton with twelve of their men, had heard that their opponents were threatening violence: "if we abode there two days we should be pulled out by the heads."[22] As a public gesture of defiance, Calle stayed for five, and took care to speak personally to all the tenants. They were well disposed, he told John, but apprehensive about what would happen once the Pastons' men were gone.

The villagers were right to be frightened. A few days after Calle left, Jenney's men moved into Cotton. Seven or eight of them took over the manor house; "they melt lead and break down your bridge," John was told, "and make that no man may go into the place but on a ladder."[23] The occupation did not last—it was not sufficiently well organised to have been intended as a long-term enterprise—but it had served its purpose: the Pastons' possession of the estate, and their ability to collect any revenue there, were now extremely fragile. Not only that, but Yelverton and Jenney—a judge and a successful lawyer, both ideally placed to use the law as a political weapon—brought felony charges against Richard Calle, alleging that his conduct at Cotton had been riotous and illegal. Calle was an experienced and usually imperturbable man, but he was shaken by the prospect of facing a criminal trial, especially because he had heard from the sheriff that John thought he was somehow complicit in his own arrest. "And God knows it was never my will nor my intent, as I might be saved at the dreadful Day of Doom," he wrote in obvious anguish, "for there is no man so sore hurt as I am by the taking."[24]

Calle's distress emphasised yet again the deficiencies in John's handling of the people around him. If it was true that he suspected Calle of conspiring with his enemies, it was a groundless and utterly implausible accusation against a servant who had proved his loyalty time and again, most recently at significant personal cost. John's inability to see the world from any perspective but his own—something that compromised his political judgment, and made him capable of great tactlessness—was becoming increasingly marked in his dealings from the lowest to the highest social levels. At the beginning of December, Margaret had to remind him to write to the townspeople who had stood bail for John Pamping when he was arrested at Ipswich in September, to express his appreciation for their support and to reassure them that, whatever happened, they would suffer no financial loss as a result: ". . . saving your better advice," she suggested carefully, ". . . it were well done that you sent a letter to Ipswich . . . thanking them for their good will . . . ; for, as I heard say, they marvel that they hear no word from you."[25] John was no more diplomatic with great men. Earlier in the year, his young brother Clement had decided against delivering a letter that John had written to the chancellor; "methought your letter was not most pleasantly written to take to such a lord," he said sharply.[26] John was under stress—and when he was stressed he was more and more likely to revert to the refrain of what he believed to be legally right, while at the same time becoming less and less adept at managing the relationships that might have allowed him to achieve what he saw as justice.

Margaret and Clement were not the only ones attempting to persuade John to conduct himself in a more politic fashion. The vicar of Caister, a priest named Robert Cutler, tried to alert him to the urgent need to pay more attention to Thomas Howes, whose support John was still taking for granted despite repeated intimations that Howes's loyalties were now deeply divided. At the very least he was not reliably discreet; "for Our Lady's love, beware what you utter unto him but only in matters that he needs must know," Cutler wrote anxiously in the spring of 1463, "for he is not secure in the bite." Howes was a good-hearted but impressionable man whose career had been defined by his devotion to his master—and the more bitter the conflict over the will became, the harder it was for him to know what he should do in order to remain loyal to Fastolf's legacy. Now that battle lines were drawn, it was not realistic for John to assume that Howes would simply sever all ties with those members of the Caister household who were opposing the Paston claim: ". . . in truth," Cutler told John, "he works much by William Worcester"—who was, of course, Howes's nephew by marriage as well as a friend and colleague of many years' standing. John had given too little thought to the need to sustain Howes's trust and confidence, and it seemed that he might now be paying a heavy price. Howes had reportedly agreed to accept William Jenney and John Heydon as arbitrators in his long-standing legal battle with John Andrew, "and methought, if he were as he should be in all matters," Cutler remarked pointedly, "all these should not be his good friends but rather his enemies."[27]

Despite this explicit and timely warning, John's relationship with Howes deteriorated still further by the end of the year. "I understood by him that he is disposed to excuse Yelverton in all matters rather than you," the vicar reported in December. A date for the probate hearing had finally been set—witnesses were called to appear in the archbishop of Canterbury's court in January 1464—which should have been good news for John, had it not been for the fact that the estrangement of his co-executor, Howes, was now threatening to undermine his entire case. Cutler desperately tried to persuade him of the need to tread carefully; "make good cheer to the parson as though you understood that he were your friend, till time you have your intent," he wrote, "but beware and trust him not, but make you so strong in lordship and in the law that you reck not much whether he be good or bad." The obvious risk was that John would take a characteristically narrow and technical approach to the legal proceedings. Cutler was an astute man who recognised only too well the intensely political nature of the process, and he pleaded with John to be pragmatic in the attempt to keep key players on side: ". . . it is a common proverb, 'A man must some time set a candle before the devil,' and therefore, though it is not most meet and profitable of all, yet of two harms the least is to be taken."[28]

Four years earlier, John Stokes, the judge in the archbishop's court who advised John Paston on the business of the will, had been optimistic about the likely outcome of the hearing. John would need no witnesses to testify in support of his claim to the inheritance, Stokes said, unless someone contradicted his account of Fastolf's final intentions; "and, if there is a contradiction, three or four witnesses is enough."[29] If that had ever been true, it was no longer the case by January 1464, when Judge Yelverton and William Worcester mounted a formal challenge to John's application for probate on the revised will. John had already secured written statements from a number of people who could testify that Fastolf had spoken of his plans to make John his heir in the months before his death, but the critical question was what had happened in Fastolf's bedchamber on the morning of Saturday, 3 November, when the new will had allegedly been dictated. On that key issue, John had the support of Friar John Brackley and the vicar Robert Cutler, as well as of John Russe, the Yarmouth merchant who was responsible for provisioning the household at Caister. All three men claimed to have been in Fastolf's room that Saturday morning, and to have heard him make his last wishes known.

In response to John's evidence, Yelverton and Worcester produced a succession of witnesses who were examined by the court during the spring, summer, and autumn of 1464. Their strategy was a simple one: to undermine as many aspects of John's case as they could. The details of his claims were raked over and any vulnerable points picked out for particularly intense scrutiny. One stipulation in the revised will—that John should be excused the payment of four thousand marks to Fastolf's executors if he succeeded in founding the college according to his patron's wishes—appeared to be a last-minute addition to the deal even by John's own account, and Fastolf's servant John Bocking, who testified for Yelverton and Worcester in May, declared that he, for one, did not believe it, on the unarguably plausible grounds that "in his whole life he had not known such generosity in the said lord John Fastolf."[30] The character of John's witnesses came under sustained attack; the priest Robert Cutler, they said, was an unreliable man with little moral judgment and a history of perjury. The merchant John Russe had provided crucial evidence for the Paston case, and Yelverton and Worcester made a great effort to discredit him in particular. Those called upon to testify that he had not been present in Fastolf's chamber on the Saturday morning in question included Sir John's barber Harry Wynstall, and his manservant Nicholas Newman—Friar Brackley's much-loathed "Colin the Frenchman"—who had now moved on to more glamorous employment as an usher of the chamber to the dowager duchess of Norfolk. Still more witnesses were called in an attempt to demonstrate that Russe had been at Yarmouth rather than Caister that morning, buying food for the household as he usually did on Saturdays.

Amid the claims and counterclaims, one piece of testimony mattered above all: that of Thomas Howes, with whom John Paston maintained he was to share the administration of the estate. Howes was called to appear before the court in April 1464. John made a last-ditch attempt to put pressure on him before the hearing, sending his brother Clement to see him at his inn when he arrived in London; but Howes pretended to be out rather than face the conversation. Clement resorted to writing him a letter to remind him of his responsibilities—"to remember what his witnesses had said for his sake," Clement told John, "and what shame it should be to him to say the contrary, and also if he said the contrary you would hereafter prove the truth and contrary to his saying, and prove him in a perjury." There was no response from Howes, but a few days later, Clement bumped into him in the street: ". . . I found him passing strangely disposed," he reported in some irritation. Yet again, it was abundantly clear that the heart of the matter—for Howes, as it had been for Worcester, and Bocking, and so many others—was whether John would recognise the validity of claims on the estate other than his own: "I felt by him that all his strangeness from you is for that he deems that you would part from nothing." Clement denied it—"I told him the contrary thereof to be true"—but words could do nothing at this late stage to repair the calamitous breakdown of trust between

John and his former colleagues.[31] If there remained any doubt that Howes was now lost to the Pastons, it was dispelled when he gave his evidence. He declared under oath that he had seen neither John Russe nor Robert Cutler, John's key witnesses, in Fastolf's chamber on the Saturday morning before his death.

John's problems were mounting. The opposition of Yelverton, Worcester, and now Howes meant that there was no prospect of the probate case being resolved quickly. Given the trouble John was facing on so many fronts, it was, if anything, in his opponents' interests to ratchet up the pressure by spinning out the proceedings for as long as they could. And to make matters worse, the Pastons were beginning to run short of money. The cost of defending the Fastolf estates in both physical and legal terms was multiplying exponentially, while at the same time the persistent harassment of their tenants at a growing number of manors was making it increasingly difficult for them to collect rents and other income. Already in February 1464, the legal fees that John owed in the court of King's Bench were in arrears, "and that makes the clerks and your attorney weary," Clement told him.[32] Meanwhile, further threats were emerging. In the summer, news came that the duchess of Suffolk was intending to seize the estate of Caldecott Hall, of which Yelverton's new ally Gilbert Debenham claimed to be the rightful owner, and to keep it (and its revenues) until the dispute could be resolved. John's sons managed to avert the danger, at least temporarily, by moving into the manor house themselves, but their father had more trouble dealing with charges brought against him by William Jenney as a result of the confrontations at Cotton. Jenney succeeded in having John outlawed in the autumn of 1464, and he spent another couple of days in prison in London before the decision was finally overruled at the end of November.

The difficulty was that he was having to work increasingly hard simply to maintain his position, running faster and getting nowhere. As his opponents forced him into ever more frantic defence on an expanding succession of fronts, his hopes of securing the inheritance in the foreseeable future—or perhaps at all—grew fainter. Margaret was becoming acutely concerned; "at the reverence of God, arm yourself as mightily as you can against your enemies," she told her husband anxiously in June 1464, "for I know verily that they will do against you as mightily as they can with all their power."[33] She was not alone in her fears. John Russe was John's staunch supporter, but he was not afraid to speak his mind in plain terms.

"Men say you will neither follow the advice of your own kindred nor of your counsel," he wrote baldly in July, "but only your own wilfulness, which, but grace, shall be your destruction." Russe knew that John would hardly welcome such unsparing criticism, but he was not about to back down: "it is my part to inform your mastership as the common voice is," he added resolutely. John was by no means a stupid man, but he was extremely stubborn. He could not see, and would not accept, that his tactics were misguided. He persisted in his belief that the case would be lost or won in a court of law in London, despite Russe's warning that his presence was urgently required to defend his interests in person in Norfolk ("the longer you continue there, the more hurt grows to you").[34] Of course, as John was well aware, his father had always opted to use the courts as his battleground of choice; but that was because the courts were home territory for a vastly experienced lawyer and judge like William Paston, whereas John—who had never practised as an attorney, despite his legal training—could find no advantage there over Judge Yelverton and William Jenney. William Paston had also enjoyed the benefit of powerful connections at the highest levels of government to back up his legal manoeuvres. John, on the other hand, was still struggling to attract any influential support for his cause.

The toll that years of conflict were now taking was clear by the beginning of 1465. John's mood was not improved at Christmas 1464 by an acrimonious falling-out with his eldest son—something that had threatened to happen for years—as a result of which he threw John II out of the house. By the middle of January, John was back in London and enraged with the world. He was very short of cash, and he convinced himself that Margaret and Richard Calle were mismanaging his affairs in his absence. He lashed out at them—his devotedly courageous wife and his loyal servant—with bitter, impotent fury. They were inept with money, he said, whether because they were incompetent at collecting it or foolish in spending it ("either you gather shrewdly or else you spend lewdly"). Not only that, but they clearly cared little about his welfare, or else they would be managing his affairs more attentively: "you may remember . . . how you should do if this were yours alone," he wrote coldly, "and so do now."[35] The letter was a long and angry diatribe, both offensive and unfair to two people who were defending his interests with a tenacity and determination to match his own. It was also totally unrealistic in its assessment of the immense strain that the conflict was putting on the family's resources, both personal and financial. Evident in every word was the distress of a man under intense pressure—and if the situation in which John found himself was largely self-created, that only compounded his problems, since he was utterly incapable of modifying his behaviour.

John Russe tried again to talk him round in May 1465. His advice was that John should negotiate, and by Russe's account Yelverton and Jenney were more than willing to talk; "they many times have moved a treaty," he said, "and never it takes to no conclusion." At the very least, he suggested, if John agreed to a meeting he would have a chance to discover what his opponents wanted, and for what they might settle. He pressed the point despite the fact that he knew his advice was likely to fall on deaf ears; anyone who suggested reaching any kind of deal, Russe pointed out in acute frustration, was likely to be dismissed by John as a traitor to his cause. More than anyone else, Russe was prepared to tell John to his face that he was his own worst enemy. The letter itself was torn at both sides at some point after it was written, making it impossible now to reconstruct everything Russe wrote, but the force of his interrupted prose is unmistakable:

> Sir, at the reverence of Jesu consider how many years it is past that my good lord and master deceased, and how little is done for [text missing] of the great substance that he had; it is heavy to remember. You say the default is not in you, after your conceit; but I can hear no [text missing] in that of your opinion, for this I know for certain, if it had pleased you to have ended by the means of treaty, you had made [text missing] peace to the great wellbeing of the dead with the fourth part of the money that has been spent, and as men say only of very wilfulness [text missing] own person. For the mercy of God, remember the unstableness of this world, how it is not a minute's space in comparison to ever [text missing] leave wilfulness, which men say you occupy too excessively.

He had no hesitation, either, in telling John that his reputation was suffering. "It grieves me to hear that you stand in no favour with gentlemen nor in no great awe with the commons," Russe declared bluntly. ". . . It is a death to me to remember in what prosperity and in what degree you might stand in Norfolk and Suffolk if you had peace and were in heart's ease."[36]

But, by the time John received Russe's letter, peace was a more remote prospect than ever. The pressure on John and Margaret intensified sharply in February 1465, when the young duke of Suffolk resolved—as it had always seemed likely that he would—to revive his father's claim to the manors of Drayton and Hellesdon, near Norwich. Suffolk sent a small force under the command of a priest named Philip Lipyate to take control of Drayton in his name, and Lipyate let it be known that he intended shortly to follow suit at Hellesdon. John, who was still in London, convinced himself that this was merely a diversionary tactic to distract him from his continuing fight to reclaim the Essex estate of Dedham. Accordingly, he sent word to Margaret to reassure their tenants at Drayton that their best interests lay in keeping their distance from Suffolk's men, and in maintaining their loyalty to the Paston cause; "if they will be so steadfast to me, and keep them strange and forward from the duke's council," he said, "all this matter shall turn to a jape and not hurt them near."[37] But it was not quite that easy for the tenants to take comfort from John's assurances. They were now caught in the middle of a war of attrition, as Suffolk and the Pastons competed to demonstrate their authority over the manors by demanding rents from the villagers and seizing the property of those who would not pay. And given John's continued refusal to countenance any kind of negotiation, it seemed inevitable that such competition would lead to an alarming escalation of hostilities.

By the spring, Margaret at least had a little more assistance at home in Norfolk. After a four-month standoff, she finally succeeded in persuading her husband that their eldest son, now a young man of twenty-three, should be allowed to return home. But as soon as one family rift was patched over, another gaped open. The tensions between John and his mother, Agnes, which went back twenty years to their disagreement over the terms of his father's will, were bubbling to the surface again, something about which Margaret sounded despairing. "In good faith, I hear much language of the demeaning between you and her," she told her husband wearily in May. "I would right fain, and so would many more of your friends, that it were otherwise between you than it is, and if it were I hope you should have the better speed in all other matters." Margaret was now approaching a point of exhaustion. The inescapable consequence of John's blinkered determination to focus on their legal battles in London was that she was left in the front line in Norfolk, dealing with the hostility of their enemies face to face at Hellesdon just as she had done almost twenty years earlier at Gresham. She coped, as she always did, and remained uncomplaining even when John vented his frustration at her, but the strain was beginning to show. "I pray God be your good speed in all your matters and give you grace to have a good conclusion of them in haste," she wrote on 10 May, "for this is too weary a life to abide for you and all yours."[38]

Nevertheless, despite her fatigue, she had not lost her resourcefulness. She continued to search for help where she could, appealing—as John had done thirteen years earlier, when he was struggling against the energetic aggression of Thomas Daniel—to the subtly astute figure of Walter Lyhert, bishop of Norwich, in the hope that he might exert a restraining episcopal influence on the duke of Suffolk's priest, Philip Lipyate. The bishop, as always, seemed sympathetic—"My lord of Norwich said to me that he would not have abided the sorrow and trouble that you have abided," not even "to win all Sir John Fastolf's goods," Margaret reported in May—but his advice, like John Russe's, was that John himself should return from London; he "said to me that it should be a great comfort to your friends and neighbours," she told her husband, "and that your presence should do more amongst them than a hundred of your men should do in your absence."[39]

But any faint hope that John might be persuaded to leave his lawsuits for long enough to take the bishop's advice evaporated completely at the beginning of June, when he was yet again committed to prison in London. He had found himself behind bars twice before, but for no more than a couple of days on each occasion. This time, it was a great deal more serious. Out of nowhere, the accusation which John Wyndham had hurled at Margaret in the street in Norwich years earlier—that "the Pastons and all their kin were churls of Gimingham"—had come back to haunt them. If it was true that John had unfree blood in his veins, if the Paston family were indeed of villein stock, then he had no right to own manorial land or exercise manorial lordship. All his estates—not merely the Fastolf inheritance—were in jeopardy, and King Edward ordered that he be kept in custody while the charge was formally investigated.

The source of the allegation is now shrouded in obscurity, but it seems likely that Judge Yelverton was implicated one way or another, perhaps in concert with a young nobleman named Anthony Woodville. Woodville was the son and heir of Richard Woodville, Lord Rivers, a landowner from the midland county of Northamptonshire, who had grown rich under the Lancastrian regime. Both father and son had fought in Queen Margaret's defeated army at Towton, and were captured for their pains; but Edward was now offering a judiciously magnanimous welcome to old enemies who were prepared to pledge him their allegiance, and both the older and the

younger Woodville were beginning to prosper in their new Yorkist identi-
ties. Anthony had married Elizabeth, daughter and heiress of the murdered
Lord Scales, and had acquired her father's title and estates along with her
hand. Whether or not he was involved in levelling the charge of villeinage
against John, he certainly tried to capitalise on John's imprisonment by
seeking to confiscate some of the Pastons' property in Norfolk.

Whoever was responsible—and, after all, there was no shortage of possible candidates—John's arrest was a crippling blow that gave renewed
heart to their enemies. "They are much the bolder, I suppose, because you
are where you are," Margaret reported unhappily. "At the reverence of
God, if you may by any worshipful or reasonable means, come out thereof
as soon as you may, and come home among your friends and tenants, and
that should be to them the greatest comfort that they might have, and the
contrary to your enemies." John hardly needed telling that prison was not
the ideal place in which to find himself, but there was nothing he could yet
do to secure his freedom. He did what he could to encourage Margaret to
hold fast in Norfolk, and she did her best to respond in kind—"I would
fain do well if I could, and as I can I will do to your pleasure and profit"—
but the effort it took to sound positive was now visible: she signed herself,
in an uncharacteristic moment of vulnerability, "your faint housewife at this
time."[40]

In public, however, there was no room for faintness. The duke of
Suffolk's hold over the tenants at Drayton was now established so firmly
that an advance on Hellesdon could not be long in coming. With John
under lock and key in London, it was left to Margaret and her sons,
together with Richard Calle and John Daubeney—the younger son of a
local gentleman, who had joined the Pastons' household some years earlier
and was now one of their most trusted servants—to organise the defence of
the manor. The expected assault materialised on Monday, 8 July, when the
duke's priest, Philip Lipyate, rode to Hellesdon at the head of a dauntingly
large company of Suffolk's men. Their weapons were not yet drawn, but the
hot summer sun glanced menacingly off swords, pikes, cuirasses, and helmets. However, Suffolk's army found that Margaret and her eldest son were
prepared for their arrival. The Pastons had mustered sixty stout-hearted
men of their own "and guns and such ordnance so that if they had set upon
us they had been destroyed," Calle reported. Lipyate was taken by surprise;
he was prepared for a confrontation, but not for a pitched battle. After
some hasty negotiations conducted by two priests dispatched hurriedly by

Bishop Lyhert to ride the two miles from Norwich to Hellesdon, both sides agreed to disperse their forces, and Lipyate and his men retreated.

But the respite lasted barely a matter of hours. Suffolk's men made their presence felt in Norwich instead, "and face us and fray upon us daily," Calle told John two days later. The sheriff had already had to rescue Calle from one attack, "and they make their avaunt where that I may be gotten I shall die, and so they lie in wait to mischief me." He asked John urgently for advice, "for you must seek some other remedy than you do, or else in my conceit it shall go to the devil and be destroyed, and that in right short time." It was not like Calle to write to his master in such forthright terms, but it was bluntness born of desperation: "I beseech you to pardon me of my writing, for I have pity to see the tribulation that my mistress has here, and all your friends, etc."[41]

His message was echoed emphatically on 12 July by Margaret herself—"praying you heartily," she wrote, "that you will seek a means that your servants may be in peace, for they are daily in fear of their lives." She had refused to be intimidated at Hellesdon, but in private she was suffering; "what with sickness and trouble that I have had, I am brought right low and weak," she told her husband, "but to my power I will do as I can or may in your matters."[42] On its way to London, her letter crossed with one travelling in the opposite direction from John himself. News of her illness had already reached him, "which I like not to hear," he wrote with genuine concern, "praying you heartily that you take what may do you ease . . . , and in any wise take no thought nor too much labour for these matters, nor set it not so to your heart that you fare the worse for it." His solicitous tone was welcome—as was the fact that he was no longer accusing her of neglecting his business while he was away—but it was hard to avoid the conclusion that his lengthy, and now enforced, absence in London had left him unable to comprehend the reality of Margaret's situation in Norfolk or the scale of the problems she was facing. Much of his letter was taken up with recounting details of the technical deficiencies in the duke of Suffolk's claim to Drayton—but however right he was, in practice Drayton was already lost. Margaret now had to find a way of protecting Hellesdon against the same fate, and John's suggestion that she should lecture Bishop Lyhert on the subject—"let my lord of Norwich know that it is not profitable nor becoming well of gentlemen that any gentleman should be compelled by an entry of a lord to show his evidence or title to his land"—was not likely to be the answer.[43]

Margaret tried again in August to underline the need for John to come home as soon as he could—"men cut large thongs here of other men's leather," she remarked acidly—but there seemed to be little he could do about his captivity, and it was clear that he, too, was sometimes in need of consolation and encouragement; "trust verily by the grace of God," Margaret wrote in a gentler moment, "that you shall overcome your enemies and your troublous matters right well, if you will be of good comfort and not take your matters too heavily."[44] At least his situation was not intolerably unpleasant, since the jail in which he found himself—the Fleet Prison in London—was probably the most comfortable prison in the capital, at least for those who had money to spend. Lying just outside the city walls to the west, near Ludgate, the prison itself was bounded on one side by the River Fleet and on the other three by a moat, which had originally been navigable but was now so choked with sewage and refuse—including animal carcasses dumped by the butchers who rented a wharf on the riverfront nearby—that it was possible to wade across the filthy water. Inside the walls, shielded a little from the stench, stood what was by contemporary standards a genteel establishment, which typically housed prisoners condemned in civil rather than criminal cases.

Comfort and gentility, however, came at a price. Inmates had to pay for their board and lodging; they were also expected to contribute tips for the servants, and were charged one-off fees when they entered the prison and when they left it—a regime so costly that those imprisoned for debt could find themselves trapped behind bars by their spiralling expenditure there. All the charges were calculated on a sliding scale to reflect the range of accommodation within the prison buildings, from luxurious private rooms reserved for the wealthy to dormitories where the less well-off slept two to a bed. Those who were destitute paid nothing for their lodging but received nothing in return; they were allowed to beg through a grate in the prison wall for money to pay for food, but even they had somehow to find a discharge fee of more than two shillings—twenty-eight pence, to be exact, at a time when just a couple of pennies would buy a hearty meal at an inn or an entire gallon of ale—once the order came for their release. The huge profits to be made from the running of the prison meant that the wardenship of the Fleet was a covetable position. Unusually, it was a hereditary appointment, which in the 1460s, even more uncommonly, was held by a woman, Elizabeth Venour—"my fair mistress of the Fleet," as John III called her when he sent his regards from Norfolk in September.[45]

As a gentleman of means, John Paston had a private room to himself, and he kept his servant John Pamping to wait on him. Within the prison close he had a fair measure of freedom, and spent time with other well-to-do prisoners, including Sir Henry Percy, the sixteen-year-old heir to the earldom of Northumberland, whose father had been killed fighting for the Lancastrians at Towton. John was still able to supervise his legal business, and gave his own statement about Fastolf's will to the ongoing probate hearing at a deposition held in the Fleet, at Elizabeth Venour's comfortable house within the prison grounds, that summer. He was also allowed to receive visitors. In September Margaret left her sons to protect Hellesdon for a few days, and rode to London to see him.

John and Margaret had not met for a long time, possibly as much as nine months. They were both stoical, practical people for whom personal pleasure would never come before duty, but it was nevertheless clear quite how much this brief meeting meant after such a long separation. Its effects suffused the letter John sent while Margaret was still travelling on her way back to Norfolk—the most openly affectionate and playful letter he ever wrote to her. He was suddenly almost unrecognisable as the dour, critical, and humourless man he had so often seemed in the last few years. His letters usually began with a succinct and functional "I recommend me to you," but this one was addressed to "mine own dear sovereign lady"; "I recommend me to you and thank you of the great cheer that you made me here," he continued—adding teasingly, "to my great cost and charge and labour." The bulk of the note was, inevitably, taken up with business, much of it dealt with in characteristic style; his sons, for example, had written to ask for money to help with the defence of Cotton, a request about which he was scathing ("remember them that they have divers times had money thitherward and do right naught, and my adversaries sent thither men without money and had their intent"). At the end of all the reminders and the advice, however, he launched into a cheerfully dreadful piece of self-penned poetry. He could not resist devoting his first twelve lines to the supposed inadequacies of Richard Calle's financial management, but his intention was clearly to make Margaret smile:

> And look you be merry and take no thought,
> For this rhyme is cunningly wrought.
> My lord Percy and all this house
> Recommend them to you, dog, cat and mouse,

And wish you had been here still,
For they say you are a good Jill.
No more to you at this time,
But God him save who made this rhyme.
Written the vigil of St. Matthew by your true and trusty husband, J.P.[46]

Margaret, too, showed the benefits of the visit, if in rather more sub-dued fashion. "Right worshipful husband, I recommend me to you," she wrote a week later, "desiring heartily to hear of your welfare, thanking you of your great cheer that you made me . . ." "God give me grace," she added with her usual stalwart courage, "to do that may please you." It was harder for Margaret to remain buoyed up by their meeting, given that she was plunged back into the maelstrom of their affairs the minute she set foot in East Anglia, although the lingering effects of her trip were perhaps visible in her unusually light-hearted account of a threatening incident at Caldecott Hall on 24 September: "you will laugh to hear all the process of the demeaning here," she told John, a reaction that would hardly have seemed plausible two weeks earlier.[47]

The pressure, however, was mounting. The confrontation at Caldecott Hall had been precipitated by William Jenney's attempt to hold a manor court there, and the Pastons' man John Daubeney was forced to muster sixty men from Hellesdon and Caister to ward him off. Only a week later, John Paston III had to gather more armed men at short notice and use all his political skills to hold Jenney and Gilbert Debenham out of Cotton. No one in the family was now thinking in terms of positive advances for their cause; their successes were measured in terms of averting the threats that came thicker and faster with each passing month—and the risk in moving men around from manor to manor was always that in protecting one front, they might leave themselves exposed on another.

As Richard Calle had warned John three months earlier, it was Hellesdon that was their most vulnerable point. There they faced their most powerful opponent, the duke of Suffolk, whose own property at Costessey lay only a mile away, close to the manor of Drayton which his men had already overrun. On the other side of Hellesdon from Drayton and Costessey lay the city of Norwich, where the mayor, Margaret believed, was in the duke's pocket; he had visited Suffolk's occupying forces at Drayton in May, and said "that if my lord of Suffolk needs a hundred men he would purvey him thereof, and if any men of the town would go to Paston he would lay them fast in prison."[48] Despite the mayor's hostility, the Pastons were not completely bereft of support among the townspeople, but no amount of sympathy there would have enabled them to resist the duke when he arrived in the city on the morning of Tuesday, 15 October—accompanied, Margaret told John, by five hundred men. Even allowing for the possibility that this intimidatingly large number was intended to give an impressionistic sense of scale rather than an accurate headcount, this was an ominous show of strength, and their old enemies within Suffolk's household were helping to ensure that the duke and his mother remained implacable in their determination to wrest Hellesdon from the Pastons' hands: "the old lady and the duke are set fervently against us," Margaret reported.[49]

The final attack came later that day. When it was over, Hellesdon was not only lost, but destroyed. The duke's men smashed their way through every house in the village, looting as they went. There were guns and armour stored in the church steeple, but the parishioners had no chance to reach them; the invaders swarmed into the building, even climbing onto the altar to reach the precious images displayed high above, while the priest looked on in helpless despair. But their principal target was the manor house. When she saw what had been done to a place that had been a home to her during the last six years, Margaret was deeply distressed: ". . . in good faith there will no creature think how foully and horribly it is arrayed unless they see it. There come much people daily to wonder thereupon, both from Norwich and from other places, and they speak shamefully thereof." There had to be some remedy for such wanton destruction, she thought, and urged her husband to arrange that "some men of worship might be sent from the king to see how it is both there and at the lodge, before any snows come, that they may make report of the truth; else it shall not more be seen so plainly as it may now."[50] But the unpalatable truth was that the duke of Suffolk was an immensely powerful man, who was married to the king's sister. The Pastons' own right to Hellesdon was no clearer than it had been six years earlier—less so, in fact, given how fiercely John's claims were now being contested by Yelverton and Worcester—and while that remained the case, they stood no chance of persuading the king to help them.

Margaret retreated to Caister, keeping with her a garrison of thirty men "for salvation of us and the place," she told John, "for in very truth, if the place had not been kept strong, the duke would have come hither."[51] She drew up an inventory of the possessions they had lost at Hellesdon, among them featherbeds, bolsters, blankets, and pillows; napkins, basins, knives, and spoons; clothes of fine fabrics—velvet, sarsanet, holland, and fustian; a "book of French" belonging to her eldest son; and "a great comb of ivory" of her daughter Margery's. And she begged John to renew his efforts to find a solution to their problems: "at the reverence of God, speed your matters now, for it is too horrible a cost and trouble that we have now daily, and must have till it be otherwise."[52]

Over the winter, John did at last manage to obtain his release from prison—probably by 10 December, when he again testified at the probate hearing, but this time outside the high walls of the Fleet. But he was unable to achieve anything more. The charge that he was a bondman still hung over him. Worse, his hopes of securing the Fastolf inheritance for his family were in shreds. Six years on from the old man's death, Dedham and Drayton were gone; Hellesdon was destroyed; Cotton and Caldecott Hall were under constant threat; Caister was under armed guard; Fastolf's college was not yet founded there; and John's relationship with his closest colleagues in his patron's service had broken down irretrievably. Along the way, he had ignored every piece of good advice he had been given, and it was hard to see from where help might now come.

In May 1465, in his bluntest and most critical letter, John Russe told John that persisting in his fight was making Margaret ill: ". . . by my troth," he wrote, "the continuance of this trouble shall shorten the days of my mistress, and it shall cause you to great loss; for certain she is in great heaviness."[53] Russe was almost right. It was not Margaret but John himself whose life was cut short. He had marked his forty-fourth birthday in prison, five days before Hellesdon was destroyed by the duke of Suffolk's men. Seven months later, on 22 May 1466, he died suddenly in London. Margaret's worst fears had been realised: his health had given out under the protracted strain of conflict and imprisonment. No record survives of his mother's reaction to his death, but Agnes, too, seems to have had a premonition that all might not be well. Her last surviving letter, written to her firstborn in his quarters in the Fleet, makes haunting reading: "By my counsel, dispose yourself as much as you may to have less to do in the world. Your father said, 'In little business lies much rest.' This world is but a thoroughfare and full of woe; and when we depart therefrom, right naught we bear with us but our good deeds and ill. And there knows no man how soon God will call him, and therefore it is good for every creature to be ready."[54]

It was William Worcester—who understood far more about what had happened to them all since his master's death than John ever did—who found a telling epitaph for his former friend. Worcester made careful notes in his copy of a book of philosophical maxims translated by Fastolf's stepson, Stephen Scrope. Where the text said, "a man should not enforce him in this world to make great buildings nor great gettings the which after his death are left to serve others," Worcester wrote, "for John Fastolf, the very rich knight who acted against this advice."[55] Next to the saying that "heaviness is a passion touching things past, and sorrow is a fear of things to come," he wrote his own name. But it was by a dictum on the subject of trust—or, rather, the lack of it—that Worcester wrote the initials "J.P.": "to be suspicious makes man to be evil conditioned and to live evil."[56] Only a man who felt betrayed, as Worcester did, could think of John Paston as evil—and perhaps Fastolf's extraordinary wealth would always, in the end, have come between those he left behind. Certainly, though, John's inability to see that he could not demand the trust of those around him without giving trust in return turned his friends into enemies. In the process, it helped to destroy his life.

a drone among bees

*J*OHN PASTON WAS BURIED in splendour. A priest and twelve poor men bearing torches walked beside his coffin for six days as it was carried in solemn procession more than a hundred miles from his lodgings at the Inner Temple in London to his parish of St. Peter Hungate in Norwich. There, behind the sombre façade of the black flint church, with thirty-eight priests in attendance, the Office of the Dead was sung. As the cortège rested briefly in the city, intensive preparations were under way twenty miles farther north, within the forbidding walls of Bromholm Priory, just outside Paston village, for the burial and the funeral feast. The family's most trusted employees, Richard Calle, James Gloys, and John Daubeney, threw themselves into the massive task of securing the necessary provisions. So many animals were slaughtered—forty-nine pigs, forty-nine calves, ten cows, thirty-four lambs, twenty-two sheep—that two men worked for three days to flay them. More than ninety servants were paid to wait on the guests; a barber was hired for five days, and fourteen bell ringers were employed at a cost of half a shilling each. When John's body arrived at the priory, it was laid on a hearse draped in fine grey linen fringed with silk, lit with candles that alone had cost more than twenty-two pounds. In the first week of June, the elaborate arrangements complete, John was laid to rest. The church was so ablaze with torches that afterward the stench of tallow was overwhelming; two panes of glass had to be removed "for to let out the reek," and soldered back into place once the air had cleared.[1]

Margaret kept precise notes of the funeral expenses, down to the twenty pence it cost to replace eight pieces of the prior's pewter tableware that had somehow been mislaid. The final total, including black gowns for the mourners and a new robe for the prior, came to almost £250—a staggeringly vast sum, which represented more than a year's income from John and Margaret's estates. It was a defiant display, as though the strain of her husband's last years, and the stain of his imprisonment, could be wiped away in death by the dignity of his burial. The Pastons' determination to hold their heads high is manifest, but the grief and shock of a husband and father dying so young and so suddenly are much harder to recapture; there are no surviving letters written by Margaret or by anyone else in the family for five months after the funeral. In any case, Margaret herself was not prone either to emotional introspection or to self-pity, but she and John had been married for more than twenty-five years, and his death could not have been anything but a devastating blow. Their relationship had never been one of high romance, but from the beginning it was a real partnership based on mutual respect and deep affection. At forty-four, she was left a widow with five children still to care for, as well as her two grown-up sons. Her loss was unequivocal—but the reaction of her eldest son to his father's death was a great deal more ambivalent.

John Paston II was twenty-four when his father died, just two years older than John himself had been when Judge William's death left him at the head of the family. But the similarities between father and son ended there. John Paston at twenty-two had been a married man with two small children; he was serious, careful, even careworn, from his first moments in charge of his inheritance. John II at twenty-four was unmarried, and showed no sign of any inclination to settle down. Not only was he not following in his father's footsteps, but he had gone far enough in the other direction to precipitate a period of bitter estrangement. Temperamentally, John II was his father's polar opposite: this son of a man who had never been young in some ways never grew up. He was, of course, intelligent and well educated; the son of John and Margaret and the grandson of William would have been nothing less. However, he was also impulsive, irrepressibly optimistic, and impatient with the minutiae of managing business and finance—all of which made him, in his father's eyes, careless and reprehensibly irresponsible. It was not that John II deliberately set out to defy his father—after his own fashion, he made desperate efforts to please him—but in outlook on the world they were so fundamentally at odds that they never came close to understanding each other.

John II and his younger brother John Paston III were educated first in Norfolk, and then in Cambridge, almost certainly under the individual instruction of a private tutor rather than in the more luxurious and much more costly surroundings of a college. Next, they moved to London for some basic schooling in the principles and practice of the law, but not the specialist training provided by the Inns of Court; at least, if they were members of an Inn, they never took advantage of its London lodgings as their father had done at the Inner Temple. It is entirely possible that plans for their further education were disrupted by the upheaval in the family caused by Fastolf's death in November 1459 and the debilitating demands, personal and financial, of John's campaign to secure the inheritance. Certainly, the two boys were back at home not long after the old knight's funeral.

Only a few weeks later, Margaret was preoccupied with the need to ensure that her arrangements for the festive season were appropriately sober and subdued, and dispatched her sons to ask advice from two distinguished local households—seventeen-year-old John II to Lady Morley, and fifteen-year-old John III to Lady Stapleton—about what Christmas entertainments should be permitted, given the constraints of public mourning. Isabella, Lady Morley, who had lost her husband shortly before Christmas seventeen years earlier, confirmed that in her house "there were no disguisings nor harping nor luting nor singing, nor no loud disports, but playing at the tables"—backgammon—"and chess and cards, such disports she gave her folks leave to play, and none other." Margaret passed the information on to her husband in London, but was just as concerned to tell him that "your son did his errand right well, as you shall hear after this."[2] Perhaps this was simply an expression of maternal pride, but—given that she took the trouble to point out the success of John II's mission, while that of his younger brother attracted no comment, favourable or otherwise—it seems likely that their eldest son's conduct and reliability had already come under disapproving scrutiny. The pattern of maternal defence against paternal criticism was one that would play itself out over and over again in John II's troubled relationship with his parents.

It was fitting that this first semipolitical errand should concern Sir John Fastolf. The battle for Fastolf's estates, which had utterly consumed John Paston's last six years, dominated his eldest son's life from the very moment he reached adulthood. In the summer of 1461, at the age of nineteen, John

II was sent to join the new Yorkist court in the hope that he would find chances there to further his father's cause. John Paston himself, travelling anxiously between his estates in Norfolk and his legal business in London, could not hope to stay in close personal touch with those around the king, especially since Edward spent the first months of his reign almost constantly on the move around his disordered kingdom. However, if his eldest son now succeeded in securing a place within the royal household, John would have a permanent representative near the heart of government to pace the corridors of power in his stead, eavesdropping on telltale whispers about the latest political developments, and seeking friends in high places on the family's behalf.

A great weight of expectation lay on John II's shoulders—but the task he faced was not an easy one. As the Yorkist regime began to take shape, the political world remained intensely volatile, and the court was a complex, subtle, even dangerous place. The Pastons had one immediate contact there—a friend and distant relative named John Wykes, an usher of the king's chamber—but John II would need to work hard to secure the help of more powerful men. It would take social poise to cultivate valuable friendships among those close to the king, and diplomatic skill to exploit such personal contacts to his family's advantage; he would also require a ready supply of money to enable him to live in the flamboyant style appropriate to a gentleman in royal service. He had not been at court long before it became clear that he was running into serious difficulties on all three fronts.

John Paston II and the young king were almost exactly the same age—John II was older by just a few weeks—but the contrast between them made that fact difficult to remember. At nineteen, King Edward was an imperiously commanding figure who had won his throne on the battlefield, and was now stamping his personal authority on a country that had not experienced strong royal leadership for the past forty years. Often exhilaratingly charming in person, he was nevertheless capable of brutal ruthlessness, and as John Paston had discovered to his cost when he ignored a royal summons, his temper was not to be provoked lightly. In comparison, John II seemed like a lost child, floundering out of his depth in the dazzlingly competitive world of Edward's new court. In August 1461, his uncle Clement—John Paston's youngest brother, who was only a little older than John II, and studying in London—sent word that what he had heard of his nephew's activities was not reassuring. John II was travelling with the royal household but had not yet succeeded in finding himself a place within its establishment, even to the extent of securing his board and lodging: ". . . my nephew is not yet verily acquainted in the king's house," Clement wrote uneasily, "nor with the officers of the king's house. He is not taken as none of that house, for the cooks are not charged to serve him." Nor had he so far been able to capitalise on the Pastons' lone contact within the household itself: ". . . he is not acquainted with nobody but with Wykes," Clement reported, "and Wykes had told him that he would bring him to the king, but he has not yet done so."[3]

If John II was socially too reticent to make friends easily in the sophisticated circles of the new royal entourage, he was also too naïve for the fine art of political lobbying. His instructions from his father were to bring the duchess of Suffolk's seizure of Dedham to the king's attention, and—in his anxiety to preempt suggestions that he was not trying his utmost—he wrote home with a blow-by-blow account of the exhaustive representations he had made to the Lord Treasurer, the earl of Essex. "I laboured daily my lord of Essex . . . every morning before he went to the king," he told his father earnestly, "and often times inquired of him if he had moved the king in these matters." Every day the answer was the same: Essex was doing everything he could, he said, but had not yet found an opportune moment to raise the issue with Edward, "so often delaying me," John II went on indignantly, "that in truth I thought to have sent you word that I felt by him that he was not willing to move the king therein. Nevertheless, I laboured to him continually, and prayed Baronners, his man, to remember him of it."[4]

John II's desperation to convince his father that no one could have done more to press the Paston case was rapidly becoming part of his problem. The earl of Essex might well have been trying to fob him off, but his message— that timing was everything in presenting petitions to great men—was no less true for that; and what applied to the earl's conversations with the king should also have applied to John II's dealings with the earl, since increasingly insistent daily reminders were more likely to amount to pestering than effective lobbying. Even worse, when these incessant inquiries produced no immediate results, John II redoubled his efforts. "I told often times to my said lord that I had a man tarrying in town that I should have sent to you for other sundry matters," he told his father, "and he tarried for nothing but that I might send you by him an answer of the said matters; other times beseeching him to speed me in those matters for this cause that you should think no default in me for remembering."[5] The hope that one of the most influential noblemen in England might be swayed by the prospect either of a Paston messenger kicking his heels, or of a teenager getting into trouble with his father for forgetfulness, demonstrated an alarming degree of political gaucheness.

Whatever the deficiencies in John II's political judgment, it became clear when he did finally manage to get a response from the king on the subject of Dedham—"as for favour, he will not be understood that he shall show favour more to one man than to another, not to one in England"— that there could be no realistic expectation of imminent royal intervention in what, seen from Edward's perspective, was a petty dispute of minimal significance.[6] If no immediate help for the family was likely to be forthcoming, the question was whether John II's continuing presence at court might prove beneficial in other ways. Clement Paston initially thought that it would be better for his nephew to leave the royal household than to persevere there as an unsuccessful hanger-on: ". . . it were best for him to take his leave, and come home till you had spoken with somebody to help him forth," he told John bluntly, "for he is not bold enough to put forth himself." But that strategy had its own disadvantages, since John II's ignominious departure from the fringes of the court would not now go unnoticed. Edward might be reluctant to entrust him with any responsibility in the future, Clement pointed out, if it seemed likely that he might be summoned home again at any moment, "the which would cause him not to be had in favour"; meanwhile, malicious court gossip might leap to the unkind conclusion that he had been sent away in disgrace. Clement's judgment, on balance, was that John II should stay—but that would require more funds, "for the costs are greater in the king's house when he rides than you thought it had been," he told his brother flatly.[7] That message was hammered home in typically forthright terms by the merchant John Russe, who had heard from an acquaintance at court about John II's progress, or lack of it: ". . . there shall nothing hurt him but your straitness of money to him . . . ," Russe wrote; "there are gentlemen's sons of less reputation that have money more liberal ten times than he has."[8]

It was decided that John II should remain where he was in the royal household, for the time being at least; but as so often, his father proved stubbornly resistant to good advice. He chose to interpret his son's impecuniousness as the result of his profligate extravagance rather than as an inevitable reflection of the costs of court life, and as a result, John II's financial difficulties were, if anything, worse by the following spring. In March 1462, King Edward was on his way north to reinforce a campaign led by the earl of Warwick against Lancastrian loyalists still holding out in the north-eastern county of Northumberland. John II, riding among the jostling carts and packhorses of the royal entourage, was acutely short of cash, and wrote to his father to ask for help. His letter makes clear how distant their relationship now was; he sounded at once formal, ostentatiously respectful, and plaintive in trying to convince his father that his need was genuine. "Please it you to understand the great expense that I have daily travelling with the king," he wrote, ". . . beseeching you to consider these causes and so to remember me that I may have such things as I may do my master service with and pleasure, trusting in God it shall be to your worship and to my avail. In especial, I beseech you that I may be sure where to have money somewhat before Easter."9

By the beginning of 1463, John II was back at home, and Margaret pointedly reported to his father that he had made a positive impression on Agnes and others in Norfolk polite society. "My mother and many other folks make much of your son John the older," she said, "and right glad of his coming home, and like right well his demeaning."10 His time at court did finally seem to be paying some dividends by the spring of that year, when he was knighted, probably to mark his formal coming of age on his twenty-first birthday. Knighthood was an undoubted honour, but it made no practical difference to the complex problems in which his father was so exhaustingly entangled, and the new title seems to have done nothing to mitigate John's plummeting estimation of his son's abilities.

By May the tense relationship between the two was beginning to cause scandalised local gossip. "And of one matter, at reverence of God, take heed," John was warned by Robert Cutler, the vicar of Caister, "for in truth I hear much talking thereof . . . ; and that is of my master your son Sir John, because he is so at home and no otherwise set for." None of the speculation about the reasons for John II's presence in Norfolk was flattering—"some say that you and he both stand out of the king's good grace, and some say that you keep him at home for niggardliness, and will nothing spend upon him"—while the vicar's flustered attempts to explain the situation for public consumption were unconvincing at best: "I have answered and said the most cause is in part because you are so much out that he is the rather at home for the safeguard of the coast." His advice was that, "for eschewing of common language," John II should "worshipfully be set for, either in the king's service or marriage."11 John had tried the first, and felt that the spiralling costs he had incurred had produced unimpressive returns. The second—which would, of course, have been even more expensive, requiring estates to be set aside for a prospective bride's jointure, and a new household to be staffed and furnished for the happy couple—appealed neither to John, focused as he was on the shortfall in his accounts, nor to his son, whose appreciative eye for the varied delights of the female form was already becoming apparent.

John II was therefore left to cool his heels in Norfolk, away from the beguiling pleasures and intrigues of the court, where he had so recently begun to feel at home. But patience had never been prominent among his virtues, and he left home abruptly in the autumn of 1463 to rejoin the king's household without his parents' knowledge or permission. His father was furious, and this time Margaret, too, was incensed. John already thought her overly indulgent, and John II's impetuous departure merely served to rob her of credibility in her attempts to act as his advocate. "I let you know I was right evil pleased with you," Margaret told her son heatedly on 15 November. "Your father thought, and thinks yet, that I was assented to your departing, and that has caused me to have great heaviness." Most of her letter was taken up—clearly not for the first time—with advice about how to repair his disastrously fractured relationship with his father. John II should write to him "as lowly as you can, beseeching him to be your good father," and sending whatever news he could glean from those close to the king; it was also an absolute necessity to be careful with his money—"that you beware of your expense better than you have been before this time." But she found it difficult to stay angry with her firstborn for long. Above all, she wanted news of John II himself, however much trouble it might end up causing with her husband. "I would you should send me word how you do," she said, "and how you have managed for yourself since you departed hence, by some trusty man, and that your father have no knowledge thereof. I dared not let him know of the last letter that you wrote to me because he was so sore displeased with me at that time."[12]

Despite the gravity of John II's misjudgment in leaving, Margaret had some success in her role as intermediary by the following spring, when John allowed their son to return home, even if under a heavy cloud. On 6 May, Margaret sent her husband a careful report of his behaviour. "As for his demeaning since you departed," she wrote, "in good faith it has been right good and lowly, and diligent in oversight of your servants and other things the which I hope you would have been pleased with if you had been at home." "I beseech you heartily that you vouchsafe to be his good father," she added circumspectly, "for I hope he is chastised and will be the warier hereafter."[13] John II remained in Norfolk over the summer, attempting to prove that he deserved his father's trust by riding with his younger brother to defend the Fastolf estates against the aggression of their rivals. But the pressure on John's possession of the inheritance, and therefore on John himself, increased markedly during the second half of 1464. Quite apart from the threat to the manors themselves, Thomas Howes had now defected to the enemy camp in the dispute over the will; the family's finances were increasingly precarious; and in the autumn, John was outlawed and spent a couple of days in prison as a result.

Perhaps unsurprisingly, given the unpropitious circumstances, the chilly reconciliation between father and son broke down completely under the strain of a family reunion that Christmas. By January 1465, John had banished John II from home and was refusing to have anything more to do with him. Their surviving correspondence gives no clue about what particular episode precipitated the breach, but the friction between them was now so deep-rooted that it need not even have been a major incident. Certainly, there was a familiar litany of complaint—if unfamiliar in its intensity—in John's letters to Margaret in the first two months of the new year. The long, forensically detailed, and violently angry letter he wrote on 15 January was concerned mainly with the inadequacies he perceived in her management of the household in his absence, but the vehemence of his outrage was fuelled by deep frustration with his son. What infuriated him more than anything was John II's failure to subscribe to his own profound sense of duty. For John himself, life was serious, effortful, and laden with responsibility for the security and advancement of his family. "Also, remember you in any household, fellowship or company that will be of good rule," he told Margaret sternly, "purveyance must be had that every person . . . is helping and furthering after his discretion and power, and he that will not do so . . . should be put out of the household or fellowship."

If it was not already abundantly clear of whom he was thinking, the next paragraph put it beyond doubt. Margaret had yet again attempted to intercede on their son's behalf, and this provoked her husband to what was for him—practical, prosaic John—an emotional and finely expressive outburst. Their son's sins, it seemed, were legion. By "his presumptuous and indiscreet demeaning," John II had not only displeased his parents, but set a bad example to the Pastons' servants, and undermined the family's reputation by making it publicly apparent "to all men's understanding that he was weary of biding in my house," despite the distressing fact that he had secured himself no reputable means of support elsewhere: ". . . yet that grieves me not so evil as does that I never could feel nor understand him politic nor diligent in helping himself," John went on, his every word suffused with frustration and fury, "but as a drone among bees which labour for gathering honey in the fields, and the drone does nothing but takes his part of it."14

John's patience was exhausted. So, too, after years of stinging disappointment, was his hope that his son might one day live up to his expectations: ". . . if this might make him to know the better himself, and put him in remembrance what time he has lost, and how he has lived in idleness," he wrote bitterly, ". . . it might fortune for his best. But I hear never yet, from no place that he has been in, of any politic demeaning or occupation of him." His decision was made, and he was unmoved by Margaret's heartfelt pleas for forgiveness: ". . . as for your house and mine," John told her with grim determination, "I purpose not he shall come there, nor by my will none other, unless he can do more than look forth and make a face and countenance."15

They were now going round in circles, Margaret refusing to give up her attempts to reconcile her husband and son, and John reiterating the principles on which he was judging John II and finding him wanting. "Item, as for your son," he wrote coldly on 21 February, ". . . I understand nothing of what disposition he purposes to be, but only I can think he would dwell again in your house and mine, and there eat and drink and sleep." Amid all his other struggles, the idea that his own son was adding to his troubles was too much to bear. "Every poor man that has brought up his children to the age of twelve years waits then to be helped and profited by his children . . . ," he wrote, with an uncharacteristic touch of self-pity. "As for your son, you know well he never stood you nor me in profit, ease or help to the value of one groat." John was determined that, this time, his son should have to prove himself—his character, his intentions, and his reliability—before he would be readmitted to the family: ". . . give him no favour," he told Margaret, "till you feel what he is and will be."16

Less than a fortnight later—undoubtedly at Margaret's prompting—John II wrote to beg his father's forgiveness. "Might it please your fatherhood," he said, in the humblest tone he could muster, "to remember and consider the pain and heaviness that it has been to me . . . here abiding till the time it pleases you to show me grace, and till the time that by report my

demeaning has been to your pleasing." He could not quite conceal the sub-
text that John's demands were impossible to satisfy—how, after all, could
he demonstrate his trustworthiness to his father's exacting standards if he
were excluded from the family and all its activities?—but wisely, or under
maternal pressure, ended on a note of abject supplication. ". . . I beseech
you of your fatherly pity to tender the more this simple writing, as I shall
out of doubt hereafter do what shall please you to the uttermost of my
power and labour."[17]

Despite this appeal, or perhaps because it was all too dispiritingly familiar, John remained implacable. A month later, Margaret sent her husband a
letter full of practical business: developments relating to the duke of
Suffolk's seizure of Drayton, the price of malt, the need for repairs to the
tenants' houses at Mautby. She left the subject of their son until last, but
tackled it in the same direct and businesslike manner. It was an issue they
had discussed many times before, but Margaret was no less stubborn than
her husband, and it was clear in every word that she would not let the matter drop until his answer was the one she wanted. "Item," she began stoutly,
"I understand . . . that you will not that your son be taken into your house
nor helped by you till such time of year as he was put out thereof"—
December, eight months away, which Margaret plainly felt was far too long.
"For God's sake, sir," she went on, "have pity on him, and remember you it
has been a long season since he had anything from you to help him with,
and he has obeyed him to you and will do at all times, and will do what he
can or may to have your good fatherhood. And, at the reverence of God, be
his good father and have a fatherly heart to him."[18]

For all John's determination that his son should be taught his lesson, it
was Margaret who got her way. Perhaps John's anger had blown itself out;
perhaps the indignity of being the subject of local gossip became harder to
bear in the face of the battles they were fighting on so many fronts; perhaps
the need for an extra pair of hands to help fight those battles became more
pressing; perhaps, simply, Margaret's resolve proved impossible to resist
indefinitely. If there were fireworks in the course of the discussions leading
to John II's return home, they have left no surviving trace. Nor was the
prodigal son welcomed back with open arms—or not, at any rate, when his
father was looking. On 3 May, Margaret once again tackled the subject as
one among many items of business, and reassured her husband that she
understood the stringent conditions on which John II was being permitted
to return. "Your son shall come home tomorrow . . . ," she wrote carefully,

"and as he demeans him hereafter I shall let you have knowledge; and I pray you think not in me that I will support him nor favour him in no lewdness, for I will not. As I find him hereafter, so I will let you have knowledge."[19]

John II spent most of the rest of the summer in Norfolk helping to defend the Fastolf estates, first taking charge at Caister and then, in July, at Hellesdon, where he stayed until the duke of Suffolk's men launched their final destructive assault in October. He was at last applying himself conscientiously, as his father wanted, to the family's business, even if John himself— who was in London, and from the beginning of June incarcerated in the Fleet Prison—was not there to see it. The whole household, though, now shared Margaret's ingrained habit of making sure that any successes were relayed in full to his father: ". . . my master Sir John . . . has gotten him as great worship for that day as any gentleman might do, and so it is reported of their party and in all Norwich," Richard Calle wrote after a confrontation with Suffolk's belligerent priest Philip Lipyate in July.[20] Communications between father and son remained formal and distant, but at least the bitterness of the early months of the year did not resurface, even when John II joined John in London after his release from prison at the beginning of 1466.

Four months later, not long after John II's twenty-fourth birthday, his father died. The sudden bereavement was as much of a shock for John II as it was for the rest of the family, but for him it was a liberation as well as a loss. At last he was free from the oppressive weight of his father's negative expectations. This was his chance to prove that John had been wrong—that he could, after all, be trusted to shoulder the responsibility of the family's interests—and to do so on his own terms. Admittedly, the position in which he found himself was, in all too many ways, unenviable: his inheritance included all of the crippling problems that had driven his father into an early grave. On the other hand, John's own misjudgments had helped to create those difficulties in the first place, and the fact that John II was instinctively a more flexible character might now serve him well in tackling them. John II also had one major political advantage over his father: after five years, he had finally succeeded in finding his way into the intricate political networks of Edward IV's household.

The benefits of this privileged access at court became cheeringly apparent almost at once. In July 1466, only two months after John's death, John II appeared before the king to refute the "surmise of great charge"—the allegation that his father was a villein by birth—which had resulted in John's imprisonment. John himself had struggled for six months even to secure his freedom, but John II immediately won a sympathetic hearing for the family's case, arguing that the Pastons were "gentlemen descended lineally of worshipful blood since the Conquest hither," when "their first ancestor Wulstan came out of France." The many documents he produced attested to a lengthy and complex family tree descended from this Norman lord; the leap of faith—or, rather, of fiction—was the assertion that "Sir John Paston was heir to all those, for they died sans issue." But it was a fiction that King Edward was now prepared to accept as "openly proved and affirmed, without contradiction or proof to the contrary."[21] With the dismissal of the charge came formal restitution of the family's property. Royal letters were issued ordering that "our trusty and wellbeloved knight Sir John Paston" should have full possession of his lands, including Caister and the other Fastolf estates, "like as the said John Paston deceased had in any time of his days."[22] This was not a verdict that had implications for the family's battles with Yelverton and Worcester, or the duke of Suffolk and his mother—possession "like as the said John Paston deceased had" was, after all, contested possession—but, whatever else happened, John II was now safe from the imprisonment that had so blighted the last year of his father's life.

But despite this success, John II was still not free from fretful parental advice. Now that there was no longer any need to defend him against his father's relentless criticisms, Margaret found it impossible to contain her own reservations about her eldest son's conduct and judgment. She had no confidence in his common sense over even the most elementary things—the need to keep crucial documents safe and out of unfriendly hands, for instance—and such exhortations were invariably accompanied by an appeal to the example of her dead husband: "Your father . . . in his trouble season set more by his writings and evidence than he did by any of his moveable goods," she admonished her son, as if the idea might not otherwise have occurred to him. Money was short, as ever these days, and she was tired and worried: ". . . at the reverence of God, speed your matters so this term that we may be in rest hereafter," she wrote wearily, ". . . and remember the great cost and charge that we have had hithertoward, and think verily it may not long endure." When John was alive, it had always been clear that Margaret's duty was to support him and represent him wherever he needed her to be, and she had never once baulked at the challenge; but the responsibility of mother to son was less clear-cut, and signs were beginning to emerge that John II could not simply rely on her to be at his beck and call. Her letter ended with a pointed reminder that it was "written at Caister . . . where I would not be at this time but for your sake."[23]

In one important respect, for which Margaret in the course of her strictures made no allowance whatsoever, John II's situation was even worse than his father's had been. John himself had not inherited all of the Paston estates, partly because a substantial proportion of them were in the hands of his mother, Agnes—who was still hale and well in her mid-sixties—and partly as a result of his father's bequests to his younger siblings. Nevertheless, the Paston lands he did receive, together with Margaret's Mautby inheritance, gave him an income of probably two hundred pounds a year, and it was from this annual sum that Margaret and all their children had to be provided for after his death. Margaret's share was clear: she retained possession both of her own valuable Mautby lands and of Gresham, the jointure she had received when she married—estates that together accounted for more than half of John's landed revenue. The problem that John faced on his deathbed, just as Judge William had done before him, was how to distribute the rest of his properties between his heir and his younger children.

Extraordinarily, for a man who had fallen out with his mother over the ambiguities of his father's will and was embroiled in a ferocious dispute over that of his patron, John left no written will of his own, probably because his final illness was so sudden and unexpected. But it seems that he did have time to express his last wishes, and looking at the dilemma now from the other side, John made exactly the same decision as his father: that he was not prepared to risk impoverishing his younger sons, even if it meant leaving his eldest with perilously little. One manor—Swainsthorpe, near Norwich—was to go to John III; other lands, worth a few pounds a year in each case, were earmarked for Edmund, now in his mid-teens, and ten-year-old Walter; while the youngest, seven-year-old William, was to receive an annuity of ten marks from the manor of Sporle. With characteristic generosity—or what his father might in other circumstances have called negligent disregard of his own interests—John II made no protest at these arrangements, despite the fact that, if his mother and grandmother were still alive when his brothers all came of age, his share of the Paston lands would amount to no more than two manors: Sporle, in western Norfolk, from which he would have to pay his brother William's annuity, and

Snailwell, in Cambridgeshire. It was not until seven years later, under financial pressure more intense than any his father had experienced, that John II
was driven in exasperation to point out explicitly to his mother that "my
father, God have his soul, left me scant £40 land in rest, and you leave me as
pleases you, and my grandam at her pleasure. Thus may I have little hope of
the world."[24] If John Paston had chosen to stake his career and reputation
on his claim to the Fastolf inheritance, the fight to secure at least some of
those estates was, for John II, a matter of financial survival.

Margaret was not utterly unwilling to help, but in the midst of reprov-
ing her son for his profligate habits, she seems barely to have noticed that
his income was a mere fraction of the revenues her husband had had at his
disposal. Luckily for John II, however, his mother was not his only lieutenant in Norfolk. He had a more cheerful and much less critical ally in the
person of his younger brother John. Before their father's death, while John
II spent time—with permission and without—in the glittering surroundings
of the royal household, John III had stayed mostly at home in Norfolk, quietly and efficiently becoming indispensable to the family's affairs. At fifteen,
he was acting as his mother's secretary, and by 1461, at the age of seventeen,
he was closely involved in the management of the family's estates in his
father's absence. Such responsibility was perhaps unexceptional in a country ruled by a nineteen-year-old king, but within a family where his older
brother was struggling to find his feet as an adult in the wider world, John
III's competence was striking.

By the following autumn, at eighteen, he was working with Richard
Calle not only to supervise the running of the Paston and Fastolf estates,
but also in the dangerous and politically sensitive task of defending them
against his father's rivals. Calle, an older, more experienced, and extremely
able man, took John III seriously as an ally and—however respectfully,
given the relationship between employer and employee—a friend. He was
not the only one to appreciate John III's abilities. John and Margaret's
approbation is harder to demonstrate directly, but the fact that their letters
barely mention their younger son speaks volumes by contrast with the
heated prose generated by his older brother. As the second son, John III
was of course under less pressure and less scrutiny than his brother, but in
any case it is clear how capable and likeable he was; he shouldered his
responsibilities lightly, rather than taking them lightly as his father believed
John II did.

John III's talents were social as well as practical. In the spring of 1462, he made a great success of entertaining John Wykes, the usher of the king's chamber who had been his brother's first contact at court, on a visit to Norwich. And he made an equally positive impression on the teenage duke of Norfolk. At the beginning of this new reign, the combination of simple chance and the murderous effects of civil war meant that the political stage on which the Paston brothers stood was overwhelmingly populated by young men. Presiding over them all was King Edward, who in 1462, like John II, had just turned twenty. Just a few months younger was the duke of Suffolk, who celebrated his twentieth birthday that September, while the duke of Norfolk turned eighteen in October, six months after John III had reached the same age. Of the other noblemen with great estates in their region, Anthony Woodville, the new Lord Scales, cut a glamorously dashing figure at the age of twenty-two; and the earldom of Oxford had newly passed (albeit under a menacing cloud) into the hands of the twenty-year-old John de Vere, whose father and brother had been arrested and beheaded on a charge of treason at the beginning of the year. If this concentration of youthful blood did nothing to exert a steadying influence on local affairs, it did at least mean that the Paston boys had the chance to find their political feet in a world dominated by young men of exactly their own generation.

At eighteen, three years away from legal adulthood, the duke of Norfolk had not yet taken possession of his inheritance, and his political influence was still therefore limited—but that did not mean his lordship was worthless. Any positive contact at this early stage in Norfolk's career might help to dissuade him from reviving his father's designs on Caister, or perhaps even convince him to champion the Pastons' cause against his rival the duke of Suffolk. In the autumn of 1462, John III was sent by his father to appeal for Norfolk's support against their opponents at the manor of Cotton—a meeting which had little practical effect in terms of the dispute, but produced immediately beneficial results for John III himself. By December, he had entered the young duke's service, and travelled three hundred miles north with him to join a military campaign led by the earl of Warwick—in the temporary absence of the king, who had been sidelined by a dangerous attack of measles—to retrieve the castles of Alnwick, Dunstanburgh, and Bamburgh, imposing fortresses that dominated the windswept northeastern coast, from forces loyal to King Henry.

John III spent another few months with Norfolk in the winter of 1463–1464 at the duke's castle of Holt, in north Wales, a great pentagonal bastion known as Castel Lion after the ferocious stone beast that loomed over its gateway, from where the duke and his men made sorties to suppress pro-Lancastrian disturbances in the west. But the main focus of his activities remained at home, working with his mother and Richard Calle, and (when relations with their father allowed) his brother, to defend the Fastolf estates. It was a campaign in which his relationship with Norfolk added another string to his bow, and he was repeatedly dispatched as an envoy to the duke in 1464 and 1465. For the time being, his visits achieved little, but there was every reason to hope that Norfolk's influence would grow; he came of age only in October 1465—and it was a mark of the favour in which he now held John III that the latter was summoned to attend the formal ceremony by which the duke received possession of his estates.

In May 1466, when John Paston died, a division of labour between his two eldest sons was so natural as to seem inevitable. John II—now, nominally at least, head of the family—spent most of his time in London, at his lodgings in Fleet Street. In the light of his protracted absences, and his lack of either the inclination or the skills needed to do the job well, it made sense that John III should take the lead in managing the family's interests in Norfolk, with the family servants Richard Calle, John Daubeney, and John Pamping answering to his proficient command. On the whole, the system worked. The brothers got on well, with an easy banter, and kept their spirits up more successfully than their beleaguered father had ever managed. Unsurprisingly, however, there were also moments of tension. Always practical and focused on the task in hand, John III tried in March 1467 to secure money for repairs to the fabric of the buildings at Caister. "Sir, etc," he began testily, "it is so that, without you have hasty reparation done at Caister, you are likely to have double cost in haste, for the rain has so moisted the walls in many places that they may not tile the houses till the walls are repaired . . . ; and if it is not done this year many of the walls will lie in the moat before long." His difficulty was that John II controlled the family purse strings, and it was no easy matter to persuade him of the urgency of domestic concerns from which his metropolitan life left him semidetached. "Pamping and I shall clout up your houses as we may with the money that we have till more comes," John III wrote in exasperation, "but you should do better yourself. I pray, read this bill once a day till you have sped these matters written herein."[25]

In response, John II was heroically vague. "Right worshipful and verily wellbeloved brother," he wrote, in an apparent attempt at a soothing tone,

"I heartily commend me to you, thanking you of your labour and diligence that you have in keeping of my place at Caister so surely, both with your heart and mind, to your great business and trouble; and I againward have had so little leisure that I have not sped but few of your errands, nor cannot before this time." Despite his lack of leisure, he devoted the rest of the letter to advising his brother on how best to go about wooing a young gentlewoman named Alice Boleyn, on whom John III had set his sights as a potential bride ("... bear yourself as lowly to the mother as you like, but to the maid not too lowly, nor that you be too glad to speed nor too sorry to fail ...").[26] Another letter arrived in Norfolk soon afterward, this time full of excitement about a tournament at the king's palace of Eltham, a few miles southeast of London, at which John II had received the honour of an invitation to fight. He had hurt his hand in the mêlée, but "I would that you had been there and seen it," he told his brother breathlessly, "for it was the goodliest sight that was seen in England these forty years."[27] All in all, he accorded the difficulties with which John III was dealing no more than a cursory postscript: "I suppose if you call upon R. Calle he shall purvey you money. I have written to him enough."[28] John III could not suppress his irritation: "... whereas it pleases you to wish me at Eltham at the tourney for the good sight that was there," he snapped, "by troth I had rather see you once in Caister Hall than to see as many king's tourneys as might be between Eltham and London." If John II had been cursory, John III was more than prepared to be curt: "... as for R. Calle," he went on, "we cannot get half a quarter the money that we pay for the bare household, beside men's wages. Daube nor I may no more without money."[29]

It was a characteristic exchange. John II, the inexperienced teenager who had been too shy to make his mark in Edward IV's household, had become something of a courtier, an accomplished fighter with a passion for books and an eye for female company—"the best chooser of a gentlewoman that I know," according to a friend in London.[30] He had never had the patience or the commitment to devote himself to the day-to-day mundanities of estate management, and at a distance it was easy for him to forget how draining they could be. His brother, to whom patience and commitment were second nature, was having to shoulder heavy responsibilities for an inheritance that was not his own. Characteristics can all too easily become caricatures, however, and the brothers had more in common than their different circumstances suggested. John III—prudent and practical though he was—was a stylish dresser who cared enormously about his appearance, and often sent to London's more sophisticated shops for finer clothes than were available in Norwich. He took the opportunity of his mother's visit to see his father in the Fleet Prison in the autumn of 1465, for example, to ask her to pick up two pairs of hose for him, one black and one a delicate rose pink; "I beseech you that this gear be not forgot," he reminded her, "for I have not a whole hose to put on."[31] And despite his brother's vaunted expertise with women, it was John III who seems first to have fathered an illegitimate child: ". . . mother, I beseech you that you will be good mistress to my little man," he asked Margaret, with touching concern, during a trip away from home in 1468, "and to see that he goes to school." There are few other mentions of his "little Jack" in the letters— and no clue about the identity of the boy's mother—but enough all the same to suggest that some of his more po-faced asides to his brother ("God keep you this Lent from lollardy of flesh") were written with tongue firmly in cheek.[32]

John III's impatience with his brother was at times heartfelt, but so, always, was his affection. In the end, too, John II was doing more in London than merely gadding about. The Eltham tournament—however irritating from the point of view of his younger brother, trying to hold back the spreading damp at Caister—was far more significant than simply a chance to enjoy himself amid the splendour and excitement of the court. With hard-won experience under his belt, and liberated at last from his father's frowning disapproval, John II was proving that he could be just as charming and relaxed in powerful company as his brother. The fact that he was chosen as one of only three knights to fight at the side of King Edward himself, against a team led by the king's childhood friend and most trusted lieutenant, William, Lord Hastings, demonstrated not only his impressive physical prowess but the political progress he had made—and such marks of royal esteem could only improve his chances of securing influential support in his battle to save the Fastolf inheritance.

It had to be said, however, that there was little reason otherwise to feel cheerful about the progress of the dispute. The probate hearings ground on inexorably in London during the course of 1466, uninterrupted either by the death of John Paston, or by that of Friar John Brackley a little earlier in the year. Whatever his faults, Brackley's loyalty to the Paston cause had been absolute, and he upheld the justice of John's claim to the very end; "I desire you that you will report after my death that I took it upon my soul at my dying that the will that John Paston put in to be proved was Sir John

Fastolf's will," he told his confessor, in characteristically dogmatic style, hours before he died.[33] Nevertheless, twenty more witnesses paraded into the archbishop's court to testify for Yelverton and Worcester in May and June, most of them alleging that the evidence produced to support John's claim was false and, in some cases, procured by bribery. The judges remained unconvinced by most of these depositions, but so much mud had already been thrown by both sides that the facts of the case now appeared more obscure than when the hearings started. Meanwhile, Judge Yelverton's men were extending their campaign of harassment from Fastolf's Suffolk estates to two of his Norfolk manors, Saxthorpe, and Guton Hall in Brandiston, northwest of Norwich. "There dares no poor man displease them," John III told his brother grimly in January 1467, "for whatsoever they do with their swords they make it law."[34]

If the legal deadlock were to be broken in the Pastons' favour, John II would have to exploit all his newfound political contacts to secure more powerful backing for his cause. In 1467 it seemed at last as though he had found the answer to his prayers in the ostentatious person of the earl of Warwick's younger brother, George Neville, archbishop of York, who held office as Lord Chancellor in King Edward's government. Like the rest of his large and formidable family, Archbishop Neville, at thirty-five, was a flamboyant character driven by boundless ambition and the healthiest of egos. At his enthronement as archbishop two years earlier, he had presided over a feast that far outstripped even his cousin Edward's coronation banquet in its magnificent scale and marathon duration. Over the course of five days of elaborate celebration, more than two thousand guests were served with twenty-five thousand pounds of beef, twenty-four thousand pounds of mutton, and fifteen thousand pounds of pork, as well as a thousand capons, two thousand geese, four hundred swans, and one hundred and four peacocks, accompanied by the roasted carcasses of young herons, curlews, cranes, egrets, and bitterns. As the archbishop presided over a top table decked out with shimmering silverware, the endless courses were interspersed with edible "subtleties" including a silver-coated dolphin, a figure of Samson, and an image of St. William holding a suit of armour in his hands. Clearly, the archbishop lacked neither political weight nor the confidence to use it. If he could be persuaded to take up the Pastons' cause, it suddenly did not seem too much to hope that an end to their troubles might be somewhere on the horizon.

There had been indications that Neville was well disposed toward the family even before John Paston's death—in February 1466 he was reported to be the Pastons' "singular good lord"[35]—and John II took great pains to cultivate the fledgling relationship. His uncle William Paston, who had inherited all of Judge William's acumen and was carving out a profitable career for himself in London as a lawyer and administrator, knew Archbishop Neville well, and worked hard in the summer of 1467 to secure his help for his nephew. William arranged, for example, for John II to lend the archbishop the huge sum of 1,000 marks (the equivalent of £666)—Neville's extravagance being such that, in spite of his lavish income, a supply of ready cash on this scale would be cause for grateful archiepiscopal benevolence in return. In view of John II's chronic financial problems, and the difficulty of enforcing repayment from such a powerful man, this cripplingly large loan was clearly a political investment rather than a business deal, but it was one that soon seemed to be producing cheering results. Archbishop Neville declared himself ready to arbitrate in the dispute with Yelverton and Worcester over Fastolf's will, and set about brokering a deal with the dowager duchess of Suffolk by which she and her son would abandon their claim to the sacked manor of Hellesdon in return for a nominal payment of 100 marks (£66).

In just a couple of months, Paston hopes had been raised higher than they had been for years. It was only a few weeks more before they were utterly dashed. At the end of July, it emerged that, unbeknown to the archbishop or to the Pastons themselves, Duchess Alice and Judge Yelverton had been in secret contact, and an agreement had been made that, in their capacity as Fastolf's executors, Yelverton and Worcester would sell Hellesdon to the duchess and her son. The prospect of such an unholy alliance between the Pastons' opponents was profoundly alarming. The duke of Suffolk's claim to Hellesdon would be bolstered by what he would argue was a legitimate purchase from Fastolf's estate, and Yelverton and Worcester would in turn be able to draw on the duke's influence to reinforce their position in the probate case.

John II could at least console himself with the knowledge that Archbishop Neville was not wavering in his support: ". . . my lord wills in any wise that you keep well all the livelihood that you have of Sir John Fastolf," John Daubeney reported confidently. ". . . You may verily think he is your special good lord, and that you shall know in time coming."[36] On the other hand, it was also becoming disconcertingly apparent that the expansive archbishop was too sure of himself, even blasé, for the intricate work of unravelling the tightly wound knot of disputes in which the Pastons were now entangled. He was initially unable to believe that Duchess Alice had double-crossed him over Hellesdon—"I dare swear upon a book that the duchess of Suffolk has no knowledge thereof," he exclaimed—and when presented with incontrovertible evidence, "he marvelled sore of her disposition," Daubeney told John II, but "bade me not care, you should do well enough."[37] That was certainly what John II, with his own marked tendency towards the blasé, wanted to hear; but given the duchess's steely intelligence and vast political experience, it was a far from adequate response.

More worrying even than this were indications that the structure of power within which they were all manoeuvring was itself beginning to suffer major convulsions. By the mid-1460s, King Edward had made giant strides in securing his rule throughout England. Lancastrian resistance in the north had been all but wiped out by the late summer of 1464, and a year later the fugitive ex-king Henry VI was captured in the northwestern county of Lancashire and imprisoned within the forbidding walls of the Tower of London. Queen Margaret had escaped to France with their nine-year-old son in 1463, but in the absence of significant Lancastrian support among the nobility in England, her chances of mounting another challenge to Edward's hold on the throne were slim. One intractable problem, however, remained for the king to face: his relationship with his cousin Richard Neville, earl of Warwick.

Warwick had played a pivotal role in Edward's victory in 1461, and the king had rewarded him accordingly: the earl was now great chamberlain and admiral of England, warden of the Cinque Ports (the country's key harbours for trade and defence on the southeastern coast), warden (together with his brother John Neville) of the Scottish borderlands in the north, and captain of Calais. Edward had already proved himself to be a charismatic leader and a brilliant general, but his powerful cousin was older and more experienced, and in the early years of the reign, the king leaned heavily on the resources at Warwick's disposal and the expertise with which the earl commanded them. But it was now becoming ominously clear that Warwick saw his dominant role in Edward's government as one held as of right rather than royal command. In England "they have but two rulers," one observer reported archly to King Louis XI of France, "Monsieur de Warwick and another, whose name I have forgotten."[38] The earl was arrogant, ambitious, able, and spectacularly wealthy, but—however much he might see himself as the power behind the throne—he was not the king. And if Edward were ever to exercise the untrammelled authority of a legitimate monarch, he could not continue to accommodate his cousin's pretensions.

Signs that all was not well between the two began to appear as early as the spring of 1464, when the twenty-two-year-old king made the astonishing decision to marry in secret, without either consulting or informing his magnates and advisers. Equally extraordinary was his choice of bride. This was no diplomatic union with a foreign princess or an impeccably blue-blooded noblewoman of the highest birth: the king's new wife was Elizabeth Woodville, the sister of Anthony, Lord Scales, a twenty-seven-year-old widow with two young sons whose husband, Sir John Grey, heir to the baronial house of Ferrers of Groby, had been killed fighting in the Lancastrian army against the earl of Warwick's forces at St. Albans in 1461. The motive behind this impetuous and politically inappropriate match was probably entirely personal. Elizabeth was an exquisitely beautiful woman, elegant, spirited, and intelligent, who allegedly refused Edward's advances unless he married her. But when news of the wedding finally emerged into the light of day four months later, it had the added effect of proclaiming all too publicly the king's independence from Warwick, who was left embarrassingly stranded in the midst of negotiating a match for Edward with the French king's sister-in-law.

In public at least, Warwick had no choice but to accept the marriage as a fait accompli, but he could hardly be expected to swallow this slight to his political standing and his amour propre without demur. By 1466, the increasing personal tensions between the two men were developing into a dangerous rift over the direction of foreign policy. Warwick continued to press forcibly for a treaty with France, while Edward became increasingly explicit about his inclination toward an alliance with France's enemy Duke Philip of Burgundy, the ruler not only of the great independent duchy of Burgundy on France's eastern border, but also of the northern European territories of Flanders and the Netherlands. In the summer of 1467, this divergence of opinion between king and earl was laid bare in the pitiless glare of public scrutiny. Warwick left England in state to lead an embassy to France, and in his absence Edward entertained Duke Philip's illegitimate son, Anthony, Bastard of Burgundy, with magnificent ceremony when he visited London to joust with the king's brother-in-law Lord Scales. Scales was rapidly acquiring a reputation as a brilliant exemplar of the chivalric arts, something in which he took after his father Earl Rivers, who had in his day been a champion in the lists. (Indeed, in the Bastard of Burgundy's entourage was a Castilian knight named Pedro Vasquez de Saavedra, with whom Rivers had fought a celebrated bout at Westminster more than twenty-five years earlier.) Over two days at Smithfield, just outside the capital's walls, on a tournament field ninety yards long by eighty yards wide, Scales and his Burgundian opponent fought each other to a standstill, and honours were even when the two champions retired to a dazzling feast given by the king and queen, attended by more than sixty fair ladies of the court.

The glittering welcome accorded to the Bastard of Burgundy was an unambiguous statement of King Edward's intent to direct his own diplomacy, which reduced his cousin of Warwick to the status of an impotent observer from the unhappy vantage point of his own fruitless mission to France. But Edward was no less determined to be master of his own government within England. On 8 June 1467, three days before the lavish tournament was held at Smithfield, Archbishop Neville of York—the earl of Warwick's brother—was abruptly dismissed from the chancellorship, which he had held since the beginning of Edward's reign.

From the Pastons' point of view, the timing of the archbishop's loss of office could not have been more disheartening. His sudden sacking probably explains why the duchess of Suffolk and Judge Yelverton felt at liberty to go behind his back a month later to agree upon the sale of the disputed manor of Hellesdon from under the Pastons' noses. They were not the only ones to see the opportunity presented by the discomfiture of the family's new patron. Word reached Margaret at Norwich in July that Thomas Fastolf of Cowhaugh, Sir John Fastolf's distant relative, was preparing to claim Caister by force. "It is said that he has five score men ready," she told her eldest son anxiously, "and sends daily spies to understand what fellowship keep the place. By whose power or favour or supportation he will do this I know not, but you know well that I have been affrayed there before this time, when I had other comfort than I have now."[39]

Margaret may not have known for certain who was behind Thomas Fastolf's plans, but her mention of previous threats to the castle—together with the fact that Thomas had supported the old duke of Norfolk when he seized Caister briefly in 1461—suggests that the new duke was the prime suspect. This was a disastrous turn of events. Norfolk had represented the Pastons' best prospect of local support against Suffolk and his mother, and

John III's success in securing the personal favour of the young duke had appeared to make that hope realistic. All things being equal, John III's service—and the prospect of bloodying Suffolk's nose—should have disposed Norfolk well toward the Pastons' cause. All things were not equal, however, when properties as valuable as Fastolf's were at stake, especially given the shortcomings of the duke's own financial situation. Two formidable dowager duchesses—his mother, Eleanor Bourchier, and grandmother Catherine Neville—were still alive and in possession (as their jointures) of two-thirds of his lands. Until they died—something of which there seemed no imminent likelihood—Norfolk faced the challenge of maintaining the power and influence of his dukedom with only a third of its revenues. In other circumstances, John Paston II, most of whose estates were in the hands of a powerful mother and grandmother of his own, might have sympathised. As it was, this statement of the duke's threatening intent came as a bitter blow.

Confronted with this renewed danger, Margaret sounded utterly drained. She had faced attack before—long ago at Gresham, and much more recently at Hellesdon—but that had been in partnership with her husband, "when I had other comfort than I have now." Now John was dead, and Margaret, having to make a new life for herself as a widow, was no longer willing to stand in the front line. "And I cannot well guide nor rule soldiers," she told John II emphatically, "and also they set not by a woman as they should set by a man. Therefore I would you should send home your brother or else Daubeney to have a rule and to take in such men as were necessary for the safeguard of the place." She had other business to attend to—estates of her own to run—and she wanted her son to know that he could not simply take her presence for granted. "I have been about my livelihood to set a rule therein as I have written to you," she said, "which is not yet all performed after my desire, and I would not go to Caister till I had done." She was not completely unwilling to help, but she was not prepared to be her son's right hand as she had been her husband's. At the same time, she did not find it easy to let go—nor was she confident that John II could be trusted to deal with the dangers that the family faced. Her letter pulled in two directions at once, resisting the demands being placed on her, but at the same time insisting that her son follow the advice she offered. "I marvel greatly that you send me no word how you do," she rebuked him, "for your enemies begin to wax right bold, and that puts your friends both in great fear and doubt. Therefore purvey that they may have some comfort that they be no more discouraged, for if we lose our friends it shall be hard in this troublous world to get them again."[40] As it turned out, the threat from Thomas Fastolf came to nothing, but there could be no guarantee that the ambitions of the duke of Norfolk would be so easy to shake off.

Nor was that the last of the shocks which the summer of 1467 had in store. On 26 August, nearly eight years after Fastolf's death, the legal battle over the administration of his will at last came to judgment. The long-awaited ruling of the archbishop's court awarded probate jointly to John Paston II and Fastolf's chaplain, Thomas Howes. This was a decision that should straightforwardly have been a victory for the Pastons' cause; after all, it had been John Paston's version of events that named John himself and Howes as Fastolf's sole executors. It was a long time, however, since anything to do with Fastolf's will had been straightforward. More specifically, it was years since the family had been able to rely on Thomas Howes for any kind of support, and John II now had to face the fact that, after all their struggles, this was not victory but at best another move in the game. Only two months earlier, John II had formally accused Yelverton and Worcester of bribing witnesses to testify against the Pastons' version of the will, and Howes had responded by giving a lengthy statement repudiating the allegations. He had asked the witnesses to come forward himself, Howes declared, "for great remorse I have in my soul of the untrue forging and contriving of certain testaments and a last will by naked words in my said Master Fastolf's name after he was deceased."[41] He went on to give a detailed rebuttal of the Pastons' claims—for the first time, not only denying that their key witnesses had been present in Fastolf's chamber when the new will had allegedly been made, but explicitly accusing John Paston of forgery and deception. If John II could now argue that he had the court's sanction to administer what he believed to be Fastolf's last will, then Yelverton and Worcester could—through Thomas Howes—maintain exactly the same thing. There was no disguising the fact that, little by little, the Pastons' hold on the Fastolf lands was becoming more tenuous. They had no option but to keep up their defences as best they could, and watch and wait for a new opportunity to seek powerful help.

The new year brought with it, if not a new opportunity, then at least a fillip for John II and John III in the form of a diversion from their troubles. In the course of the negotiations with the duke of Burgundy that King Edward had pursued, much to the earl of Warwick's fury, in 1467, a marriage was proposed between Edward's twenty-year-old sister Margaret—the girl who had stayed at Fastolf's Southwark town house with her mother and younger brothers almost seven years earlier—and Duke Philip's son Charles, count of Charolais and heir to the duchy of Burgundy. John II, now every inch the worldly courtier, wagered half the price of "an ambling horse" that Warwick's pro-French policy would prevail and the marriage would not take place.[42] He lost the bet, but won a place in the princess's huge entourage when she travelled to Flanders in June 1468 for her sumptuous wedding to Charles, now duke of Burgundy in his own right after his father's sudden death the previous year. Chief among the ladies who attended her was Elizabeth, the young duchess of Norfolk. The duchess seems to have taken a particular liking to John III during the time he spent in her husband's service, and, despite the previous year's tensions over Caister, she invited him to travel with the wedding party in her own retinue.

Both brothers therefore witnessed Princess Margaret's ceremonial entry into the great trading city of Bruges, carried on a litter of crimson silk shot through with gold thread, drawn by six white horses and attended—despite a heavy downpour—by a train of almost two thousand noblemen, knights, and musicians. There, in streets ablaze with riotously coloured flags and flowers, she was greeted by ten elaborately staged pageants depicting celebrated unions from scripture and history, from Adam and Eve to Antony and Cleopatra. She was received into the ducal palace, gleaming with the precious metals woven into its rich tapestries, for more than a week of festivities, with jousting by day and feasting by night. The wedding tournament was named after the golden tree that stood at the entrance to the lists, on which every knight who came forward to break a lance hung his coat of arms. The Bastard of Burgundy, organiser of the entire spectacle, seized the opportunity to extend his chivalric renown by fighting with energetic enthusiasm until he was forced onto the sidelines by a broken leg. Declared "Prince of the Tourney" was Sir Edward Woodville, younger brother of Lord Scales and the new English queen—a dashingly elegant gentleman who would later be cast into a deep depression by the loss of his front teeth at a Spanish siege. John III was dazzled. "And as for the duke's court," he told his mother, "as of lords, ladies and gentlewomen, knights, squires and gentlemen, I heard never of none like to it save King Arthur's court. By my troth, I have no wit nor remembrance to write to you half the worship that is here."[43]

The respite was brief. Only a couple of months after the Paston brothers returned from Flanders, the duke of Norfolk's speculative interest in Caister suddenly took more concrete and much more intimidating form when

Yelverton, Worcester, and Howes agreed to sell the castle and a number of other Fastolf properties to the duke for the bargain price of 500 marks (a little less than £350). Thomas Howes explained their decision by arguing that the Paston claim to the estates was "not just nor true," and that he and Fastolf's other executors needed money "to dispose in charityful deeds to do for his soul."[44] It seems more likely that Yelverton and his allies were seeking to win the dispute by proxy, or at least, after nine exhausting years, to extract themselves from the legal mire and end their own liability. By selling the estates they could indeed secure the means to make some sort of provision for Fastolf's soul, but also pay off their own obligations and reward themselves as they believed the old knight had wanted, while passing on the battle against the Pastons to more powerful men. In fact, it seems that Norfolk's purchase of Caister was one part of a more comprehensive projected sale of Fastolf's lands: the archbishop of Canterbury had his eye on the manor of Guton Hall, while the duchess of Suffolk, to no one's surprise, was circling acquisitively around her husband's birthplace of Cotton. Whatever the arguments over the Paston claim to the inheritance, Caister in the hands of the duke of Norfolk, and the rest of the estates carved up between other great lords, clearly did not satisfy any version of Fastolf's last wishes.

Nine years into the dispute, this was a price that Yelverton at least was prepared to pay, although Thomas Howes seems to have been more anxious about the deal. An anonymous but well-informed correspondent urged John II to arrange for pressure to be brought to bear on Howes, the last to join the anti-Paston alliance, and always potentially its weakest link. If he were "made believe and put in hope of the moon shone in the water and I know not what," John II was told, "that such labour were made that either he should be a pope, or else in despair to be deprived of every ecclesiastical benefice for simony, lechery, perjury and double variable peevishness, and for administering without authority"—if all of this were impressed upon him "half in game and half in earnest, it should make him to depart, for Yelverton and he are half at variance now."[45] However, even if it was true that Howes and Yelverton were on the brink of falling out, the Pastons' opportunity to exploit the differences between the two men was snatched away almost immediately. Howes died on 4 February 1469, too soon to see what would become of the legacy of a master to whom he remained devoted to the very end. All hope of undermining Yelverton's position by regaining his support died with him.[46]

At least Caister itself was still in Paston hands. The duke of Norfolk had paid only five hundred marks, such a small fraction of the estate's real value, because what he was buying was a disputed title, not possession of the property itself. But a duke whose income was a fraction of what it should have been would not lay out what was, after all, a serious amount of money without expecting to realise his investment. Caister's long-suffering tenants soon found themselves harassed by Norfolk's men, and the possibility that he might make some move to seize the castle was sufficiently threatening that in November 1468 John II engaged four professional soldiers to help his brother protect it: ". . . they are proved men and cunning in the war and in feats of arms," he told John III seriously, "and they can well shoot both guns and crossbows, and mend and string them, and devise bulwarks or any things that should be a strength to the place; and they will, as need is, keep watch and ward." He was concerned that the local men on whom his brother could call might be too afraid for the safety of their own property to be reliable beyond question in the face of attack; these men-at-arms would provide leadership and expertise to shore up Caister's defences—albeit that John II's efforts at recruitment had characteristic drawbacks. "They are . . . well advised men," he wrote optimistically, "saving one of them which is bald and called William Penny, which is as good a man as goes on the earth, saving a little he will, as I understand, be a little cupshotten"—in other words, too fond of his drink.[47]

Despite its small size and potential deficiencies, the new garrison provided reassurance in case the worst should happen, and in the meantime acted as a deterrent by making clear to the duke of Norfolk that the castle could only be taken with a degree of force to which the king was unlikely to turn a blind eye. But it also represented a significant new drain on resources, which could not easily be met. In May 1469, only six months after the soldiers had been retained, Richard Calle wrote from Caister to tell John II that money was needed urgently "that men's wages might be paid, for they complain grievously," he said with obvious concern; ". . . there is like to grow right an evil noise of it if it should endure any while." The family's finances were now so precarious that, as Calle trenchantly pointed out, his own job was costing him money; he had spent forty shillings out of his own funds, "and of all this twelvemonth I have not had one penny for my wages."[48] John II and his brother were caught in a vicious circle: without money, they would struggle to protect their tenants from their enemies' demands, but the attempt to squeeze money out of their harassed estates risked alienating or ruining the tenants altogether. "And labour hastily a remedy . . . ," Margaret warned her eldest son, "or else Sir John Fastolf's livelihood, though you enter it peaceably, shall not be worth to you a groat this year without you will undo your tenants."[49]

Exactly what that remedy should be, however, was not at all clear. John II could still count on support from Archbishop Neville, who reacted with fury when he heard of the duke of Norfolk's deal with Yelverton and Worcester. With vociferous support from his brother the earl of Warwick, the archbishop lambasted Norfolk when he encountered the duke at court in October 1468, John II was told; "and . . . my lord of York said, rather than the land should go so, he would come dwell there himself." Norfolk was unprepared for the vehemence of this attack, and responded limply by implying that it was his wife rather than he who was set on the purchase of Caister ("he would speak to my lady his wife and entreat her").[50] But it was difficult to feel confident that the archbishop's outrage would produce tangible results for the Pastons' cause, since the Nevilles' fiery relationship with the king had deteriorated still further since the tensions of the previous year. Edward was hoping that Warwick could gradually be brought to accept honourable participation in his government rather than the controlling share the earl wanted. To that end, the king had not turned a completely cold shoulder to his cousin, but had been careful to offer him continuing marks of trust and favour. But Edward's determination to rule independently of Warwick's influence was unmistakable. The earl was no longer the irresistible force he had once been, and as a result, there was more room for manoeuvre in the power structures around the king than had been the case for years.

A volatile new element had also been introduced into the dynamics of Edward's regime by his unexpected marriage to Elizabeth Woodville four years earlier. Leading members of the nobility scrambled to ally themselves with the new queen's many relatives, a process in which the king's need to provide for his wife's two sons, five brothers, and seven sisters coincided with his magnates' concern to position themselves advantageously at the reconfigured court. The rapid series of betrothals included, in 1465, a startling match between Catherine Neville, dowager duchess of Norfolk, the young duke's grandmother, who was in her late sixties and had already survived three husbands, and the queen's brother Sir John Woodville, who was only just out of his teens. This ill-assorted wedding—which shocked contemporaries, with one chronicler dubbing it a "diabolical marriage"[51]—can have done nothing to endear the queen's large brood to the redoubtable old lady's nephew, the earl of Warwick. A gentleman of such modest standing as John Paston II could not, of course, hope to compete in this stampede for the members of the queen's immediate family, but it was with some political savvy that he realised that a more distant Woodville connection might not be beyond his reach. He had never before shown any inclination to find himself a wife, but at the beginning of 1469 he sought the hand in marriage of one of the queen's cousins, a gentlewoman named Anne Haute. By the end of February he was engaged.

The benefits of his strategy were instantly apparent. The king and queen for the first time showed a benevolent interest in the Pastons' troubles. News reached John II via one of Anne Haute's brothers that King Edward had sent a letter to the duke of Norfolk ordering him to put "all manner of matters" into abeyance until the king "shall take a direction therein." Queen Elizabeth, meanwhile—well aware that there were powerful female influences behind the young dukes of Norfolk and Suffolk—wrote to Norfolk's wife and Suffolk's mother, requiring them to exert a restraining feminine hand on the conduct of their husband and son, "so that no default be found in them."[52] The dowager duchess of Suffolk, one of the canniest political operators even on this tempestuous political scene, indicated immediately that she was prepared to soften her previously aggressive stance to one of gracious friendship—"it is told me that my lady of Suffolk has promised you her goodwill if your bargain of the marriage holds," Margaret reported, with cautious approbation, in March—before retreating to her home at Ewelme in Oxfordshire "that she might be far and out of the way, and the rather feign excuse because of age or sickness, if the king would send for her for your matters."[53]

There was reason to hope that these expressions of royal concern might at least curb the two dukes' ambitions in relation to the Fastolf estates, but John II also secured more explicitly partisan support from the queen's brother, Lord Scales. Despite the fact that Scales's only previous intervention in the family's affairs had been predatory—he seems to have been involved in pressing the charge of villeinage against John Paston in the last year of his life—he responded to his cousin's engagement by offering John II his protection. This was not simply a matter of charity on Scales's part: his marriage to the Scales heiress had brought him estates in western Norfolk along with his title, and he saw in the Pastons' predicament an appealing opportunity to exhibit his own influence in the region at the duke of Norfolk's expense. It was with some relish, therefore, that Scales wrote to one of Norfolk's counsellors in April, requiring—with a hint of steel behind the genial tone—that, "forasmuch as marriage is fully concluded between the said Sir John Paston and one of my nearest kinswomen," and that "nature must compel me the rather to show my goodwill, assistance and favour to the said Sir John in such things as concern his inheritance," the duke should end his harassment of the tenants at Caister until a settlement could be found "to the saving of the right title of the said Sir John Paston."[54]

Margaret, who was scarcely able to believe that help was at last in sight, could not stop herself from telling her son that Scales's support was more than he merited. "You are beholden to my lord of his good report of you in this country," she scolded, "for he reported better of you than I think you deserve." She was pleased about John II's engagement—"I pray God send you joy and worship together"—although she was also, as ever, worried, partly about whether he would commit himself to the costs of married life before he was sure enough of his lands, and partly about whether he was temperamentally ready for the commitment: ". . . before God," she reminded him, "you are as greatly bound to her as if you were married; and therefore I charge you upon my blessing that you be as true to her as if she were married unto you in all degrees."[55]

John III, on the other hand, sounded distinctly amused at the prospect: "I pray you send me word whether you shall be made a Christian man before you come home or not." He was under a great deal of pressure at Caister, both because money was so short and as a result of Norfolk's aggression, but he still managed flashes of his usual resilient humour: ". . . whoever sends you word that I have spent any money since you went hence," he told his brother cheerfully, "they must give you another reckoning, saving in meat and drink, for I eat like a horse on purpose to eat you out at the doors; but that needs not, for you come not within them, wherefore, so God help me, the fellowship here think that you have forgotten us all." But strain and frustration were beginning to show through the familiar banter. He knew the duke and duchess of Norfolk better than anyone in the family, and was convinced that John II was mishandling the situation, taking the risk of causing grave offence by enlisting Scales's high-handed support without first petitioning the duke and duchess directly: ". . . by God that redeemed me, the best earl in England would not deal so with my lord and my lady as you do . . . ," he wrote in exasperation; "so God help me, whosoever advises you to do so, he is not your friend." Still, if he was miserable, he would not let it show in public. He asked his brother to send him a stiffened hat and a soft bonnet from London—the messenger, by John III's specific instruction, was to wear the hat rather than carry it, lest it be squashed out of shape in transit. "I have need of both," he said in mock despair, "for I may not ride nor go out at the doors with none that I have, they are so lewd; a mulberry bonnet, and a black or a tawny hat." It took two months, but John II got them for him—"To begin, God yield you for my hats," John III wrote in June.[56]

It was fortunate that the fashionable new hats arrived when they did, since John III was required to make a good showing when King Edward paid a royal visit to Norfolk that same month, on his way to deal with an outbreak of disorder in the northern county of Yorkshire. After several years during which Edward had succeeded in bringing much-needed stability to his realm, the political world was again becoming more uncertain. The unsettling effects of the growing tension between the king and the earl of Warwick were compounded in 1468 by an attempted Lancastrian invasion of Wales, led by Henry VI's loyal half-brother Jasper Tudor, with assistance from King Louis XI of France, who had been deeply alarmed by the alliance between his traditional enemies England and Burgundy, and was now eager to destabilise the Yorkist regime before Edward had a chance to muster any more active threat to French interests. Tudor's small force was repelled before it could do any serious damage, but the threat which further French support for the Lancastrian cause might pose was underlined by fresh fears of pro-Lancastrian conspiracies within England. One of those who came under suspicion of treason was the earl of Oxford, Warwick's brother-in-law, who was arrested in November 1468 and imprisoned in the Tower. His father and brother had been executed as traitors in the first year of Edward's reign, but Oxford managed to avoid following them to the scaffold, even if it was at the cost of sending others to their deaths; "he has confessed much things," it was reported in December, and he was pardoned and released early in 1469.[57]

Meanwhile, for the first time there were serious rumblings of popular discontent with Edward's government, largely because he had demanded a heavy grant of taxation from his subjects to pay for an invasion of France which then failed to materialise once the money lay safely in the royal coffers. In April 1469, risings erupted in the northern counties of Yorkshire and Lancashire, led by men calling themselves Robin of Redesdale and Robin of Holderness, both pseudonyms evoking popular legends of the folk hero Robin Hood. The rebellions were suppressed easily enough, but by the beginning of June, news reached the capital that the Redesdale rising was beginning to reanimate itself. This time, King Edward intended to deal personally with what he saw as no more than a little local difficulty, but decided on his leisurely way north to make pilgrimages to the great shrine of St. Edmund, a venerated Saxon king of East Anglia murdered by the Vikings, at Bury St. Edmunds in Suffolk, and to the holy site of Walsingham in north Norfolk, stopping at Norwich en route.

John II hoped to travel from London in the king's entourage, even though it would mean somehow finding the money to deck out twenty servants in brand new livery. He proposed that Margaret should take temporary charge of the garrison at Caister during the royal visit, "as there shall be no doubt for the keeping of the place while the king is in that country," leaving his brother, he thought, optimistically as ever, with the possibility of rejoining the duke of Norfolk's household: ". . . whether you will offer yourself to wait upon my lord of Norfolk or not, I would you did what best were to do," he suggested.[58] In the event, the idea that John III could move seamlessly from defending Caister against the duke to serving in his retinue proved a bridge too far, and he was not offered Norfolk's blue-and-tawny livery for the royal visit. But a substantial Woodville contingent accompanied the king to Norwich, and in the absence of John II, delayed yet again by legal business in London, John III busied himself in discussion with the family's new patrons about how best to take advantage of the king's presence in Norfolk to press the Paston case.

Lord Scales and his brother Sir John Woodville—the young husband of the elderly duchess of Norfolk—whom John III entertained to lunch with a number of other gentlemen from the royal household, were particularly reassuring. "And when I prayed them at any time to show their favour to your matter," he reported back to John II, "they answered that it was their matter as well as yours, considering the alliance between you," and "bade me that I should cast no doubts but that you should have your intent." But concrete action proved harder to come by than comforting words. Scales's father, Earl Rivers, promised to ask the king to speak to the dukes of Norfolk and Suffolk on the Pastons' behalf, but John III could not be sure whether he had done so before his departure, and when he checked with Scales himself, the response he received was worthy of Archbishop Neville in its airiness: "he gave me this answer, that, whether he had spoken to the king or not, that the matter should do well enough."[59]

From King Edward himself there were conflicting signals. William Brandon, one of the most hot-headed gentlemen in the duke of Norfolk's household and no friend to the Pastons, found an opportunity to ask the king to favour the duke in his claim to Caister, but the king took the request very badly. "Brandon," he said coldly, "though thou can beguile the duke of Norfolk, and bring him about the thumb as thou like, I let thee know thou shall not do me so, for I understand thy false dealing well enough." If this was cheering news, John III was quick to warn his brother against any complacency. An acquaintance in the king's household had promised to draw Edward's attention to the ruined lodge at Hellesdon when the royal party rode past the sacked manor on the road out of Norwich toward Walsingham, but the sight of their damaged property did not have the effect for which the Pastons were hoping: ". . . my uncle William says that the king told him . . . that he supposed as well that it might fall down by itself as he plucked down," John III reported unhappily. And when William persisted, telling Edward that his nephew hoped to have royal help in negotiating a settlement with the two dukes, "the king answered him that he would neither treat nor speak for you but for to let the law proceed."[60]

It was a disingenuous response. The Pastons' difficulty was yet again one of timing: in 1469, as had been the case in 1461, when John II sought the king's help on his first tentative visit to court, Edward was under severe pressure. Until the earl of Warwick had been conclusively brought to heel, the threat of a Lancastrian resurgence averted, and the unrest in the country stamped out, the king would not risk alienating magnates as powerful as the dukes of Norfolk and Suffolk, even had the justice of the Pastons' case been clear beyond doubt, which of course it was not. In these circumstances, the command to "let the law proceed" allowed Edward to opt out of engaging with the politics of the dispute and the niceties (or otherwise) of his lords' behaviour. He would not condone the duke of Norfolk's actions, but neither would he slap him down, which in practice meant that the duke could continue to make the Pastons' lives extremely difficult at Caister, just as the duke of Suffolk had already done at Hellesdon. Despite the Woodvilles' fine speeches, John III was concerned: ". . . labour your matters effectually, for by my troth it is need," he told his brother fretfully, "for, for all their words of pleasure, I cannot understand what their labour in this country has done good."[61]

The great opportunity of the king's visit to Norfolk had come and gone, and the brothers had little to show for it, other than that John III had made his customarily good impression, personal and political, on those he had met. Lord Scales had spoken to him about the possibility of entering the king's service for the coming campaign to suppress the northern rising, but as ever, John III put his family responsibilities first. "I made no promise so to be," he told John II, "for I told him that I was not worth a groat without you, and therefore I would make no promise to nobody till they had your goodwill first; and so we departed." He was unwilling to leave his post at Caister, but also aware that apparent signs of favour might not always be what they seemed; he had heard a rumour that royal letters had been issued summoning his brother to attend on the king, but "if it be so," he reported uneasily, "I think verily it is done to have you from London by craft, that you shall not labour your matters to a conclusion this term but put them in delay."[62]

John III could not have known it, but the disruption of being away from London turned out to be the least of the Pastons'—or the country's—problems stemming from the king's meandering journey to the north. All still seemed well when Edward left Walsingham to make his unhurried way northwest to Lincolnshire, and then spent a week with Queen Elizabeth, who had recently given birth to their third daughter, at Fotheringhay, an imposing twelfth-century castle in Northamptonshire. From there he moved on to Newark, in the midland county of Nottinghamshire. There, at the beginning of the second week in July, he received devastating news. The second wave of the Redesdale rising was no local disturbance: it was a full-scale revolt fomented and orchestrated by the earl of Warwick. Edward had hoped that his cousin would come to accept that he could no longer dictate royal policy, and was prepared to allow Warwick an influential—if no longer dominant—role within his government if he did so. The inescapable and horrifying conclusion in July 1469 was that his strategy had utterly failed. In the end, it seemed, Warwick could not tolerate his royal protégé's determination to rule for himself. The northern rebels were no peasant rabble but a well-equipped and well-organised force bigger than Edward's own. Rather than press on to meet them, the king retreated to the city of Nottingham to await reinforcements.

Warwick himself had spent most of June on the south coast, in Kent, ostensibly supervising the refitting of one of his ships. His brother, Archbishop Neville of York, joined him there. So, too, did King Edward's twenty-year-old brother, George, duke of Clarence—who, until such time as Queen Elizabeth should produce a son, was also the next male heir to

252 / BLOOD AND ROSES

Edward's throne. Two years earlier, Warwick had planned that Clarence should marry Isabel, the elder of his two daughters. The earl had no son of his own; all Warwick's dynastic ambitions therefore rested on his daughters' slender shoulders, and—with so many noble heirs snapped up by the swarm of Woodville brides—he was convinced that the king's brothers were the only fitting husbands for his girls. Clarence, meanwhile, was understandably attracted by a match with one of the wealthiest heiresses in the country. But Edward was seeking to restrain Warwick's aspirations rather than encourage them with a royal marriage, and he refused permission for the wedding to take place. Unfortunately for the king, Clarence—who was vain, ambitious, and profoundly immature—took the refusal as badly as his prospective father-in-law, to such an extent that he was now, astonishingly, prepared to join Warwick in rebellion against his own brother. On 6 July, Warwick, Clarence, and Archbishop Neville sailed to Calais where, less than a week later, in open defiance of the king's command, Clarence married Isabel Neville. Also present at the ceremony was the Nevilles' brother-in-law, the young earl of Oxford, whom Edward had released from the Tower only months earlier.

By the middle of July, Warwick and his allies arrived back in England. They sent ahead a manifesto claiming they wanted only to remedy the ills of Edward's government by freeing the king from "the deceivable covetous rule and guiding of certain seditious persons"—in other words, those, including the Woodvilles, who Warwick believed had supplanted his rightful role in government.[63] Edward—still hoping against hope to avert the crisis, or at least to buy himself some precious time—had written on 9 July in temperate terms to Warwick, Clarence, and the archbishop, requesting that they should come to him "as soon as you goodly may." "We trust not," he told Warwick in conciliatory tones, "that you should be of any such disposition towards us as the rumour here runs, considering the trust and affection we bear in you. . . . And cousin," he added as an afterthought, "think not but you shall be to us welcome."[64] But the damage was far too deep to be repaired by warm words. Warwick ignored Edward's summons, and—extraordinary as it was that the two great architects of the Yorkist regime, these cousins who had once been so close, should come to blows—armed confrontation now seemed inevitable.

With his recent patron Archbishop Neville on one side, and his new lords the Woodvilles on the other, John Paston II was caught, agonisingly, in no man's land. The archbishop's brother-in-law Oxford, with whom John

II had had friendly dealings over the past couple of years, wrote on 18 July to ask him to procure some horse armour—a letter that the earl addressed to "my especial true-hearted friend," adding, "I trust to God we shall do right well."[65] But, if Oxford confidently expected John II's support, so, too, did King Edward. A few days later, John II received a royal summons to join the king's forces at the town of Doncaster in Yorkshire on 3 August, "with as many men defensible in array as you can bring to us," to resist "the malice of our enemies, traitors and rebels."[66]

Edward himself never arrived at Doncaster. On 26 July, at Edgecote, in the midland county of Northamptonshire, a division of his army on its way to his muster was defeated by the earl of Warwick's northern supporters. Three days later, the king—who had not yet received news of the battle—set out from Nottingham to join reinforcements that no longer existed. Edward was captured on the road, seized by his own subjects in the heart of his own kingdom, and taken under armed guard to his cousin's formidable castle at Warwick. The king had already sent away for their own safety those members of the Woodville family who had attended him in Norfolk: Lord Scales escaped, but his father, Earl Rivers, and his young brother, Sir John Woodville, were caught and beheaded—the latter leaving his elderly bride, the dowager duchess of Norfolk, a widow for the fourth time. With King Edward a prisoner, the normal rules of government were effectively suspended. If the Pastons had any doubts about what this chaos would mean for them, those doubts were quickly dispelled. On 21 August, the duke of Norfolk dispatched an army to lay siege to Caister Castle.

John Paston II, the gawky teenager turned cultured courtier, had come a long way since his father's death, but he had arrived precisely nowhere—or worse than nowhere: the fabric of politics had been ripped to tattered shreds for the second time in a decade, and this time his family could not choose to lie low until the fighting was over. This time, the battle had come to them.

till better peace be

THE PASTONS' IMPROVISED GARRISON at Caister, under the unwavering command of John III, numbered about thirty men. Their makeshift troops included the ever-loyal John Daubeney and John Pamping, as well as Margaret's cousin Osbert Berney, the illegitimate son of her maternal uncle, who had served the family for years. The rest of the castle's defenders ranged in experience and expertise from the four professional soldiers hired by John II eight months earlier, to the indomitable figure of Thomas Stumps, so called because he had no hands, who nevertheless doughtily insisted he could shoot a crossbow. Between them, they had twenty guns of various sizes, and had taken their training so seriously over the summer that they had broken three steel bows practising their shots. The castle—complete with its moat, tower, and crenellations—was designed to be defensible, and they had hoped that their resolute presence would convince the duke of Norfolk that he could not take it without breaching the peace spectacularly enough for King Edward's fury to be unavoidable. By August 1469, however, the peace had been shattered by the earl of Warwick's rebellion, and the king was no longer in a position to object to anything Norfolk cared to do. As a result, the thirty men of the Caister garrison found themselves staring bleakly over the battlements at an army hundreds strong, with field artillery deployed in three positions around the castle walls.

If it seemed unlikely that the duke would risk wholesale damage to a house he wanted for himself, that did not mean the siege was a sham. The feast of St. Bartholomew, which fell three days after the army first encamped itself at Caister, "was a cruel day," William Worcester recorded in one of his notebooks, "with guns fired at the castle."[1] Rather than an all-out assault, the plan seemed to be to prevent food and ammunition from reaching John III and his men, and in the meantime to intensify the physical and psychological pressure on them as much as possible by making it inescapably clear that their lives would be at risk for as long as they refused to surrender the castle into Norfolk's waiting hands. John III, meanwhile, was determined to hold out until his brother could muster help. What form that help might take, however, was far from obvious.

The difficulty was that the circumstances which had allowed the duke to embark on this campaign of domestic warfare in the first place—the disintegration of political order at the highest level—also made responding to his attack deeply problematic. Control of government now lay in the implacably ambitious grip of the earl of Warwick, who was attempting to stave off the spectre of anarchy that had been unleashed by his own ruthless self-aggrandisement. To that end, he sought to rule in the name of his cousin Edward—now chafing under lock and key at Warwick's northern fortress of Middleham, in Yorkshire—by taking charge of the royal council with the support of a motley coalition of noble allies: his flamboyant brother Archbishop Neville; his narcissistic new son-in-law George, duke of Clarence; and his brother-in-law the earl of Oxford, whose loyalty to the king who had been responsible for the execution of his father and brother had, perhaps unsurprisingly, proved ephemeral.

Warwick, Oxford, and the archbishop had been sympathetic to the Pastons' cause in the recent past, but their new eminence did not straightforwardly bode well for the family's interests. In his determination to regain what he believed to be his rightful place at the heart of government, Warwick had overlooked the fact that trying to govern in King Edward's name, when Edward was all too obviously neither incapable of ruling for himself nor content to be sidelined in this way, left Warwick himself bereft of authority. The council of lords was just that—a council of lords—rather than an anointed sovereign, and their ability to command the acquiescence of the duke of Norfolk, their peer rather than their subject, was therefore extremely limited.

The prospect of negotiating a resolution to the siege was difficult even in the practical terms of how talks should be conducted, let alone the thorny matter of their substance. The duke of Norfolk's men would allow no messages to pass in or out of Caister's walls. John II, frantically searching for support in London, was therefore attempting to negotiate without any clear sense of exactly how long his brother might be able to hold out, while John III was trying to hold out without any clear sense of the progress of negotiations. Margaret, staying at her mother-in-law Agnes's house in Norwich, was stuck in the middle—closer to the military action at Caister, about which she was desperately worried, but farther away from the political manoeuvres in which her eldest son was engaged. Predictably enough, she had little confidence either that he understood the gravity of the situation, or that he would respond with sufficient urgency or judgment.

Ten days after the siege began, the duke of Norfolk—who was directing operations in the field at Caister from more comfortable lodgings a couple of miles away, at the port of Yarmouth—sent an envoy to Margaret at Norwich with an offer for John II: if he would allow the duke to take possession of Caister peacefully, Norfolk would agree to pay compensation for all wrongs done to the Pastons if the law courts subsequently found in the family's favour. This was so bad a deal as to be no deal at all. If possession was nine-tenths of the law—and more than nine-tenths, if the person in possession were a duke at a time when there was no higher authority in the land to overrule him—then this would be not compromise but capitulation. Margaret had an alternative proposal, suggested, she told John II, by "a faithful friend of ours": that a neutral party should hold the castle and take the profits until the title to the estate could be determined in the courts. Margaret thought this a good idea—or, at the very least, preferable to the current situation: "they must needs have hasty succour that are in the place," she urged her son in evident disquiet, "for they are sore hurt and have no help. . . . Therefore take it in your mind and purvey therefor in haste." Her tendency since her husband's death to think the worst of John II's good sense, or lack of it, was compounded by the fact that he was such a bad correspondent. A Paston servant had just returned to Norwich from London, dusty and stiff from three days in the saddle, but yet again bearing no letter or message from John II—"which grieves me right ill," Margaret told her son sharply, "that I have sent you so many messengers and have so feeble answer again."[2]

John II was a bad correspondent, it was true—but in this instance he could perhaps be excused for feeling that writing to his mother was not his first priority. By the beginning of September—having resuscitated the contacts with Archbishop Neville that had lapsed in recent months in favour of his new Woodville connections—John II had secured some assistance from the lords of the council in the person of Walter Writtle, a gentleman in the service of the duke of Clarence. Writtle was dispatched from London to Caister, armed with the authority of the council, such as it was, to broker an end to the siege. Whatever Margaret believed, John II's letters to Writtle make clear how intensely anxious he was, and how deeply he was torn between, on the one hand, the need to ensure that his brother and his men were safe, and on the other, the fear—after everything his family had been through—of losing Caister completely. Always, incorrigibly, the optimist, he was hoping that the intervention of the royal council might persuade the duke of Norfolk to withdraw, and in the meantime urged Writtle not to cut a deal on the duke's terms if John III could continue to hold the castle against him. "Wherefore, Master Writtle, all our welfare rests in you, beseeching you to remember it," he begged, "for this matter is to all of us either making or marring."[3]

The proposal which Writtle took with him to Yarmouth was that the duke should lift the siege while the dispute was adjudicated by the lords of the council. Several days passed without news, which John II, with more than a little wishful thinking, took to be a good sign that negotiations were progressing well. He was wrong. When a message finally arrived, it was to say that the duke thanked the lords for their gracious offer, but preferred not to accept it. Instead, he was pugnaciously insisting that Caister should be handed over to him until the question of title was determined by law. As John II pointed out in utter frustration, this was exactly the deal that the duke had proposed to Margaret at the end of August, and Norfolk and his advisers had therefore moved not an inch in response to the council's intervention. The impotence of Warwick's regime—attempting to act on the royal authority of a king whom the earl himself was holding captive—could not have been more clearly demonstrated.

Writtle's advice, nevertheless, was that the duke's proposal should be accepted, as much as anything to rescue John III and his men, who were beginning to run low on even basic foodstuffs—bread and ale, salt fish, and vegetables to make a rudimentary pottage—as well as shot for their guns and bolts for their crossbows. They had always known they might have to withstand the brute aggression of a direct assault, but a long-drawn-out siege was a test of a quite different nature: a searching examination of their capacity to endure creeping hunger, fear, tension, and exhaustion. John

II—under another kind of pressure in London, and unable because of the siege to communicate directly with his brother—was incredulous that it could yet be a question of safeguarding their lives, "marvelling sore," he said in disbelief, that their supplies could be failing "in this short season, or in four times the season hithertoward."[4]

Writtle had achieved nothing, but felt that he could do no more, protesting weakly that he dared not exceed the authority he had been given. John II, with as much respect as he could muster given his shock and disappointment, told Writtle he protested too much: "You write in your letter that you dare not pass your credence. Please you to remember, your credence before the lords was right large, and as large as might well be in this matter." The problem was that, however great the goodwill of Archbishop Neville and his allies, their attention was consumed elsewhere, in their over-ambitious attempt to govern in the name of a king whom they had imprisoned. They had instigated the breakdown in royal authority that had allowed the duke of Norfolk to put an army into the field at Caister; and the compromised nature of their regime now meant that they lacked the power to compel his cooperation. As a result, Writtle's failure left John II chasing his own tail. Nothing, he said, should take precedence over the safety of his brother and the castle garrison, if it really was the case that they were on the brink of starvation—"which should be half impossible in my mind that they should misuse so much stuff in four times the space," he repeated, seeking reassurance as much as venting irritation. But he could not bring himself to accept that the loss of Caister might now be inevitable: "I would not that my brother and servants should give up the place, not for £1,000, if they might in any wise keep it and save their lives."[5]

If John II was sure that the situation could not yet be so grave, he was about to be disabused of that certainty. On Tuesday, 12 September, Margaret wrote to her son in London to say that a messenger had reached Norwich with appalling news. The destructive force of land disputes, however brutal or vicious, was usually unleashed on property rather than people. If an unlucky individual did take the brunt of an aggressor's violence, the loss was generally borne by a household of much lower status than the Pastons'; poor men could not afford costly weapons and armour to minimise their chances of injury in a fight, and poor men's families lacked the money and influence to insist that those responsible for the death of a husband or brother should face the full penalties of the king's law. But in September 1469, the king was a prisoner and the Caister dispute now a full-blown siege, beyond all normal parameters of convention or expectation. There had been an exchange of fire at the castle, and two men lay dead, Margaret was told, both of them gentlemen's sons and both among the Pastons' most trusted retainers: John Daubeney, younger son of a north Norfolk landowner, who had given the family a decade of faithful service; and Osbert Berney, born out of wedlock but Margaret's cousin nonetheless. Others lay hurt; the garrison lacked food, gunpowder, and arrows; and the walls of the castle itself were "sore broken with guns of the other part."[6]

Margaret was at the end of her tether. The situation at Caister was parlous, and the loss of two such loyal friends as Daubeney and Berney utterly devastating. Her usual manner of writing to John II was weary and critical, but this was different: she was sick with worry, and desperate that he should do something—anything—to rescue the men at Caister from the duke of Norfolk's guns. Without help, she told her son frantically, "they are likely to lose both their lives and the place, to the greatest rebuke to you that ever came to any gentleman, for every man in this country marvels greatly that you suffer them to be so long in so great jeopardy without help or other remedy." Writtle, she was convinced, had done more harm than good— "the duke has been more fervently set thereupon, and more cruel, since Writtle, my lord of Clarence's man, was there than he was before"—and Norfolk had summoned more men and more ordnance to the castle for a "great assault" planned for the following Thursday morning. Margaret's advice was to accept Norfolk's terms—to let him have Caister until the law should determine title—but she was even afraid that this arrangement would not now be acceptable to the duke, given that it had already been refused twice. If there were any sign that the duke might indeed seize the castle without binding himself to a future legal judgment, Margaret counselled her son, then the duke of Clarence or Archbishop Neville should dispatch the earl of Oxford to rescue the Caister garrison, even if it meant in return giving the castle itself to Oxford for his lifetime. She barely had time for reproaches in her urgency: "Spare not this to be done in haste if you will have their lives and be set by"—that is, respected—"in Norfolk," she said bluntly, "though you should lose the best manor of all for the rescue. I had rather you lost the livelihood than their lives."[7]

For John II, pacing the floor of his London lodgings as he read Margaret's letter, this was the last straw. His customary mode with his mother was deferential and placating—the product of a lifetime's practice of fending off parental criticism. This time, though, he was angry. Margaret was neither at Caister with his brother, nor in London with him in the attempt to find a solution; she was misinformed and she was panicking, and he was having to find time amid everything else to write to tell her so. For once, the reply he sent on Friday, 15 September, observed none of the niceties of formal and respectful greeting. "Mother," he began curtly, "upon Saturday last, Daubeney and Berney were alive and merry, and I suppose there came no man out of the place to you since that time that could have ascertained to you of their deaths." Not only were Daubeney and Berney still alive, he believed, but hostilities were temporarily stopped, rather than spiralling out of control. Writtle had secured a truce, he told her firmly, which would hold for more than a week, "by which time I hope a good direction shall be had." And there were other flaws in her proposals. It was all very well instructing him to seek the intervention of Clarence and the archbishop, he said defiantly, but "they are not here; and if they wrote to him, as they have done two times, I think it would not avail."[8]

John II had been told since his teens that he was irresponsible and lazy, and now—when he was doing his utmost both to protect the family's interests and to rescue his brother and his men from mortal danger—he had had enough: "But, mother, I feel by your writing that you deem I should not do my duty unless you wrote to me some heavy tidings; and, mother, if I had need to be quickened with a letter in this need, I were myself too slow a fellow. . . . I take God to witness that I have done my duty as I would be done for in like case, and shall do till there be an end of it." He had answered back to his mother for the first and only time in his life. Once he had let off steam, his good nature and his optimism, irrepressible even under these bleak circumstances, began to reassert themselves. He could see, after all, that anxiety and fear lay behind Margaret's criticisms, and he did what he could to reassure her. "And with God's grace it shall be remedied well enough," he wrote; "for by my troth I had rather lose the manor of Caister than the simplest man's life therein, if that may be his salvation."[9]

— But, whatever he did, the awful truth was that he was not in a position to guarantee his men's safety. The news of the casualties at the castle, when it was finally confirmed, was better than Margaret had feared but far worse than John II had hoped: Osbert Berney was safe, but John Daubeney— loyal "Daube," who had given devoted service to the Pastons for the best part of ten years—had been killed by a crossbow bolt, probably on Saturday, 9 September. In response, the Caister garrison was returning fire: two men among the duke of Norfolk's forces had already been killed by gunshots from the castle. John II wrote to his brother on Monday, 18 September, hoping that the letter would somehow get through and that his words of comfort would be believed. The duke of Norfolk's men had been publicly shamed by what they had done, he said in what he hoped were stalwart tones, "and I promise you that the duke's counsel would that they had never begun it." John III and his band of brothers-in-arms, meanwhile, had done nothing but demonstrate their valour: "there is neither you nor none with you but, if he knew what is generally reported of him, he or you—and God fortune you well—may think him four times better in reputation of all folk than ever he was." And John III should be assured that tireless efforts were being made to secure the intervention of lords powerful enough to stay the duke of Norfolk's hand. The lords of the council had sent the duke letters—"as special writing as might be," given the myriad uncertainties of such a turbulent world—and forbidden him to harm a hair on the head of the castle's defenders.[10]

But even this attempt at reassurance could not conceal the difficulties of their situation. John II had certainly acquired "as special writing as might be," but it was not special enough. In calmer times, the violent events at Caister would have left the duke of Norfolk exposed in the blinding glare of royal disapproval—or, more likely, the fear of royal reprisal would have prevented their happening at all. Now, however, they were little more than a tawdry sideshow compared with the rollercoaster ride of national politics. While King Edward was held securely out of the way, an unwilling guest at Warwick's palatial home at Middleham, the earl's attempt to rule in his stead was falling apart. East Anglia was not the only region in which serious disorder had erupted, and it was not only private disputes that were threatening to escalate out of control. At the end of August, Lancastrian sympathisers—unable to believe their luck as the Yorkist regime tore itself apart—began to organise themselves in the far north for another assault on the throne in King Henry's name. And a grim-faced Warwick discovered that no one would answer a call for troops to suppress the revolt on his own questionable authority while King Edward remained a prisoner. As a result, he had no option but to release Edward from custody.

As soon as the king showed himself in public in the northern city of York—which he did during the week after John Daubeney's death at Caister—forces rallied in his name to defeat the Lancastrian rebels. Having taken the genie out of the bottle, however, Warwick found that he could not put it back. Edward would not meekly submit to imprisonment for a second time. The king was taking great pains to maintain a public show of conciliation with his cousin—there could be no benefit, after all, in provoking Warwick to further military action before Edward was in a position to counter him—but he summoned a number of his nobles, including his youngest brother, the duke of Gloucester, and his brother-in-law, the duke of Suffolk, to join him in Yorkshire to shore up his newly regained freedom of action on his journey back to the capital.

Back at Caister, meanwhile, hope was fading. The council under Warwick had already tried and failed to persuade the duke of Norfolk to back down. If King Edward—preoccupied as he was with the battle for supremacy in his own government—even gave Caister a second thought, it was probably to note that Norfolk's resort to violence had, if anything, helped Edward's cause by demonstrating that Warwick could not keep order without him. And the king's most urgent concern was to gather as much noble support as he could, in order to isolate Warwick and bolster his own newly restored autonomy. For the time being at least, conciliating Norfolk was likely to take priority over disciplining him. It was becoming chillingly clear that there was no one to whom the Pastons could appeal who had both the will and the authority to help them.

By the third week in September, almost five weeks into the siege, there was no avoiding the shattering conclusion that negotiations would now have to focus on terms for surrender. The objective had been reduced to the bare minimum: to get John III and his remaining men out of the castle in safety. The message was relayed to Norfolk's headquarters at Yarmouth, and on 26 September 1469, formal letters setting out the conditions of the Pastons' capitulation were drawn up under the duke's seal. The document left no room for doubt about the extent of Norfolk's victory. John Paston III and his small garrison had, "against the peace, kept the manor of Caister with force against the will and intent of us, the duke of Norfolk, to our great displeasure," the text ran sternly. But the duke would not seek retribution for this violent and unlawful behaviour; instead, he had consented to be merciful—a benevolent response, the document explained, to the request of the lords of the council, "and also at the great labour and instance of our most dear and singularly beloved wife."[11] Perhaps the duke wished to appeal to the well-worn chivalric trope of a knight sparing his enemy at the intercession of his noble lady; or perhaps the duchess's fondness for John III had left her genuinely anxious for his well-being. Either way, John III and his men were graciously permitted to give up the castle into Norfolk's possession—the duke's self-satisfaction sticking in their throats as they went—and to depart under his safe conduct.

It was over. John III—of whose feelings during the siege no record exists, since he had no means of communicating with the world beyond Caister's walls—wrote immediately, with extraordinary composure, to let his brother know what had happened. He had had no choice, he said, but to admit defeat: "we were—for lack of victuals, gunpowder, men's hearts, lack of surety of rescue—driven thereto." But he would hear no word of criticism against the men who had served under his command; it had simply proved impossible to sustain their resolve indefinitely, especially once they had seen the russet of Caister's bricks stained crimson with their friend Daubeney's blood. Despite the ordeal they had all endured, John III was calm, collected, and full of praise for the four professional soldiers who had helped him to lead the castle's defence—"I pray you give them their thanks," he told John II, "for by my troth they have as well deserved it as any men that ever bare life." Unbelievably, he even tried to lift his brother's spirits. "God preserve you, and I pray you be of good cheer till I speak with you," he wrote warmly, "and I trust to God to ease your heart in some things."[12]

But there was little comfort to be found. Almost exactly ten years after Fastolf's death, the family's prospects had never looked bleaker. After a decade of struggle, Caister—Fastolf's home, and the greatest prize of the entire inheritance—was gone. John Daubeney had been killed in the attempt to keep it, and Norfolk's servants were still issuing threats against the remaining members of the garrison, despite the duke's safeguard which, in any case, John III had not accepted for himself—"it were shame to take it," he told his brother.[13] Meanwhile, in what increasingly seemed to be a looking-glass world, John II found himself under threat of arrest for his "riotous and disorderly" conduct in ordering his men to resist the duke of Norfolk's army.

Yet there was no question but that they would cope. From the beginning of October, John II, John III, and Margaret slipped quietly back into their familiar routines—with John II in London doing what he could to push their cases forward in the courts, while John III handled the family business in Norfolk. The bonding effects of his recent gruelling experiences were evident in John III's anxiety to ensure that the men who had served under his command at Caister were properly looked after, even though the household of which they had been a part no longer existed. There were no contractual rights or benefits to which redundant employees could appeal, but the Pastons clearly felt a powerful moral and emotional obligation to recognise loyalty given, danger endured, and services rendered. Margaret promised to give the garrison a month's board in her own household while they sought work, and John III urged his brother to help find alternative employment for those he could not afford to retain. "If I were of power to keep them," he said feelingly, ". . . they should never depart from me while I lived."14 And at least one of the castle's defenders was kept on in Paston service: the hardy and devoted Tom Stumps, of whom the brothers seem to have been especially fond, rode to London to attend John II.

John III's deep concern for his small band of volunteer soldiers extended to the dead as well as the living; he was determined to ensure that John Daubeney's will was properly fulfilled as his friend had wanted. Otherwise—superficially, at least—he showed remarkably little sign of the trauma of the last two months. There even, astonishingly, seemed to be a possibility that he might reenter the duke of Norfolk's service. The conflict, after all, had never been personal; and if it might appeal to the duke's ego to emphasise the extent of his victory over a family who had dared to defy him by readmitting one of their number to serve in his household, it might also suit the Pastons to have personal access to Norfolk's inner circle.

John II and Margaret, too, soon settled back into normality after the barbed outbursts that the siege had precipitated. Margaret, of course, had to have the last word: ". . . you think that I should write to you fables and imaginations," she told him severely, "but I do not so; I have written as it has been informed me, and will do." But when her lectures resumed, they were in relatively subdued mode, exhorting a son whom she still thought of as wayward to abandon frivolous pursuits amid the temptations of the capital for a life of sober responsibility. "God visits you as it pleases him in sundry wises," she wrote solemnly. "He would you should know him and serve him better than you have done before this time, and then he will send you the more grace to do well in all other things."15 For his own part, John II was keen to make amends, and made sure to offer an elaborate olive branch at the start of his next letter ("Right worshipful mother, I commend me to you and beseech you of your blessing, and God thank you for your tenderness and help both to me, my brother and servants").16

It was vital that their differences be forgotten as quickly as possible, since the project now was bare survival. Money was desperately tight. The family's accounts have not survived, but even in happier times, the cost of running households of a style and substance appropriate to their status—the conspicuous consumption essential to proclaim, and therefore maintain, gentility—could swallow up hundreds of pounds in wages, fees, and liveries for staff (maids, valets, grooms, cooks, and bailiffs); food and drink to provide suitably aristocratic hospitality for the household and its guests; and capital expenditure to keep manor houses, barns, and byres from crumbling. Expenses, for a fifteenth-century gentleman, rose relentlessly, hand in hand with income and aspiration. And for the Pastons, these were not happy times. The Fastolf inheritance had promised to boost the family's revenues to the stratospheric levels of the super-rich. Instead, the costs of battling to defend the estates in the courts and on the ground were spiralling, while fewer and fewer of Fastolf's manors were yielding any rents to replenish Paston coffers. It was John II—nominally the head of the family, but holding only a small fraction of the Paston lands, thanks to the claims of his mother and grandmother—who felt the pinch in his pocket most acutely. John III, visiting his brother in London in October, wrote to tell Margaret that "so God help me, he has at this season not a penny in his purse, nor knows not where to get any."[17]

They also now had to handle their affairs without the help of John Daubeney. The same qualities that made his death such a grievous personal loss—his honesty, intelligence, versatility, courage, and the respect in which he was universally held—were keenly missed in the management of the family's business. Daubeney had been John III's right-hand man, trusted to stand in for his master and friend in his dealings with noblemen and tenants, allies and rivals. The Pastons could ill afford to lose his experience—particularly since, with disastrous timing, they had also lost the service of Richard Calle, the man who knew more about the running of their estates than anyone else. He had been in the family's employment for fifteen years; his family were shopkeepers in the Suffolk village of Framlingham, close by the duke of Norfolk's castle, and Calle himself had originally been recommended to John Paston by the duke's father. But it was not the conflict with Norfolk, nor anything so violent as a crossbow bolt, that parted Calle from the Pastons. Instead, it was a marriage proposal.

The first hint that something was amiss in Margaret's household had come six months earlier, when Margaret asked her eldest son to find his sister Margery somewhere else to live. "I would you should purvey for your sister to be with my lady of Oxford or with my lady of Bedford, or in some other worshipful place where you think best," she told John II carefully,

"... for we are either of us weary of other. I shall tell you more when I speak with you. I pray you do your duty herein as you will my comfort and welfare and your worship, for divers causes which you shall understand afterward, etc."[18] At first sight, this seemed a move that was long overdue. Girls of gentle birth were often sent to board in a noble household, a domestic finishing school where they learned the refined manners and courtly accomplishments—music, singing, dancing, and needlework—expected of an aristocratic lady. But Margery was already twenty, and might reasonably have expected by now to find herself on the brink of an independent life as a married woman, at the head of a household in her own right. However, neither her mother nor her brothers had had the time, amid the devastating upheavals of the past three years, to give any thought to her future. Even if they had done so, the family's finances were now so strained—with John II lacking even a few pennies to cover his costs in London—that there was no chance of finding a lump sum large enough to serve as a dowry. Her aunt Elizabeth's long-delayed dowry of two hundred pounds, after all, had represented the best part of a year's income from the Paston lands—and for Margery, without a dowry there could be no marriage.

But if Margaret had paid little attention to her daughter in recent months, the same was not true of everyone in the Paston household. There was no impermeable upstairs-downstairs divide in a gentry establishment; family and servants ate together in the great hall (however keenly distinctions of menu and seating arrangements at table might be observed), and worshipped together at mass in the parish church on Sundays, while the family's most senior and trusted officers had the run of the household in the execution of their duties. And a headstrong girl with a distracted mother would not find it difficult to seek out a servant whose company she enjoyed. In the spring of 1469, Margaret discovered, to her utter dismay, what had been going on under her nose for almost two years: Margery and Richard Calle had fallen in love.

Margaret's plan—which she had suggested to her eldest son in guarded terms in order to avoid the possibility that the shameful secret might be discovered if her letter fell into the wrong hands—had been to stamp out this unsuitable romance by dispatching her daughter to be trained in more appropriate conduct under the watchful eye of a great lady. But she had reckoned without her daughter's stubborn determination. Margery and Calle were now so deeply committed to each other that they had decided to face down the family's displeasure by seeking permission to marry. Their request was met with horror.

Surprisingly, the most extreme reaction to Calle's request for Margery's hand came from the usually equable person of John III. "I conceive by your letter . . . that you have heard of R.C.'s labour which he makes by our ungracious sister's assent," he wrote to his brother angrily in May; "but whereas they write that they have my goodwill therein, saving your reverence they falsely lie of it, for they never spoke to me of that matter." The only person who had approached him on the subject was a family friend, but "I can think that it was by Calle's means," he said, "for when I asked him whether C. desired him to move me that question or not, he would have got it away by hums and by hays." John III's response was implacable. "I answered him that if my father, whom God pardon, were alive and had consented thereto, and my mother and you both," he told John II, "he should never have my goodwill to make my sister sell candles and mustard in Framlingham."[19]

The family felt they had good reason to be outraged. Their objections were not to Calle in person: he was an intelligent, capable, and likeable man, on whom they had relied heavily for years. He was much older than Margery—probably in his late thirties—but that hardly mattered. What did matter was that he was a servant. The Pastons' gentility was so recently acquired, and potentially still so fragile, that the idea of Margery wilfully throwing away her status by marrying into a family of shopkeepers was appalling and distressing in equal measure. If John III's reaction sounds like small-minded snobbery—which comes as a shock by contrast with the easy generosity, warmth, and humanity that characterised most of his dealings— it is at least comprehensible in terms of the damage Margery could do to the family's good name. His bitterness may also speak of personal hurt, perhaps less at Margery's conduct than at Calle's. He had worked closely with Calle since his teens, a relationship that had always been one of trust and camaraderie and respect. But Calle had not spoken to him about his intentions toward Margery—probably, of course, because he feared exactly this response. Margery and Calle were left in no doubt that they could not hope to secure the family's blessing for their plans.

But in the late summer of 1469—at the worst possible moment, given that Caister was besieged by the duke of Norfolk's men on 21 August—it became shockingly clear that the couple were not prepared to take no for an answer. They married in secret. When Margaret discovered what had happened, Margery—who was evidently too like her strong-willed mother for either's comfort—utterly refused to acquiesce in the face of the family's demands that she disown her new husband. They were kept apart, with Calle banished from the household to wait for news in London, and Margery kept under watch in her mother's home. One letter from Calle survives among the family papers from this period, despite the fact that he urged Margery to burn it as soon as she had read its intensely private contents. Perhaps it was intercepted before it reached her, or perhaps she could not bring herself to destroy it, only for it to be discovered and confiscated by her enraged mother. Either way, it is apparent how much pressure the couple were under, and how difficult it was to cope with a situation where they were each being told that the other was betraying them. Calle was suffering, not least because the separation from Margery was almost more than he could bear:

> My own lady and mistress, and before God very true wife, I with heart
> full sorrowful recommend me unto you as he that cannot be merry,
> nor naught shall be, till it be otherwise with us than it is yet; for this
> life that we lead now is neither pleasure to God nor to the world, con-
> sidering the great bond of matrimony that is made between us, and
> also the great love that has been, and as I trust yet is, between us, and
> as on my part never greater. . . . it seems a thousand years ago since I
> spoke with you.[20]

He could not tolerate the thought of what Margery was enduring for his sake. "I understand, lady, you have had as much sorrow for me as any gentlewoman has had in the world," he told her; ". . . it is to me a death to hear that you are treated otherwise than you ought to be." All the same, he felt justified in what they had done: they loved each other, and had acted honourably by marrying. Calle must have known exactly what he was jeopardising—his career, his friends, his standing—and was prepared to risk it all; but he was also a proud man, who would not accept that Margery was ruining herself by becoming his wife. "I marvel much," he said with quiet dignity, "that they should take this matter so heedfully as I understand they do." Isolated as he was, his mood swung between despair, resignation, defiance, and hope. "And therefore, good lady, at the reverence of God be plain to them and tell the truth, and if they will in no wise agree thereto, between God, the devil and them be it."[21]

The difficulty for the family was that no priest or witnesses were required to make wedding vows binding: the couple's promises to each other, and the consummation of the relationship, were enough to make the union irrevocable. That had left Margaret and her sons powerless to prevent the marriage, but it also offered them a loophole. If Margery could be persuaded to deny that such promises had been made, the validity of the union would depend on her word against Calle's, and escape would be possible. By the end of the first week in September—with John III defending Caister against the duke of Norfolk's forces, and John II urgently searching for help in London—Margaret and Agnes were grappling with the problem of Margery's wilfulness and resolve.

The question of whether or not the marriage had in fact taken place had been referred for judgment into the diplomatic hands of Margaret's old acquaintance Bishop Lyhert of Norwich. Margaret and Agnes were trying to stave off his investigation until the crisis at Caister had been defused, so that Margery's brothers could participate in the discussions. The bishop was sympathetic—"he knew well that her demeaning had staked sore at our hearts," Margaret reported—but the case was now so much a matter of public scandal that he felt compelled to act: "he had been required so often to examine her that he might not, nor would, no longer delay it." Margaret and Agnes, meanwhile, were indulging in some wishful thinking on the subject, informing the bishop that, so far as they could tell from Margery's own account of her clandestine wedding, she had never uttered the fateful words "I take you to be my husband," a simple statement of present consent, that would have bound her irretrievably to Calle. They sustained their hopes as best they could until Friday, 8 September, when Margery was brought before the bishop.

Lyhert did his utmost to remind her what was at stake: ". . . how she was born, what kin and friends that she had, and should have more if she were ruled and guided by them; and, if she did not, what rebuke and shame and loss it should be to her . . . and therefore he bade her be right well advised how she did, and said that he would understand the words that she had said to him, whether it made matrimony or not." Whatever the truth of the matter, the choice now lay in Margery's hands: she could repudiate her marriage, and secure her status, reputation, and prospects; or she could stand by her lover, and face an uncertain future. She did not hesitate for an instant: ". . . she rehearsed what she had said, and said, if those words made it not sure, she said boldly that she would make it surer before she went thence." This defiance was the last straw for her mother. "These lewd words grieve me and her grandam as much as all the remnant," Margaret told John II.[22]

The investigation proceeded. Bishop Lyhert interrogated Calle separately, asking when and where they had married and exactly what words they had used, to see whether his story matched Margery's. Clearly, it did. The bishop said "he would not be too hasty to give sentence thereupon," on the vague but hopeful grounds that something else might emerge to stand in the way of the marriage, and postponed his decision for a month. Margery and Calle both protested; "they would have had their will performed in haste," Margaret reported, deeply unimpressed by their ardour, but the bishop stood his ground. There could be no doubt now of Margery's unyielding determination to make a new life with the man she loved. As a result, Margaret refused to receive her daughter back into her house, sending messages to friends that they, too, should refuse to take her in. "I had given her warning," she said coldly; "she might have been ware before if she had been gracious."[23]

For all that, she did care where Margery went. At the bishop's request, the young woman was given temporary lodging in the household of Roger Best, a prominent citizen and former mayor of Norwich. "I am sorry they are encumbered with her," Margaret wrote, "but yet I am better pleased that she is there for the while than if she had been in other place, because of the . . . good disposition of himself and his wife"; there, she believed, no insolent or unchaste behaviour would be tolerated. The situation was deeply painful, but she was determined to stand firm; no compromise was possible given the extent to which, in Margaret's eyes, her daughter had betrayed the family by her duplicity and disobedience. "I pray you and require you that you take it not pensively," she told John II sternly, perhaps as much to convince herself as him, "for I know well it goes right near your heart, and so it does to mine and to other; but remember you, and so do I, that we have lost of her but a brothel"—a good-for-nothing wretch—"and set it the less to heart." Compassion and forgiveness were not, yet, emotions that Margaret could bring herself to contemplate: "if he were dead at this hour," she wrote with chilling austerity, "she should never be at my heart as she was." John II had suggested they might find other ways to undo the damage, but Margaret would not countenance the idea that they should place their immortal souls in jeopardy by seeking to annul a marriage that—however objectionable it might be—was nevertheless lawful in the eyes of

God: ". . . as for the divorce that you wrote to me of, . . . I charge you upon my blessing that you do not, nor cause no other to do, what should offend God and your conscience . . . ," she told him solemnly. "For know well, she shall full sore repent her lewdness hereafter, and I pray God she must so."[24] Despite Margaret's confidence, there is no sign that Margery did repent. The couple's resolve held, in spite of all the pressures on them and the fact that their future—Margery with no prospect now of any inheritance, and Calle without employment, his reputation in ruins—was uncertain at best. Neither would give up on what was clearly, however great the difference in their ages and their status, true love.

In the end, there was nothing the family could do. For Margery's mother and brothers, the trauma caused by her headstrong behaviour was compounded by the disastrous timing of the breach with Calle. For more than a decade, with unobtrusive but unquestionable competence, he had compiled their accounts, supervised agricultural production on their estates, and arranged the sale of their surplus produce on the open market. Now, the sudden loss of his expertise while the battle for Caister was in the process of being fought—at the very point when the death of John Daubeney deprived them of another of their most trusted servants—could hardly have been worse. The complications of his sudden departure from their employment took weeks to resolve. Calle was doing all he could not to alienate the family further, but he also needed to protect himself in terms of the large sums of money for which his business dealings on their behalf had left him liable. For their part, the Pastons had to be careful to retrieve all the valuable documents—property deeds and financial accounts—that Calle had in his keeping, and would not hand over until he had been indemnified against his financial obligations. Margaret initially handled the negotiations, since John III—fresh from the siege—was still too angry to deal with him: ". . . as for me, I had rather he were hanged than to be bound to him," he wrote heatedly on 5 October.[25] Once Calle had delivered the documents, however, John III seemed to be softening a little; even he had to admit that, unsurprisingly, Calle was behaving with characteristic integrity. Margaret was not prepared to say the same of her daughter: ". . . as for your sister, I can send you no good tidings of her," she wrote to John II grimly on 28 October. "God make her a good woman."[26]

Despite his best efforts, Bishop Lyhert had been unable to find any impediment to the marriage, and Margery and Calle had now been reunited: ". . . as for his abiding," John III told his brother, "it is in

Blackborough nunnery a little from Lynn, and our unhappy sister's also; and as for his service, there shall no man have it before you, if you will."27 Calle had never wanted to leave the Pastons' household, and by his own lights he had done nothing wrong. He also knew his own worth, and realised that, given time, deep-rooted Paston pragmatism might come to the fore. The damage to Margery's status and reputation could not now be avoided, but the same was not true of the harm to the family's affairs that the loss of his experience would entail. The rift was too deep to be smoothed over immediately, and in the meantime he would have to take employment wherever he could find it—but with humility and patience, Calle made it clear that his service would be at the family's disposal whenever they might choose to call on it.

In the meantime, there was plenty to occupy the Pastons' attention while they considered Calle's offer. The political situation remained in turmoil. King Edward was still playing a double game, offering fair words to his cousin of Warwick while at the same time making clear—with steel behind the public smiles—that, now he was at liberty, he would no longer be the earl's puppet. In mid-October he returned from Yorkshire to London, "accompanied in all people with a thousand horse," John II told his mother, to be greeted by the mayor and twenty-two aldermen of the city, all arrayed in scarlet, and two hundred of the capital's craftsmen decked out in blue. Despite the splendour of his arrival, the struggle for power still teetered on a knife's edge. Warwick had demonstrated that Edward had much to fear from his military might, should he again choose to use it; but the earl had also learned that, while Edward remained king, he could not govern without him. John Paston II was as confused as anyone else about what it all meant. "I know not what to suppose therein," he reported from London with disarming honesty. "The king himself has good language of the lords of Clarence, of Warwick, and of my lords of York, of Oxford, saying they are his best friends. But his household men have other language, so what shall hastily fall I cannot say."28

The "other language" circulating privately in the royal household was much more plausible than the idea that Edward might be best friends again with the brother and cousins who had imprisoned him, but for the time being the king had adopted a policy of self-restraint on an epic scale. Instead of seeking revenge for the humiliations of the past four months, he sought to maintain at least a front of unity while he rebuilt his government, rather than risk further confrontation before he had mustered the military resources to deal with it. As a result, it was difficult for John II to know which way to turn. Should he pursue his contacts with Archbishop Neville, now staying at a tactful distance from London in his magnificent palace of the Moor, just north of the capital in Hertfordshire? Or should he renew his acquaintance with the queen's brother Lord Scales (who had now—after his father's execution on Warwick's orders—inherited the title of Earl Rivers)? Woodville connections had temporarily become a liability rather than an asset under the earl of Warwick's regime, and John II had therefore been very quiet for a number of months on the subject of his engagement to Scales's cousin, but, with his usual optimism, he was hoping now to revive the relationship. "As for my good speed, I hope well I am offered yet to have Mistress Anne Haute," he told his brother brightly in the new year.[29]

Despite John II's cheerfulness, there was little sign of any practical improvement in the Pastons' situation. The duke of Norfolk's strategy in the attempt to reinforce his possession of Caister was guided, it seemed, by the maxim that attack was the best form of defence. At the end of 1469, he threatened to seize the Fastolf manor of Guton Hall, ten miles northwest of Norwich; and he was also bringing personal pressure to bear on the Paston brothers, by making arrangements for the widows of the two men in his service who had been killed by gunfire from the Caister garrison to bring charges against John III for the murder of their husbands: ". . . the cause is this," John III told his brother, "as it is told me by divers, that you make no more suit to my lord for yourself than you do, and therefore they do the worse to me for your sake."[30] If John II was wondering why he should contemplate going cap in hand to a man who had forced him out of what he considered to be rightfully his own property, his younger brother—who was more diplomatic, and more philosophical about the ways of great lords—knew that they had little alternative.

For once, John III sounded weary, asking his brother to make inquiries for him about the possibility of finding honourable and gainful employment by serving as a soldier in the English garrison at Calais. The prospect that he might be readmitted to the duke of Norfolk's service had proved prohibitively far-fetched—perhaps unsurprisingly, given that he and his former fellows in the duke's household had so recently surveyed one another down the barrel of a gun. But with no fees or wages to his name, and with the Paston finances currently in so precarious a state, he found himself out of money. As always, though, he managed to find a stoical word or two. "Item," he told his brother, "you must purvey a new attorney in this country"—in other words, John II should find someone else to represent his interests in Norfolk—". . . for our matters and clamour is too great and our purse and wit too slender; but I will rub on as long as I may"—at least "till better peace be."[31] Discretion dictated that John III should try to make his peace with the duke and duchess of Norfolk, but they were not yet willing to receive him, despite the fact that the duchess's fondness for him was undiminished; "every man tells me that my lady says passingly well of me always," he told John II, with a hint of wistfulness. To add insult to injury, the duke—preoccupied as he now was with the uncertain power play in London, and perhaps conscious of the need not to parade his ill-gotten gains too ostentatiously—had done nothing with Caister other than shut it up. "There is now but three men in it," John III reported, "and the bridges always drawn."[32]

There was, however, one flicker of hope. John II, the flexible pragmatist, had finally reached the conclusion that his father had never come close to accepting: that the only prospect of securing even a part of the Fastolf inheritance lay in agreeing upon a compromise. Caister had been lost to the duke of Norfolk because those among Fastolf's executors who opposed the Pastons' claim, represented principally by Judge Yelverton, had been willing to sell their putative title to the duke. The Pastons' only chance of loosening Norfolk's hold on Caister now was to make their peace with Yelverton, get him to ratify their claim, and thereby undermine the duke's legal position. Peace with Yelverton would undoubtedly come at a price— but whatever it cost, failing to accept that would mean losing everything. After so many years of deeply entrenched hostility, the family desperately needed powerful help to persuade Yelverton of the merits of such a deal, and not just the nebulous benevolence of a patron such as Archbishop Neville who had far too much else to do. What they needed was the support of a lord with his own stake in seeing that their claims were pursued— a possibility that finally appeared on the horizon at the beginning of 1470.

William Wainfleet, bishop of Winchester—still as acute as ever at the age of seventy—had a long-standing interest in Fastolf's affairs as one of the old knight's trustees, and as the most senior of the executors named in the revised will of November 1459. He also, like everybody else involved in the dispute, had his own agenda. In his case, it was his foundation of a new college of priests and scholars, dedicated to St. Mary Magdalen, within the university of Oxford. There the fruits of Wainfleet's labours can still be seen today: the gracefully soaring tower of Magdalen College is the highest point amid Oxford's dreaming spires. But in 1470, the college's very existence still hung in the balance. Only three years of preliminary building work had so far been completed, and Wainfleet would need to secure major further funding if the project were ever to be completed. Meanwhile, Fastolf's plan for his own college at Caister had not yet come to fruition, and might never do so if the duke of Norfolk's seizure of the castle proved to be permanent. Wainfleet's suggestion was that the needs of Fastolf's soul might be better served by committing his lands to pay for prayers at Wainfleet's own college rather than at a foundation at Caister which did not yet exist—a proposal, he must have thought, of conveniently mutual benefit. Not only that, but the bishop was also an ideal person to act as an intermediary between William Yelverton and the Pastons, since he was a man of undoubted integrity whose relationship with both sides went back years to the days when John Paston had been Yelverton's colleague in Fastolf's service.

Two conditions would have to be met before the negotiations could move forward: Wainfleet needed to secure some kind of formal authority over the disposition of Fastolf's estate to underpin his position as an arbiter in the dispute; and the proposed displacement of Fastolf's college from Caister to Oxford required approval from the pope. The bishop tackled both issues in the first months of 1470. In January, he sent a servant to Rome to seek papal dispensation for the move to Oxford. In the following month, although the probate hearings in the archbishop of Canterbury's court had come to judgment more than two years earlier, Wainfleet secured the intervention of the archbishop himself in the case, on the grounds that the two executors appointed by the terms of the revised will to take charge of its administration—John Paston and Thomas Howes—were both now dead. On 13 February, sole administration of Fastolf's estate—which had, in effect, hung in limbo during the vicissitudes of the past two years—was awarded to Bishop Wainfleet.

Only a week or so later, discussions between the various parties were already well advanced. "Item, there is a way moved by the means of my lord of Winchester between Sir William Yelverton and me," John II told his brother buoyantly, "and both Sir William Yelverton and I agreed to abide his award." Wainfleet had so far played his hand with enough skill that both sides believed he looked favourably on their claims. "I hope this next term there shall be a way taken and an end, and . . . I fear not the award," John II went on—while, at almost exactly the same time, Yelverton's ally William Worcester was telling Margaret that "he thinks that the bishop will be against you," John III reported back to his brother from Norwich.[33] Despite the negative sentiment, the very fact that Worcester had renewed contact with Margaret—after the long years of hostility provoked by her husband's refusal to countenance his claims on their old master's estate— was itself an encouraging sign. Worcester, like Yelverton, was now cooperating with Bishop Wainfleet's attempt to find a lasting solution to the conflict. He was still holding fast to his claim that Fastolf had promised him a modest living from his estates, and complained mournfully to the bishop that a decade of conflict had utterly impoverished him:

> Item, my lord, the costs and charges that I have borne these ten years in London and in ridings when I awaited upon the infinite process of the deciding of my Master Fastolf's testaments in the Court of Audience, that I am so indebted and so unpurveyed of goods to live that I may not ride nor continue in London, but am fain to withdraw me for my poor solace to Cambridge, . . . and to eschew greater costs to abide me there till I may be purveyed of a competent living . . .[34]

Nevertheless, Worcester's emotional and financial exhaustion was likely, if anything, to encourage him to sign up to a settlement, if the bishop could find some basis for agreement.

The deal that Wainfleet hammered out over the following months was this: John II would be confirmed in his right to Caister—which of course he no longer held—and one other Fastolf manor at Herringby, four miles west. Bishop Wainfleet would then do everything he could, mustering all his influence and experience as a spiritual peer of the realm and a former chancellor of England, to help the Pastons retrieve the castle from the duke of Norfolk. The bishop also promised to help John II recover the manors of Hellesdon and Drayton, on condition that those properties would then be shared between them. Of the other Fastolf lands, John II, with Caister and Herringby, would receive as much as would provide an income of fifty pounds per year. All that remained of this once-great estate—which, back in Fastolf's heyday, had given him an annual income of a thousand pounds— would go to the bishop, to be used to endow his new college in Oxford for the benefit of Fastolf's soul. John II would therefore be relieved of his obligation to found and fund Fastolf's college at Caister (a responsibility that, truth be told, would always have weighed heavily on a man of his blithely lighthearted temperament). If Wainfleet could not reclaim Caister for the Pastons within a fixed period, John II would have the right to the manor of Guton Hall instead—not that Guton in fact represented any kind of fair exchange for Caister's fine castle, staring out toward the sea at a key point on the coast, though it would undoubtedly be better than nothing— or to receive financial compensation in lieu of the estate. John II would also be released from any obligation to pay the sum of 4,000 marks (more than £2,500) that had originally been specified in his father's bargain with Fastolf. Details of Wainfleet's negotiations with Yelverton, Worcester, and Fastolf's lawyer William Jenney do not survive, but it is clear that the settlement made some provision for their interests; Worcester, for example, did eventually receive the lands he claimed Fastolf had promised him. Certainly, the bishop succeeded in securing their assent to the agreement. Once John II's deal with Wainfleet was concluded, it was formally set out in legal documents to which both parties put their seal on 14 July 1470.

In just six months, a resolution had at last been found for a dispute so bitter that it had festered for a decade. Exhaustion, of course, now played its part in persuading both sides of the need to accept a compromise. But John Fastolf and John Paston would have been outraged. This, after all, was what Fastolf had been afraid of all along: that once he was gone, his executors' commitment to realising his plans for the college at Caister would falter in the face of the complexities of dealing with his estate. Fastolf's soul would now be remembered at Magdalen College in Oxford, but Magdalen was not Caister, and Wainfleet's foundation was a long way in nature and purpose from Fastolf's vision of seven priests and seven poor men living together at his birthplace within an institution expressly dedicated to perpetual prayer for his soul and those of his family. Fastolf's college—the scheme that had been at the heart of his will and therefore of the whole dispute—was now abandoned. It was exactly the outcome that the old man had hoped to avoid by giving John Paston a personal investment in its foundation, but his reluctance to give his intentions legal form in good time before his death had left what proved to be an open invitation for his wishes to be challenged.

John Paston, meanwhile, would surely have seen the agreement as one more example of his eldest son's lack of responsibility. The castle at Caister and lands worth an annual sum of fifty pounds represented a small fraction of the prize that had once been within his grasp. Nor would he have accepted the language in which the agreement was framed, referring as it did to a bargain "alleged to be made" between himself and Fastolf.[35] Nevertheless, it was his own obduracy and persistent misjudgments that had gone a long way toward undermining his case and leaving his son in a position that had turned out to be indefensible. Of the properties to which John II's title was confirmed by the terms of the deal with Wainfleet, he was in possession of hardly any—but that was part of the point: he now had a claim to Caister, and to Hellesdon and Drayton, which was uncontested by any of Fastolf's executors, and he had the bishop's backing in his attempt to enforce it. It was a gamble, but it was also the only chance he had left to retrieve anything from the debâcle which his father's claim to Fastolf's lands had now become.

Or so it seemed. What he could not know in July 1470 was that all political certainties were about to be swept away with terrifying speed. The uneasy reconciliation between King Edward and the earl of Warwick at the end of the previous year had lasted only until March. By then, disorder had erupted again in the northeast Midlands, when a feud between two Lincolnshire landowners exploded into a private war, culminating in the sacking and pillage of a local manor house. The victim of this assault was the master of the king's horse, and Edward declared his intention to settle the dispute in person, partly out of concern for his servant's interests, and partly in order to demonstrate the majesty of the king's justice as a deterrent to other gentlemen who might consider taking the law into their own hands. But news of Edward's imminent arrival at the head of a body of troops caused widespread panic in Lincolnshire and further north in Yorkshire, where many men had been embroiled in the revolt of 1469, and now feared that the king might cast aside the mask of magnanimity and seek revenge for their insubordination.

Meanwhile, Warwick and his son-in-law Clarence—knowing now that their ambitions would never be fulfilled while Edward remained in power, and fearing that it could be only a matter of time before he took decisive action to punish them for their disloyalty—seized the opportunity of the unrest to instigate a second rebellion against him. They covered their tracks so well that their intentions were not clear for some weeks. "I cannot tell you what will befall the world, for the king verily is disposed to go into Lincolnshire and men know not what will fall thereof nor thereafter," John II told his brother apprehensively late in February. ". . . my lord of Warwick, as it is supposed, shall go with the king," he reported. ". . . Some men say that his going shall do good, and some say that it does harm."[36] The king himself found it particularly difficult to believe that his own brother—vapid and totally self-centred though Clarence was—would choose to betray him for a second time. However, the king had little choice but to come to that unpalatable conclusion after his decisive defeat of the Lincolnshire rebels on 12 March. So many of the rebel soldiers dropped their jackets as they fled the rout that the battle was named "Losecoat Field"—and it was their flight that provided damning evidence of their masters' perfidy: several of those who discarded clothes as they made their frantic escape had been wearing the livery of Clarence and Warwick. Not only that, but among the dead was one of Clarence's servants, in whose possession were found incriminating letters from the duke and the earl. Interrogations carried out after the battle suggested that the plan—for which there could be no public justification whatsoever, driven as it was purely by Warwick and Clarence's overweening ambitions—had been to depose Edward and install Clarence on the throne in his place.

For all that the king had an instinctive careless generosity, he could no longer hide from the fact of their treachery: his brother and his cousin had flung his forgiveness back in his face. He set out in force after them, and "it was said that were never seen in England so many goodly men and so well arrayed," John III was told.[37] In public, Warwick and Clarence continued to proclaim their willingness to cooperate with Edward, but they dared not confront him in person. When they found that they could command no support among the wider political community, they fled. The king pursued them westward across country as fast as he could, only to discover when he arrived on 14 April at the city of Exeter, just ten miles from the southwestern coast, that Warwick and Clarence had already set sail for Calais—of which Warwick, who had held the captaincy there for more than a decade, was still officially in command. But the Calais garrison held fast to its loyalty to Edward and refused them entry, leaving Clarence's wife, Warwick's eighteen-year-old daughter Isabel, to give birth to her first child on board ship. The terrified young duchess survived the experience, but her baby son died shortly afterward.

Warwick, who had become so uncompromisingly accustomed to being master of his own fortunes, had finally run out of options. His only hope now lay in seeking help from the French king, Louis XI, whose subtle mind and predilection for intrigue earned him the nickname of "the Spider." As Warwick well knew, Louis would be only too pleased to see the downfall of King Edward and the end of the English alliance with France's enemy, Duke Charles of Burgundy. The earl's small fleet sailed on, reinforced by

Warwick's capture in the Channel of thirty or forty Burgundian ships, a piratical exploit which had the happy triple effect of securing a lavish haul of booty at the same time as establishing the earl's credentials with the king of France and embarrassing Edward in the eyes of his Burgundian ally. At the beginning of May, Warwick's flotilla at last dropped anchor at Honfleur, on the Normandy coast.

Also in France, living in a château in Bar belonging to her father, the duke of Anjou, were Henry VI's exiled wife, Margaret, and their sixteen-year-old son, Prince Edward. She had never given up on her husband's cause, but its apparent hopelessness—with Henry himself still a prisoner in the Tower of London, and no more capable of leadership than he had ever been—meant that she had made little headway in recent years in securing any international interest in her family's plight. Her situation changed dramatically, however, with the earl of Warwick's arrival on French soil. Warwick's attempt to rule in King Edward's name while keeping his cousin under lock and key had proved unworkable, and since then it had become clear that the earl's idea of replacing Edward with his more malleable brother Clarence was too implausible and unpopular to be viable. If Warwick were to try his hand at kingmaking yet again, he would need to find a more credible contender for the throne. And he was not slow to realise that the most convincing candidate—convincing, that is, not in terms of his personal qualities but by virtue of the fact that he had held the crown once already—was the deposed king Henry VI.

For King Louis of France, the prospect that Warwick, whose pro-French sympathies had been evident for years, and Henry's French-born queen, Margaret of Anjou, might form an alliance to reestablish Lancastrian rule in England was a tantalising one. In the short term, the implosion of the Yorkist government would remove at a stroke the persistent threat of Anglo-Burgundian aggression against France via a pincer movement from the north and east. In the longer term, a friendly Lancastrian regime might prove a vital ally in pursuit of Louis's ambition to overthrow his Burgundian enemy and reclaim the duchy for the crown of France. But his chances of brokering such a treaty between Warwick and Margaret seemed remote, given that for years they had regarded each other with virulent animosity. Not for nothing, however, was Louis nicknamed the Spider King. After weeks of patient negotiation, he succeeded in bringing these two bitterest of enemies face to face at his palace at Angers, beside the River Loire. There, on bended knee, the earl offered his renewed allegiance to King

Henry VI, and undertook to lead an invasion of England to restore him to the throne. In return, Margaret gave her consent to the betrothal of her son Edward to Anne Neville, the younger of Warwick's two daughters. Given that King Henry was manifestly incapable of ruling, it was further agreed that the young Prince Edward should act as regent on his father's behalf, and his prospective father-in-law, Warwick, would stand at his right hand in the new Lancastrian government.

It was an extraordinary and profoundly unlikely alliance. Warwick had been one of the greatest enemies of the Lancastrian cause ever since he had first fought for the duke of York at St. Albans in 1455, and his own father and brother had been slaughtered by Lancastrian hands. After so much Neville blood had been spilled to win a Yorkist victory, his defection was an astonishing step in personal as well as political terms. But Warwick's ambition, and his self-belief, were implacable. It was his utter conviction that the role he had played in bringing down the Lancastrian regime entitled him to more power than Edward was now prepared to allow him, and he was resolved to go to any length to achieve what he felt was rightfully his, even if it meant reestablishing the regime he had fought so hard to topple, and compromising his own integrity in the process.

His was not the only spectacular volte-face. Queen Margaret had been outraged at the very suggestion that she should have anything to do with the man she saw as "the greatest causer of the fall of King Henry, of her, and of her son." It took King Louis several weeks of painstaking work—"His Majesty has spent and still spends every day in long discussions with the queen," it was reported at the end of June—to convince her that the potential benefits of Warwick's help outweighed her revulsion at the alliance.[38] Nevertheless, when the earl knelt before her at Angers to ask her forgiveness and pledge his loyalty, Margaret kept him on his knees for more than fifteen minutes. She consented to the marriage between her son and Warwick's daughter only with the greatest reluctance, and could not be brought to agree that Prince Edward should accompany Warwick when he invaded England in her husband's name; instead, the prince would remain safely with her in France until King Edward had been defeated.

It was abundantly clear that the animosity between the queen and the earl had not been dispelled by a deal based on expediency rather than trust. The agreement also had the disadvantage of undermining the whole basis on which the duke of Clarence had offered Warwick his support. Vanity and ambition had led the duke to betray his brother in the hope of securing the crown for himself, but his father-in-law's decision to throw in his lot with the Lancastrian cause cut adrift Clarence's personal pretensions. For the time being, it seemed that—having shown such outrageous disloyalty to his brother that he perhaps had little choice—he could be placated with a promise that he would be granted the duchy of York under the new regime. But Clarence's usefulness to Warwick had been based from the beginning on the fact that he was both self-centred and impressionable, and the risk was that he would no longer be a dependable ally if asked to fight in some-one else's cause.

Whatever doubts remained, the deal was done. With help from the French king, Warwick gathered his fleet and set sail for England on 9 September, accompanied by his son-in-law Clarence, his brother-in-law the earl of Oxford—who had fled the country soon after Warwick and Clarence to join them in France—and Henry VI's half-brother, Jasper Tudor. They landed in the southwest four days later, declaring ominously that they had come in the name of "our most dread sovereign lord, King Henry the Sixth" to resist "his great rebel and enemy Edward, late earl of March, usurper, oppressor, and destroyer of our said sovereign lord and of the noble blood of all the realm of England and of the good, true commons of the same."[39] King Edward himself was in Yorkshire, the heartland of Warwick's regional power, where he had gone a month earlier to put down yet more pro-Neville disturbances, and now began to move south, giving every appearance of confidence in his ability to resist Warwick's attack.

However, as he paused at the Yorkshire town of Doncaster to await reinforcements, he received the shocking news that one of his most trusted lieutenants had defected to join the rebellion against him. John Neville, another of the earl of Warwick's many siblings, had demonstrated impecca-ble loyalty to Edward throughout his reign—loyalty that had not wavered even in recent months, when it meant taking the field against his own brother. He had played a key role in the early 1460s in the suppression of Lancastrian resistance in the northeast, and Edward had rewarded him with the earldom of Northumberland, of which the Percy family had been deprived because of their adherence to Henry VI. This eclipse of Percy influence had allowed the Neville family to stand as the greatest bulwark of Yorkist rule in the north of England; but now, across huge swathes of Neville land, Neville tenants were being confronted with an intractable choice between their allegiance to the king and their loyalty to their local lord, the earl of Warwick. As a result, the problem of keeping order in the north had now grown so acute, and had played such a significant part in Warwick's capacity to undermine Edward's rule, that the king had been forced to rethink his strategy there.

In March 1470, Edward had deprived John Neville of the earldom of Northumberland in order to restore Henry Percy—formerly John Paston's fellow prisoner in the Fleet—to the title and lands, believing that only the Percys had the depth of support along the eastern border with Scotland to hold the region securely against Warwick's now-hostile influence, and seeking through this policy of reconciliation to attach the Percy family to his own cause. The king did not completely ignore the need to provide John Neville with compensation for his lost title: Neville himself became Marquis Montagu, and his ten-year-old son was created duke of Bedford and betrothed to King Edward's eldest daughter. But Neville was deeply unimpressed with the way he had been treated. Despite his immaculate record in Edward's service, one of the greatest estates in England had been taken from him, and he saw the reparation he had received—which was long on glittering titles and short on the practical power conferred by land—as wholly inadequate. ". . . he had many fair words and no lordships," he was later reported to have claimed bitterly; his new title was all very well, but the king had given him no more than "a magpie's nest to maintain his estate with."[40] The extent of Neville's unhappiness and Edward's miscalculation became clear only in September, as Neville and his troops advanced toward the king at Doncaster. They were within six or seven miles of Edward's position by the time the king learned that Neville had declared for Henry VI, and was coming not to help but to capture him.

Neville's defection was a crippling blow. Edward was now caught between two hostile armies, with Neville approaching from the north and Warwick from the south. The king's own troops, dispersed in billets to wait for Neville's arrival, were not ready to fight. Rather than face battle against overwhelming odds, or submit to imprisonment for a second time— especially given that his personal safety would be less than assured now that Warwick had discarded all pretence of loyalty and declared him a usurper—Edward decided to run. Accompanied by his youngest brother, Richard, duke of Gloucester, his friend Lord Hastings, and his wife's brother Earl Rivers, he fled east. He nearly drowned crossing the Wash, the shallow but unpredictable bay that separates Lincolnshire from the Norfolk coast, where rivers flowing out to sea compete with incoming tides, and where, more than two centuries earlier, King John had lost the crown jewels of England in the treacherous waters. Narrowly avoiding the same fate, Edward managed to reach the Norfolk port of King's Lynn, where, on 2 October, he and his small company took ship for the Netherlands to seek refuge and support from his brother-in-law Duke Charles of Burgundy.

Amid riots in the capital, Queen Elizabeth, who was eight months pregnant, fled in the middle of the night from her apartments in the city's royal residence, the Tower of London, to take sanctuary at Westminster Abbey with her three small daughters. So long as she stayed there, within the abbey's walls, she would be safer even than within the Tower's most closely guarded precincts, since no assailant could remove her without risking excommunication and eternal damnation. She had not moved a moment too soon. As Warwick and his army approached the capital, the earl's brother Archbishop Neville seized control of the Tower. Bishop Wainfleet of Winchester was among those who conveyed the hapless and dishevelled figure of Henry VI from his prison quarters there to the royal chambers that Queen Elizabeth had so recently been forced to abandon. On 6 October, the earl of Warwick arrived in London, and immediately went to kneel at King Henry's feet to offer his allegiance. Five years earlier, Henry had been in Warwick's charge when he was brought into London as a captive, his feet tied to the stirrups of his horse. Now, on Saturday, 13 October, the earl carried his train when Henry was crowned for a second time in St. Paul's Cathedral.

The course of politics had been chaotic and unpredictable ever since Warwick had taken up arms against Edward fifteen months earlier, but these were upheavals of an entirely different order: the world had been turned upside down in a matter of weeks. John Paston II had made his career at the Yorkist court, but the Yorkist court was now irrevocably split in two, and John II found himself with a foot in each camp. His Woodville connections—he was, after all, still engaged to Queen Elizabeth's cousin—had suddenly become dangerous, with the queen herself sheltering in the Westminster sanctuary and her brother Earl Rivers a fugitive with King Edward in the Netherlands. But John II could also call on the goodwill of Archbishop Neville, who had just been appointed chancellor in the new Lancastrian government. Whatever the Pastons' feelings about the deposition of King Edward—thoughts which, prudence dictated, should not be committed to paper—it was clear that the Nevilles now represented their best hope of retrieving Caister from the duke of Norfolk.

In fact, it was not Archbishop Neville himself but his brother-in-law the earl of Oxford—the new constable of England—who emerged as the Pastons' principal champion. John II and John III had enjoyed a warm relationship with the earl and members of his household for years, but Oxford's political influence had remained limited as he slowly rebuilt his family's position after the execution of his father and brother in 1462. At last he had a chance to demonstrate the benefits of his lordship. Oxford had estates of his own in Norfolk, and he savoured the opportunity to exercise his authority there—especially at the expense of the duke of Norfolk, whose identification with Yorkist interests was so close that he was briefly placed under arrest on Warwick's orders. By Friday, 12 October—only a week after Warwick's arrival in the capital, and the day before Henry VI's second coronation—John II and John III were in London and full of excitement at what Oxford's help might mean. "I trust that we shall do right well in all our matters hastily," John III told Margaret eagerly, "for my lady of Norfolk has promised to be ruled by my lord of Oxford in all such matters as belong to my brother and to me." He sounded exhilarated; after a deeply traumatic year, they could never have imagined such a dramatic transformation in their prospects. "And as for my lord of Oxford, he is better lord to me, by my troth, than I can wish him in many matters," he wrote, "for he sent to my lady of Norfolk . . . only for my matter and for none other cause, my unwitting or without any prayer of me, for when he sent to her I was at London and he was at Colchester, and that is a likelihood he remembers me." The idea of a lord who would help without even being reminded to do so seemed almost too good to be true—as was the effect on the duke of Norfolk and his wife. "The duke and the duchess sue to him as humbly as ever I did to them," John III reported; the couple were so desperate to find favour with this new regime that "my lord of Oxford shall have the rule of them and theirs" at their own request, he added, with understandable satisfaction.[41]

Margaret was not so easily impressed. The day after her son's letter was written, Norfolk's men at Caister had stolen sixteen sheep from her manor of Mautby, a mile away, and had taken pot shots at her farmer there as he rode past the castle on his way home from Yarmouth. "They stuff and victual sore the place, and it is reported here that my lady of Norfolk says she will not lose it in no wise," she told John III apprehensively.[42] Margaret had a point. The authority of the new government was precarious in the extreme—not least because, to achieve any kind of lasting stability, it would have to find some way to reconcile competing noble interests divided by bitter personal enmities: Lancastrian lords returning from exile, Yorkist lords newly reborn as Lancastrians under the earl of Warwick's leadership, and those Yorkist lords—such as the duke of Norfolk—who had not supported Warwick's rebellion, but who might now be prevailed upon to accept the restoration of King Henry as a fait accompli. In the attempt to secure the broadest possible support for his rule, Warwick could not afford to take too hard a line with former opponents, and the duke of Norfolk was freed from prison after only a few days.

If the duke's release came as a disappointment to the Pastons, they also had to contend with the possibility that the return of a Lancastrian government might mean the return of those who had been powerful when Henry VI was last on the throne—including, among others, their old enemy John Heydon, the family's most hated opponent during the dark days of the sack of Gresham. Heydon had retreated almost entirely from the political arena since the fall of the regime under which he had built his career. Years earlier, in his bleakest moments, John Paston had suspected that he might somehow be pulling strings behind the scenes of the young duke of Suffolk's occupation of Drayton and Hellesdon, but it seems more likely that Heydon had merely enjoyed the spectacle of Fastolf's executors squabbling among themselves, and the resulting devastation of the Pastons' hopes; "he has a great while laughed at us both," John II told Judge Yelverton sharply during the negotiations brokered by Bishop Wainfleet earlier in the year.[43]

However, Heydon's renewed capacity for dirty tricks became a matter of concern when the earl of Oxford visited Norwich in late November. John II had hoped to attend on the earl himself, but was unable to travel after a fortnight's illness; "I have gone with a staff as a ghost, as men said," he told his brother ruefully, "more like that I rose out of the earth than out of a fair lady's bed." John III was to represent the family in his stead, but "then must you beware of one pain," John II warned him, "and that is this: Heydon will of craft send among you perchance six or more with harness"— that is, men wearing armour and carrying weapons—"to slander your fellowship with saying that they are riotous people and not of substance." Not only should John III take precautions against the possibility of such infiltration by troublemakers, John II wrote anxiously, but he should "cause the mayor in my lord's ear to tell him . . . that the love of the country and city rests on our side, and that other folks are not beloved nor never were."[44]

Margaret had never been convinced by her sons' confidence in the new political order, but she was left frantic by reports of John II's illness—about which sinister rumours reached Norfolk—and an attack on John III by unknown assailants: ". . . it was told me this day that you were hurt by affray that was made upon you by fellows disguised," she wrote to her younger son on 1 December. "Therefore in any wise send me word in haste how your brother does, and you both, for I shall not be well at ease till I know how you do. And, for God's love, let your brother and you beware how you walk and with what fellowship you eat or drink, and in what place; for it was said here plainly that your brother was poisoned." She already blamed the conflict over Fastolf's estates for the premature death of her husband, and could not bear the idea that she might now lose a son to the same cause. "I had rather you had never known the land," she told John III. "Remember it was the destruction of your father." She certainly had no faith in the stability or the integrity of the new Lancastrian world. "Trust not much upon promises of lords . . . ," she wrote. "A man's death is little set by nowadays. Therefore beware of simulation, for they will speak right fair to you that would you fared right evil."[45]

Despite her misgivings, only ten days later her sons' greatest hopes were realised at last. The combined support of the earl of Oxford, Archbishop (now Chancellor) Neville, and Bishop Wainfleet proved enough to persuade the duke of Norfolk that the surrender of Caister would be a price worth paying to secure his position under the new regime. On 11 December 1470, the duke put his seal to a document which declared, with wide-eyed sincerity, that new information had come to light about his purchase of the castle from Judge Yelverton and his allies two years earlier:

> . . . forasmuch as by our dear uncle and cousin the archbishops of Canterbury and York and the bishop of Winchester we are informed that the said bargain was made contrary to the last will of Sir John Fastolf, . . . therefore at the especial request of the aforesaid reverend fathers in God, and to accomplish the said Sir John's last will, and in discharging of our conscience, we agree . . . to depart from all the said manors etc unto the said bishop of Winchester, who has taken upon him to execute the will.[46]

In return, Bishop Wainfleet graciously agreed to repay the duke the purchase price of five hundred marks (more than three hundred pounds, a sum that would not take too long to recoup from his new share in the Fastolf estate). Just over a year since John III had led his men, defeated and dejected, from the castle gates, the Pastons were once again masters of Caister.

In only two short months, their situation had been completely transformed. Thanks to the unforeseeably tortuous process of national politics, the deal with Wainfleet had paid off spectacularly. The duke of Norfolk had been forced to relinquish Caister. The castle's exterior was a little more battered and broken than it had been in Fastolf's day, and its interior stripped of the sumptuous furnishings with which the old knight had surrounded himself in retirement, but John Paston II would at last be able to walk through Caister's towering gate, under the watchful gaze of the gargoyles that stared down from the corbels, as its rightful owner with the support of all Fastolf's executors. "I am right glad that Caister is and shall be at your commandment, and yours in especial," William Worcester told Margaret that Christmas. He wrote warmly, despite the fact that the passage of the years had done nothing to ease his bitterness at the way he had been treated. "Would Jesu, mistress," he wrote, "that my good master that was sometime your husband . . . could have found in his heart to have trusted and loved me as my master Fastolf did, and that he would not have given credence to the malicious contrived tales that Friar Brackley, W. Barker and others imagined untruly, saving your reverence, of me." But he was now willing to accept a reconciliation, so long as his integrity and his honesty were recognised. "And now you may openly understand the truth," he went on, "and your son Sir John also. And yet, for all that, I put never my master Fastolf's livelihood in trouble, for all the unkindness and covetousness that was showed me."[47] More than ten years after the old knight's death, the rift that had torn apart the formerly close-knit circle of his friends and servants was finally beginning to heal.

But the Pastons had little time to enjoy their good fortune. The earl of Warwick was not finding it easy to establish secure foundations for his rule. He could not restore the estates of returning Lancastrian exiles without depriving those—himself included—who had benefited from their forfeitures. The position of the duke of Clarence, the most conspicuous Yorkist cuckoo in this supposedly Lancastrian nest, was becoming increasingly invidious; quite apart from the fact that Warwick's conversion to the Lancastrian cause had deprived him of all hope of achieving the crown for himself, Clarence was said to be "held in great suspicion, despite, disdain and hatred with all the lords . . . that were adherents and full partakers with

Henry."[48] The impending arrival from France of Queen Margaret and her son promised to introduce a forceful and unpredictable new element into a government that was already acutely unstable. Meanwhile, King Edward was not about to give up on the throne from which he had been ousted so suddenly. He had not been met with an effusive welcome on his arrival in Holland; his brother-in-law, Charles of Burgundy, had no wish to be drawn into all-out war on Edward's behalf, and refused to meet him for almost three months, at the same time sending conciliatory messages to the Lancastrian regime in England. However, Warwick had secured French backing for his coup on the basis of his commitment to an Anglo-French alliance against Burgundy. He therefore had no choice but to rebuff the duke's overtures, and made clear his intention to support King Louis when the latter declared war on Burgundy in December. Duke Charles's response to this aggression was, belatedly, to offer Edward his help, in the form of money and ships. On 11 March 1471, after an agonising nine-day wait for favourable winds, Edward set sail to reclaim his kingdom.

He aimed for the Norfolk coast in the hope of joining forces with the dukes of Norfolk and Suffolk, but found that the duke of Norfolk had been placed under arrest for a second time as soon as news reached England that Edward's arrival was imminent. Instead, the earl of Oxford was raising men in East Anglia in King Henry's name. Edward's small fleet therefore turned away from this inhospitable shore and headed north. On 14 March—having survived a violent storm at sea, at the cost of one ship full of drowned horses—he landed at Ravenspur, in Yorkshire. The situation in which he found himself was intensely dangerous. "It is a difficult matter to go out by the door and then try to enter by the windows," was the laconic comment of the Milanese ambassador in France on first reports of Edward's landing. "They think he will leave his skin there."[49] Edward had only a thousand or so soldiers under his command in what proved to be hostile territory; the city of Hull barred its gates against him, and scarcely any local men rallied to his cause. But the fragility of Warwick's regime was equally apparent. Two northern lords could have taken decisive action against Edward in the first few days after his landing: Warwick's brother John Neville, whose defection had precipitated Edward's deposition six months earlier; and Henry Percy, whose restoration to the earldom of Northumberland had provoked Neville's discontent. Neither made any move at all, either to stop Edward or to join him. Edward was therefore able to move southward, gathering support at last as he moved through the Midlands.

He marched on to the city of Coventry, where his enemy Warwick was waiting for the duke of Clarence to arrive with reinforcements. Warwick shut himself within the city walls and refused to respond to Edward's challenges—a strategy of uncharacteristic timidity which proved to be a costly mistake when word at last came that Clarence and his troops were approaching. On 3 April, Edward rode out to meet the brother who had betrayed him. Clarence—who had been under concerted pressure for months from his mother and sisters to abandon Warwick, and was looking now to save his own skin—threw himself onto his knees and begged for his brother's mercy. Even a man of Edward's magnanimous temperament might have found Clarence's repeated duplicity hard to stomach, but a combination of family feeling with hard-headed political calculation made the case for accepting Clarence's ostentatious show of repentance unanswerable, and the king embraced him with "right kind and loving language."[50]

With his army now swelled by Clarence's forces, and Warwick still refusing to fight, Edward turned south to London. News of the approaching Yorkist army threw the city into a panic; the mayor had already taken to his bed, claiming weakly that he was too ill to make any decisions. In desperation, Archbishop Neville paraded King Henry through the streets in a last attempt to rally the Londoners, but Henry—wearing "a long blue gown of velvet, as though he had no more to change with," and clinging nervously to the archbishop's hand—now cut such a frail and pathetic figure that the sight of him went a long way to persuade the city's inhabitants that they would do well to throw in their lot with his Yorkist rival.[51] On 11 April, when Edward finally rode into the capital, he encountered no resistance. (Given the terrifying reverses of the past two years, it was perhaps not surprising that he was greeted with little celebration either, unless a Burgundian commentator was right that the ladies of the city were overjoyed to see the return of their handsome king.) He made his way to Westminster Abbey, pausing there for a brief moment to allow the archbishop of Canterbury a chance to place the crown ceremonially on his head once more, before hastening to the abbey's sanctuary to be reunited with his wife and daughters. There, for the first time, he saw the baby boy—his son and heir Edward, Prince of Wales—to whom Elizabeth had given birth in the sanctuary five months earlier. On Edward's orders, King Henry was returned to the Tower under guard, scarcely, by now, in a state to understand what was happening to him. Archbishop Neville and Bishop

Wainfleet, as men of the cloth, were safe from the scaffold; but neither Neville's glib fluency nor Wainfleet's age and integrity could save them from imprisonment, and they joined Henry in custody.

It seemed barely credible that another reversal of power could be possible only six months after Edward's forlorn flight to the Netherlands as a refugee from his own realm—and certainly his victory was not yet assured. Warwick, who had recovered his composure after the debâcle of Clarence's defection at Coventry, was now advancing on London, with his brother John Neville and his brother-in-law Oxford in his company. He had long ago passed the point of no return; his only hope even of safety, let alone of the power he had craved so fiercely, now lay in the utter destruction of the cousin for whom he had once fought so steadfastly. Meanwhile, Queen Margaret—whose departure from France had been repeatedly delayed by bad weather—was expected to land on the south coast any day, bringing more troops to swell Warwick's forces. It was clear that the rule of England would yet again be contested on the battlefield.

Until now, John Paston and his sons had kept their heads down when political division gave way to open warfare. Wherever their sympathies lay, they had always known that they had nothing tangible to gain by committing themselves in battle, and potentially everything to lose if they backed the wrong side. Now it was different. The restoration of Lancastrian government had meant the restoration of Caister to the Pastons, and had brought them for the first time, in the person of the earl of Oxford, a truly powerful lord who welcomed their service and went out of his way to further their interests. They had spent most of their adult lives under the rule of Edward of York, but a victory for him now would be a victory for the duke of Norfolk, and all the family's achievements of the past few months would disappear without trace. It was not a question of being "Lancastrian" or "Yorkist": the relationship between the two sides was in any case more complex than that, now that the Yorkist earl of Warwick had seized power in the name of the Lancastrian Henry VI. The Paston brothers had no option but to follow the lords—the earl of Oxford, Archbishop Neville, and Bishop Wainfleet—who had championed their interests and offered hope for the future.

By the time Edward swept into London on 11 April, therefore, John II and John III had already left the city to serve under the command of the earl of Oxford in the earl of Warwick's army, now marching south from the Midlands. On 12 April, Good Friday, Warwick's forces—perhaps numbering as many as ten or fifteen thousand men—reached the town of St. Albans, whose streets had rung with the clash of steel more than once in the past two decades. The next day they pressed on as far as the town of Barnet, ten miles away from the capital, where Warwick drew up his troops on a ridge of high ground just north of the town. That same afternoon, Edward moved north from London, accompanied by his brothers Clarence and Gloucester, his brother-in-law Rivers, and his friend Hastings. As night fell, the Yorkist army—a smaller force of perhaps nine thousand men—advanced through Barnet itself and, under cover of darkness, took up position immediately opposite Warwick's troops. During the night, the earl ordered his gunners to blast the Yorkist lines, but Edward's troops were nearer than Warwick realised, and the cannon shot harmlessly over their heads, while the king ordered his men to stay still and silent to conceal their true position. A few hours later, at around four in the morning on Easter Sunday—in semi-darkness, the field shrouded with densely swirling fog—Edward gave the order to attack.

When the fighting began, it gradually became clear that, not only had the two armies been encamped closer together than Warwick had thought, but unbeknown to both sides, they were not facing each other in exact alignment. The right flank of Warwick's army—commanded by the earl of Oxford and including among its number John Paston II and John Paston III—extended beyond the left flank of Edward's forces by some distance, giving Oxford an advantage that he was quick to exploit, his men hacking their way, with the sickening thud of steel on flesh, into Yorkist lines that were soon overwhelmed by sheer weight of numbers. But as the Yorkist left crumbled, an identical scenario was playing itself out in reverse on the other side of the battlefield. There, the right flank of Edward's army reached beyond the left flank of Warwick's, which in turn began to buckle under the pressure. As each army pressed forward on one side of the field and gave way on the other, the two lines wheeled round until they faced east–west rather than north–south.

At the same time, the vicious mêlée, and the disorientating effects of the fog, meant that the commanders on both sides could neither see nor hear exactly what was happening. Oxford's men, who had now routed the Yorkist left, pursued their fleeing opponents a mile southward into the town of Barnet, and it was some time before the earl succeeded in regrouping his jubilant forces to return to the field. By the time he did so, the force of the fighting had swung the battlelines so far from their original position that, without realising what they were doing, Oxford's charging troops smashed into the rear of their own army. They were not the only ones fatally confused by the appalling conditions. Warwick's men mistook the livery their attackers were wearing—emblazoned as it was with Oxford's badge of the Enrayed Star—for the Sun in Splendour, the personal emblem of King Edward. They opened fire, and Oxford and his soldiers fled in disarray, while cries of treason began to spread among Warwick's army. The earl's brother John Neville, who had abandoned Edward's cause so late and so unhappily, now paid the ultimate price for that unwilling betrayal. Cut down amid the bloody chaos, his corpse lay on the battlefield beside the bodies of two thousand of his countrymen. Learning of his brother's death, and realising that Edward had now decisively secured the upper hand, Warwick tried to escape. But he was cornered by Yorkist soldiers and killed—a dagger thrust into his face through his open visor—before Edward could reach him. It was a brutal and ignominious end for a man who had cast himself as arbiter of the nation's fate.

It was the best part of a week later before Margaret received word that her sons were safe: ". . . blessed be God, my brother John is alive and fares well, and in no peril of death," John II wrote from London on 18 April. "Nevertheless he is hurt with an arrow on his right arm beneath the elbow, and I have sent him a surgeon which has dressed him, and he tells me that he trusts that he shall be all whole within right short time." He was doing what he could to reassure her; despite the catastrophic reversal in their fortunes, they were at least alive, and John III's wound was not serious. Their situation—with Warwick dead, Oxford on his way to seek shelter in Scotland, and Archbishop Neville and Bishop Wainfleet incarcerated in the Tower—was far from good. On the other hand, Lancastrian hopes had not been completely obliterated by Edward's victory. With dreadful irony, Queen Margaret—who had refused to bring her son back to England until the country was safely in Warwick's hands—finally landed on the south coast on the day the earl died at Barnet. As Margaret advanced, gathering armed support from the southwestern counties of Devon and Cornwall as she went, Edward responded by mustering fresh troops of his own—and until the two armies met, all conclusions were provisional and all political activity dangerous: ". . . the world, I assure you, is right queasy," John II told his mother. Nevertheless, his instinctive optimism shone through, even if he had to choose his words with great circumspection. "God has showed himself marvellously, like him that made all and can undo again when he pleases," he wrote carefully, "and I can think that by all likelihood shall show himself as marvellous again, and that in short time. . . . Be you not doubted of the world, for I trust all shall be well. If it thus continue I am not all undone, nor none of us; and if otherwise, then, etc."[52]

By the end of the month, John III had almost recovered, and added his voice to his brother's attempt to set their mother's mind at rest. "If it please you to have knowledge of our royal person," he wrote with deliberate cheerfulness, "I thank God I am whole of my sickness, and trust to be clean whole of all my hurts within a sevennight at the furthest." He was also so desperately short of money—"in my greatest need that ever I was in"—that he found himself forced to ask Margaret for help; "I have neither meat, drink, clothes, leechcraft nor money but upon borrowing." But he was convinced—or perhaps doing his utmost to convince his mother—that it would be only days before Queen Margaret's forces delivered the news for which they had been waiting: ". . . with God's grace it shall not be long before my wrongs and other men's shall be redressed," he wrote confidently, "for the world was never so like to be ours as it is now."[53]

He was right that it would be a matter of days, but wrong about the outcome. On 4 May 1471, Edward succeeded in intercepting the northward march of Queen Margaret's army at Tewkesbury in Gloucestershire, little more than twenty miles east of the Welsh border. It proved to be the final disaster for the Lancastrian cause. The queen herself was captured, and her seventeen-year-old son—the Lancastrian heir to the throne, fighting in his first battle—was killed in combat. The events of the past two years had warned Edward about the dangers of being overmerciful, and on the night he arrived back in London, Henry VI—now an ex-king twice over, and once again a prisoner in the Tower—was murdered. With him died all the Pastons' hopes. The heady experience of powerful patronage had persuaded them to fight against the Yorkist king to whom they had offered loyal service for a decade, but getting too close to powerful men in dangerous times meant that risks, as well as rewards, were great. It was a gamble they had been forced to take, but they had lost in spectacular fashion. The duke of Norfolk was quick to seek his revenge. On 23 June 1471, he seized Caister Castle again, and this time the Pastons—with all hope of protection gone—dared offer no resistance.

CHAPTER II

✌

the matter of Caister

KING EDWARD HAD WON HIS THRONE on the battlefield for the second time. It had come at a heavy price. Only ten years after the bloodletting of 1459–1461, thousands more Englishmen had been slaughtered, cut down by English hands on English soil. And for Edward, like many of his subjects, the conflict had brought personal betrayal and loss. The bodies of Warwick and his brother John Neville—the cousins who had once been Edward's brothers-in-arms—had been brought back to the capital in rough wooden coffins, stripped of their armour, still spattered with the mire of the battlefield and the dark stains of their own clotted blood. They were left for two days on the floor of St. Paul's Cathedral, so that the people of London could see for themselves that the great kingmaker was dead. But their corpses were spared the full penalties of treason; they were not carved up to be displayed on city gates around the country as macabre totems of victory. Instead, they were buried with quiet dignity at Bisham Abbey thirty miles west of London, beside the graves of their father and brother, who had died fighting for Edward's father at Wakefield a decade before.

The absence of vengefulness was characteristic of Edward, but so was his resolute determination that his hold on the crown should never again be challenged. The Lancastrian line—which fifty years earlier, at the height of Henry V's glorious victories, had seemed to contemporaries to be marked by God's blessing—had been wiped out. Poor, fragile Henry VI and his young son were dead, and Edward ordered that Henry's body be publicly displayed on a bier at St. Paul's, its face uncovered, to forestall seditious rumours that the former king might still be alive. The loss of her husband and son left Queen Margaret a spent force and a broken woman. With no one left to fight for, she was no longer a threat to Edward's rule, but remained a prisoner, held first at the royal palaces of Windsor Castle and the Tower of London. Later, extending his usual generosity even to this bitterest of enemies, the king delivered Margaret into the more congenial custody of her old friend Alice Chaucer, dowager duchess of Suffolk, at Wallingford Castle forty miles west of London, with an allowance of five pounds a week for her upkeep.

Meanwhile, as Edward yet again set about the task of reimposing his authority on the country, the Pastons were left to contemplate what might have been. Power had changed hands so often and so rapidly during the past two years that the topsy-turvy course of politics might have seemed almost farcical, had it not been for the fact that the rule of England, and thousands of lives, were at stake. At stake for the Pastons, of course, was Caister. The family had sacrificed much, and John Daubeney had died, in the attempt to keep hold of the castle. Now it was gone. More than a decade after John Paston had first claimed the Fastolf inheritance, scarcely any of the old knight's estates were left in Paston hands.

John II and John III lay low during the summer of 1471, doing what they could to secure formal pardons for having taken up arms against King Edward at Barnet. They were in no immediate danger, since the king's concern—which he was pursuing with the same remarkable magnanimity evident in his treatment of his cousins' remains—was to reunite his subjects under his rule, not to engage in a witch hunt. Much more powerful men than the Paston brothers had already been forgiven, officially at least: their patrons Archbishop Neville and Bishop Wainfleet, for example, were pardoned and freed in the months after Edward's final victory at Tewkesbury. Nevertheless, the Pastons' situation would remain uncomfortably vulnerable until they could obtain royal documents absolving them of any possible charges of treason. "I pray you beware of your guiding, and in chief of your language," John II warned his brother grimly that autumn, "so that from henceforth by your language no man perceives that you favour any person contrary to the king's pleasure." The threat was not an idle one; word had reached John II from Norfolk that dangerous accusations had been made in public against John III. "I heard yesterday," he wrote, ". . . that at Norwich one had large language to you and called you traitor, and picked many quarrels to you. Send me word thereof. It were well done that you were a little surer of your pardon than you are."[1]

It did not help the Pastons that, although Archbishop Neville and Bishop Wainfleet were now at liberty, neither was in a position of sufficient trust with the king to intercede with him on their behalf. Given how deeply the two prelates had been implicated in Warwick's treachery, that was hardly surprising—but much more disappointingly, the Pastons' one former patron who had fought at King Edward's side proved to be just as ineffectual. The queen's brother Earl Rivers—or Lord Scales, as he was still better known in Norfolk—had declared his intention to go to Portugal on crusade against the Moors, "and because he thinks that I would go with him," John III told his mother in July, ". . . this is the cause that he will be my good lord and help to get the pardon." However, Edward was unimpressed by his brother-in-law's plan to leave the country when there were so many challenges still to face at home, commenting acidly that his valour was all surface and no substance. "The king is not best pleased with him," John III reported, ". . . in so much that the king has said of him that, whensoever he has most to do, then the Lord Scales will soonest ask leave to depart, and thinks that it is most because of cowardice."[2]

Rivers, who prided himself on his carefully cultivated chivalric reputation, can hardly have been pleased by this disparaging interpretation of his motives, especially when Edward responded by dismissing him from the lieutenancy of Calais—a key strategic appointment in command of the permanent garrison there—in favour of the king's closest friend, William, Lord Hastings. It was perhaps because of the fact that Rivers was under such a cloud at court that John II made no urgent attempt to revive his relationship with the earl's cousin Anne Haute, to whom he was still formally engaged—a match, it had to be said, for which he had never shown any pressing personal enthusiasm. The young woman herself seemed equally ambivalent, and the couple were considering the possibility of seeking an annulment of their betrothal, something that would require a papal dispensation. "I had almost spoken with Mistress Anne Haute," John II told his brother in September, "but I did not. Nevertheless, this next term I hope to take one way with her or other. She is agreed to speak with me, and she hopes to do me ease, as she says."[3] It was clearly no grand romance—but when they did finally meet in February 1472, three years after they were first engaged, both parties seem to have surprised themselves by agreeing that the marriage should go ahead after all. ". . . as for tidings," John II reported cheerfully to John III, "I have spoken with Mistress Anne Haute at a pretty leisure and, blessed be God, we are as far forth as we were heretofore, and so I hope we shall continue; and I promised her that at the next leisure that I could find thereto that I would come again and see her."[4]

John II had other reasons too for his good spirits in the early months of 1472. Despite their political miscalculations, the brothers had not lost all their friends among the gentlemen of King Edward's household. John II and John III were not, after all, full-blooded Lancastrians, but renegade Yorkists who were now keen to demonstrate their repentance of their misdeeds. As a result, they finally succeeded in securing official pardons, John III in February and his brother two months earlier, "for comfort whereof I have been the merrier this Christmas," John II told Margaret at the beginning of January.[5] He was still spending most of his time in London, often staying at the Black Swan Inn where he became so friendly with the landlady, Elizabeth Higgins, that he took the trouble to send news of her family back to his brother in Norwich: "Mistress Elizabeth" herself had just given birth to a healthy baby boy, he reported, but her grown-up daughter had lost a son, born eleven weeks prematurely. "It was christened John, and is dead. God save all," John II added soberly.[6]

However, he spent Christmas itself at Betchworth in Surrey, twenty miles south of the capital, with his aunt Elizabeth Paston and her recently acquired second husband, a gentleman named Sir George Browne. Twelfth Night, the lavish feast that marked the end of the Christmas season, was celebrated in great households under the anarchic direction of the King of the Bean, otherwise known as the Lord of Misrule, who was chosen at random from the assembled company by hiding a bean in a rich fruitcake. Whoever found the bean in their own slice of cake would delight the guests by presiding over games and entertainments, dancing and "disguisings," in which decorum was forgotten. For these raucous festivities John II moved on from his aunt's home to the Moor, Archbishop Neville's magnificent house in Hertfordshire, "where I have had as great cheer, and been as welcome, as I could devise," he reported happily to Margaret. He signed off with a solicitous attempt to transmit his positive mood to his mother: "I beseech God send you good health and more joy in one year than you have had these seven."[7]

But, as so often, Margaret was not convinced by his optimism. Her relief at her sons' survival on the battlefield at Barnet had quickly evaporated under the accumulating pressures of the months since King Edward had reclaimed his throne. In the autumn of 1471, while John II and John III were nervously awaiting news of their hoped-for pardons, a frightening outbreak of plague swept the country. Fragmentary references in the surviving documents make it impossible to be sure how many people perished, although the king was so alarmed that he spent the hefty sum of ten pounds on prophylactic medicine to ward off the pestilence. Certainly, the Pastons and their friends were terrified by its virulence; "the most universal death that ever I knew in England," John II called it. "Wherefore, for God's sake," he told his brother, "let my mother take heed to my young brethren, that they be not in no place where that sickness is reigning, nor that they disport not with no other young people which resort where any sickness is."[8] In November, Margaret reported four deaths among their acquaintances in Norwich, although she and the children had so far escaped. "All this household and this parish are safe, blessed be God," she wrote on 5 November. "We live in fear, but we know not whither to flee to be better than we are here."[9]

Not that the younger Pastons were all still children. William, the baby of the family, was eleven, and Walter and Anne were both teenagers. Edmund was twenty and had completed his education, but his further prospects had so far been blighted by the fact that his mother and brothers had been too preoccupied with the family's difficulties at Caister to help find him some honourable and remunerative position, perhaps in the service of a great lord. "Also my brother Edmund is not yet remembered," John II had noted as an afterthought at the end of a letter to John III more than a year earlier. "He has naught to live with; think on him, etc."[10] Nothing had been done by November 1471, when Edmund himself asked John III if he could secure him "any profitable service." He still owed money to the Staple Inn in London, where he had spent some time as a student learning the basics of the law, but he did not allow his financial straits to compromise his exuberant taste in clothes. He included a lengthy shopping list in his letter to John III, who was staying in the capital for a few weeks: three yards of purple camlet—a lightweight cloth—at four shillings a yard; a "bonnet of deep mulberry" for two shillings and fourpence; woollen cloth, in yellow, to make a pair of hose; a belt made out of ribbon in a grey-blue colour known as "plunket"; three dozen "points"—laces by which hose were tied onto other garments at the waist to prevent them falling down—in white, red, and yellow; and three pairs of pattens, wooden overshoes worn to raise the wearer's feet above the mud and refuse in the streets.[11] He, too, sent his regards to Elizabeth Higgins at the Black Swan, and was clearly chafing at the restrictions of life at home in Norfolk.

Edmund was made particularly unhappy in the spring of 1472 by his mother's outraged insistence that he dismiss his manservant Gregory, whom Margaret held responsible for the fact that a prostitute had recently spent the night in the stables of her manor house at Mautby. Gregory had availed himself of the woman's services in the enclosure of the rabbit warren there when two ploughmen saw what was happening "and desired him to have part." It was with the ploughmen that she stayed overnight in the stable, "and Gregory was clean delivered of her," Edmund pointed out indignantly, "and, as he swears, had not ado with her in my mother's place." He blamed the loss of a man from whom he was "as sorry to depart . . . as any man alive from his servant" on the growing influence of his mother's chaplain, James Gloys, on whom Margaret had come to rely heavily in recent years.[12]

Gloys was no longer the hothead he had been in his twenties when he provoked a fight by refusing to doff his cap to the Pastons' loudmouthed enemy John Wyndham—although, from the point of view of the Paston brothers, it seemed that his arrogance was undiminished. He was of their mother's generation—Margaret was now fifty, and Gloys cannot have been much less—and was asserting his authority in the household to an extent that Edmund thought excessive and profoundly irritating. He was not the only one. In July, John III reported to his older brother that he, too, had argued with "the proud, peevish and evil disposed priest"; "we fell out before my mother with 'Thou proud priest' and 'Thou proud squire,'" he told John II gloomily, "my mother taking his part." That was the heart of the problem. Margaret had coped with the traumas of the past three years with her usual fortitude, but she had also found them exhausting; and while she leaned on her chaplain for practical and emotional support, she was less appreciative of her sons' continued presence in her household. They were full-grown men—John III twenty-eight, and Edmund now twenty-two—and should renew their efforts to find honourable employment in a great lord's service, she felt, rather than continue to live at home at her expense. "Many quarrels are picked to get my brother E. and me out of her house," John III wrote in exasperation. "We go not to bed unchidden lightly. All that we do is ill done, and all that Sir James and Pecock do"—"Sir" being the honorific form of address to which priests as well as knights were enti-

tled, and Pecock a Mautby man who had been in Paston service for years—
"is well done."[13]

John III and Edmund were just as keen to leave as Margaret was eager
to secure a little more peace and quiet in her household, but the difficulty
they faced was that, until the passing of time had dissolved the black mark
with which Barnet had blotted the family name, a position in noble service
would be hard to come by. Until then, they had nowhere else to go, and no
income on which to live independently. There seemed to be no possibility
that they might receive the lands allotted to them in their father's will while
they were still unmarried and had no household of their own to support.
And given the family's political disgrace and current penury, no well-
connected gentlemen would easily be persuaded of their merits as potential
sons-in-law. In the meantime, friction with their mother was doing their
prospects no good at all. Margaret had recently declared her intention to
draw up her own will, "and, in this anger between Sir James and me, she
has promised me that my part shall be naught," John III told John II
resignedly; "what yours shall be, I cannot say."[14]

There was some consolation in the fact that one older breach within the
family had begun to be mended. As Richard Calle had hoped—and thanks,
perhaps, to the disastrous turn the family's affairs had taken, which made
competent and loyal service all the more valuable, whatever its source—
Margaret's hostility to her own unwanted son-in-law had now subsided far
enough for him to return to the Pastons' employment. He was not yet
accorded the same level of responsibility that he had once enjoyed, and
Margaret's forgiveness may not have extended as far as her wayward daughter, since she made no mention of Margery in her letters. Nevertheless,
Calle's experience and his capabilities were such that his return could only
be a relief, in practical terms at least—although Edmund, impetuous and
volatile as always, quickly managed to fall out with him, too ("there has
been a great break between Calle and me, as I shall inform you at my coming," he told John III testily).[15]

However trying she found the squabbles within her household,
Margaret was preoccupied above all with the need to find some kind of
answer to the reverses the family had suffered. So far, there was no sign of
any improvement in their fortunes. In the autumn of 1471, John II had suggested to John III that he should sound out the duchess of Norfolk and
other members of the duke's household to see "whether it be possible to
have Caister again, and their goodwills, or not."[16] Even by John II's stan-

dards, this seemed wildly over-optimistic. After everything that had happened, it was hardly likely that Norfolk could simply be persuaded to
accept a deal that involved his giving up the castle, let alone to do so with
good humour. It was far from clear even by what means the Pastons might
succeed in bringing the duke to the negotiating table. Without doubt,
Norfolk's claim to Caister was technically weak (albeit that the duke himself, determined as he was to assert the validity of his purchase, would never
admit as much). On the other hand, the fact of the matter was that the castle was now in his possession. Even if King Edward could be persuaded of
the justice of the Pastons' cause, his principal preoccupation, for the
moment at least, was the consolidation of his hold on power after the chaos
of the past few years—a process in which the support of the duke of
Norfolk weighed more heavily than the claims of a minor gentleman who
had forfeited Edward's goodwill when he took the field against him at
Barnet.

It was not even that the king was particularly impressed by Norfolk's
political talents. At twenty-seven, the duke displayed an awkwardly unpredictable combination of impulsiveness and mulish stubbornness. He was no
more a subtle politician than his blundering father had been, nor did he
show much sign of emerging as a charismatic leader of men. Certainly,
Norfolk was entrusted with no major responsibilities as Edward rebuilt his
regime, unlike many of the other noblemen who had supported the Yorkist
cause during the conflict of 1470–1471. Nevertheless, even if the duke was
not high in the king's esteem, that was all the more reason for Edward not
to risk alienating him by insisting that he restore Caister to a family whose
own title to the castle had been in dispute for a decade, and who had abandoned their Yorkist allegiance to support the restoration of Henry VI.
Discouraging as it was for the Pastons to admit, there was no indication that
the king had any immediate intention to discipline Norfolk. The duke had
acted with egregious aggression, but the chaotic circumstances that had
allowed him to do so—the vicious struggle for the throne itself—both overshadowed and, it seemed, excused his conduct. Instead, Edward found a
way to bestow public honour upon Norfolk without delegating any practical power into his hands: on St. George's Day, 23 April 1472, in a splendid
ceremony at Windsor Castle, the duke was created a knight of the Order of
the Garter, the elite chivalric brotherhood founded more than a century
earlier by the warrior king Edward III in homage to Arthurian legend.

Two days later, any lingering hope that Archbishop Neville might eventually recover enough influence to press the Pastons' case suddenly vanished. The archbishop had been employing all his diplomatic wiles in the attempt to rebuild his relationship with his royal cousin, and Edward—driven by some combination of his characteristic clemency and an instinct to keep this slippery opportunist under close observation—had responded warmly to his overtures, seeking out the archbishop's company on his frequent hunting trips into the royal forests around Windsor. That April, Edward suggested that they move their sport to Neville's luxurious palace of the Moor, north of London, and the archbishop hurried home to prepare his household, ordering copious supplies of food and drink fit for a king, the banquet to be served on the silver plate that he had stashed away for safekeeping ever since his brother's death at Barnet a year earlier. But his illustrious guest never arrived. The day before Edward's breathlessly anticipated visit was due to begin, the archbishop received a peremptory summons to return at once to Windsor. There, he was placed under arrest: ". . . my lord archbishop was brought to the Tower on Saturday at night," John II reported uneasily to his brother, "and on Monday at midnight he was conveyed to a ship and so into the sea, and as yet I cannot understand whither he is sent nor what is befallen of him."[17]

The news, when it came, was not good. The archbishop was now a prisoner in Hammes Castle, the fortress just to the west of Calais that lay within the English-controlled militarised zone around the port itself, stretching eighteen miles along the coast and ten miles inland, known as the Calais Pale. He had been taken into custody on suspicion of treasonable conspiracy with his brother-in-law the earl of Oxford, who had fled via Scotland to France after the disaster at Barnet and was now launching raids on Calais with the support of the French king. Louis XI was delighted to use any means at his disposal to destabilise Edward's rule and keep him occupied within his own borders, with no opportunity to turn an aggressive eye toward France; and to achieve that end by sponsoring attacks on an English stronghold that was a perennial thorn in French flesh merely made Oxford's tactics still more appealing. Whether or not Archbishop Neville had been embroiled in treacherous intrigue with Oxford and the French—and it was all too likely that he had, given his track record of limitless ambition and dangerous over-confidence—it was abundantly clear that, this time, his disgrace was permanent. Edward lost no time in seizing the lands Neville held as archbishop, and the opulent jewels and plate he had amassed for his personal use; his mitre, encrusted with gemstones, was broken up and refashioned, on Edward's orders, into a new crown for the king's own head. As the archbishop contemplated the wreckage of his hopes from behind Hammes's impregnable walls, John II and John III had no option but to face the fact that none of their former patrons was in any position to help them.

By the beginning of June, not much more than a month after the archbishop's arrest, Margaret sounded distressed about how little they had to show for all their years of labour, and how remote the prospect now seemed that they might salvage anything from the Fastolf inheritance for which they had struggled so long. She had heard that Bishop Wainfleet, under pressures of his own, had agreed to sell two Fastolf manors from his share of the estate (which he still retained, under the terms of the agreement of 1470) to John Heydon's son Henry. The idea that some of the property for which her husband had fought so hard should go to the family of his oldest rival was almost heartbreaking. "We beat the bushes, and have the loss and the disworship, and other men have the birds," she told John II bleakly. "My lord has false counsel and simple that advises him thereto. . . . What shall fall of the remnant, God knows; I think as evil or worse. We have the loss among us." Not only that, but the duke of Norfolk's men were threatening her own manor of Mautby only a mile away from Caister, where she now spent much of her time; "and if we lose that," she wrote, ever the proud Mautby heiress, "we lose the fairest flower of our garland." If her home and its estates were to be kept safe from damaging harassment while the wrangle over Caister continued, she said, John II should do everything he could to secure the retreat of Norfolk's occupying forces from the castle—perhaps ceding it temporarily to a third party, as she had suggested when the siege was at its height—"whatsoever fortune hereafter."[18]

But that, like every attempt they had ever made to persuade the duke to come to some kind of compromise, was easier said than done. In practice, there was little John II and his brother could do but be patient, be careful, cope as best they could with the little money they had, and take what few political opportunities came their way to press their case. However, Margaret's confidence in her eldest son's handling of the family's affairs had been badly eroded over the previous year. Her natural conservatism, and her responsibilities as custodian of many Paston estates as well as her Mautby manors, left her preoccupied with the urgent need not to put the family's own lands at risk in the wild goose chase that the quest for the Fastolf inheritance had now become. Meanwhile, for John II—an instinctive risk-taker, and one who saw little benefit from his Paston lands while his mother and grandmother still held more than two-thirds of the family's estates—it must have seemed that he had little to lose by gambling everything on the fight for Caister.

The relationship between mother and son deteriorated still further under the strain of their increasingly desperate financial difficulties. Seven months earlier, in the autumn of 1471, Margaret had been thrown into panic when her friend Elizabeth Clere suddenly found that she needed to reclaim a loan of one hundred marks—the equivalent of sixty-six pounds, about half Margaret's annual income from her lands—which Margaret had borrowed in order to pass the money on to John II. Usury—that is, lending at interest for certain gain—was forbidden by the church (although the element of risk inherent in all transactions between different currencies allowed international banking houses, the Medici of Florence prominent among them, to evade this stern prohibition). But interest-free loans between friends were commonplace, helping to ease the cash shortages which landowners inevitably suffered from time to time, given that their incomes were both seasonal and unpredictable. Their tenants' rents were paid twice yearly, and could be severely depleted by the costs of running repairs on barns and byres, hedges and ditches, walls and mills; and the profits to be made from the produce of estates that landlords retained under their own cultivation depended not only on waiting for harvest time or sheep shearing, but also on the vagaries of the local market: "as for your barley in this country, it cannot be sold above 10d or 11d; that is the greatest price of barley here," Margaret reported gloomily to John II one year.[19] But the strain on the Pastons' finances was much more acute than these quotidian pressures. Their costs, including legal fees, wages for the men they had taken on to help defend their properties, and political payments to grease influential palms (including the huge loan to Archbishop Neville, which they now stood no chance of recouping), had been running at what should have been abnormally high levels for years. Meanwhile, the Fastolf estates, for the sake of which all these extraordinary costs had been incurred, were barely adding any revenues at all to the family's rapidly emptying coffers.

In the circumstances, Margaret found, to her horror, that she did not have the means to make good what she owed. "And I know not how to do therefor, by my troth," she wrote frantically to John III during his trip to London that November, "for I have it not, nor I cannot make shift therefor"—

not even "if I should go to prison."[20] She sounded agitated and over-wrought: she could raise a lump sum by selling all the timber from her woods, she said, but there was a glut on the market in Norfolk and she would not get a good price. In any case, carefully managed woodland was a precious asset, and future years of valuable supplies would be lost if the trees were chopped down to their stumps and sold off wholesale: there would be no brushwood for fuel and fencing, no carefully managed stocks of timber for building and repairs; and without their woodland home, there would be no pigs fattening themselves for slaughter on acorns and beech mast, nor bees producing honey for everyday sweetening (imported sugar being an expensive luxury reserved for special occasions). The short-term financial benefit of disposing of the wood was obvious, but fine trees would take years to grow again, and while they did so, the annual value of the whole manor would suffer.

The proposal was too shortsighted to warrant serious consideration, but Margaret was worryingly bereft of realistic alternatives. Her anxieties were compounded by the prospect of public humiliation, since gentlemen and gentlewomen of standing were expected to be responsible financial man-agers. No landowner could hope to avoid borrowing against future income at one time or another, but from year to year those with a cash surplus would extend favours in the form of loans for reasons of policy or friend-ship, while those who found themselves short of money would accept them, in the expectation that their roles would soon be reversed. This was a credit network into which credit of every kind was inextricably woven. Reputations were at stake just as much as money: "as for Paston," a friend had once, in much happier days, said admiringly of Margaret's husband, "he is a squire of worship, and of great livelihood, and I know he will not spend all his goods at once."[21] It was not "worshipful" to extend one's finances to a point where valuable assets—principally silver plate, which conveniently doubled up as a cash reserve as well as a glittering display of a household's magnificence—might have to be forfeited in lieu of repay-ments. A gentry household without silverware would lose face; but if, God forbid, land had to be sold, a family risked losing everything. The Pastons had made themselves conspicuous by setting their sights on Fastolf's riches, and friends, neighbours, and enemies alike had watched as their dreams were trampled into the dust under the feet of the duke of Norfolk's men. The last thing they now needed was to find the full extent of their financial woes mortifyingly exposed to public view. The only escape Margaret could see from the hole in which she suddenly found herself was that John II himself would have to find the money—but she no longer had any faith that she could rely on him to help her. "And when I remember it, it is to my heart a very spear," she wrote accusingly, "considering that he never gave me comfort therein, nor of all the money that he has received will never make shift therefor. If he had yet before this time sent me fifty marks thereof yet, I would have thought that he had had some consideration of my danger that I have put me in for him."[22]

She was so unhappy with her eldest son's behaviour that she was now communicating with him only through his younger brother. "Methinks by your brother that he is weary to write to me," she told John III with some hauteur three weeks later, "and therefore I will not encumber him with writing to him. You may tell him as I write to you."[23] John III's role as go-between was profoundly unenviable. His mother's messages were increasingly angry and censorious, while his brother was simply unable to raise the money she needed. John II's failure to repay the loan was hardly a surprise, given how limited his resources now were. While Margaret and his grandmother Agnes were still alive, he held only a tiny fraction of his Paston inheritance, and virtually all of the Fastolf estates to which he still had a claim had now been taken from him. Margaret, however, persisted in believing that extravagance lay at the root of his financial problems. "He writes to me also that he has spent this term £40," she told John III disapprovingly. "It is a great thing. Methinks by good discretion there might much thereof have been saved. Your father, God bless his soul, has had as great matters to do as I think he has had this term, and has not spent half the money upon them in so little time, and has done right well." The comparison with his dead father—against whose criticisms she had once defended John II so tenaciously—was deeply unfair, not least because it involved a substantial rewriting of history: John Paston could hardly be said to have "done right well" in his handling of the Fastolf dispute, however economical his methods had been. Nevertheless, unfair though they were, her reproaches were an expression of genuine distress. "So may I answer before God, I know not how to do for the said money . . . ," she wrote in evident anguish; "it is a death to me to think upon it."[24] They also served to demonstrate how estranged she now felt from a son who spent so little time at home in Norfolk that she scarcely had a chance even to try to see the world from his point of view.

John II sought to rebuild bridges with his mother with his cheerful message from Archbishop Neville's house that Christmas, adding some good intentions to accompany the good wishes he sent her. If all went well, he said, "I purpose me to come home and see you this Lent, and set my land in better rule than it has been heretofore."[25] He also renewed his efforts to lay his hands on some money. Over the past few years, he had already been forced to supplement his landed income by pawning a substantial amount of the family's silver plate—£90 worth in a single week in July 1470, for example. Now, although Margaret was unwilling to contemplate despoiling her woodlands to raise the cash they needed, John II saw no alternative but to do so on his own estates, and he set about finding a buyer for the timber at his manor of Sporle. John III, always more attuned to the practical realities of agriculture and husbandry, thought the proposal to surrender future income for cash in hand unwise: ". . . by God, if I were you, I would not sell it for a hundred marks more than it is worth," he told his brother earnestly.[26]

Despite his objections, there was little else John II could do if he were serious about securing a lump sum with which to settle his debts, especially once all hope of further help from Archbishop Neville had been dashed by his arrest in the spring of 1472. John II found a purchaser and agreed the sale by the end of that summer, all the while making every effort to keep the deal secret from his mother. In the end, however, his subterfuge was exposed by the Norfolk rumour mill. Word of his plans reached Margaret in October. She was distraught—"my mother weeps and takes on marvellously," John III reported—and threatened to cut her eldest son out of her will altogether: "she says that she will purvey for her land that you shall none sell of it, for she thinks you would if it came to your hand."[27] When Margaret herself wrote to John II, it was to speak her mind in no uncertain terms. If what she had heard was true, she told him, "it . . . should cause both your enemies and your friends to think that you did it for right great need, or else that you should be a waster and would waste your livelihood. . . . Wherefore, in eschewing of the great slander and inconvenience that may grow thereof, I require you and moreover charge you upon my blessing, and as you will have my goodwill, that if any such sale or bargain be made . . . that you restrain it." And it was abundantly clear that she meant what she said: ". . . whosoever will counsel you the contrary," she wrote vehemently, "do as I advise you in this behalf or else trust never to have comfort of me."[28]

John II could have been forgiven for feeling that, whatever he did, he could not win. On the other hand, Margaret was undoubtedly right that it would damage him politically to expose his need for money as a subject for speculative chatter in the great houses of Norfolk and London by going ahead with the deal. She got her way, and the trees at Sporle remained unfelled. As a result, it became all the more urgent that he should make some progress in the attempt to put pressure on the duke of Norfolk over his continuing occupation of Caister. A month earlier, in September 1472, John II had written to Norfolk's council to propose a settlement by which he would reclaim the castle from the duke in return for some token financial compensation—perhaps as little as forty pounds—and the promise of his own future service. John III took the letter to Framlingham on his brother's behalf and received a surprisingly encouraging response. Norfolk's counsellors referred him to the duchess, who was not willing to broach the subject with her husband herself, but "this she promised, to be helping if it were first moved by the council." When John III returned to the council, "they answered me your offer was more than reasonable," he told John II, "and, if the matter were theirs, they said they knew what conscience would drive them to."[29] It seemed that the duke's advisers were beginning to feel that the best way of dealing with the transparent frailty of his claim to Caister was to settle the dispute on his own authority, rather than wait for the undesirable possibility that King Edward, once incontrovertibly secure on his throne, might intervene to take the castle from him.

Meanwhile, Duchess Elizabeth herself had other priorities. Her marriage was a grand noble alliance—he the heir to a powerful dukedom, she the daughter of the earl of Shrewsbury—and as often happened in such rarefied social circles, political strategy had dictated that the wedding should take place when the bride and groom were barely out of the nursery: Norfolk had been just four years old when their vows were made, and the duchess almost certainly a similar age. Like many other unions between blue-blooded children who grew up knowing that their duty lay in a destiny mapped out for them from the cradle, their partnership was a successful one, at least within the boundaries of convention and shared expectation. By the early 1470s, now in their late twenties, their dynastic marriage had failed in only one crucial respect: they had no children. But in the spring of 1472, the duchess at last discovered that she was pregnant. If it had ever been true, as her husband had once weakly suggested to Archbishop Neville, that she was the driving force behind his occupation of Caister, it was certainly no longer the case. Against all the odds, the signs emanating from the ducal household at Framlingham Castle seemed positive for the Pastons' cause—but within days it became depressingly clear why the duchess and the council had each suggested that the other should be the one to raise the issue with the duke. His counsellors finally agreed to "move my lord with it, and so they did," John III reported despondently; "but then the tempest arose, and he gave them such answer that none of them all would tell it me."[30]

Even though the duke had dismissed the petition—and had done so in terms too intemperate to be repeated—John III remained hopeful. As always, he was patient and diplomatic, with his characteristic unselfconscious charm, and the fact that the duchess still showed a particular liking for him was one of the strongest cards in the family's hand. A month later, however, it seemed that John II might have undone all his brother's good work when he bumped into the duchess and her attendants in the street on a visit to Yarmouth. She was now almost eight months into her pregnancy, and John II made an elaborate attempt to pay her a gallant compliment. "I should have said that my lady was of stature good, and had sides long and large," he told his brother, "so that I was in good hope she should bear a fair child; he was not laced nor braced in to his pain, but that she left him room to play him in." John II was usually confident and debonair in the company of women—at least, women who were not his mother—but when maliciously amused gossip began circulating shortly after their encounter, it became horribly clear that on this occasion he had miscalculated badly. "They say that I said my lady was large and great, and that it should have room enough to go out at." He was aghast at the idea that he might have caused offence on the inevitably sensitive subject of the duchess's size—"I meant well, by my troth, to her and to that she is with, as he that owes her best will in England," he protested in paroxysms of embarrassment—and appealed to John III to find out how much harm had been done.[31]

The faux pas knocked his usual cheery self-assurance to such an extent that four days later he was still trying to find the right form of words with which to convey his respects to the duchess, but this time with unmistakable courtesy. John III was about to attend the ceremony that would accompany her formal retreat into confinement—the period of a month before the birth that she would spend closeted in the privacy of her own apartments in exclusively female company. A suite of richly furnished rooms had been made ready at Framlingham Castle, kept warm and dark with carpet spread on the floor, and finely worked tapestries hung on the walls and stretched across the ceiling. There the duchess would eat, sleep, pray, and rest, attended by her ladies, until she went into labour. When the time came for the confinement to begin, lords, ladies, gentlemen, and gentle-women would come to pay their respects at mass celebrated in the castle's chapel, before accompanying the duchess to the threshold of her chamber where more prayers would be said and the doors would be ritually closed to shut out all the gentlemen present. As John III prepared to leave for Framlingham, his brother was still rehearsing courtly phrases: ". . . and where you go to my lady of Norfolk's and will be there at the taking of her chamber," John II wrote, "I pray God speed you, and Our Lady her to her pleasure, with as easy labour . . . as ever had any lady or gentlewoman save Our Lady herself. And so I hope she shall to her great joy and all ours, and I pray God it may be like her in worship, wit, gentleness, and every thing except the very very thing"—in other words, that the baby should be the much-desired son and heir, but resemble its mother in every way other than its sex.[32]

But John II's preoccupation with restoring the duchess's good opinion of him did not prevent him from achieving what appeared to be a major breakthrough in the fight for Caister. In late November, for the first time, he secured an expression of concern from King Edward that the castle was being kept from its rightful owner, in the form of royal letters addressed to the duke and duchess. The missives themselves have not survived, but whatever the tenor of their contents, John II was thrilled. "The king has specially done for me in this case," he told his brother excitedly, "and has put me, and so have the lords, in right great comfort that, if this fail, that I shall have undelayed justice."[33] John III suggested he should bring the letters to Framlingham himself, "as hastily as you may, so that you may be at the christening of the child that my lady is with." His brother's attendance at the baptism, John III said, would be a mark of respect that "shall cause you great thank, and a great advantage in your matter."[34] Delayed still in London, John II did not take his advice, but when the duchess gave birth on 10 December—to a daughter named Anne—it was the Pastons' good luck that Bishop Wainfleet of Winchester was invited to stand godfather and baptise the baby. It was a fleeting visit: he arrived on the evening of Wednesday, 17 December, and left the following lunchtime after a morning christening. However, he did find time to speak to the duchess about Caister, "as well as he could imagine to say it, considering the little leisure that he had with her." It seemed to be the perfect opportunity to lobby the duchess on the subject, but Wainfleet proved disconcertingly evasive about her response: ". . . he told me that he had right an agreeable answer of her," John III wrote, "but what his answer was he would not tell me."[35] But when more details emerged of the duchess's conversations with the bishop and his servants, it became clear quite how far away the Pastons still were from any prospect that Norfolk might agree to relinquish the castle. The duchess had explained that she and the duke were planning soon to visit London, and proposed that, once they were in the capital, she would advise the bishop of the most politic way to tackle her husband, in order to max-imise the chances that Wainfleet "should speed of his intent." In other words, no one had yet dared even to broach the subject of the Paston claim to Caister with the duke himself since his furious outburst in September, and all the brothers' efforts of the last two months had so far achieved pre-cisely nothing. Not only that, but John III's foothold in Norfolk's house-hold again seemed to be becoming less secure. "I let you plainly know I am not the man I was, for I was never so rough in my master's conceit as I am now," he reported miserably.[36]

As if that were not enough, it was also becoming painfully apparent that the king's promise of "undelayed justice" was not about to materialise. Edward had written to the duke to ask him to attend to the Pastons' com-plaints, but it was far from clear that he would contemplate any more force-ful intervention. It also remained the case that the king had other, more pressing concerns of much greater significance for the security of the realm. The earl of Oxford was still at large, and made an attempt with French help to land on the southeastern coast in the spring of 1473. Although he was quickly repulsed, he and his small fleet spent the summer harrying and rob-bing English ships in the Channel. Meanwhile, Edward was also having to deal with a vicious dispute between his two younger brothers, George, duke of Clarence, and Richard, duke of Gloucester, over the rich inheri-tance of the earldom of Warwick. Clarence was married to Isabel Neville, the elder of the dead earl's two daughters, and early in 1472, Gloucester married her sister Anne, who had previously been betrothed to the Lancastrian prince of Wales under the terms of her father's alliance with Queen Margaret. Isabel and Anne were each entitled to inherit half of the Warwick estate, but Clarence—who seemed to have no inkling of how for-tunate he had been to escape punishment for his double rebellion against his brother—objected furiously to the idea that the lands should be split between himself and Gloucester, insisting that he should keep his father-in-law's property in its entirety.[37] Biting back his anger at Clarence's aggressive importunity, the king sought to keep the ship of state steady in troubled waters by brokering a compromise in the spring of 1472. But the ill feeling between the two dukes continued to simmer, and in 1473 whispers were beginning to spread that Clarence might yet again be involved in treasonable correspondence with his old ally the earl of Oxford, and through him with King Louis of France. In the circumstances—and despite the hopes inevitably raised by the arrival of King Edward's letters at Framlingham in December 1472—it would have been foolish to expect a speedy settlement at Caister by royal means.

John II and John III were therefore left to pursue their own petitions to the duke and duchess as best they could. Their efforts were not helped by the fact that relations between John II and Margaret remained tense and distant, not least because the business of Sporle wood was still rumbling on. By the autumn of 1472, when John II halted the sale of his timber there at his mother's insistence, Margaret's own finances seem to have recovered a little, since he agreed not to sell the wood on the understanding that in return she would lend him the large sum of a hundred pounds, to be repaid from the manor's revenues over the next five years. Six months later, however, Margaret was utterly refusing to advance him the money, either because she had changed her mind or because the promise had never been made in the first place. John II believed the former and Margaret the latter— a mix-up which had been made possible only by the fact that yet again they were not in direct contact with each other. Instead, increasingly frosty messages were passing back and forth via John III and the family's lawyer, Thomas Playter. "My mother does me more harm than good," John II told his brother with uncharacteristic bitterness in April, by which time he had defiantly embarked on another attempt to find a buyer for the wood at Sporle.[38]

There were other issues on which their exchanges were becoming more barbed, among them the question of John Paston's tomb at Bromholm Priory. The place where John had been buried in the priory church had been covered with a cloth after the lavish funeral, but more than six years after his death, no monument to mark the grave had yet been commissioned. In September 1471, John II had gotten as far as asking his brother to measure the precise dimensions of the site, "both the thickness and compass of the pillar at his head and from that the space to the altar, and the thickness of that altar and imagery of timber work, and what height the arch is to the ground of the aisle, and how high the ground of the choir is higher than the ground of the aisle."[39] But he had done nothing further by the end of November, when Margaret added pointed reproaches on the subject to her recriminations over John II's financial mismanagement. "It is a shame," she wrote, "and a thing that is much spoken of in this country, that your father's gravestone is not made. For God's love, let it be remembered and purveyed for in haste—there has been much more spent in waste than should have made that."[40] By April 1473, after six months of unrelieved tension over Sporle, John II's patience was exhausted, and he threw the criticism back. "I pray you remember her for my father's tomb at Bromholm," he told John III angrily. "She does right naught."[41] Margaret's point was that the grave was John II's responsibility as head of the family; John II's rejoinder was the not unreasonable one that his mother's income was larger than his own, and that she herself might therefore bear the cost of his father's memorial. Both were under pressure, and each felt let down by the other. It was John II who finally made an attempt to make peace—"I heard not from you of long time, which causes me to be right heavy," he wrote in July 1473—although his letter was noticeably short on apologies and long on self-justification.[42]

That summer he was at least enjoying a few pleasant distractions from his financial troubles and his mother's rebukes. His letter to Margaret was written not from London but from the great port of Calais, where he had contracted to serve in the English garrison under the command of the king's friend Lord Hastings. It was an imposing stronghold. Beyond the entrance to the harbour, where the Rysbank Tower stood lookout over two curved breakwaters, lay a city of four thousand inhabitants behind battlemented limestone walls punctuated by towers, both round and square, which provided secure accommodation for the garrison's soldiers and their guns. Fifteenth-century Calais had two raisons d'être: war and trade. The town's massive fortifications and the bastion of its castle secured the defence of the Channel and served as a foothold from which English kings might launch yet another assault on French territory, or in the meantime spy on their continental neighbours. And its busy streets were dominated by the elegant houses and vast warehouses of the Calais merchants, whose wealth was ensured by their monopoly on the lucrative export of English wool. Seven years earlier, in a typically astute move, King Edward had bound together these two facets of Calais life by granting all the customs revenues due to the crown from the wool trade to the merchants themselves, in return for their commitment to pay the wages of the Calais garrison, some ten thousand pounds each year. Those who were best placed to collect the customs revenues were thereby given a pressing incentive to do so with the utmost efficiency, and then to use them to cover essential military costs that had been a perennial drain on crown resources.

The garrison itself numbered about five hundred men in peacetime (double that in time of war), many of them retained by a system of subcontracting. Each gentleman who offered his service there as a man-at-arms undertook to equip himself with the full range of knightly accoutrements: a suit of plate armour; a twelve-foot wooden-handled lance; a sword with a steel blade more than two feet long; and a poleax, a vicious weapon developed less than a century earlier to counter plate armour's evolving defences, with a hammerhead to deliver crushing blows, an axe-blade for slicing, and at the top, a lethal sharpened point for jabbing and piercing. In wartime, the most expensive needs of a man-at-arms were his horses—he would require at least two, of a strength and temperament to withstand the violent cacophony of battle—although the different demands of urban defence meant that many of the garrison's soldiers left their mounts behind in England. But each gentleman also undertook to recruit and bring with him a number of archers, men of lesser birth but no less vital to the English military machine, equipped with an armoured jacket and helmet, a dagger, an axe, and most important, a six-foot longbow made of yew, oak, or maple, the deadly weapon with which Englishmen were legendarily skilled. On campaign, a man-at-arms would expect to receive wages of between one and two shillings a day, and archers a daily rate of half a shilling each. The rates of pay for the Calais garrison were somewhat lower—perhaps a little more than a shilling a week for an archer, for example—but their duties were less onerous and less dangerous than those of an army in the field. True, the port was surrounded by potentially hostile territory (although marshes to the west and forest to the east provided valuable natural defences), and its garrison had to contend with periodic raids and skirmishes. But for much of the time the soldiers' responsibilities were those of watch and ward, leaving them plenty of opportunity to sample the many pleasures—the obvious combination of wine, women, and song—available to an expatriate military community in such a wealthy town.

For John II, the prospect of spending time at Calais had multiple attractions. By offering military service to King Edward's government, he might help to expunge Barnet from his record and speed up his political rehabilitation. At the same time, he would have the chance to renew his acquaintance with Lord Hastings, one of the king's most trusted friends, whom he had known at court in the 1460s and who might now be a powerful ally in his campaign to reclaim Caister. It also gave him something adventurous to do in congenial company that would help to pay his expenses and take him away, physically at least, from the stresses he faced at home. The idea had occurred to him as early as the summer of 1472, but his plans made slow progress during the autumn, preoccupied as he was with his unsuccessful attempt to petition the duke and duchess of Norfolk about Caister. As a result, he did not take ship for Calais until January 1473, and then only for an initial visit of a month or so.

By June of that year he was impatient to return, but delayed by the fact that he was having trouble persuading likely members of the Paston household to serve as the small company of archers he had contracted to bring with him. "I hoped to have been very merry at Calais this Whitsuntide," he told his brother in exasperation, "and am well apparelled and appointed save that these folks fail me so."[43] One servant, William Wood, had been in Paston employment ever since the siege at Caister; he had begged to be kept on when the castle was lost, pledging that he would never leave the family's service, and had proved to be a talented actor in the masques and pageants with which gentry households entertained themselves at Christmas and other great holidays. "I have kept him these three years to play St. George and Robin Hood and the sheriff of Nottingham," John II grumbled—but now, when it was a question of a military posting overseas rather than amateur dramatics at home, Wood had rapidly absented himself. "I have been and am troubled with my over-large [in the sense of *largesse*—that is, liberal] and courteous dealing with my servants, and now with their unkindness," John II wrote with some asperity.[44]

Nevertheless, he was using his enforced stay in London to free himself from other potential ties to domestic life in England. The attempt to renew his lacklustre relationship with Anne Haute had not, after all, proved a success, and he was now negotiating the terms under which her family would agree to seek an annulment of the betrothal. The discussions went well enough that arrangements to apply for a papal dispensation were in place by the autumn—"I have answer again from Rome that there is the well of grace and salve sufficient for such a sore," John II told his brother somewhat ungallantly in November—although the process was expensive, threatening to become yet another alarming drain on his resources.[45]

However fragile his financial position, the good sense of John II's decision to join the Calais garrison was confirmed by political developments at
the end of the year. The earl of Oxford's piracy in the Channel, together
with the increasing uncertainty about the intentions of the duke of
Clarence, had made the capital a tense place to be in the spring and summer of 1473; "there are in London many flying tales," John II reported.[46]
On 30 September, the threat from Oxford suddenly crystallised—albeit on
a much smaller scale than many had feared—when he seized the fortress of
St. Michael's Mount, off the rocky coast of the southwestern county of
Cornwall. Having failed to persuade the kings of France and Scotland to
back a full-scale invasion, the earl had decided to do what he could with his
own tiny force of about eighty men. Once taken, the castle on its towering
rock was all but impregnable in the hands of determined defenders, but the
problem facing Oxford was what to do next, especially when the king sent
troops and ships to besiege the fortress and stop supplies getting through to
the rebels. In February 1474, after four months of dogged resistance,
Oxford was left with little choice but to capitulate. Edward spared his life,
but he was imprisoned in Hammes Castle without hope of release. With the
lord for whom the Paston brothers had fought at Barnet, and from whom
they had once hoped so much, now under lock and key, John II's decision
to busy himself in the service of Lord Hastings at Calais was a diplomatic
one. As he had remarked to his brother the previous summer, ". . . some
men think it wisdom and profit to be there now, well out of the way."[47]

"Calais is a merry town," John II told his brother cheerfully, and life
there suited him.[48] He could enjoy the camaraderie of arms, for the most
part without its usual risks; there was no shortage of willing female company; and he had plenty of free time—at least while England remained at
peace—in which to amuse himself, or even to spend a few days travelling in
the Low Countries, part of the domains of King Edward's brother-in-law
and ally, Duke Charles of Burgundy. On his first trip to Calais in January
1473, John II took the opportunity to return to some old haunts in
Flanders, which he had last visited with his brother in the entourage of the
king's sister Margaret when she married Duke Charles in such splendour in
1468. He sent back news of mutual friends in the great trading city of
Ghent to John III in Norfolk. "Peter Metteney fares well and mistress
Gretkin both, and Babkin recommends her to you. She has been very sick,
but it has done her good, for she is fairer and slenderer than she was. And
she could make me no cheer, but always my sauce was, 'How fares Master

John your brother?', wherewith I was wroth and spoke a jealous word or two, disdaining that she should care so much for you when I was present."[49]

The brothers had slipped back into their old familiar banter along with their old division of labour—John II living the glamorous life of the cosmopolitan gentleman (albeit at the moment an impecunious one), while John III stayed in Norfolk taking care of the family's business. In the autumn of 1472, John III complained with mock despair that Norwich offered so little in the way of entertainment that he was in urgent need of a hawk with which he could at least go hunting. "Now think on me, good lord," he told his brother reproachfully, "for if I have not a hawk I shall grow fat for default of labour and dead for default of company."[50] He asked John II to buy one for him in London or Calais, and they spent two months in half-joking correspondence on the subject, partly because it took John II that long to make any progress with his brother's errand. "I thought to have had one . . . before this time; but far from eye, far from heart," John III observed caustically in October.[51] A bird finally arrived in Norfolk in November—"as for the hawk that I sent you, thank me for it, God save it," John II wrote—but it proved to be a poor specimen; "she shall never serve but to lay eggs," John III reported with a mixture of regret and exasperation, before taking his brother to task for his indolence. "Now, if you have as many ladies as you were wont to have, I require you for her sake that you best love of them all, once trouble yourself for me in this matter, and be out of my clamour."[52]

However sharp the teasing became, it was full of affection, and for John III it perhaps went some way toward alleviating the frustrations of life at home. His difficult relationship with his mother's chaplain, James Gloys, had not improved: "Sir James is ever chopping at me when my mother is present," he wrote in October 1472, "with such words as he thinks wroth me and also cause my mother to be displeased with me. . . . And when he has most unsitting words to me, I smile a little and tell him it is good hearing of these old tales."[53] This annoyance, it turned out, was one he had to tolerate for only another year, since Gloys died in November 1473—a painful loss for Margaret, but a relief for her sons, and one that offered John III an opportunity to reclaim a position of greater trust and responsibility in his mother's household: ". . . I am right glad that she will now do somewhat by your advice," John II told his brother; "wherefore beware from henceforth that no such fellow creep in between her and you, and if you like to take a little labour you may live right well, and she pleased. It is as good that you ride with a couple of horse at her cost as Sir James or Richard Calle."[54]

It seems that John III had at least managed to escape briefly from Norfolk earlier that year by travelling on pilgrimage to the great shrine of St. James at Santiago de Compostela, in northwestern Spain. None of John III's surviving letters mention this voyage, far removed as it was from his daily life in Norfolk; the only references to the trip can be found in letters written before the event by John II, who was looking forward to seeing his brother when he visited Calais on the way home. As a result, it is impossible to know exactly what the experience—if in fact he did take ship for Spain as planned—meant to John III. But he had also made a pilgrimage on foot in the summer of 1470 to the jewel-encrusted shrine of St. Thomas Becket at Canterbury Cathedral, in the southeastern county of Kent—from Norwich, an arduous walk of about 150 miles on hot, dusty roads. It may not be stretching interpretation too far to see these devotional journeys as an attempt to make some sort of penitential reparation for the death of John Daubeney under his command at Caister in the autumn of 1469. There was nothing intrinsically unusual in John III's decision to visit two of the most famous holy places in Europe, both of which attracted thousands of pilgrims each year, but the specific timing of his travels perhaps indicates that his emotional recovery from the ordeal of the siege may not have been as untroubled as his outwardly calm and collected letters suggest.[55]

Memories of the siege would not fade easily, of course, while Caister remained in the hands of the duke of Norfolk. The brothers did not give up their efforts to pursue their claim to the castle, but while the duke himself continued to be so fiercely intransigent, they had little prospect of success. John II's customary optimism was beginning to sound more like blind faith than anything grounded in a realistic assessment of their chances. "Item, as touching Caister, I trust to God that you shall be in it to my use before Christmas is past," he told John III confidently in November 1473.[56] Three months later he assured his mother that, "as for the having again of Caister, I trust to have good tidings thereof hastily."[57] By the autumn of 1474, however, nothing had changed, and even John II was becoming defensive on the subject. "Item, as for Caister, it needs not to spur nor prick me to do aught therein," he told Margaret in November. "I do that I can with good will, and somewhat I hope to do hastily therein that shall do good."[58]

Whatever it was that he was planning—if indeed he had anything in mind other than the need to convince his mother that he was on top of the situation—had no effect. Norfolk's men still held Caister at the beginning of 1475, four years after the Battle of Barnet, and almost six since the duke had first sent his forces to besiege the castle, while John II and John III were still going through the motions of trying to find influential support for their cause. Their old patron Archbishop Neville had at last been freed from the fortress of Hammes and allowed to return to England in November 1474, but he could offer the Pastons no help: at forty-one, he was a broken man who took no further part in political life, and died less than two years after his release. Meanwhile, John II's service at Calais had earned the benevolence of Lord Hastings in general terms—"if there is anything that I can and may do for you, I shall with right good will perform it to my power," Hastings wrote in a genial note in the autumn of 1473—but it was apparent that it would take a great deal more than that to force Norfolk to reconsider his position.[59]

However, one thing at least had changed by the beginning of 1475: Margaret and John II had finally found a way out of the spiralling recriminations that had threatened to overwhelm them. The turning point seems to have come in the autumn of 1474, when John II was taken ill on a rare visit to Norfolk. On his return to his lodgings in London—he now rented rooms at the George Inn, near Lord Hastings's house in the southwest of the city, on the river at St. Paul's Wharf—he thanked his mother for "the great cost and the great cheer that you did to me . . . at my last being with you, which cheer also has made me perfectly whole, I thank God and you." He had been worried, "so green recovered of my sickness" as he was, that the journey back would be too much for him, "but, God thank you, I took so my crumbs while I was with you . . . that God and you had made me stronger than I thought," he told her warmly.[60] Their surviving letters shed no light on exactly what had happened when they met, but the effect was a startling transformation in Margaret's feelings—whether because she had at last had a chance to spend time with the son she now hardly saw, or because his illness conjured up the threat of losing him completely. Their increasingly acerbic exchanges of the last three years—usually conducted via the long-suffering John III—were suddenly replaced by correspondence full of solicitous affection. Previously, Margaret's letters to her sons had invariably begun with an unadorned and functional "I greet you well," but when she wrote to John II, by this time back at Calais, in January 1475, she addressed him in markedly different style: "Right wellbeloved son, I greet you well and send you God's blessing and mine, letting you know that I marvel that I have had no writing from you."[61] For once, it was not a reproof but an expression of genuine eagerness to hear from him.

The contents of Margaret's letter were even more extraordinary. John II's financial woes continued, but for the first time, his mother was taking them in her stride, offering constructive advice and concrete help, and sounding sanguine and cheerful as she did so. Not only had she agreed to stand surety for him for another loan, but she was now, after all the months of misery the subject had provoked, calmly organising the sale of some of the timber at Sporle on his behalf. "I shall be as good a housewife for you as I can," she told him, "and as I would be for myself."[62] It seemed suddenly obvious that money had been a symptom of her unhappiness with her eldest son, not its root cause. She had always expended more energy worrying about him than about any of her other children, and perhaps as a result found it all too easy to fall back on her husband's conviction that John II was irredeemably unreliable when her son was not there in person to reassure her. But it is hard to avoid the conclusion—although she probably would not have admitted it—that John II, her firstborn, was her favourite child. Whatever it was that had happened on his visit in October, it had at last succeeded in reminding her of his good nature and convincing her of his good intentions, and in response she became as protective of him as she had once been in defending him against his father.

For his part, John II was keen to let his mother know that he was—and always had been—appreciative of everything she was doing for him. "I have put you to cost, charge and loss enough, God thank you of it," he told her in February; "wherefore, if Sporle wood spring any silver or gold, it is my will that first of all you be your own payer of all that is behind."[63] He also had to cope with the fact that her renewed affection was manifesting itself in ways that, for John II, probably verged on the alarming. "Send me word how you do of your sickness that you had on your eye and your leg," she told him in January, "and, if God will not suffer you to have health, thank him thereof and take it patiently, and come home again to me, and we shall live together as God will give us grace to do."[64] It took all John II's charm and courtesy to sidestep the suggestion while simultaneously assuring her of his devotion. "God thank you of your large proffer," he wrote carefully, "whereof I would be right glad if I might"—but the military commitments he had taken on for the coming months made it impossible for him to return. However, "that journey with God's grace once done," he said, "I purpose verily with God's grace thereafter to dance attendance most about your pleasure and ease."[65] Deeply fond though he was of his mother, the weight of expectation which she heaped on his shoulders had strained their relationship since he was a teenager; and he had no wish to swap his life in London and Calais—where the cares of the struggle for Caister were leavened with entertaining friendships, romantic dalliances, and proximity to the political intrigues of the court—for the slower pace and stifling domesticity of the Paston household in Norfolk.

It was perhaps lucky for John II that he could claim the pressing excuse of duty to his sovereign to explain his reluctance to return to the bosom of his family. It had not taken King Edward long after he regained the throne to consider the possibility of renewing war against France—a scheme which offered the dual attraction of recapturing the English territories that had been so humiliatingly lost during the previous thirty years, and of moving the arena of Anglo-French conflict back into the domains of the French king whose support for the earl of Warwick had cost Edward his crown, however briefly, in 1470–1471. Three years had gone by while he levied taxes to pay for a major campaign: by 1475 the vast total of £180,000 had been promised, though by no means all of it paid. During that time he also tried to persuade his two potential allies for such an ambitious project—his brother-in-law Charles, duke of Burgundy, and Francis, duke of Brittany, the independent duchy at France's northwestern tip—to commit themselves to his plans.

By the beginning of 1475, preparations were well under way. Edward's army numbered almost fifteen thousand men, and hundreds of others were recruited for their technical expertise, among them armourers, smiths, tent makers, saddlers, bowyers, fletchers, carters for the artillery train, and miners to dig tunnels and trenches. The king was determined to ensure not only that his forces were well supplied with provisions and ammunition—779 stone cannon balls and more than 10,000 sheaves of arrows were shipped across the Channel, along with gunpowder, sulphur, brimstone, and saltpetre—but also that he would lead his army in appropriately sumptuous style: campaign expenses included more than four hundred pounds spent on cloth of gold for the king's wardrobe and the interior of his pavilions. Edward also ordered a portable house made of wood and covered with leather, impermeable to the weather and the enemy's arrows alike, for his personal use in the field. Almost all of his nobles agreed to serve on the expedition, each bringing with him men-at-arms and archers to join the "finest, largest and best appointed force that has ever left England," an Italian observer reported from Bruges.[66]

Among the soldiers were John II, John III, and their younger brother Edmund. John II probably took his place in Lord Hastings's retinue, and John III may have joined him, although it is difficult to be sure given that Earl Rivers and the duke of Norfolk—both of whom he had previously served—were also recruiting men for their contingents. Edmund, meanwhile, was retained by King Edward's youngest brother, the duke of Gloucester. There may even have been four Pastons among the king's forces, if Walter, who was still not quite twenty, accompanied his brothers to France. It seems unlikely that he did so, given that he was now studying at Oxford and intended for the priesthood, but on the other hand it is otherwise hard to explain the letter Margaret wrote to her eldest son at Calais in May 1475, while the newly recruited forces that included Walter's brothers were gathering at Canterbury, near the south coast, in readiness for the crossing to France: "For God's love," she wrote, "if your brothers go over the sea, advise them as you think best for their safeguard, for some of them are but young soldiers and know full little what it means to be a soldier, nor to endure to do as a soldier should do."[67] John II and John III, now in their early thirties, had both been in battle before, under the earl of Oxford's command at Barnet, and Edmund had already gained some relevant experience by joining John II at Calais in the summer of 1473—although admittedly life in the garrison there could not be said to be active service in the sense which Margaret had in mind, and it is possible that Edmund rather than Walter was the "young soldier" of whom she was thinking. Nevertheless, however many of her sons travelled to France that summer, it is clear that she was troubled at the prospect of any of them going to war.

As it turned out, she had little to fear. Even before Edward's army began to move slowly out of Calais in mid-July, it had become apparent that the support of the dukes of Brittany and Burgundy would not, after all, be forthcoming. The duke of Brittany had committed himself to Edward's cause so much at the eleventh hour that their treaty of alliance had not yet been formally ratified by the time the king embarked for France, and in the end the duke made no move to assist the English invasion. Meanwhile, the duke of Burgundy was preoccupied with his own interests further east in the Rhineland, in particular his attempt to secure control of the city of Neuss, to which he had laid siege in July 1474. The duke persisted in his campaign throughout the winter; John II had hoped to see the besieged city for himself in January 1475, on a trip into Flanders to buy himself a horse and armour for the coming English expedition. (". . . perchance I shall see the siege at Neuss before I come again if I have time," he told his brother cheerfully; ". . . I think that I should be sick unless I see it.")[68] Duke Charles did not finally admit defeat there until the middle of June, by which time he had neither the troops nor the money to help Edward against the French. Given the circumstances, Edward made the pragmatic decision to use the presence of his army on French soil to press his advantage in negotiating a settlement with King Louis, who was anxious to see off the English threat before the Anglo-Burgundian alliance could resurrect itself. As a gesture of goodwill while the diplomatic preliminaries began, Louis ordered that the gates of the town of Amiens, seventy miles south of Calais, be opened to the English army. Huge tables loaded with food were set out in the streets, and the French king dispatched cartloads of wine to entertain his English visitors. It proved to be an irresistible invitation. Four days later, Edward himself was forced to order that his happily inebriated troops be thrown out of the town, and he posted guards on the gates to prevent their return.

With talks between the two camps now well under way, arrangements were made for a meeting to be held on 29 August at the village of Picquigny, near Amiens, where a bridge over the Somme had been hurriedly built on which Edward and Louis would come face to face, their forces drawn up on either side of the river. In similar circumstances fifty-six years earlier, the duke of Burgundy's grandfather John the Fearless had stepped onto a bridge at Montereau, near Paris, for what he thought was a diplomatic meeting with the French dauphin, only to be attacked and murdered by the dauphin's entourage. Edward and Louis were taking no chances of such treachery: a tall wooden screen was constructed across the middle of the bridge at Picquigny with a grating through which the monarchs could talk without fear of assassination. Awnings had also been erected to shelter the royal parties from the weather, but they proved too short to cover all the kings' attendants, and several fine outfits were ruined by a sudden downpour—although not, of course, Edward's robe of cloth of gold lined with red satin, with a jewelled fleur-de-lis sparkling in his black velvet cap as he exchanged pleasantries with Louis, in reasonable French, through the wooden partition. Terms had already been agreed by delegates from both sides, and the treaty was rapidly concluded: England and France were to observe a truce for the next seven years; and the king of England would receive a sum of fifteen thousand pounds from the king of France before his departure, to be followed by a pension of ten thousand pounds each year. In effect, Louis was paying Edward handsomely to take his army home.

The end of the campaign meant the safe return of all Margaret's sons. ". . . blessed be God, this voyage of the king's is finished for this time," John II wrote from Calais on 11 September, the same day that his brothers took ship back to England. Margaret should perhaps have been more worried about the climate at Calais than about the French king's guns, since both John II and John III fell ill on their return there. "I . . . mislike somewhat the air here," John II told her gloomily, "for by my troth I was in good health when I came hither, and all whole, and to my knowledge I had never a better stomach in my life, and now within eight days I am crazed again."[69] John III blamed the temperature: "all my sickness that I had at Calais, and since I came over also, came but of cold," he reported to his brother from Norwich a month later; "but I was never so well armed for the war as I have now armed me for cold."[70] Despite his precautions, he was still ill a fortnight later. "It will not out of my stomach by no means," he wrote miserably. ". . . I may not eat half enough when I have most hunger. I am so well dieted, and yet it will not be. God send you health, for I have none three days together, do the best I can."[71] Margaret, meanwhile, remained unnervingly keen to have her eldest son at home in Norfolk: ". . . she would fain have you at home with her," John III wrote, "and if you be once met she tells me you shall not lightly depart till death depart you."[72]

The brothers themselves were preoccupied with the urgent need to make one more attempt on Caister. By gathering the great men of England in one place, the abortive invasion had offered an unparalleled opportunity to seek powerful help, and it seemed at last that King Edward might be prepared to put pressure on the duke of Norfolk. "I was in good hope to have had Caister again," John II told Margaret on his return. "The king spoke to my lord of Norfolk for it, and it was full like to have come, but in conclusion it is delayed till this next term, by which time the king has commanded him to take advice of his council and to be sure that his title is good, or else the king has ascertained him that for any favour he must do me right and justice."[73] It was not yet the result they wanted, but even the duke's acceptance that there was a case to answer represented substantial progress. In the meantime, they still had the significant advantage of the duchess's support. In early October, John III visited her at Norwich, where she was staying during her second pregnancy; "she would as fain you had it as anybody," he told his brother.[74] Two weeks later, he wrote again to John II—but this time with shattering news. He had seen the duchess of Norfolk for a second time, "and she told me that the king had no such words to my lord for Caister as you told me," he said. Instead, a startling scene of defiance had unfolded at Calais as King Edward and the duke were preparing to leave for England: ". . . the king asked my lord at his departing from Calais how he would deal with Caister," John III reported, "and my lord answered never a word." While Norfolk maintained a mulish silence, Edward forced an answer out of one of his retainers, Sir William Brandon. According to Brandon, the duke had declared "that the king should as soon have his life as that place"—and when Edward asked Norfolk "whether he said so or not," the duke confirmed that he had. "And the king said not a word again, but turned his back and went his way," John III went on. "But my lady told me if the king had spoken any word in the world after that to my lord, my lord would not have said him nay."[75] Perhaps the duchess was right; or perhaps she was trying to put a positive spin on her husband's dangerous intransigence. Either way, Norfolk's brinkmanship confronted Edward with an uncomfortable dilemma. Insisting on the duke's compliance would risk precipitating serious political conflict with a magnate who, despite his questionable judgment, had at least been consistently loyal. Edward was determined to be master in his own kingdom, but as the French expedition had just demonstrated in no uncertain terms, he was a pragmatist who knew that he had to pick which battles to fight. In the end, there was no reason for him to stake his authority on the Pastons' claim to Caister. As always, the Pastons' problem was that they were not important enough—either in their own right or in the service of anyone more influential—to force concessions from a more powerful opponent. As a result, it suited the king better to let it be known that he had commanded Norfolk "to take advice of his council," and then to walk away, than to make an issue of the duke's recalcitrance.

At least it was now clear that there was no point in continuing to petition the duke in the hope that he might one day relent. John III immediately told the duchess that, in the circumstances, he could not offer his service to her husband any longer. She was so sorry to see him go that she made him promise to talk to her again before committing himself to the service of any other lord. John II, meanwhile, for the first time drafted a formal petition to the king detailing the losses he had suffered as a result of

Norfolk's seizure of Caister—a total, he said, of more than £1,300—and setting out his grievances "for redress whereof your said supplicant has, this said space of four years, sued to my said lord and his council," he wrote dejectedly, "and of all that time . . . my lord would never suffer him to come in his presence nor hear him, nor none other for him, to declare or show his grief."[76] But there was little chance that a public complaint would succeed where private manoeuvres had failed. There was nothing more they could do except wait and hope for a miracle.

They did not have to wait long. On Tuesday, 16 January 1476, the duke of Norfolk was suddenly taken ill at Norwich. He died the same night, at around midnight, at the age of thirty-one.[77] John II managed to compose himself well enough the next morning to cast his letter reporting the news to his mother in appropriately respectful terms ("it is for all that loved him to do and help now that which may be to his honour and weal to his soul"). However, he was already—only hours after the duke's death—deep in plans to take full advantage of an opportunity which was so momentous and so fortuitous that it seemed scarcely credible. The duke's heir was his three-year-old daughter, Anne, the baby who had indirectly caused John II such embarrassment with Duchess Elizabeth in the winter of 1472. The duchess herself was pregnant again and might yet have a son, but even if she did, the political power of the dukedom would be in abeyance, or at least much reduced, for many years. It had been the duke himself—not his wife or his council—who had been immovable on the subject of Caister, and if the Pastons were ever to have a chance to make their claim good, this was surely it. John II immediately threw himself into action on two fronts. First, he sought to do what service he could to the newly widowed duchess and her shocked household: ". . . it is so that this country is not well purveyed of cloth of gold for the covering of his body and hearse," he told his mother, "wherefore, every man helping to his power, I put the council of my lord in comfort that I hoped to get one for that day." As luck would have it, he had bought some silk woven with gold for his father's uncompleted tomb, and he now offered it for use instead at the duke's funeral. The purchase had clearly been made a while before, since he was not certain "if it be not broken or put to any other use," but he asked Margaret to send it, and promised that "it shall be saved again for you unhurt at my peril. I deem hereby to get great thanks and great assistance in time to come."[78]

The second step he took was less likely to be received with favour by the duchess and her advisers. Three days after the duke's death, John II left

Norwich for London to present his claim to Caister to the king, and sent a servant to assert his rights at the castle itself. John III—who was temperamentally more cautious than his brother, and personally much closer to the duchess—was convinced that the move was hamfisted and premature. "... I assure you your sending to Caister is evil taken among my lord's folk," he wrote in some irritation a few days later, "in so much that some say that you tendered little my lord's death, in as much as you would so soon enter upon him after his decease without advice and assent of my lord's council."[79] John II was stung by the criticism, but rejected out of hand the suggestion that he had acted without courtesy or judgment. He had been patient for more than six years since Norfolk had first seized the castle, and during that time diplomacy had gotten him nowhere. He sounded defiant and angry: "where that some towards my lady of Norfolk noise that I did unkindly to send so hastily to Caister as I did," he wrote, "there is no discreet person that so thinks; for if my lord had been as kind to me as he might have been, and according to such heart and service as my grandfather, my father, yourself and I have owed and done to my lords of Norfolk that dead are—and yet if I had wedded his daughter—yet must I have done as I did." He was certain that his tactics were necessary if they were to succeed in recovering Caister, but he had also been rattled by the emergence of yet another potential threat to their hopes. The king had proposed that if the duke's small daughter did in the end inherit her father's estates, she should marry his second son, two-year-old Richard, duke of York, and John II feared that Edward might therefore have an acquisitive eye of his own on the castle along with the rest of the Norfolk inheritance. It was clear that a little more patience would be required, since the Pastons could not be sure what attitude the king and the widowed duchess would adopt toward their claim until the fate of the dukedom itself was decided by the birth of her baby: "... let us all pray God send my lady of Norfolk a son," John II told his brother anxiously, "for upon that rests much matter."[80]

As winter gave way to spring, John II continued to press his case as forcefully as he could—"I pray you send me some word if you think likely that I may enter Caister when I will, by the next messenger," he asked his brother in March—while John III still tried to restrain him ("take not that way if there be any other").[81] John III himself was back in the service of the duchess, and it seemed a hopeful sign for the family's prospects that she had asked Margaret to attend on her when she went into labour: "... and if it were your ease to be here I would be right glad ...," John III told his mother earnestly, "for I think your being here should do great good to my brother's matters that he has to speed with her."[82] If Margaret did join the duchess's attendants, her help could not secure a happy outcome for the birth, either for the expectant mother or for Margaret's own family. The baby did not survive, and the king therefore pursued his plans for the marriage of the three-year-old heiress to his toddler son—exactly the course of events that the Pastons had feared.

But John II's irrepressible optimism—which he had somehow maintained despite the crushing setbacks of the previous ten years—was about to be vindicated at last. He worked hard to avert the possibility that Caister might be swept into the king's hands by playing down the castle's charms— King Edward "was informed of the truth and that it was not for a prince," John II reported—and playing up the financial compensation he would demand in return for relinquishing his own title to the estate.[83] Whether or not the king was convinced by these protestations, Edward was a shrewd politician who knew that the duke of Norfolk's death offered a chance to settle once and for all a dispute which had festered, in one form or another, for as long as he had ruled England. He secured the dukedom for his son, but graciously allowed the Pastons' claim to Caister to be heard without challenge from the crown.

By the end of May, John II was at last sounding genuinely confident, if also more than a little weary: ". . . as for my matters," he told his mother and brother, ". . . they do, blessed be God, as well as I would they did, save that it shall cost me great money"—yet more palms to grease and lawyers to pay—"and it has cost me great labour."[84] It took one more month, but on 30 June 1476, almost seventeen years since the death of Sir John Fastolf, and more than ten since that of their father, John II was finally able to send his brother the good news for which they had been waiting so long. "Item, blessed be God, I have Caister at my will," he wrote. "God hold it better than it was done heretofore."[85]

✢

CHAPTER 12

I pray get us
a wife somewhere

JOHN PASTON II TURNED THIRTY-FIVE in the spring of 1477. The battle for the Fastolf inheritance had overshadowed his entire adult life, but at last it was over. He was left exhausted rather than triumphant: the human cost of the struggle—in lives cut short, friendships broken, and opportunities missed—had been high, and the prize itself was not what it had once been. Most of Fastolf's lands were now helping to pay for the construction of Magdalen College in Oxford under the direction of Bishop Wainfleet, at seventy-seven still as energetic as ever in his desire to see his project come to fruition. The foundation stone had been blessed and laid three years earlier in the centre of what would become the high altar in the college's chapel; wooden cranes with rope pulleys were now in use to lift intricately carved masonry for the pinnacles and crenellations that surrounded its leaded roof, while nearby, the great hall and the shaded quadrangle of the cloisters were beginning to take elegant shape.

Caister, by contrast, was no longer quite the graceful and luxurious home of Fastolf's original design. John III had thought a number of repairs to be necessary ten years earlier, but since then the buildings had been damaged during the siege, and for all the duke of Norfolk's obdurate insistence that it was his property, he had shown little inclination to spend either time or money there. Now that it was back in Paston hands, none of the family took up permanent residence in the castle. Margaret's household was already well established a mile away at her own manor of Mautby, from where she and her servants could at least keep a close eye on the estate, but there was no sign that her eldest son had any imminent intention of making Caister his home.

Quite apart from John II's lack of enthusiasm for the domestic tenor of country life, the fact that the castle was back in his possession did not mean that he was suddenly freed from legal entanglements in the London courts. Even after the duchess of Norfolk's men had left Caister in the summer of 1476, it took more than a year to secure formal ratification of John II's title. Not only that, but in the early months of 1478 he was precipitated into further litigation over the manors of Drayton and Hellesdon, just outside Norwich, which had been lost to the duke of Suffolk for more than a decade, apparently without hope of recovery. The duke's redoubtable mother, Duchess Alice, had died in 1475 at the age of seventy-one, and was buried under an exquisite alabaster monument in the church near the Chaucer family home at Ewelme, in Oxfordshire. Three years after her death, it appeared that the Pastons might at last stand a chance of retrieving the estates when the duke—who seems to have inherited the political talents of neither of his formidable parents—ran short of money. Despite their own financial worries, John III urged his brother to seize the opportunity that the duke's difficulties presented by offering cash to secure the manors' safe return: ". . . A hundred marks will do more now . . . than you shall peradventure do with two hundred marks in time coming, if this season be not taken," he wrote urgently.[1] John III believed that their best hope lay in petitioning the duke's wife, King Edward's sister Elizabeth; it seemed that, yet again, they might find more favour with a powerful and pragmatic duchess than with her stubborn husband.

However, the parallel with their dealings with the duke of Norfolk proved all too exact. Suffolk reacted to his need for cash not by agreeing to part with Drayton and Hellesdon, but by selling cartloads of timber there (a policy of which it is tempting to believe that his mother, like her equally formidable Paston counterpart, would not have approved). He also took the opportunity to reassert his ownership of the estates by visiting them in person. Despite the fact that he was ill and, on a hot May afternoon, needed the support of two strong men simply to keep him on his feet, the duke made great show of being as implacable as Norfolk had been at Caister: ". . . he would meet you with a spear, and have none other amends for the trouble that you have put him to but your heart's blood, and that will he get with his own hands," John II's servant John Wheatley reported to his master in London; "for if you have Hellesdon and Drayton you shall have his life with it." Wheatley was distinctly unimpressed with the duke's bullying behaviour: no one, he said caustically, had ever played the villainous King Herod in a mystery play on the feast of Corpus Christi "better and more agreeable to his pageant" than Suffolk in his posturings. And the menaces were continuing; John III and Wheatley himself were now facing persistent threats and harassment from Suffolk's servants on the streets of Norwich.[2] In the attempt to protect his men and what he considered to be his property—which was rapidly being devalued as the wood at Drayton was cut down—from such ostentatious aggression, John II was left with little option but to start new legal proceedings to challenge the duke's hold on the manors.

He had continued to divide his time between London and Calais over the past couple of years, although life in the garrison seemed to have lost some of its excitement along with its novelty. He had been ill there again in the spring of 1476; ". . . in truth I am somewhat crazed, what with the sea and what with this diet here," he told his brother dolefully.[3] His reluctance to return was more marked by February 1477, when Lord Hastings was planning a personal visit to Calais, and John II thought—rightly, as it turned out—that his own presence would be required in his lord's retinue for the trip. "I fear that I cannot be excused," he reported to John III, "but . . . if I go, I hope not to tarry long."[4] However jaded he felt, it remained the case that his attachment to Hastings was too valuable to put at risk. Hastings had known the king since childhood, and was now one of the most powerful and prominent members of Edward's inner circle, entrusted with wide-ranging responsibilities not only as the king's lieutenant in charge of the Calais garrison, but also as lord chamberlain (an office that gave him control of the royal household) and as the leading magnate across a huge swathe of the north and east Midlands.

Service to Hastings, potentially at least, offered political access of a kind that John II's old patron, the queen's brother Earl Rivers, could not have provided. Since the controversy over his crusading plans in 1471, Rivers's relationship with the king had recovered enough for him to be put in charge of the household of Edward's eldest son, the six-year-old prince of Wales, an appointment that brought Rivers substantial authority in the Welsh borders, where many of the prince's lands lay. However, the earl was not even a constant presence in England, let alone at the heart of government. He spent much of 1476 travelling in Italy on an expedition that was part pilgrimage, part sightseeing tour—a trip marred only by a frightening encounter with thieves on the road outside Rome, who relieved him of plate and jewels worth more than £650 (although the earl later received a gracious offer of compensation from the senate of Venice, where some of the gems had reportedly been put up for sale).

If Rivers had proved to be of little help in John II's attempt to rehabilitate himself after the traumas of 1470–1471, the Paston brothers had other contacts from those years that they were even more keen to leave behind. The duke of Clarence—whose servant Walter Writtle had unsuccessfully tried to broker an end to the siege at Caister in 1469—had learned no lessons whatsoever as a result of his lucky escape from the consequences of his own treason. With his ambition and self-regard now verging on the delusional, the duke's public behaviour remained provocatively confrontational, while whispers persisted in England and on the Continent of his continuing disloyalty. Every attempt Edward made to curb his brother's excesses was met with petulant defiance, and by the summer of 1477, the king's patience was finally exhausted. Clarence was arrested and held in the Tower of London until January 1478, when he was found guilty of high treason at a specially convened meeting of parliament. It was another month before Edward could bring himself to order his execution, but on 18 February, the duke was put to death privately in the Tower—probably, as rapidly spreading rumour soon had it, drowned in a barrel of sweet malmsey wine. If contemporaries were shocked at the king's destruction of his own brother, it had to be remembered that Edward had extended the hand of forgiveness toward Clarence repeatedly for almost a decade, and that the duke's incorrigibly erratic behaviour was much more than eccentric indiscretion. Clarence had not only rebelled against his king, but also betrayed his own blood—"a much higher, much more malicious, more unnatural and loathly treason," as the king declared in parliament, his rhetoric infused with obvious emotion.[5]

A few months after the duke's execution, news reached London that the earl of Oxford—Clarence's former ally and the Pastons' former lord—had evaded his guards at Hammes Castle for long enough to jump from the battlements into the moat; ". . . he leapt the walls and went to the dyke and into the dyke to the chin," John II reported to his brother, "to what intent I cannot tell—some say to steal away, and some think he would have drowned himself."[6] Whether the earl had intended escape or suicide, he achieved neither, but was caught and returned to his prison quarters. For John II, it was a potent reminder that, whatever trials he had faced over the past seven years, he was fortunate to have found the chance in Lord Hastings's service to resuscitate a political career that might have ended amid the carnage of the battlefield at Barnet.

By the end of 1477, John II had also secured his freedom from his long-drawn-out betrothal to Anne Haute. They had been engaged for nearly nine years, the last six of which had been spent trying to obtain official sanction for their separation. The delay in procuring a dispensation from Rome had prevented him from embarking on other matrimonial plans, but that fact appeared to trouble him little. His engagement had been a matter of political advantage rather than personal inclination, and the idea of settling down seemed to hold no greater appeal for him at the age of thirty-five than it had ten years earlier. He was not short of female company: in the summer of 1473, for example, he had asked his brother Edmund to send news from Calais of one of his conquests there (". . . I pray you send me word . . . of her welfare, and whether I were out and other in, or not").[7] Letters he received from a friend in London when he was back in Calais himself in the spring of 1477 were full of laboured innuendo on the subject (". . . we have heard say that the fraus of Bruges with their high caps have given some of you great claps, and that the feat of their arms doing is such that they smite all at the mouth and at the great end of the thigh . . .").[8] Meanwhile, a liaison in England with a woman named Constance Reynforth produced at least one illegitimate child, a daughter named Constance after her mother.

But it is clear that, tired though he was after the years of struggle over Caister, the prospect of a more permanent relationship and greater domesticity was not an enticing one. Instead, as a gentleman in London and a soldier at Calais, he preferred to live the courtly life, or at least whatever version of it he could afford. He indulged his love of books, collecting not only fine manuscript volumes—chronicles, chivalric romances, devotional texts, and works by Cicero—but also a copy of *The Game and Play of the Chess,* one of the first books produced by William Caxton's revolutionary new printing press at Bruges. He also pursued his enthusiasm for knightly feats of arms. The two passions were combined in the "Great Book" he had commissioned several years earlier from a scrivener named William Ebesham—"my book of knighthood," John II called it—which contained copies of treatises on war, tournaments, and chivalry.[9] John II enjoyed music and masques and hunting and good company, both male and female, and it was sufficiently clear to his mother that he was unlikely to change his ways that she was deeply sceptical when she heard rumours of another engagement in the spring of 1478. Whatever the possible advantages of the match, she said sternly, he should contemplate marriage only ". . . if you can find in your heart to love her, so that she be such one as you can think to have issue by; or else, by my troth, I had rather that you never married in your life."[10]

On the face of it, Margaret's lack of enthusiasm at the prospect of seeing her eldest son settled at last was surprising, but by now her hopes that he would come home for good had given way to the bitter realisation that, whatever he might say, it was unlikely to happen. At the end of 1475, she had still expected his imminent return; "my mother would fain have you at Mautby," John III told his brother in October. "She rode thither out of Norwich on Saturday last past to purvey your lodging ready against your coming."[11] The prospect of the recovery of Caister after the duke of Norfolk's death may have raised her hopes further, particularly given John II's increasing disenchantment with life at Calais. He sent profuse apologies for a lengthy stay there in the spring of 1476, claiming that it was driven solely by political necessity ("mother, I beseech you to take no displeasure with me for my long tarrying, for I dare do none otherwise for displeasing of my lord. I was nothing glad of this journey if I might goodly have chosen").[12] However, by the summer of 1477, as he continued to make excuses for his absence, the warmth and optimism of Margaret's earlier letters were replaced by weary resignation, and she gave up asking when he would come back to Norfolk.

As so often before, her distress manifested itself in her husband's old complaints, unfair though they were: her son was negligent, extravagant, and unreliable; he paid little attention to her advice, and cared less about her welfare. Inevitably, given the circumstances, his financial troubles again became a source of conflict. John II owed money to a man named Cockett, a debt that he was struggling to repay, and he was hoping for help from his mother. Two years earlier the request might have elicited a positive response, but now it merely served to make Margaret angry. "I put you in certain that I will never pay him penny of that duty that is owing to him, though he sue me for it," she declared, "not of my own purse, for I will not be compelled to pay your debts."[13] John II insisted that he was doing his best, but his attempts to raise cash had already forced him to mortgage the manor of Sporle, a tactic with which Margaret was so unhappy that she made scarcely veiled threats to withhold his inheritance as a result:

> I marvel much that you have dealt again so simply with Sporle. . . . It causes me to be in great doubt of you what your disposition will be hereafter for such livelihood as I have been disposed before this time to leave you after my decease, for I think verily that you would be disposed hereafter to sell or set to mortgage the land that you should have after me, your mother, as gladly and rather than that livelihood that you have after your father. It grieves me to think upon your guiding . . .

Acute though their money problems were, the emotional charge of Margaret's reproaches was clearer than ever. "I think you set but little by my blessing," she told him, "and if you did you would have desired it in your writing to me. God make you a good man."[14]

If John II would not come home, Margaret was all the more adamant that he should not escape what she saw as his responsibilities. His father's tomb had still not been constructed, and in 1476 word came from Bromholm Priory that "the cloth that lies over the grave is all torn and rotten, and is not worth 2d." Despite the "ill speech" to which this upsetting and damagingly embarrassing state of affairs gave rise, two years later the monument had not yet even been commissioned, let alone built.[15] John II was full of good intentions—"there shall be a tomb and somewhat else over my father's grave, on whose soul God have mercy, that there shall none be like it in Norfolk"—but his plans depended on money that he did not have.[16] Margaret was keenly aware of the stigma, particularly since her friend Elizabeth Clere and her old enemy John Heydon had both recently made lavish gifts to the church at Bromholm, "and if there should nothing be done for your father, it would be too great a shame for us all, and in chief to see him lie as he does."[17] Nevertheless, however exercised she was, there was no sign that she might relent and pay for the tomb herself.

Nor was this the only family expense that Margaret now refused to shoulder: in 1477 she told John II that she was no longer willing to support his youngest brother William out of her own pocket. William's school fees had not been paid for more than six months, and he needed new clothes, but Margaret insisted that it was her eldest son's duty as head of the family to meet the cost of his brother's upbringing. "I would you should remember it and purvey therefor," she wrote sharply; "as for me, I will not."[18] Five years earlier, in the midst of their first altercations over Sporle, John II had had similar arguments with his mother about which of them should provide for his sister Anne, in terms of either her board and lodging or the cost of finding her a husband. Concerned though he was to do the right thing, it was clear that John II felt more than a little resentful of the suggestion that the burden should lie on his shoulders alone. "I will purvey for her . . . ," he told John III, "and yet she is not my daughter."[19]

The question of Anne's future was one issue at least that had been resolved by the summer of 1477. She was now twenty-three, and various potential matches had been suggested for her over the previous five years, ever since her mother and brothers had been prompted into action by the fear that she might otherwise follow too closely in the footsteps of her disgraced sister Margery. The first sign of any concern over Anne's behaviour had come in the autumn of 1471, when Margaret asked John III to find employment in London for their servant John Pamping, ostensibly because "he loses his time here" in Norfolk. She made it abundantly clear, however, that there was more to her request than she was prepared to commit to paper: ". . . for divers other causes I would he were hence in haste, for all manner of haps," she wrote. "Construe you, etc. I shall tell you more hereafter."[20] Two years later, John II felt able to be less discreet: "I pray you take good heed to my sister Anne, lest the old love between her and Pamping renew," he told his brother in November 1473.[21]

Pamping had worked hard for the family for more than a decade, attending John Paston in the Fleet Prison in 1465 and helping John III to defend Caister against the duke of Norfolk's forces. Nevertheless, despite his loyalty and his manifest capabilities, Margaret and her sons were not prepared to take any chances; the similarities between Anne's situation and her older sister Margery's romance with Richard Calle were too close for anyone's comfort. Yet again, a young Paston daughter had fallen in love with an older man whose undoubted personal qualities could not make up for the crucial issue of his status, or lack of it. This time, however, there would be no clandestine marriage. By the autumn of 1472, Pamping had gone from Margaret's household to serve John II in London and Calais, and a year after that he left the Pastons' employment altogether. Once the couple had been separated, the next priority was to find Anne a more suitable husband—not an easy task, given the precariousness of the family's finances and therefore the difficulty of providing her with an acceptable dowry. One possibility that emerged very quickly was a match with Judge Yelverton's grandson William, an alliance that would serve to cement the reconciliation between Yelverton and the Pastons after the long years of conflict over Fastolf's will. Even leaving aside the question of Anne's feelings for Pamping, it was clear that the Yelverton marriage would not be a love match on either side; "as for Yelverton," John II reported bluntly in November 1473, "he said but late that he would have her if she had her money, and else not."[22] Nevertheless, the proposal had Margaret's backing, and in the end she got her way: in the spring of 1477, Anne Paston finally became Anne Yelverton.

By that stage, however, negotiations for another marriage were causing much greater tensions within the family. It had been apparent for some time that John III—unlike his elder brother—was keen to find himself a wife. Domesticity did not hold any fears for him; despite the occasional frustrations of his mother's household, life in Norfolk had never left him restless as it did John II. His eagerness to marry was partly a matter of personal preference, but it was also grounded in pragmatic judgment: a wife with a dowry would allow him at last to take possession of the manor earmarked for him in his father's will, and to set up his own household there with some measure of independence from his family. His problem was that, personable and talented though he was, he was a younger son. It had to be assumed that one day, even if it was in the far-distant future, his older brother would marry and produce an heir, and consequently John III's prospects—and therefore his appeal as a potential husband—were limited. Property attracted property in the marriage market, and certainly John III could not offer enough of an estate to secure the hand of an heiress. The question was whether he could find a bride whose family would provide a sufficient dowry to establish the new couple's household on a solid financial footing, but would also be prepared to accept the limitations of the resources which he himself would bring to the marriage.

The difficulties he faced were obvious as early as 1467, when he made a tentative approach to Alice Boleyn, the daughter of a local man who had made his fortune as a mercer in London and used the money to establish his family at the north Norfolk manor of Blickling. The response John III received was disheartening. Alice's mother would not overrule her daughter if Alice herself were determined on the match, John II reported from London, but would "never advise her thereto in no wise."[23] The Pastons' financial and political problems over the next few years did nothing to improve John III's chances, and by 1470 he sounded half-jokingly despairing on the subject: "I pray get us a wife somewhere . . . ," he asked his brother that spring.[24] Other proposals came and went: in the summer of 1474 John III was juggling two potential matches in London, one a widow named Agnes—he did not even seem to be sure of her surname—at Blackfriars, the other a draper's daughter named Elizabeth Eberton. This seemed promising, not least because London merchants who were rich in cash but short on the status conferred by land and birth might be prepared to offer a substantial sum to secure their daughter's marriage to a gentleman, even a relatively impoverished one such as John III. However, despite his best efforts, nothing came of either possibility, nor of any of the other options he pursued, and by February 1476 he was ruefully asking his brother to keep an eye out for "some old thrifty alewife" for him.[25] Then, at the beginning of 1477, he met Margery Brews.

Margery—who was probably in her late teens, and certainly not more than twenty—was the daughter of a Norfolk knight, Sir Thomas Brews. She was not an heiress, and had three sisters for whom her father would also have to provide, but her family was of good local standing. So far, so moderately encouraging, although John III had been here before and, on those previous occasions, had made no further progress. However, this rapidly proved to be different from all of his previous courtships: he and Margery fell headlong in love. By February, Margery's mother, Elizabeth Brews—who was clearly already as fond of John III as her daughter was smitten—was scolding him for making her life so difficult while the financial terms of the marriage contract had yet to be agreed: ". . . you have made her such advocate for you," she chided him affectionately, "that I may never have rest night nor day for calling and crying upon to bring the said matter to effect."[26]

For his part, John III was just as impatient. At nearly thirty-three, he had been overwhelmed by the strength of his feelings for Margery, and sounded almost breathless as he wrote urgently to his mother about the progress of negotiations. "Mother, the matter is in a reasonable good way," he reported from the Brews's home at Topcroft, ten miles or so south of Norwich, "and I trust, with God's mercy and with your good help, that it shall take effect better to my advantage than I told you of at Mautby, for I think there is not a kinder woman living than I shall have to my mother-in-law if the matter take, nor yet a kinder father-in-law than I shall have, though he be hard to me as yet."[27] John III's optimism was touching, but

Margery's father was determined to drive a tough bargain—or, from his point of view, a fair one: ". . . I were right loath to bestow so much upon one daughter that the other her sisters should fare the worse," he wrote firmly in March. The difficulty was that Swainsthorpe, the manor bequeathed to John III in his father's will, had by now been mortgaged, and a sum of £120 was required to pledge it out before the couple could live there and receive an income from the land. Thomas Brews was unhappy at the prospect that almost all of his daughter's dowry might be consumed by the cost of recovering the manor, telling John II that he "would be sorry to see either my cousin your brother or my daughter driven to live so mean a life as they should do if the £120 should be paid of their marriage money."[28] On the other hand, if Sir Thomas himself put up the cash to reclaim Swainsthorpe, perhaps as a loan to be repaid over a period of some years, he would require a quid pro quo from the Pastons in the form of a larger jointure for his daughter than simply that single estate.

The details of the settlement hardly mattered to Margery and John III. Margery said as much in two tender and heartfelt letters to her "good, true and loving Valentine": her mother had argued their case as well as she could, she reported, but her father would not budge from his demands, "for the which, God knows, I am full sorry. But, if that you love me, as I trust verily that you do, you will not leave me therefor; for if that you had not half the livelihood that you have . . . I would not forsake you."[29] Meanwhile, Margaret was worried that, despite all his experience, her son's judgment would prove to be equally clouded by his emotions. "I know well, if it is not concluded in right short time, that, as for my son, he intends to do right well by my cousin Margery and not so well by himself," she told Elizabeth Brews.[30] The two mothers were now determined that the marriage should take place—partly because of the evident intensity of the personal commitment between John III and Margery; partly because it would not reflect well on either family if negotiations that had been so widely reported within local society came to nothing; and partly because, in essence, it was a good match for both sides. Elizabeth Brews therefore renewed her efforts to persuade her husband to compromise, while Margaret agreed to enhance Margery's prospective jointure by granting her own manor of Sparham to the couple, on top of the estate that her husband had left John III at Swainsthorpe.

Given Margaret's customary strictures about financial caution, this was unlooked-for generosity. When objections to the cost of the match were eventually raised, they came from a much less likely source. Over the years, John II had applied himself cheerfully to the task of trying to find a bride for his brother—an assignment that he certainly found more diverting than looking for a wife for himself: ". . . I always shall be your herald," he told John III expansively in 1467, and he had been as good as his word, suggesting names of potential brides and making courtly overtures to a number of gentlewomen on his brother's behalf.[31] But once it became clear that John III needed no help to win Margery's heart, and that it was now a question of agreeing upon a financial settlement to enable the wedding to take place, John II suddenly seemed a great deal less sanguine. To begin with, he had appeared reluctant to take the relationship seriously, referring to Margery as just one among three possible matches currently under consideration for his brother, and comparing the candidates' merits with almost ostentatious flippancy ("I had rather you had her than the Lady Waldegrave; nevertheless, she sings well with a harp . . .").[32] However, his letter crossed in transit with one from John III which—in asking John II's indulgence for the scribblings produced by a love-addled brain—left no room for doubt about the depth of his feelings.

In response, John II abandoned his frivolous tone, and along with it his usual lightness of spirits. He was happy at the prospect of John III's marriage to Margery, he told his mother soberly, "considered her person, her youth, and the stock that she is come of, the love on both sides, the tender favour that she is in with her father and mother, the kindness of her father and mother to her in departing with her, the favour also and good conceit that they have in my brother, the worshipful and virtuous disposition of her father and mother, which prognosticates that of likelihood the maid should be virtuous and good."[33] This uncharacteristically solemn exposition of Margery's virtues proved to be a prelude to his serious reservations about the financial agreement that his mother and brother were proposing to conclude with the Brews family. Margaret's decision to grant Sparham to John III and Margery and their future children was overhasty and ill-considered, he said: what if, for example, the couple had a daughter, and Margery then died; any son John III might have by a second marriage would then have no right to inherit the estate, despite being his father's heir. It was not, he said, that he minded his mother giving away property that otherwise might have been his own; "I would be as glad that one gave you a manor of £20 by year as if he gave it to myself, by my troth," he told John III emphatically. Nevertheless, an unmistakable coolness and distance had replaced the familiar blithe fluency of his letters to his brother. "This matter is driven thus far forth without my counsel; I pray you make an end without my counsel," he wrote abruptly. "If it be well, I would be glad; if it be otherwise, it is pity. I pray you trouble me no more in this matter."[34]

John II's sudden sternness—which was disconcertingly reminiscent of his father—owed a lot to the fact that, in reality, he was not the irresponsible figure of his parents' worst imaginings. He was probably telling the truth when he claimed that he had no objection in principle to the idea of Margaret granting his brother part of the Mautby inheritance; he was nothing if not generous, and told John III with a characteristic flourish that "I will be to Sir Thomas Brews and my lady his wife a very son-in-law for your sake."[35] However, the negotiations were well under way by the time he was consulted, and it was already too late, he felt, for his legitimate concerns about the detail of the proposals to be addressed. Undoubtedly, too, there were other, more personal reasons for his anger. He had endured years of recrimination, first from his father and latterly from his mother, about his carelessness with money. Margaret had never acknowledged the fact that his financial struggles were not entirely—perhaps not at all—of his own making, and by the summer of 1477 she was refusing to lend him a single penny to help him deal with his debts. In the circumstances, her readiness to hand over an entire manor to his brother could only be hurtful.

If so, it was a hurt that was compounded, in prospect at least, by the impact that John III's marriage would have on his own life. If his brother were now to become a husband and father, and head of a family in his own right, John II would lose the constant support of his right-hand man and probably his best friend. John III had been his partner in business, in fun, and literally his brother-in-arms, through all the troubles of the previous ten years. John II was certainly not in any straightforward sense envious of his brother's situation, but John III's romance with Margery unquestionably left John II a much lonelier figure. The estrangement between the brothers did not last long: bridges were rebuilt once John III and Margery finally married in the autumn of 1477, and John II was genuinely delighted when Margery gave birth to the couple's first child, a boy named Christopher, in August 1478. Nevertheless, that summer there was real feeling as well as brotherly teasing in John II's reproach that "you have now wife and child, and so much to care for that you forget me."[36]

Even if there was little prospect that John III's domestic contentment would encourage his older brother to emulate his example, it seemed that the rest of the family did not share John II's reluctance. Anne—like John III, if somewhat less happily—had settled into marriage by 1478. Their sister Margery Calle had already been married for almost ten years and had three sons, John, William, and Richard—a new family to make up for the fact that her relationship with her mother and brothers had never recovered from the shock of her inappropriate choice of husband. Edmund, now in his late twenties, was actively looking for a wife, so far without success, although he had managed along the way to father a son by a married woman named in his brothers' letters only as "Mistress Dixon."[37] Their youngest brother, William, was a student at Eton, the great school founded almost forty years earlier by Henry VI—an educational opportunity that William perhaps owed to Bishop Wainflet, who had been provost there in the 1440s and still maintained close links with the college. Despite the fact that he was not yet twenty, William already seemed to have an eye on his matrimonial chances: in February 1479 he met a girl at a wedding, and asked John III to investigate her prospects—and offer an opinion on her looks—on his behalf.

Meanwhile, Walter was studying at Oxford. Their mother had high hopes of him: ". . . I trust to have more joy of him than I have of them that are older," she had written with some asperity several years earlier. The plan had always been that Walter should enter the church once he had taken his degree, although Margaret urged him not to put himself forward for ordination until he was old enough to be sure of the commitment. "I will love him better to be a good secular man than to be a lewd priest," she said firmly.[38] In June 1479, he graduated as a Bachelor of Arts, an achievement celebrated with a feast at which he faced a double disappointment: his brother John III, to whom he was particularly close, was unable to attend because a mix-up in their correspondence meant that he was not informed of the date; and the venison Walter had been promised for the meal failed to materialise. Nevertheless, "my guests held them pleased with such meat as they had, blessed be God," he told John III cheerfully.[39] It had now been decided—thanks, perhaps, to his mother's concerns about his vocation for the priesthood—that Walter should instead train as a lawyer, studies which he was due to begin that autumn. By then, however, fate had taken a decisive hand in the family's plans.

Plague was an inescapable fact of life, but a no less terrifying one for that. England had suffered recurrent epidemics ever since the Black Death first struck more than a hundred years earlier, but the outbreak that swept the country in 1479 was particularly virulent—one of the worst, in fact, since the cataclysmic mortality of 1348–1349. In November, John III reported apprehensively to his older brother that "the people die sore in Norwich, and specially about my house; but my wife and my women come not out, and flee further we cannot, for at Swainsthorpe since my departing thence they have died and been sick nigh in every house in the town."[40] By the time John III wrote, the Pastons already knew at first hand how terrible the consequences of infection might be. In early August, only weeks after his graduation, Walter Paston had fallen ill, and was brought from Oxford to be cared for at home in Norwich. By 18 August, it was clear that he would not survive. When he dictated his will that day, his youth was heartbreakingly evident in the fact that he had so little to leave: he carefully distributed his clothes among his teachers and friends in Oxford, and bequeathed his small share of the Paston estates to his favourite brother, John III. Shortly after the document was completed, Walter died.

Over the next three days, the family gathered at Margaret's side to prepare for his funeral. His siblings were joined by their uncle William—John Paston's younger brother, who had helped him in the early days of the Fastolf dispute and was now living in London, where his legal and administrative career continued to flourish. Missing, however—presumably because the journey would have been too much for her—was their grandmother, Agnes, now in her late seventies, who had left Norfolk several years earlier to take up residence with her son at his London home. On 21 August, while the Pastons were in church to hear mass for Walter's soul, a messenger arrived with news that Agnes, too, had died. When Edmund wrote to send word of this second bereavement to John III, who was not yet in Norwich, there was still more distressing information to add to his letter: "my sister"— Anne, it seems likely—"is delivered, and the child passed to God, who send us his grace."[41]

As if three deaths spanning four generations of the family within a single week were not enough, Agnes's will also threatened to precipitate John II into yet another bitter dispute over property. His uncle William's insistence that he should be the one to care for Agnes in her old age had been rooted not only in filial duty but also in his determination to pursue his own claim to a greater share of the Paston lands—a claim that dated back to the acrimony over Judge William's will thirty-five years earlier. Agnes always maintained that her husband's dying wish had been to leave more of his estates to his younger sons, but once John Paston had succeeded in overruling her, citing the terms of his father's written will, there was little that his brother could do to secure possession of the contested properties. But there was everything still to play for in terms of the lands that Agnes herself held—the three manors of her own inheritance, as well as Paston estates including Oxnead, with its comfortable new manor house. John II had been aware of his uncle William's intentions for ten years: "he and I are as good as fallen out," he told Margaret in the autumn of 1469, just after the siege at Caister, "for he has let me plainly know that he shall have all my grandam's livelihood of her inheritance and of her jointure also."[42] That particular argument did not prove to be a permanent breach, but the relationship between uncle and nephew remained uneasy. William was still willing to lend John II money, something that had proved a lifeline during the difficult years before the recovery of Caister. However, the debts left John II deeply uncomfortable, since he was no longer sure how far his uncle could be trusted. They also served to emphasise the fact that William had deep pockets and powerful friends, which would serve him well in any future battle for Agnes's estates. In August 1479, William served notice that it was a battle he was determined to fight: he moved to stake his claim on the very day that news of Agnes's death reached Norwich.

William's legal challenge was a blow that John II could well have done without. Together with his own continuing litigation against the duke of Suffolk over Hellesdon and Drayton, it meant that he was obliged to return to London in mid-October. For once, he seemed deeply reluctant to be there. He was yet again hopelessly short of money, to such an extent that he was having to borrow cash for his living expenses; he did not even have enough to cover the cost of his journey home, he told his mother and brother. The letter they received from him displayed none of his usual sunny confidence. For the first four days of his stay "I was in such fear of the sickness," he wrote miserably; "and also found my chamber and stuff not so clean as I thought, which troubled me sore." Confronted with the plague that was still gripping the capital, and the interminable pressure of his own business, he sounded frightened, exhausted, and alone. His lack of money, he said, had "troubled me so that it has made me more than half sick, as God help me."[43] He was right to be fearful. Less than a month later, John II died, at the age of just thirty-seven. His brother came immediately to bring his body back to his family in Norfolk, but John II had left instructions that he should be buried where he died, in London. John III had never sounded so lost as when he contemplated his lonely journey home. "I have much more to write, but my empty head will not let me remember it . . ."[44]

↰

our trusty and
wellbeloved knight

MARGARET WAS SUDDENLY GETTING OLD. She had suffered bouts of ill health a little more frequently over the past few years—at the beginning of 1475, for example, she asked John III to seek permission from the bishop of Norwich for her to hear mass in her own private chapel, "because it is far to the church and I am sickly, and the parson is often out."[1] In May 1478, at the age of fifty-six, she was so ill that she drew up her will, fearing that death was imminent—even if, by the end of the month, she had recovered enough to write a typically robust letter to John II on the subject of his father's unmade tomb. The deaths of the summer and autumn of 1479, however, were hammer blows that hit her hard. She had already come to the painful realisation that her eldest son was unlikely to return home on any kind of permanent footing, but that did not mean that she had reconciled herself to his absence. Now, suddenly, she had lost him completely. Her younger son Walter, on whom she had pinned her hopes for the future, had also been taken from her. The death of her elderly mother-in-law, Agnes, was less unexpected, and in any case Margaret had seen little of her since she had left Norwich for London five years earlier, but the two women had once been close, and her death can only have compounded Margaret's distress. Meanwhile, the consolations offered by the next generation of Pastons were fragile. Not only had Anne's baby died at birth, but John III and Margery had lost their young son, Christopher, some time after his arrival in the summer of 1478.

But Margaret had never flinched in the face of adversity, and she did not do so now in the midst of overwhelming loss. Her grief did not prevent her from recognising the need to pay urgent attention to the practical issues that arose as a result of her eldest son's death. Shortly after the news reached Norwich, her son Edmund rode to two of the manors now in dispute with William Paston to claim them for John III as his brother's heir— and Edmund did so, a friend reported to John III in London, by the advice of "my mistress your careful mother." Margaret also had an urgent message for John III himself: "my mistress your mother greets you well and sends you her blessing, requiring you to come out of that air as soon as you may."[2] The idea that she might now lose another son in the disease-ridden capital was too much to contemplate. John III could not comply with her request for his immediate return, but he did what he could to reassure her: ". . . whereas you willed me . . . to haste me out of the air that I am in, it is so that I must put me in God, for here must I be for a season," he wrote; "and in good faith I shall never, while God sends me life, dread more death than shame. And, thanked be God, the sickness is well ceased here, and also my business puts away my fear."[3]

Certainly, John III had plenty to distract his attention from the risks he was running. William was pursuing his claim to Agnes's lands with all the resources he could muster, and—whatever his personal feelings about the loss of his oldest nephew—John II's death undoubtedly presented him with a further opportunity to press his case. John II had been handling the dispute in person in London while his brother remained at home in Norfolk, and it would inevitably take John III some time to familiarise himself with the progress of negotiations—a delay that left the political initiative, temporarily at least, in William's hands. It was nevertheless clear that William's case was far from watertight. To argue that Agnes had the right to dispose of her own manors as she pleased was one thing, but the Paston estates she held—including Oxnead and lands in and around the village of Paston itself—were hers only for life, and on her death should have reverted as of right to the senior Paston line. William's claim depended on the questionable argument that he had been unjustly deprived of the estates which his father had left him on his deathbed nearly forty years earlier, and that he was therefore entitled to compensation in the form of the Paston property held by his mother.

As always, however, his chances of victory had as much to do with the political support on which he could call as with the technical viability of his case in a court of law. Unfortunately for John III, William was now a wealthy and well-connected man as a result of his professional success. A decade earlier, he had married Lady Anne Beaufort, daughter of the duke of Somerset who had dominated Henry VI's government in the early 1450s until his death at the first Battle of St. Albans in 1455. It was a glamorous match that represented something of a coup for a younger son from a parvenu gentry family, even if its political and financial benefits were severely circumscribed by the fact that Anne's brothers had been executed and their lands forfeited as a result of their adherence to the Lancastrian cause.[4] Over the years, William himself had served as counsellor and trustee to the rich and powerful—among their number Sir John Fastolf in the 1450s; the duke of Clarence, Archbishop Neville, and the earl of Oxford in the 1460s; and now, in the 1470s, the duke of Buckingham, the widowed duchess of Norfolk, and John Morton, the newly appointed bishop of Ely. In fact, as John III soon discovered, Bishop Morton had agreed to act as one of two arbitrators in William's dispute with John II; the other was John II's own patron, Lord Hastings. John III had almost no time to absorb the profound shock of his brother's death as he launched himself into the next round of political manoeuvres, petitioning both Hastings and the bishop, and seeking support wherever he could find it. "And if I may . . . cause the king to take my service and my quarrel together, I will," he told his mother with determined optimism.[5]

Despite his efforts, it became clear as the months went by that there was little prospect of a speedy resolution to the conflict. William's contacts and his political experience made him too powerful an opponent to be brushed aside either swiftly or easily. Meanwhile, an all-too-familiar scenario unfolded at the disputed manors, as the two sides competed to assert their authority over peasant tenants who were trapped helplessly in the middle. By the autumn of 1481, John III's wife, Margery, was sufficiently concerned about the situation at Marlingford, one of the manors of Agnes's own inheritance, to write to her husband twice in four days, warning him that his uncle's men were seizing wood and grain from the estate. Despite this aggression, word reached Norwich that William was now keen to find a settlement, but Margery remained sceptical about his sincerity: "trust him not too much," she warned her husband feelingly, "for he is not good."[6]

Nevertheless, she was determined to do whatever she could to help. More than one family friend had suggested that the duchess of Norfolk might agree to act as a peacemaker. So far, the duchess had offered William her support, but Margery had recently been reliably informed "that my lady is near weary of her part," and had been advised to speak to the duchess herself—so long as she could do so diplomatically—on the grounds that "one word of a woman should do more than the words of twenty men, if I could rule my tongue and speak no harm of my uncle."[7] Margery therefore proposed to take her mother-in-law, Margaret, and her mother, Elizabeth Brews, to petition the duchess for help when she next visited Norwich. Margery, Margaret, and Elizabeth together certainly made a formidable combination; but if the meeting did in the end take place, it achieved very little, whether because the duchess—whose fondness for John III does not seem to have survived the wranglings over the final recovery of Caister—was unwilling to compromise her support for William, or because William was unwilling to compromise his own campaign at the duchess's request.

However exhausting their troubles, Margery and John III could at least take comfort in each other. Their relationship had settled happily and easily into warm domesticity, but it had not lost its romance. If some of Margery's letters to her husband were conventionally formal in address ("Right reverend and worshipful sir . . ."), others were not: "Mine own sweetheart," she called him in November 1481.[8] Even where the address was properly decorous, the postscript might not be: "Sir, I pray you if you tarry long at London that it will please you to send for me," she added at the end of one letter, "for I think long since I lay in your arms."[9] By now, Margery was not the only one waiting impatiently at home for John III's return. They had had to cope with the loss of their firstborn son Christopher, but since then Margery had given birth to two more children, a boy named William and a girl named Elizabeth. The babies were flourishing, she told John III that autumn, and his mother, too, was in good health, albeit that she "thinks long she hears no word from you," Margery reported.[10]

Perhaps inevitably, Margaret's relationship with her son and daughter-in-law was gradually becoming more demanding as the years went on. Her grip on her affairs was as competent as ever, but she was weary, and increasingly preoccupied with her coming end. Given the prominent and destructive role that contested wills had played in her life, it was hardly surprising that she was deeply concerned with ensuring the fulfilment of her own wishes after her death—and, in particular, that her heir, John III, should respect her bequests to her younger children and her servants. If there was anyone in the world Margaret could trust implicitly to honour her intentions to the last detail, it was John III—and yet her need for certainty was so great that she would take nothing for granted. At the end of a visit that her son and his family paid to her household at Mautby, Margaret broached the subject with her daughter-in-law, asking Margery to speak to John III on her behalf once they returned home. He wrote immediately—half exasperated, half concerned—to try to put her mind at rest: ". . . mother," he said, "it pleased you to have certain words to my wife at her departing touching your remembrance of the shortness that you think your days of, and also of the mind that you have towards my brothers and sister . . . and also of your servants, wherein you willed her to be a means to me that I would tender and favour the same. Mother, saving your pleasure, there needs no ambassadors nor means between you and me." He would of course do whatever she wanted, he told her; he could scarcely believe that it might occur to her to doubt him, still less that she might feel unable to approach him directly, "for I know well no one man alive has called so often upon you as I to make your will, and put each thing in certainty that you would have done for yourself and to your children and servants." He even suggested—whether to jolly her along or jolt her out of her insistent concern with her own mortality—that she was as likely to outlive him as the other way around.[11]

Nevertheless, it was easy to see why she might worry about her legacy. Ten years after her husband's death, his grave had been covered only with a tattered cloth; and for all the grandeur of Sir John Fastolf's intentions, his college at Caister had in the end been swallowed up by Bishop Wainfleet's foundation at Oxford. Margaret's plans were on a much more modest scale, but to her they were no less important. The final version of her will, completed in February 1482, was characteristically purposeful. She was meticulously exact where it mattered most: she was precise to the last detail, for example, about the stone that was to be placed over the site where she wished to be buried in the south aisle of Mautby church. She was determined that she, at least, should have a fitting tomb "within a year next after my decease"—but more than that, both the location and the design of her grave would proclaim her heritage as the last heir of the Mautby line.[12] The Mautby arms were to be carved in the middle of the marble tombstone, with four more shields at its corners—displaying the Mautby arms impaled with those of Paston, Berney, Loveyn, and Beauchamp—to represent her own marriage and those of her father, grandfather, and great-grandfather. Margaret had been a devoted and dutiful wife: she had thrown herself without reservation into her life as a Paston, and had done everything she could to help secure the Paston name among the old established families of

Norfolk landed society. But she had never forgotten that—unlike her husband—she herself had been born into one of those old established families, and it was among her ancestors, rather than at her husband's side, that she now wished to be buried.

Her gifts to her family were as practical and unsentimental as she was. She made individual bequests where goods were valuable enough to be specified, but there was a limit to the detail into which she was prepared to go. Male testators, occupied principally with the important business of apportioning estates, often paid little attention to the disposition of their personal possessions: Margaret's brother-in-law William Paston, for example, did not include a single personal gift when he drafted his will in 1496. Women, on the other hand, frequently went into painstaking detail about the household goods they wished to distribute to members of their family. The will of Margaret's sister-in-law Elizabeth Paston, now Elizabeth Browne, contained an exhaustive itemised list of the silver plate, jewels, clothes, beds, bedlinen, carpets, vestments, altar cloths, napkins and tablecloths, tables, stools, coffers, candlesticks, tableware, and kitchenware (including "two colanders, two spits, two dripping pans of iron, three dressing knives, two leeching knives, two chopping knives, a trivet, a brazen mortar with a pestle of iron, two stone mortars, two gridirons, one pair of pot hooks, a flesh hook, and a coalrack") that she intended her daughter Mary to have when she married—"except," Elizabeth added as an afterthought, "such stuff as cannot be kept from moths," of which Mary was to take possession straight away.[13]

By comparison, Margaret's will seemed almost austere. As her oldest surviving son, John III would of course inherit her estates, but she also gave him a silver-gilt standing cup with "a knob like a garlic head" on its lid, and six silver goblets; and to his wife, Margery, she left her mass book, her altar cloths, and silver vessels to hold the consecrated bread and wine at the Eucharist. To their children, William and Elizabeth, Margaret left the sum of a hundred marks (sixty-six pounds) to be shared between them. Her son Edmund had at last found himself a wife, a young widow named Catherine Clippesby, and the couple now had a baby son. All three were remembered in the will: for Edmund, there was silver plate and a featherbed; for Catherine, a fine purple girdle "harnessed with silver and gilt," as well as an iron cauldron and two pestles and mortars; and to her grandson Robert, Margaret left her swans—birds so highly valued as a delicacy that a licence from the king was needed to keep them. Edmund's family were also to receive a small annual income of five marks (a little more than three pounds) from Margaret's lands. Her daughter Anne Yelverton was to have a share of her silver plate, a blue girdle adorned with silver and gilt, her primer, her enamelled silver beads, a featherbed with "two pairs of my finest sheets," "my best garnish of pewter vessels" and some pots, pans, and candlesticks, as well as ten pounds "to her proper use." To her youngest son, William, Margaret left yet more silver, a featherbed, a ewer and basin, and a hundred marks with which to buy "as much land to him and to his heirs as may be had with the same money."[14]

Margaret was tough-minded, but she had never been unemotional: she put aside ten marks (more than six pounds) for her illegitimate grand-daughter Constance, John II's only child, and twenty pounds for John Calle, eldest son of her estranged daughter Margery. To Margery herself, Margaret left nothing. It is possible that she had already died—or perhaps Margaret could still not bring herself to forgive her daughter's defiance. Beyond these bequests, and a handful of others—her quartz beads "gaud-ied with silver and gilt" to her goddaughter, and gifts for her servants—Margaret was prepared to allow John III discretion to exercise his judgment as her chief executor: "I will that the residue of the stuff of my household unbequeathed be divided equally between Edmund and William, my sons, and Anne my daughter," she wrote. John III himself, as the head of the family, had much less need of such practical assistance, but Margaret instructed that he should nevertheless be given ten pounds "for his labour" in the execution of the will.[15]

That left only the question of religious and charitable donations to ease her soul through the pains of purgatory. Those too were careful, measured, and precise. There were bequests to the churches at her own manors—principally, of course, Mautby, where she directed that "the said aisle in which my body shall be buried be new roofed, leaded and glassed, and the walls thereof heightened conveniently and workmanly." She left money to be shared among her tenants, a few pence per household; to the churches of the two parishes in which she had lived at Norwich; and to the four orders of friars at Norwich and Yarmouth. Her executors were to pay for the pro-vision of masses for her soul for seven years after her death, and she speci-fied that twelve of her poorest tenants, "apparelled in white gowns with hoods according," should hold torches around her coffin during her funeral. Her poor tenants were not only the most in need of her help but also the closest to God on account of their poverty, and their prayers of intercession were therefore particularly efficacious; the same (on account of their sickness) was true of the inmates of the leper houses at the city gates of Norwich and Yarmouth, each of whom was to receive three pence. All that remained was to commit her soul "to God Almighty, and to Our Lady his blessed mother, St. Michael, St. John Baptist, and to all saints," and to confirm that her will was composed "with perfect advisement and good deliberation."[16] It is the last surviving document to which she put her seal. Two years later, on 4 November 1484, at the age of sixty-two, Margaret died.

For John III, his mother's death marked the passing of an era. He was not left alone: he had a new and happy family of his own to console him. But he had been devoted to his mother and brother, with whom he had spent most of his life working shoulder to shoulder in defence of the family's interests—and now they were both gone. Margaret's death also, of course, left John III much wealthier. In theory, he now enjoyed what neither his father nor his brother ever had—control of all the family's estates—since he now inherited Margaret's Mautby lands and the Paston manors that she had held during her eighteen years of widowhood, on top of the properties formerly held by his grandmother. In practice, of course, given the determined challenge of his uncle William, Agnes's estates were not simply John III's to command, but he was at least spared his elder brother's peculiarly stressful existence as an heir whose inheritance was for the most part tantalisingly out of reach.

Despite their father's fears, John II's stewardship of the family's affairs had been far from disastrous, particularly in terms of his unsparing efforts to retrieve Caister from the political wreckage of the dispute over Fastolf's will. Nevertheless, it was clear that Paston interests were finally in the hands of the person best equipped to look after them. Over the years since their father's death, John III's quiet competence, his lucid judgment, and his generosity of spirit had quietly made him the backbone of the family. His talents now also attracted the attention and the friendship of one of the most powerful men in the country. By 1483, Lord Hastings valued John III's service so highly that he sent him to assist his ailing brother, Sir Ralph Hastings, in command of the fortress of Guines within the Calais Pale, just south of the port itself. Toward the end of April, Sir Ralph recovered his health, and Hastings was keen to have John III back. "I trust he may now spare you," he wrote warmly, signing the letter "your true friend Hastings."[17] For his own part, Ralph Hastings was more than sorry to see John III go, particularly since he fell ill again almost immediately, but by the time he wrote on 9 May—to "my faithful loving good cousin John Paston"—it had become frighteningly apparent why his brother wished to have men he could trust around him in England.[18]

King Edward had turned forty in the spring of the previous year. One of the mottoes that he had chosen for himself was *"confort et liesse"*—"comfort and delight"—and in the spring of 1483 it emerged that the king had taken his maxim too far for his own or his country's good. Years of overindulging his physical appetites had transformed Edward from a golden boy into a bloated man, his remarkable beauty and athletic build blurring into dissolution. Excess, it turned out, had taken its toll on his health as well as on his appearance. The king was suddenly taken ill at the end of March. He rallied enough after the first devastating seizure— probably a stroke—to revise his will, but on 9 April, three weeks before his forty-first birthday, Edward died.

As his nobles gathered, still scarcely able to believe what had happened, to honour their dead sovereign, his body lay in state in Westminster Abbey, draped in a cloth of black silk threaded with gold; next to the bier stood a life-size effigy of the king, "in habit royal, crowned with the very crown on his head, holding in that one hand a sceptre and in that other hand a ball of silver and gilt."[19] The embalmed corpse was then placed on a chariot hung with black velvet for its final journey westward to Windsor Castle. There the king was buried in the beautiful new chapel dedicated to St. George which he had commissioned with the money received from King Louis of France by the terms of the Treaty of Picquigny, and where building work was still continuing on the nave. After the elaborate and sombre rites, the king's armour was ceremonially placed on his grave: a coat of gilded mail, covered in crimson velvet embroidered with the royal arms in gold, pearls, and rubies.

Edward's charisma, his implacable resolve, his decades of political experience, and his iron grip on the affairs of his kingdom were suddenly gone. *"The king is dead: long live the king!"* the heralds cried at his funeral; but the monarch to whom he left his throne, his young son Edward, was just twelve years old. It was an appalling shock for a country which had had little more than ten years to settle back into stability since the terrifying upheavals of 1470–1471; and under the force of the unexpected blow, the powerful regime which Edward had built during that time abruptly fractured.

The difficulty was that the new boy-king, Edward V, was, in political terms, at the worst possible age to inherit the crown. It would be only two or three years before it could plausibly be claimed that he was old enough to begin to rule for himself, but on the other hand he was plenty young enough for those around him to exert a controlling influence over the exercise of his authority for some time to come. Any manoeuvring for position among the nobility would have to be done quickly before the new government took irreversible shape. The fact that the reign of the last monarch to have inherited the throne in childhood—Henry VI—had ended in disaster did not help to calm the atmosphere of rising panic. Nor did it help that the young king, who was staying at Ludlow Castle, near the Welsh border, when his father died, was currently in the care of his mother's large and assertive family, the Woodvilles. They were therefore better placed than anyone else to secure their position at the king's side; that fact, however, ensured that they were also regarded with suspicion and intense hostility by other leading members of the nobility, including the dead king's two most trusted lieutenants, his friend Lord Hastings and his younger brother, Richard, duke of Gloucester.

Both Gloucester and Hastings feared for their future under a Woodville-dominated regime, and only days after Edward's death they resolved on a preemptive coup. The new king was making his way from Ludlow to London with his Woodville uncle, Earl Rivers, when on 30 April the royal party was met at Stony Stratford in Buckinghamshire, a little more than forty miles northwest of the capital, by the duke of Gloucester, riding in the company of the duke of Buckingham and at the head of a substantial retinue. Rivers was expecting to escort his nephew to London to prepare for the coronation; instead, he was arrested. The king arrived in the capital on 4 May with his uncle Gloucester at his side, to be welcomed into the city by Lord Hastings. Less than a week later, Gloucester was named protector of the realm, with authority to rule until his nephew came of age, while Rivers and other members of the Woodville family were imprisoned, and their lands and offices confiscated.

The fall of the Woodvilles was an indication of the profound trauma that Edward IV's sudden death had precipitated within the political establishment, but they had been able to rally little support in their own defence, and the coup had been executed rapidly and ruthlessly. The stage now seemed set for the continuation of Yorkist rule in the name of Edward V under the leadership of his father's two most loyal servants. Together, Gloucester and Hastings already dominated large areas of the country,

Gloucester as the greatest magnate in the north, and Hastings as the preeminent power in the Midlands. They also had the backing of the duke of Buckingham, who could trace his descent back to the royal line of Edward III, but had so far found little favour under the Yorkist regime, whether because his father and grandfather had been killed fighting for the Lancastrian cause, or because Edward IV had not been convinced of the duke's political judgment. Buckingham was married to Rivers's sister Catherine Woodville, but he showed no inclination to throw in his lot with his wife's family. Instead, by positioning himself at the heart of the new government, Buckingham stood to reap major political rewards for the first time in his career—something which became apparent immediately when he took over from his brother-in-law Rivers as the leading power in Wales and the Welsh borders.

For John Paston III, as for other loyal subjects of the Yorkist crown, there was no reason to question his own allegiance to the newly established protectorate. It was a long time since he had had any politically meaningful contact with Earl Rivers, and it seemed that the dramatic events of the past two months had served to secure the influence in government of his current patron Lord Hastings. However, it would be some time before calm was fully restored, and meanwhile the political atmosphere remained tense. Sir Ralph Hastings had recognized as much when he wrote to John III, in suitably circumspect terms, from Guines Castle on 9 May: "praying you to advertise my lord"—his brother Hastings—"to see well to himself, etc."[20] A month later, Sir Ralph's anxiety was vindicated in horrifying fashion. On Friday, 13 June, during a council meeting at the Tower of London, the duke of Gloucester suddenly accused Lord Hastings of treason. Hastings was given no chance to respond to the allegations, still less any kind of formal hearing: on Gloucester's orders he was immediately bundled outside onto Tower Hill and beheaded. The execution proved to be the first move in a second coup—this time a coup d'état, designed to place Gloucester on the throne in his nephew's place. The duke summoned an army from his northern estates and, while his troops were mustering, proclaimed that Edward V and his siblings were illegitimate, on the grounds that their father was already promised elsewhere in marriage at the time of his secret wedding to Elizabeth Woodville. On 26 June, Gloucester took his seat on the marble throne in the great hall of the palace of Westminster. Ten days later, with his own men now in control in the capital, he was crowned as King Richard III.

It was an utterly shocking turn of events, of which it is no easier to make sense with the benefit of hindsight than it was for the new king's terrified subjects. Gloucester's political career, his entire life even, had been shaped and defined by his uncompromising loyalty to his brother; but he had responded to the crisis of the king's unexpected death by murdering Edward's best friend and deposing his son in order to take the crown for himself. The public justification for his actions—the flimsy story of Edward's alleged bigamy—was patently bogus. Probably the most plausible explanation is that Gloucester—under extreme pressure of time and circumstance—felt himself forced into radical action by the realisation that the destruction of the Woodvilles could secure his position only in the short term, since it was almost inevitable that the young king would one day seek retribution against those he perceived to be responsible for the downfall of his mother's family. Gloucester seems to have been driven by a combination of fear, panic, and an emerging conviction that his own rule was the only means of safeguarding the stability of a realm so recently recovered from the devastation of civil war. If he needed to remove Lord Hastings—who would never have accepted the deposition of Edward IV's son—in order to clear his own path to the throne, that was a price the duke was prepared to pay. He was undoubtedly encouraged to reach that conclusion by the Machiavellian whisperings of the duke of Buckingham, who had gained a great deal from the fall of the Woodvilles, and stood to gain a great deal more from Hastings's death.

If Gloucester did believe that this usurpation was the route to political security for himself and for the country, his mistake quickly became apparent. The newly crowned Richard III was an able, intelligent, and energetic man, who did his utmost to govern as effectively as his dead brother had done. But this Yorkist king had achieved the throne by dividing the Yorkist regime against itself, and without legitimacy, he could not hope to rebuild political unity. Less than a month into his reign, evidence was discovered of a plot to rescue Edward V and his brother, the ten-year-old duke of York, from the Tower of London, where they had been housed in preparation for Edward's now-abandoned coronation. The conspiracy served to emphasise the fact that, for as long as they were alive, Richard's nephews would be a powerful focus for resistance to his rule. On the other hand, it was no easy matter to dispose of the threat that they embodied. In the past, the killing of deposed kings—as in the case of Henry VI in 1471—had been tacitly accepted as a fact of life, a necessary evil on the road to political recovery. However, the murder of two children who bore no responsibility for the brutal conflict in which they had been caught up was unlikely to be accepted with any kind of equanimity or understanding—and the simultaneous deaths of two healthy boys could not easily be represented as the result of accident or coincidence. Instead, they disappeared. It is impossible to know exactly what happened, beyond the fact that sightings of them in the Tower became less and less frequent, until they were no longer seen at all. Certainly, by the end of September 1483, just five months after Edward IV's funeral, it was widely believed that his sons were dead. It quickly became apparent, however, that their removal from the political stage had not eliminated their capacity to undermine their uncle's authority. Even in the absence of conclusive proof that the princes had been murdered, rumours alone were enough to alienate support further from a king who now seemed to have the innocent blood of his own nephews on his hands.

That autumn, the instability of Richard's regime was publicly exposed by a full-scale rebellion against his government. The most frightening aspect of the revolt from the king's point of view was that it came from within, not outside, the Yorkist establishment. The rebels included prominent members of Edward IV's household in the south of England, and at their head—in what was for Richard a devastating personal betrayal—was the duke of Buckingham, whose vaulting personal ambition had made him a destabilising force throughout the entire crisis. The disappearance of Edward V and his brother proved to be no defence against this rising. Instead, Richard had achieved the unlikely feat of making a credible contender for the throne out of Henry Tudor, the last scraping of the Lancastrian barrel.

Tudor, who was in exile at the court of the duke of Brittany, was the only surviving male heir of the Lancastrian dynasty: his mother, Margaret Beaufort, was the great-granddaughter of John of Gaunt, duke of Lancaster and father of King Henry IV. However, the Beaufort line was descended from Gaunt's third marriage to his long-standing mistress, Catherine Swynford, and the couple's children, born out of wedlock, had been legitimised after their parents' wedding with the explicit proviso that they should have no right to inherit the crown. Even if this technical disqualification could be set aside, arguments for the superiority of the Lancastrian claim to the throne over that of the house of York had depended on the fact that Henry VI was descended from the third son of King Edward III in the male line, whereas the Yorkist descent from the second son of Edward III came through a woman. Given that Henry Tudor's descent from the third son of Edward III also came through a woman, it was indisputable that the Yorkist claim should take precedence.[21] In the autumn of 1483, none of that mattered. What mattered was that all those who could not accept the disappearance of Edward IV's sons and the destruction of half his regime were now looking to Henry Tudor as the only viable claimant around whom to rally opposition to Richard. Extraordinarily, the Lancastrian heir had now become a Yorkist candidate for the throne—a new political persona which Tudor immediately sought to bolster by publicly promising to marry Edward IV's oldest daughter, seventeen-year-old Elizabeth of York.

In the face of this ominous challenge, Richard could call on the support of his powerful northern retinue, and a few magnates whose personal interests were closely linked to the fortunes of his regime. In East Anglia, his principal representative was John Howard, whom he had created duke of Norfolk in June 1483, in one of his first acts after seizing the throne. Anne Mowbray, the small daughter and heiress of the last duke, had died two years earlier at the age of only eight, and Howard, whose mother was the dead duke's great-aunt, was the next heir. However, the terms of the little duchess's marriage to Edward IV's second son—which had taken place amid splendid ceremony in 1478, when the bride was five and the groom four—had been so generous to her young husband that he kept his wife's title and estates after her death. Despite Howard's twenty years of loyal service to the Yorkist regime, Edward IV had preferred to appropriate the dukedom for his own family rather than allow Howard to succeed his Mowbray cousin.

The deposition of Edward V therefore opened the way for Howard to claim his inheritance, and he supported the usurpation from the first: his son Thomas was among those who carried out the summary execution of Lord Hastings on Richard's orders, and Howard himself served as high steward at the new king's coronation. He was amply rewarded with not only the dukedom of Norfolk but also the estates of Earl Rivers, who had been beheaded without trial a few days after Hastings's death, and the East Anglian lands of the earl of Oxford, who was still in captivity at Hammes Castle. By 10 October 1483, with the rebels gathering their forces in the southeastern county of Kent, Howard was raising as many men as he could in defence of the king to whom he owed his sudden promotion. One of those who received a letter was John Paston III: "I pray you," Howard wrote urgently, "that with all diligence you make you ready and come hither, and bring with you six tall fellows in harness; and you shall not lose your labour, that knows God, who have you in his keeping." The letter was signed "Your friend, J. Norfolk."[22]

Howard, who was now in his early sixties, had known the Paston family for decades, but their relationship was not unequivocally positive: it was one of Howard's servants, after all, who had attacked John Paston with a dagger over a disputed parliamentary election more than twenty years earlier. Nevertheless, the new duke's personal dealings with John III had begun in more propitious circumstances when they were both in the late duke's service in the early 1460s; Howard had even lent "young Paston" three shillings when they were travelling together in Norfolk's household in the winter of 1463.[23] However, if Howard hoped that shared memories—or his new eminence—would persuade John III to arm himself in support of King Richard, he was to be disappointed. For John III, there was too much to lose, and nothing to be gained, by risking his life on the battlefield. Twelve years earlier, he had fought at Barnet in the service of the earl of Oxford, to whom the Pastons owed a great deal and from whom they hoped for much more under a future Lancastrian government. It was a gamble that failed, and spectacularly so. Now, John III had little incentive to repeat the experience, since he owed nothing to John Howard—quite the reverse, in fact, given the role that Howard had played in the lynching of his new patron Lord Hastings. Howard's efforts at recruitment were persuasive enough that the rebels were defeated by early November, but it was a victory achieved without Paston help.

If John III needed any reminder of the dangers of political involvement in such unstable times, it was provided by his aunt Elizabeth's second husband, Sir George Browne, who had been a knight of the body to Edward IV, and was so close to his royal master that he had carried the banner of St. George in the solemn procession which escorted the king's corpse into Westminster Abbey in April 1483. Six months later, he and his stepson Edward Poynings, Elizabeth's son by her first marriage, joined the ill-fated rebellion against King Edward's usurping brother. Elizabeth Paston had lost her first husband on the battlefield at St. Albans in 1461; now she lost her second to the executioner's axe, and her son into exile.

It was hardly surprising, therefore, that John III maintained a low political profile during the months that followed. He concentrated on pursuing his case against his uncle William over his grandmother's lands, drawing up a petition that detailed the losses he claimed to have suffered at his uncle's hands, including the thousand marks lent to Archbishop Neville at William's suggestion ("which was not paid again by the sum of £100," John III added indignantly), and more than three thousand pounds in cash that he alleged had disappeared into his uncle's pockets after Judge William's death forty years earlier. The total, he said (almost certainly with a touch of the creative accounting in which most petitioners indulged), came to more than seven thousand pounds, "beside grief, great labour and dis-ease that the said John has daily been put unto."[24] However, neither John III himself nor his uncle—whose Beaufort marriage brought him uncomfortably close connections to the camp of the king's rival-in-exile Henry Tudor—was in a position to press his claim to a successful conclusion. In November 1484, John III was also confronted with the loss of his mother. It is impossible to recapture in any detail the emotional impact of Margaret's death on the family as a whole, since in the letters—or rather the absence of them—there is silence. Apart from anything else, John III now spent most of his time at home with his wife and children, and once Margaret herself was gone, there was neither the opportunity nor the need for the kind of sustained correspondence that had become second nature during the long years of the Fastolf dispute.

Even had his mother and brother still been alive, the continuing volatility of the political world meant that John III might well have hesitated before committing too many of his thoughts to paper. The suppression of the revolt of 1483 had brought no lasting security to King Richard's beleaguered regime. The king was attempting to use his northern supporters to reimpose his authority across the south of England—a short-term fix that was already stirring up widespread resentment at the appointment of outsiders to positions of local influence, and thereby emphasising the dangerous limitations of his own power base. Meanwhile, the threat of further insurrection in support of Henry Tudor was becoming more menacing. In the summer of 1484, Richard exerted all the diplomatic pressure he could bring to bear on the duke of Brittany in the attempt to secure Tudor's arrest, but Henry instead escaped from the Breton court to neighbouring France, where Edward IV's old sparring partner, the "Spider King" Louis XI, had died just four months after Edward himself. The parallels were uncanny: Louis, too, had succumbed to a fatal stroke, leaving a twelve-year-old son, Charles VIII, to inherit his throne. But the French regent, Charles's elder sister Anne, made no attempt to seize her brother's crown. Instead, it became alarmingly clear that her government was as keen as its predecessors to seize any opportunity to destabilise English rule—which, in 1484, meant providing the fugitive Henry Tudor with both money and troops.

Tudor was joined at the French court not only by the Yorkist loyalists who had fled England after the failed rebellion of 1483, but also by the Pastons' former lord, the earl of Oxford. In November 1484, after ten years of imprisonment at Hammes, Oxford finally made his escape by the brilliantly simple manoeuvre of persuading the captain of the castle to abandon his post and defect to Tudor's cause. The earl had last tried to leave the fortress six years earlier by jumping from the battlements. Now he was a free man, riding out of Hammes with his jailer at his side, to be followed a couple of months later by most of the soldiers of the garrison. By the summer of 1485, King Richard's regime was, if not haemorrhaging support, then at least badly incapacitated, and Henry Tudor was gathering an invasion force in Normandy. His fleet landed in south Wales on 7 August.

For the second time, John Howard set about raising troops to defend his king. Once again he wrote to his "wellbeloved friend" John Paston III, summoning him to join his muster and requiring him to "bring with you such company of tall men as you may goodly make, at my cost and charge." This time, in haste and with more than a hint of desperation, he signed himself "Your lover, J. Norfolk."[25] For the second time, John III did not respond. Nor did he join his old lord the earl of Oxford in opposition to the king. When the two armies met near Market Bosworth in the midland county of Leicestershire on 22 August, the only Paston on the field was Elizabeth Paston's son Edward Poynings, who had fled into exile after the failed rebellion in which his stepfather had lost his life two years earlier, and now rode at Henry Tudor's side on his return from France.

The fundamental weakness in King Richard's position was that his authority was too flawed and fragile to command the unquestioning support of his subjects, many of whom, like John III, were waiting to see what would happen before committing themselves irrevocably to his cause. The vanguard of Richard's army was led by John Howard, the stalwart duke of Norfolk, but many other nobles had not rallied to his side, and, disastrously, not all of those who did so proved to be reliable allies. When the battle began, neither the men under the command of the earl of Northumberland nor the forces of Lord Stanley—who had ostensibly remained loyal to Richard despite being married to Henry Tudor's mother, Margaret Beaufort—joined the fighting. Stanley's men did not intervene until the king himself, with headlong, reckless courage, charged at the heart of his enemy's army, intending to kill Tudor and thereby end the conflict with a single decisive blow. Richard fought so hard, pressing forward furiously on foot even after his horse was killed under him, that he came within feet of his rival. As he did so, he discovered that he had been betrayed: Stanley intended not to destroy Henry Tudor, but to save him. As Stanley's troops swarmed at last onto the field, Richard's men were engulfed and butchered, and the king himself hacked down in the mêlée. Among the heavy casualties sustained by Richard's defeated army was his loyal servant John Howard, duke of Norfolk.

Yet again, England had a new king. Richard's naked body, mangled and filthy as it was, was left exposed in public for two days before being unceremoniously buried in an unmarked grave at the Grey Friars' church in the city of Leicester, while Henry Tudor rode south in triumph to take possession of the capital. There, on 30 October, he was crowned as King Henry VII. By then, with the new regime beginning to take shape around him, John Paston III had already been forced to show his hand. Henry was, to all intents and purposes, a foreigner in England: he had been brought up in Wales, and had spent the last fourteen of his twenty-eight years in exile as an impoverished refugee. As a result, he had little firsthand experience even of the country of which he was now king, let alone of the demands of government, but he set about establishing his authority through the resources most immediately at his disposal. In East Anglia, that meant the regional power of the earl of Oxford, who was restored to his estates and appointed lord admiral of England. Oxford, at forty-three, had also spent the last fourteen years on the Continent, at first in exile and then as a prisoner at Hammes. But he at least had political connections from the years before 1471—associations such as his relationship with John III—on which he could now draw in the service of the new king.

His task, and that of his royal master, was also made easier by the fact that Henry's accession in many ways represented a restoration of the Yorkist regime which had been shattered by Richard III's usurpation— albeit that Richard's actions had turned the natural political order on its head to such an extent that it was now a Yorkist regime with Lancastrian leadership. John Paston III was ideally placed to benefit from this hybrid political heritage: he had fought for the Lancastrian cause at Barnet under the earl of Oxford's command, before refashioning himself as a loyal subject of King Edward in the service of Lord Hastings. He therefore represented the Yorkist establishment through which the country had been governed until 1483, while at the same time his Lancastrian past recommended him to Oxford, who knew his abilities of old. The combination of Henry's decisive victory and the return of his own former lord seems to have persuaded John III finally to commit himself unequivocally to the new regime. On 12 September 1485, less than a month after the fighting at Bosworth, he was given office as sheriff of Norfolk and Suffolk for the year—that is, placed in charge of law enforcement in the two counties, with the weighty responsibility of serving royal writs, arresting malefactors, and keeping order on the king's behalf—an appointment almost certainly made at Oxford's suggestion. By the following summer, John III had been named one of the esquires of the body in the new royal household, whose duties (which included dressing the king in the morning and disrobing him at night, with especially favoured esquires required to sleep on a paillasse in the king's chamber) gave unparalleled personal access to the monarch. Five months after that, the earl of Oxford was addressing John III warmly as "my right trusty and wellbeloved counsellor."[26] It was not long before his younger brothers Edmund and William followed him into the earl's service.

But political commitment brought risks as well as rewards, especially once the aftershocks of the bloody conflict of 1485 began to make themselves felt. In the spring of 1486, Francis, Viscount Lovell—one of King Richard's closest friends and the former chamberlain of his household—raised a rebellion in the north. The rising was quickly suppressed, but Lovell himself escaped, and John III was charged with keeping watch on the East Anglian coasts in case the fugitive tried to reach the Continent. By the beginning of 1487, it emerged that the information which John III had gathered about Lovell's movements and adherents was both out of date and inaccurate—circumstances that prompted an icy letter of reproof from the earl of Oxford.

Lovell, it transpired, was already in Flanders, part of the territories of the duchy of Burgundy. Edward IV's brother-in-law and erstwhile ally, Duke Charles, had been killed in battle in 1477, leaving as his heir his twenty-year-old daughter Mary, the only child of his first marriage. Mary took up the reins of Burgundian power with the help of her stepmother, Charles's widow, Margaret of York—the graceful girl whose glamorous wedding the Paston brothers had attended, now the grande dame of Burgundian politics—who had no children of her own and became the staunchest defender of her stepdaughter's cause in the face of renewed French aggression. It was to counter the threat from France that, seven months after her accession, Mary married Maximilian, heir to the

Habsburg Holy Roman Empire; but five years later she was killed in a riding accident, leaving her three-year-old son Philip as the new duke of Burgundy. Dowager Duchess Margaret was as devoted to Philip as she had been to his mother, and played a key role in ruling the Burgundian territories in his name.

She was equally dedicated to the memory of her own dead brothers, Edward IV and Richard III. Despite Henry Tudor's claims to be the heir of Edward IV's political legacy, which were underpinned in January 1486 by his marriage to Edward's daughter Elizabeth, Margaret refused to accept that his dubious title to the throne should prevail at the expense of her own blood. The fact that Henry had deposed her brother Richard with French support also meant that Burgundian interests were well served by efforts to destabilise the fledgling Tudor government. Margaret therefore gave her powerful backing to a planned invasion of England under the leadership of her brother's friend Lovell, who had recently arrived at her court as a refugee. As their figurehead, the rebels adopted a boy who claimed to be Edward, earl of Warwick, son of the dead duke of Clarence and the next Yorkist heir in the male line after the princes who had disappeared in the Tower of London. It was not difficult for King Henry to demonstrate that this pretender was an imposter, and he did so in February 1487 by producing the real earl of Warwick, an unworldly twelve-year-old, from the apartments where he lived at the Tower—his proximity to the throne enough reason for Henry to keep him securely under lock and key—and parading him through the streets of the capital. The "Warwick" championed by the rebels was a boy named Lambert Simnel, the handsome son of an Oxford tradesman, who had been trained to conduct himself with a more convincingly regal bearing than the artless child in the Tower could ever have managed. But the truth of Simnel's identity was not enough to defuse the threat that Lovell and his allies posed to Henry's regime—a threat that was reinforced two months later by the defection to their ranks of John, earl of Lincoln, the eldest son of the duke of Suffolk. Lincoln, too, had Yorkist blood in his veins through his mother, Elizabeth, another sister of Edward IV and Richard III, and in April 1487 he fled to join Lord Lovell in Flanders at the court of his aunt, Duchess Margaret.

As Lovell and Lincoln prepared their assault on England, John Paston III was appointed to a commission charged with the task of raising men in Norfolk to resist the invasion. At the end of April, however, he found himself in danger of being swept away by increasingly treacherous currents of speculation and suspicion. Toward the end of the month he was observed leaving the port of Yarmouth by boat—an event of no moment whatsoever in normal circumstances. But with the king's enemies massing their forces in Flanders, John III's decision to travel by sea was enough to call his intentions into question. "Sir, it is so that there has been a great rumour and marvellous noise of your departing from Yarmouth," he was warned anxiously by a servant on 29 April; "for some said that you were departed in a Dutch ship and some said in a Spanish ship and some said in your ship, and some said against your will you were departed." The atmosphere was so feverish that even those with most reason to trust him were ready to jump to threatening conclusions. The steward of King Henry's household, Lord Fitzwalter, was a Norfolk man, promoted to a new eminence by the change of regime, who had extended his friendship to John III ever since they had met more than a decade earlier, to such an extent that it had even seemed possible at one stage that John III might marry his sister-in-law. However, when Fitzwalter heard of John III's embarkation at Yarmouth in the spring of 1487, he "imagined and purposed many grievous things against your mastership," John III was told.[27]

Despite the threatening gossip, it became clear soon enough that he had not in fact absconded to the Continent, and by the middle of May the muster of troops in King Henry's name was well under way. Nevertheless, there was widespread uncertainty about how many local gentlemen would prove willing to take up arms against the rebels, and it was apparent that John III remained under suspicion: ". . . you be sore taken in some place, saying that you intend such things as is like to follow great mischief," his friend Edmund Bedingfield warned.[28] It may have been John III's personal generosity that raised doubts about his political reliability. Lord Lovell's mother-in-law, Lady Fitzhugh, was the sister of both Lady Hastings and the countess of Oxford, the wives of John III's two most recent patrons, and it was perhaps through this connection that John III came to offer her his service—a relationship which Lady Fitzhugh valued so highly that she addressed him affectionately as "son Paston," and signed herself "your loving mother."[29] His unstinting friendship, both to Lady Fitzhugh and to her daughter, gave rise to politically damaging innuendo: Bedingfield's letter, for example, written on 16 May, reported the spread of rumours that John III had recently been seen returning from a visit to Lady Lovell. Whether or not it was true, the allegation could scarcely have been more dangerous. Ten days earlier, her husband had landed in Ireland with two thousand

German mercenaries provided by Duchess Margaret of Burgundy. In Dublin, on 24 May, Lambert Simnel was crowned King Edward VI of England, and less than a fortnight later the rebels set sail for the Lancashire coast.

Perhaps John III had always intended to serve in King Henry's army under the earl of Oxford's command, or perhaps he was prompted to do so by the need to silence the whispers about his suspected disloyalty. Either way, he demonstrated both his allegiance and his courage in unequivocal terms on 16 June, when the king's troops met the rebel contingent at the village of Stoke, in the midland county of Nottinghamshire. Oxford's men, John III among them, formed the vanguard of the king's forces and bore the brunt of a brutal engagement. Thousands died before the greater numbers and superior equipment of the royal army finally began to tell. After almost three hours of heavy fighting, the rebels were routed. The earl of Lincoln was killed; Lord Lovell disappeared without a trace; and the sorry figure of Lambert Simnel, a terrified boy behind his royal disguise, was captured and put to work in the king's kitchens. Once the battle was over, fifty-two gentlemen were knighted in the field by King Henry in recognition of their service. John Paston III was one of their number.

The king's victory at Stoke was a turning point, which at last established his rule on secure foundations. It did the same for John III's political career. He did not abandon his association with Lady Fitzhugh or her daughter Lady Lovell—now searching in vain for her missing husband—but no one now questioned his loyalty. He resumed his friendship with Lord Fitzwalter, its warmth unimpaired by the tensions of 1487; and he rose high in the service of the earl of Oxford, becoming steward of the earl's Norfolk estates and his deputy as lord admiral, an office in which his responsibilities ranged from the salvage of shipwrecks and the arrest of "men of war roving upon the coast," to the disposal of the valuable carcass of a whale—its meat, oil, and whalebone all prized commodities—found in shallow water off a north Norfolk beach ("a great fish and a royal . . . eleven fathoms and more of length and two fathoms of bigness and deepness in the middle fish").[30]

The new distinctions of John III's public career also seemed to bode well for his private quarrel with his uncle, although William Paston, too, had benefited greatly from the change of regime. His wife's formidable cousin Margaret Beaufort was now, as the king's mother, an extremely powerful figure, who took an active interest in the affairs of her extended family.

It was thanks to Margaret, for example, that William's eldest daughter, Mary, married the heir of the earl of Westmorland—a wedding that took place in the presence of the king himself—although the lasting significance of this stellar match was limited by the fact that Mary died before her twentieth birthday, succumbing to measles in the winter of 1489.

Perhaps, in the end, his grandmother's manors were saved for John III by an accident of fate. William had no sons—his heirs were his two surviving daughters, Agnes and Elizabeth—and the knowledge that his estates would be divided between two families, neither of which would bear the Paston name, encouraged him to accept a settlement in money rather than land. An arbitration was under way by 1489, in which John III's hand was strengthened by the support of an unlikely ally. His father's oldest and bitterest enemy, John Heydon, had died in September 1479—perhaps, like John II and Walter Paston, a victim of the devastating plague that swept the country that year. A decade after the old man's death, the Paston-Heydon feud was decisively consigned to history when Heydon's son and heir, Henry, agreed to a marriage between his own daughter Bridget and John III's young son William—an alliance which also secured Heydon's help in the conflict over Agnes's lands. The negotiations over the disputed manors and the arrangements for the wedding were pursued in parallel, Heydon writing warmly to John III not only about the progress of "your matter between you and your uncle," but to ask "in what silk or cloth you will have these two innocents married."[31] The match was an excellent one, not least because Bridget's large dowry helped to ease the financial burden of John III's eventual agreement with his uncle. John III's pleasure at seeing his son so advantageously married was tempered shortly afterward by harrowing loss, when his beloved wife Margery died in 1495. She was not yet forty. John III eventually married again, but it seems possible that this second match—to a wealthy widow named Agnes Morley—had more to do with his temporarily straitened financial circumstances than any kind of personal inclination.[32]

By 1500, John III was in his mid-fifties. The Paston name was respected and honoured, and its influence felt within the highest political circles. No one would ever again speak disparagingly of the family as "churls of Gimingham"; their place among the "right noble and worshipful blood" of the realm was assured. That spring, one more mark of distinction was accorded to a trusted servant of the crown. A marriage had been contracted between the heir to the throne, King Henry's oldest son Prince Arthur, and

Catherine of Aragon, the fifteen-year-old daughter of the Spanish monarchs Ferdinand of Aragon and Isabella of Castile. In March a royal letter arrived in Norfolk, summoning John III to attend the princess's arrival:

> Trusty and wellbeloved, we greet you well, letting you know that our dearest cousins the King and Queen of Spain have signified unto us by their sundry letters that the right excellent Princess, the Lady Catherine their daughter, shall be transported from the parts of Spain aforesaid to this our Realm about the month of May next coming for the solemnisation of matrimony between our dearest son the Prince and the said Princess. Wherefore we, considering that it is right fitting and necessary, as well for the honour of us as for the laud and praise of our said Realm, to have the said Princess honourably received at her arrival, have appointed you to be one among others to give attendance for the receiving of the said Princess; willing and desiring you to prepare yourself for that intent, and so to continue in a readiness upon an hour's warning, till that by our letters we shall advertise you of the day and time of her arrival and where you shall give your said attendance; and not to fail therein as you tender our pleasure, the honour of yourself, and of this our foresaid Realm.[33]

John Paston III was now the king's "trusty and wellbeloved knight," called to give personal service at a royal wedding. His grandfather—growing up as the son of a "good plain husbandman"—could have hoped for nothing more.

letters of good

consequence in history

*J*OHN PASTON III DIED at the age of sixty on 28 August 1504. He was survived by his second wife, Agnes, and probably by his youngest brother, William, who had served the earl of Oxford faithfully for almost twenty years until he was sent home to his family in 1503 when he became "troubled with sickness and crazed in his mind."[1] John III's other siblings, Edmund, Margery, and Anne, had predeceased him: Anne had died ten years earlier and Edmund only six months before John III himself. The date of Margery's death is unknown, but her husband, Richard Calle, was still living in 1503. John III was also survived by his two children, his daughter Elizabeth—who married William Clere, grandson of Margaret Paston's friend Elizabeth Clere—and his son and heir, William, who followed his father into royal service. William was dubbed a knight by 1520, and in that year he attended King Henry VIII at an Anglo-French summit conducted in such ostentatiously magnificent style—a glittering two-week extravaganza of feasting, tournaments, and pageantry—that it came to be known as the Field of the Cloth of Gold.

The success of Sir William's political career was matched by that of his marriage. He and his wife, Bridget Heydon, had a large family of five sons—Erasmus, Henry, John, Clement, and Thomas—and seven daughters.[2] Erasmus Paston died before his father, but his younger brother Clement gave distinguished military and naval service to the crown, and built a beautiful new house at Oxnead, the manor nine miles north of

Norwich that Judge William had bought more than a century earlier. Oxnead became the family's main seat when it was inherited after Clement's death by his nephew, Erasmus's son William.[3] The family continued to prosper until the mid-seventeenth century, when they found themselves engulfed by another terrifying civil war, this time between royalist and parliamentarian forces. Erasmus's great-great-grandson, yet another Sir William Paston, committed himself to the doomed cause of King Charles I, and as a result, a great deal of the family's property was sequestered by the victorious parliamentarian regime. William himself survived the conflict, but in 1659, exactly two hundred years after the death of Sir John Fastolf, he was forced to sell Caister Castle to a London merchant in the attempt to pay off his mounting debts. However, the family's loyalty to the Stuart monarchy meant that they benefited spectacularly from the restoration to the throne in 1660 of Charles I's son, King Charles II. William's son, Sir Robert, became a gentleman of the privy chamber at King Charles's court, and was created Lord Paston and Viscount Yarmouth in 1673. Six years later he was further rewarded, becoming the first earl of Yarmouth.

Robert's son William, the second earl of Yarmouth, at first emulated his father's success. He married Charlotte Jemima Henrietta Maria Fitzroy, one of Charles II's illegitimate daughters, and in 1687, at the age of thirty-three, became treasurer of the royal household of James II, King Charles's brother and heir. However, King James's attempts to promote a restoration of Catholicism precipitated an overwhelming political crisis, and in 1688 the king was driven into exile, leaving the throne to be taken by his Protestant daughter Mary and her Dutch husband William of Orange. William Paston's career fell with his king: he was imprisoned in the Tower of London on charges of treason in 1690 and again in 1692. He escaped execution and even achieved some measure of political rehabilitation, but he lost both his fortune and his family. He was estranged from his mother— "her son gives her no respects or holds any correspondence with her, though she lives not above two miles from him," it was reported in 1693[4]— and his son Charles died before him, leaving no male heirs of his own to inherit the family name or his father's title. Isolated and impoverished, William died on Christmas Day in 1732.

John Paston III had once, in dangerous times, reminded his brother of the uncertainty of the world with a cheerful jingle: "But Fortune with her smiling countenance strange/Of all our purpose may make a sudden change."[5] Fortune's wheel was a ubiquitous motif in medieval culture, and for the Paston brothers in 1471 it had seemed to offer the consoling prospect that triumph must one day follow the disasters against which they were struggling. Almost three centuries later, however, the wheel came full circle for the Paston family itself. From the moment when William Paston first left Paston village to embark on his legal career, it took nearly a hundred years to establish beyond question the family's position as gentlemen, landowners, and valued servants of kings and nobles. It took seven generations more for the Pastons to reach the apotheosis of a peerage in their own right. Just one generation after that—with the lonely death of another William Paston—title, wealth, and family were gone.

It was the end of the Paston dynasty. Their long years of struggle to inscribe the Paston name in the pages of history had ended in poignant defeat. Or so it seemed. In fact, the sad end of the second earl of Yarmouth marked the beginning of a historical afterlife which none of the fifteenth-century Pastons—shrewd Judge William and practical Agnes, stubborn John and redoubtable Margaret, dashing John II, or charming John III and his beloved Margery—could ever have begun to imagine.

The earl of Yarmouth had been staving off bankruptcy by the narrowest of margins for the last thirty years of his life, and after his death in 1732 the task of liquidating his estate to pay off his crippling debts fell to his son-in-law Thomas Weldon, the husband of his daughter Charlotte. Oxnead Hall was already in a state of tumbledown disrepair, and would shortly be abandoned altogether, its timbers and masonry plundered for reusable building materials until it lay, as one contemporary described it, "in the utmost ruins," "a deplorable sight."[6] By the spring of 1735, Weldon had already disposed of the earl's books, paintings, and furniture, but he found himself at a loss when confronted with the damp and chaos of the muniment room, where boxes and trunks of estate records, deeds, and court rolls stood amid heaps of loose letters and papers in no discernible order. He decided to call in an expert: the Reverend Francis Blomefield, a noted antiquarian and local historian, who spent two weeks "among the old writings" in the Paston archive, gathering material for the *Topographical History of the County of Norfolk* which he planned to publish, and bringing order to the jumbled piles of documents for the benefit of the earl's executors. At the end of the fortnight, Blomefield wrote to Weldon to report his findings.

There are innumerable letters, of good consequence in history, still lying among the loose papers, all which I laid up in a corner of the room on a heap, which contains several sacks full; but as they seemed to have some family affairs of one nature or other intermixed in them, I did not offer to touch any of them, but have left them to your consideration, whether, when I go to that part of the country, I shall separate and preserve them, or whether you will have them burned, though I must own 'tis pity they should; except it be those (of which there are many) that relate to nothing but family affairs only. I have placed everything so that now the good and bad are distinguished and preserved from the weather, by which a great number have perished entirely.[7]

Whether any of the letters which had miraculously survived the elements and the late earl's indifference were in fact burned is not clear. What is known is that Blomefield himself acquired a good number, while others passed into the hands of rival collectors; and that, in 1771, many of the manuscripts were bought by a Norfolk chemist named John Worth, as a speculative investment. When Worth himself died three years later, the papers were acquired by a local gentleman and amateur historian named John Fenn.

In May 1782, Fenn showed the collection to an eminent friend, the literary connoisseur Horace Walpole, who responded with great excitement:

I have brought you back your manuscripts myself, for I was afraid of keeping them they are so valuable, especially the Paston Letters, which are the most curious papers of the sort I ever saw, and the oldest original letters I believe extant in this country. The historic picture they give of the reign of Henry VI makes them invaluable, and more satisfactory than any cold narrative. It were a thousand pities they should not be published, which I should be glad I could persuade you to do.[8]

Fenn took him at his word, and embarked on the challenging process of preparing the manuscripts for publication. He was initially overwhelmed by the scale and complexity of the task that faced him: the sheer number of letters, and the difficulty of deciphering archaic English in centuries-old handwriting. "I must read much and I must write much, for I would not willingly publish them either in a slovenly or a careless manner," he told another friend anxiously. "I have been in some measure arranging them lately, but the heap and the crincum crancum hands fright me. However, if my friends encourage me, I think I shall venture."[9]

He was engagingly modest about his own abilities, but—in an era when a number of early manuscript collections were destroyed by antiquarians who cut up the documents, filed away the topographical references, and used what was left as scrap paper—Fenn proved to be a historian of unusual sensitivity and rigour. He transcribed a selection of the letters in their original spelling, and produced a modernised version of the text of each one, to be printed on the facing page. It took three years from the date of his first discussions with Walpole to complete his work, nine months to agree upon terms with a publishing house, and another year for the two volumes to go through the press. Finally, in January 1787, the first edition of the Paston letters appeared in print, cumbersomely entitled *Original Letters, written during the reigns of Henry VI, Edward IV, and Richard III, by various persons of rank or consequence; containing many curious anecdotes relative to that turbulent and bloody, but hitherto dark period of our history; and elucidating, not only public matters of state, but likewise the private manners of the age: digested in chronological order; with notes, historical and explanatory; and authenticated by engravings of autographs, paper marks and seals.*[10] It sold out within a week.

The Paston letters rapidly became the literary sensation of the year. Walpole rhapsodised over them: "The *Letters of Henry VI's reign* etc are come out, and to me make all other letters not worth reading," he said; "I have gone through above one volume, and cannot bear to be writing when I am so eager to be reading."[11] He was not alone in his enthusiasm. "It is with more pleasure than I can describe that I have seen your *Original Letters,*" another antiquarian told Fenn; "I think them one of the richest treasures in the English language; my attention is captivated; they cause me to forget to eat and to sleep."[12] Nor was it only those who already shared Fenn's historical interests who were entranced by the correspondence. The Paston letters became the talking point of the season in polite society: ". . . so fast went the first edition that we could not procure a copy so soon as we wished, though a friend had been written to in town upon the very first advertisement," a Suffolk gentleman wrote in May, adding that ". . . for several visits, the chat of the day was given up for the anecdotes of our ancestors."[13]

It was not long before Fenn's new celebrity status was accorded royal recognition. He had dedicated the two volumes of published letters to King George III, and—thanks to a family connection with George Pretyman, private secretary to Prime Minister William Pitt—Fenn was invited to present his books in person to the king three days before their publication. Less than a month later, with excitement about the letters running high in aristocratic circles, Fenn received another letter from Dr. Pretyman: "Dear Sir, I have three things to tell you which I must do concisely: 1st the king is much pleased with your books—2ndly he wishes to have the originals—3rd you may be knighted when you please."[14] On 23 May 1787, Fenn attended a levée at St. James's Palace in London, at which he gave the king the original manuscripts of the correspondence he had so far published, handsomely bound in three red morocco volumes. In return, he was dubbed Sir John Fenn—an honour with which he was so delighted that he broke off from his work on the remaining Paston papers for three months in order to research and write an essay on the history of knighthood.

Fenn published two further volumes of Paston letters, and was working on a fifth when he succumbed to a stroke in 1794, at the age of fifty-four. After his death, and that of his wife, Eleanor, twenty years later, his collection of Paston manuscripts disappeared from public view. Equally mysterious was the fate of the letters presented with such ceremony to King George, which had never reached their intended home in the Royal Library. By the 1860s, rumours were circulating, fuelled by the suspicious disappearance of the correspondence, that the letters had been forgeries all along. A learned investigation was launched by the august members of the Society of Antiquaries in London, as a result of which the descendants of Eleanor Fenn's nephew rediscovered the manuscripts that had lain undisturbed in their family home ever since her death half a century earlier. In 1866 the Society confirmed the letters' authenticity and recommended to the Treasury that they should be acquired for the nation. They were bought by the British Museum, and a new edition compiled by James Gairdner, a scholar at the Public Record Office, was published in the 1870s. Finally, in 1889, the lost letters that had been given to George III were found, not in the royal collection but at the home of one of the grandsons of George Pretyman, the private secretary who had been so conspicuously eager to facilitate Fenn's gift of the manuscripts to his royal master. They were purchased by the British Museum in 1933.

"IT IS VERY CURIOUS—indeed, I did not know that there was so much as a private letter extant of that very turbulent period," Horace Walpole had written when John Fenn first showed him one of the Paston letters in 1782.[15] He was right to be surprised. Given the ephemeral nature of such personal papers, the continued existence of the Paston correspondence over a period of six hundred years is little short of miraculous. It was the chance result of an unforeseeable combination of circumstances: the meticulous care with which the medieval Pastons kept their letters, and the heedless neglect of later generations who failed to clear their archive of documents that had no further practical use. Even when the papers came to light in the 1730s, it was not a foregone conclusion that they would be preserved. The antiquarian Blomefield thought it entirely possible—if regrettable—that the earl of Yarmouth's executors would choose to burn them, and even he saw no particular value in "those (of which there are many) that relate to nothing but family affairs only."[16] Forty years later, it was happy accident that brought the collection into the sensitive and conscientious hands of John Fenn; and in the nineteenth century the fame of Fenn's edition—a surprise bestseller—saved the letters from the threat that they might once again be left to moulder, forgotten and discarded, in a damp and dusty attic.

To the fifteenth-century Pastons, it had seemed that lasting remembrance would depend on the physical embodiment of their achievements: on the fine houses in which they lived and the proud memorials that marked their graves. Little now remains of the buildings and monuments on which they lavished such care, and so much of their wealth. Judge William's house at Oxnead is long gone; the manor house at Gresham is nothing but overgrown foundations; and Caister Castle is a ruin, its elegant tower overlooking no more than an outline of the great house traced in brick on the grass below. Not a single fifteenth-century Paston tomb survives. The chantry chapels and monastic institutions to which so many of the family entrusted their graves were swept away by the Reformation; and although Mautby church still stands, its south aisle—where Margaret Paston was buried under a tombstone made to her own precise specification—no longer exists. What did survive, against all the odds, was not brick or marble, but hundreds of fragile pieces of paper. As a result, the Pastons now occupy a unique place in the history of medieval England.

"So violent and motley was life," the historian Johan Huizinga famously wrote of the late Middle Ages, "that it bore the mixed smell of blood and of roses." War and dynastic conflict undoubtedly cast a long shadow over fifteenth-century England; but to listen to the Pastons describe the world in which they lived is to be reminded that blood and roses might signify family and home just as much as they represent the epic subjects of Shakespearean drama. What, then, of Huizinga's portrait of the people of the Middle Ages, oscillating "between the fear of hell and the most naive joy, between cruelty and tenderness, between harsh asceticism and insane attachments to the delights of this world, between hatred and goodness, always running to extremes"?[17] In the Paston letters there is a chorus of voices—rational, humane, amused, sceptical, pragmatic, and resilient—speaking across the centuries to contradict him.

NOTES

References are given for direct quotations from contemporary texts, and for material taken from unpublished documents. Otherwise, the principal sources used are listed in the bibliography.

The main source for the lives of the Paston family is the edition of their letters by Norman Davis (*Paston Letters and Papers of the Fifteenth Century,* 2 vols., Oxford: Oxford University Press, 1971–6, abbreviated here as *PL* Davis). Some documents omitted by Davis are printed in James Gairdner's earlier edition (*The Paston Letters,* 6 vols., London, 1904, reprinted Gloucester: Alan Sutton, 1983, abbreviated as *PL* Gairdner). Apart from references to Davis's introduction (where page numbers are used), notes refer to individual letters, which are numbered consecutively throughout the volumes of each edition.

PROLOGUE: then was a good world

1. This German woodcut, printed in 1423, is the earliest dated example of European printing. It is held in the United Kingdom by the John Rylands University Library of Manchester, and can be viewed at http://rylibweb.man.ac.uk/data1/dg/text/dg005.html.

2. Quotations from John Clynn's account, from the *Scotichronicon* of John of Fordun, and from the *Historia Roffensis* (the chronicle of the cathedral priory of Rochester), can be found in R. Horrox (trans. and ed.), *The Black Death* (Manchester: Manchester University Press, 1994), pp. 70, 82–84, 85.

3. Letter from the archbishop of Canterbury to the bishop of London, 28 December 1349: Horrox, *The Black Death,* p. 118.

4. B. Tuchman, *A Distant Mirror* (London: Macmillan, 1979), p. xiii; J. Huizinga, *The Waning of the Middle Ages* (Harmondsworth: Penguin, 1968), p. 146.

5. Quotation from the *Gast of Gy,* a fifteenth-century prose tract: E. Duffy, *The Stripping of the Altars: Traditional Religion in England, 1400–1580* (New Haven and London: Yale University Press, 1992), p. 345.

6. Duffy, *Stripping of the Altars,* p. 342.
7. Horrox (ed.), *The Black Death,* pp. 340–42.
8. Quotation from the *Anonimalle Chronicle,* the most authoritative surviving narrative of the rising: R. B. Dobson (trans. and ed.), *The Peasants' Revolt of 1381,* 2d ed. (London: Macmillan, 1983), p. 124.
9. Quotations from the *Anonimalle Chronicle:* Dobson, *Peasants' Revolt,* pp. 164–65.
10. The chroniclers agree on the king's actions: this version of his words is taken from the *Historia Anglicana* of Thomas Walsingham, a monk of St. Albans: Dobson, *Peasants' Revolt,* p. 179.
11. The words are Thomas Walsingham's: Dobson, *Peasants' Revolt,* p. 260.
12. Huizinga, *Waning of the Middle Ages,* p. 25.

CHAPTER 1: a wise man of the law

1. *PL* Davis, p. xli. The document survives in the form of a nineteenth-century transcription of a manuscript that has since gone missing.
2. Clement was named in a court case brought after the events of June 1381 by the abbot of St. Benet's, but the government's concern to pacify the country rather than punish every participant meant that reprisals against this type of local action were limited, and Clement does not seem to have suffered significantly as a result of this legal process. H. Eiden, "Joint Action Against 'Bad' Lordship: The Peasants' Revolt in Essex and Norfolk," *History* 83 no. 269 (1998), p. 22n.
3. *PL* Davis, p. xli.
4. H. T. Riley (ed.), *Munimenta Gildhallae Londoniensis: Liber Albus, Liber Custumarum, et Liber Horn,* vol. i (London: Longman, Brown, Green, Longmans, and Roberts, 1859), p. 584.
5. "London Lickpenny," an anonymous early fifteenth-century poem, printed in R. H. Robbins (ed.), *Historical Poems of the XIVth and XVth Centuries* (New York: Columbia University Press, 1959), pp. 130–34.
6. Robbins (ed.), *Historical Poems,* pp. 130–34.
7. Statute of Winchester, 1285, translated in H. Rothwell (ed.), *English Historical Documents, 1189–1327* (London: Eyre and Spottiswoode, 1975), pp. 460–62.
8. Quotation from the chronicle of Thomas Walsingham, in C. Given-Wilson (trans. and ed.), *Chronicles of the Revolution* (Manchester: Manchester University Press, 1993), p. 75.
9. *PL* Davis 423.
10. Trial by battle was still very occasionally used in cases—often treason cases—where a convicted criminal tried to save his own neck by informing on his associates. The informer (or "approver") was required to fight in person against those he accused of complicity in his crime. Judicial combat involving an approver took place in London in 1455–56, but it was probably the last such trial ever staged in England. The case in which William Paston was involved in 1423 was different in that it involved land rights rather than charges of felony or treason, which accounts for the procedural distinctions and uncertainties noted in the Year Book. The champions' heads were not shaved before the duel, for example, as that of an approver would have been, and the knob that was so controversially missing from

the end of the "baston" would have been present in an approver's case. For all details, see C. H. Williams (trans. and ed.), *Year Books of Henry VI (1 Henry VI),* (London: Selden Society 1933), pp. 95–100.

11. Williams (ed.), *Year Books of Henry VI (1 Henry VI),* p. 96.

12. L. O. Pike, *A History of Crime in England,* 2 vols. (London: Smith, Elder and Co., 1873), I, p. 389.

13. *PL* Gairdner, vol. VI, appendix I.

14. *PL* Davis, p. xli.

15. For quotation, see C. Richmond, *The Paston Family in the Fifteenth Century: The First Phase* (Cambridge: Cambridge University Press, 1990), p. 86.

16. Richmond, *The Paston Family,* p. 90.

17. *PL* Davis 870D.

18. *PL* Davis 867.

19. *PL* Davis 4.

20. *PL* Davis 2.

21. *PL* Davis 1, 2, 3, 4, 6, 8, 10.

22. *PL* Davis 7.

23. *PL* Davis 13.

24. *PL* Davis p. xli.

CHAPTER 2: no will of them in writing

1. Gonville Hall was refounded in the sixteenth century as Gonville and Caius College. A seventh college, King's, was founded by Henry VI in 1441, and another, Queens', by his wife, Margaret of Anjou, in 1448.

2. A. R. Myers (ed.), *English Historical Documents, 1327–1485* (London, Eyre and Spottiswoode, 1969), pp. 895–901.

3. *PL* Davis 14.

4. From Sir John Fortescue's *De Laudibus Legum Anglie;* excerpt printed in Myers (ed.), *English Historical Documents, 1327–1485,* p. 491.

5. *PL* Davis 439.

6. *PL* Davis 13. The report of John and Margaret's meeting is the main business of Agnes's only surviving letter to William (see chapter 1).

7. *PL* Davis 13.

8. *PL* Davis 125.

9. *PL* Davis 125.

10. *PL* Davis 126. "Scarlet" was a type of woollen cloth of the highest quality, usually brightly coloured, but not yet exclusively associated with the colour red.

11. *PL* Davis 155.

12. *PL* Davis 346.

13. *PL* Davis 127.

14. *PL* Davis 432.

15. *PL* Davis 31.

16. *PL* Davis 32.

17. Even the will of January 1444 had not been properly revised; the text of the 1441–1442 draft was not changed to take account of the time that had passed since

it was written (as reflected, for example, in his children's ages, and the birth of his first grandson): *PL* Davis, 12; *PL* Gairdner, vol. 6, appendix 2, II.

18. *PL* Davis 32.
19. *PL* Davis 31.
20. *PL* Davis 33.
21. *PL* Davis 32.
22. *PL* Davis 33.

CHAPTER 3: a perilous dwelling

1. *PL* Davis 129.
2. *PL* Davis 129.
3. *PL* Davis 129.
4. For the reconstruction of the missing words, see Caroline Barron, "Who Were the Pastons?" *Journal of the Society of Archivists,* 4 (1972).
5. *PL* Davis 23.
6. *PL* Davis 14.
7. *PL* Davis 79.
8. *PL* Davis 127.
9. *PL* Davis 38.
10. *Rotuli Parliamentorum,* V, pp. 340–41.
11. *PL* Davis 128.
12. *PL* Davis 128.
13. *PL* Davis 128. The hostility between Daniel and Tuddenham, and the rivalry between Heydon and the Pastons, became further entangled when Heydon's father-in-law, Edmund Winter, married Tuddenham's mother-in-law, Alice Woodhouse, after she was widowed in 1431.
14. *PL* Davis 36, 39.
15. *PL* Davis 130.
16. *PL* Davis 130.
17. *PL* Davis 443.
18. *PL* Davis 444.
19. *PL* Davis 36; National Archives, London, KB9/262 mm. 45–46.
20. *PL* Davis 444.
21. *PL* Davis 131.
22. *PL* Davis 131.
23. *PL* Davis 131.
24. *PL* Davis 132.
25. *PL* Davis 36.
26. *PL* Davis 133 (and, for Moleyns's letter itself, see *PL* Davis 875).
27. *PL* Davis 132.
28. *PL* Davis 133.
29. *PL* Davis 37. Edmund's will is *PL* Davis 80.
30. *PL* Davis 37
31. *PL* Davis 135.
32. *PL* Davis 136.

33. E. F. Jacob, *The Fifteenth Century* (Oxford: Oxford University Press, 1961), p. 493.
34. *PL* Gairdner 117.
35. *PL* Davis 450.
36. *PL* Davis 450.
37. J. L. Watts, "Ideas, Principles and Politics," in A. J. Pollard (ed.), *The Wars of the Roses* (London: Macmillan, 1995), p. 110.
38. *PL* Davis 450.
39. *PL* Davis 450.
40. *PL* Davis 133.

CHAPTER 4: the world is changed greatly

1. *PL* Davis 692; R. A. Griffiths, *The Reign of Henry VI* (London: A. & C. Black, 1981), p. 636.
2. *PL* Davis 455.
3. *PL* Davis 136.
4. *PL* Gairdner 122.
5. *PL* Davis 455.
6. *PL* Davis 39.
7. *PL* Davis 458.
8. *PL* Davis 460.
9. *PL* Davis 461.
10. *PL* Davis 460, 463.
11. *PL* Davis 463, 460.
12. *PL* Davis 460.
13. *PL* Davis 460.
14. *PL* Davis 463.
15. *PL* Davis 467.
16. *PL* Davis 878.
17. *PL* Gairdner 162.
18. *PL* Davis 878, 877.
19. National Archives, London, KB9/272 m. 2.
20. Magdalen College, Oxford, Hickling MS 104.
21. *PL* Gairdner 162; *PL* Davis 881.
22. *PL* Davis 471.
23. *PL* Davis 471.
24. *PL* Davis 472.
25. *PL* Davis 472.
26. *PL* Davis 473.
27. *PL* Davis 137.
28. *PL* Davis 474.
29. *PL* Davis 138.
30. *PL* Davis 139.
31. *PL* Gairdner 192.
32. *PL* Gairdner 192.

33. *PL* Davis 477.
34. *PL* Gairdner 192.
35. *PL* Davis 478.
36. *PL* Gairdner 192.
37. Magdalen College, Oxford, Hickling MS 104.
38. *PL* Davis 479.

CHAPTER 5: a squire of worship

1. *PL* Davis 141.
2. *PL* Davis 144. (For the redating of this letter from Davis's suggested date of 1452 to 1451, see C. Richmond, *The Paston Family in the Fifteenth Century: Endings* [Manchester; Manchester University Press, 2000], p. 106n.)
3. *PL* Davis 144.
4. *PL* Davis 483.
5. *PL* Davis 485.
6. National Archives, London, KB27/750 rot. 104.
7. *PL* Davis 40, 48; National Archives, London, KB9/272 m. 52.
8. *PL* Davis 40.
9. *PL* Davis 40.
10. *PL* Davis 48.
11. *PL* Davis 43.
12. *PL* Davis 43, 40, 48; National Archives, London, KB27/790 Rex rot. 43v; KB9/85/2 m. 8.
13. *PL* Davis 43 (see also 42, 44).
14. *PL* Davis 46.
15. *PL* Davis 41, 46, 882.
16. *PL* Davis 882.
17. *PL* Gairdner, 210.
18. *PL* Davis 487.
19. *PL* Davis 140. Davis suggests that this letter was written on 3 June 1451, but Margaret's reference to Charles Nowell indicates a date of 18 May 1452.
20. *PL* Davis 45 (redated to 4 or 18 July 1451: see National Archives, London, KB27/762 Rex rot. 1). Richard Southwell later married Jane's sister Amy Witchingham.
21. *PL* Davis 45, 140. Margaret's reminder about the girdle—a request first passed on to her husband by John Osbern in *PL* Davis 487 (written 14 May 1452)—confirms the date of 1452 for this letter.
22. *PL* Davis 41, 81, 142 (redated to 4 July 1452 by the references to Roger Church and Margery's girdle).
23. National Archives, London, E28/84; KB27/775 Coram Rege rot. 20v.
24. For these indictments, see National Archives, London, KB9/85/2 mm. 8, 14, 17–17v, 25, 6, 30, 33, 35, 37; KB9/118/1 mm. 16, 22, 23, 24, 28, 29, 36; KB9/118/2 m. 30; *PL* Davis 48.
25. National Archives, London, KB9/118/2 mm. 163–64.
26. *PL* Davis 146.

27. *PL* Davis 147.
28. *PL* Davis 26.
29. *PL* Davis 148.
30. *PL* Davis 149.
31. *PL* Davis 150.
32. *PL* Davis 151.
33. *PL* Davis 150.
34. *PL* Davis 150.
35. *PL* Davis 446.
36. *PL* Davis 446.
37. *PL* Davis 84. For the other proposals over the years 1449–1454, see *PL* Davis 19, 145, 150, 493, 27, 499, 50.
38. *PL* Gairdner 235.
39. *PL* Gairdner 230.
40. *PL* Gairdner 235.
41. *PL* Davis 48.
42. *PL* Davis 83.
43. *PL* Davis 83.

CHAPTER 6: the heartiest kinsman and friend

1. *PL* Davis 64; H. S. Bennett, *The Pastons and Their England* (Cambridge: Cambridge University Press, 1922), p. 111; *PL* Gairdner 389; K. B. McFarlane, "The Investment of Sir John Fastolf's Profits of War," in his *England in the Fifteenth Century* (London: Hambledon Press, 1981), p. 190n.
2. *PL* Gairdner 223.
3. *PL* Gairdner 174.
4. *PL* Gairdner 164, 173.
5. *PL* Davis 537.
6. *PL* Davis 506.
7. *PL* Gairdner 251.
8. *PL* Davis 509.
9. *PL* Davis 516.
10. *PL* Davis 520.
11. *PL* Davis 525.
12. *PL* Davis 536.
13. *PL* Davis 509.
14. *PL* Davis 28.
15. *PL* Davis 121.
16. *PL* Davis 512.
17. *PL* Gairdner 282.
18. *PL* Gairdner 283.
19. *PL* Davis, 522.
20. *PL* Gairdner 287.
21. *PL* Davis 527.
22. *PL* Davis 528.

23. *PL* Davis 528. The word used in the original text was "*wood* as a wild bullock," a now-obsolete adjective meaning "mad" in both modern senses—that is, insane and/or violently angry.

24. *PL* Gairdner 299.

25. *PL* Gairdner 322.

26. *PL* Davis 553. Many of the surviving letters from 1456–58 are difficult to date conclusively and precisely. They are attributed here to the most plausible date within that period.

27. *PL* Davis 556.

28. *PL* Davis 571, 572. (Worcester's text gives the last phrase in Latin—*de malo in peius.*)

29. *PL* Davis 572.

30. *PL* Davis 566.

31. Fastolf's Yorkshire estates had formerly belonged to his wife, Millicent Scrope; for John's visit there, see *PL* Davis 53.

32. *PL* Davis 550.

33. *PL* Davis 558.

34. *PL* Davis 537.

35. *PL* Davis 570.

36. *PL* Gairdner 340 (dated to 1457 by reference to Davis 569 and 570). The royal administration was allegedly demanding the vast sum of five hundred marks for each one hundred marks of annual landed income with which the college was to be endowed. Fastolf was planning an endowment to produce a net income of three hundred marks a year, which would mean paying at least 1,500 marks—the equivalent of £1,000—for the licence, an amount that might justifiably be thought outrageously high.

37. National Archives, London, C1/19/115.

38. *PL* Davis 25.

39. *PL* Davis 569.

40. There is a difficulty about the date of this written will, since *PL* Davis 54 reports that it was sealed on 14 June in the thirty-fifth year of the reign of Henry VI—the thirty-fifth year being 1457. However, all other evidence dates the will to 14 June 1459, which suggests that the reference in Davis 54 is no more than a slip of the pen.

41. *PL* Gairdner 385.

42. *PL* Davis 578.

43. *PL* Davis 54. The purchase price of land was usually calculated as twenty times its annual income. On that basis, Fastolf's estates (including his properties in London and elsewhere, as well as in Norfolk and Suffolk) would have been worth about twenty thousand pounds on the open market.

44. *PL* Davis 25.

45. *PL* Gairdner 385.

46. During a period of "great sickness" while Fastolf was still living at Southwark, for example, a proclamation was made on his instructions at St. Paul's Cathedral offering restitution to anyone he had wronged, and a number of people came forward to ask for redress. When they did so, however, Fastolf gave them "sharp and

bitter answer"—whether because illness had made him more than usually irritable, or because by then he had recovered and was therefore no longer so acutely conscious of the need to make amends before his time ran out. The presumably confused and disappointed petitioners "naught had but rebukes." C. Richmond, *The Paston Family in the Fifteenth Century: Fastolf's Will* (Cambridge: Cambridge University Press, 1996), p. 88n.

47. The unsettling effects of this deliberately maintained ambiguity were apparent in a letter that John Paston received from Henry Windsor, a chancery clerk who had served Fastolf for some time, asking whether Fastolf intended to keep his promise that Windsor should have charge of one of the inns he owned in London: ". . . if it please you to remember my master, at your best leisure, whether his old promise shall stand as touching my preferring to the Boar's Head in Southwark," Windsor wrote. "Sir, I would have been at another place, and of my master's own motion he said that I should set upon the Boar's Head; in the which matter I report me to William Worcester, Bocking and William Barker, and most specially to my master's own remembrance": *PL* Davis 574.

48. *PL* Davis 578—and see also Fastolf's own detailed list of instructions for John on a variety of legal and other matters, written on 3 July 1459 (*PL* Davis 579).

49. *PL* Davis 583.

50. *PL* Davis 901.

CHAPTER 7: neither in trust nor favour

1. Richmond, *Paston Family: Fastolf's Will*, p. 137.

2. *PL* Davis 54; *PL* Gairdner 387.

3. *PL* Davis 86. William Paston and William Worcester must have left Caister on Tuesday in order to arrive in London by 8:00 A.M. on Friday, as William Paston describes in his letter. Thomas Howes later alleged that Worcester spent that Tuesday night at Caister (see *PL* Davis 901), but his declaration was made seven years after the event to serve a particular political purpose, and his evidence cannot therefore be taken to override that of William Paston's letter.

4. *PL* Davis 86.

5. *PL* Davis 152.

6. *PL* Davis 584.

7. *PL* Davis 153.

8. The passage in full reads: "*Propter Deum caveatis a confidentia in illo nigro Hibernico oculis obliquo et lusco, qui utinam corde, ore et opere non esset obliquior, qui heri misit litteram Colino Gallico, de quibus dicitur quod singuli caccant uno ano*": *PL* Davis 612.

9. *PL* Davis 86. For Worcester's absence when Fastolf died, see *PL* Davis 612.

10. *PL* Davis 88.

11. *PL* Davis 604.

12. *PL* Davis 604.

13. Or (another version given elsewhere in the same letter) "Who that ever says so, I say he lies falsely in his head": *PL* Davis 705.

14. *PL* Davis 88.

15. *PL* Davis 88.
16. *PL* Davis 705.
17. *PL* Davis 88.
18. *PL* Davis 89.
19. *PL* Davis 705.
20. *PL* Davis 89.
21. *PL* Davis 609.
22. *PL* Davis 154.
23. *PL* Davis 157.
24. *PL* Davis 624.
25. *PL* Davis 612: "*Item, dicit quod cum pater vester fuerit iudex ditissimus, quasi nihil fecistis pro eo in distribuendo elemosinam pro anima eius, et cum nihil feceritis pro patre vestro, quomodo pro Magistro Fastolf aliquid facietis?*"
26. *PL* Davis 114.
27. Quotation from Gregory's Chronicle: see C. L. Scofield, *The Life and Reign of Edward IV*, 2 vols. (London: Longmans, Green, and Co., 1923), I, p. 139.
28. *PL* Davis, 114.
29. *PL* Davis 317. The letter was written in the name of one of John's sons, but corrections to the text in John's own hand make clear that he was responsible for drafting it.
30. *PL* Davis 158.

CHAPTER 8: the infinite process

1. "*Je n'ai pas souvenance d'avoir jamais vu un plus bel homme*": Scofield, *Edward the Fourth*, I, p. 127.
2. *PL* Davis 114.
3. *PL* Davis 632.
4. R. E. Archer, " 'How Ladies . . . Who Live on Their Manors Ought to Manage Their Households and Estates': Women as Landholders and Administrators in the Later Middle Ages," in P.J.P. Goldberg (ed.), *Woman Is a Worthy Wight: Women in English Society, c.1200–1500* (Stroud: Alan Sutton, 1992), p. 154.
5. *PL* Davis 611. "*Ipse enim* [the bishop of Norwich] *cum ducissa Suffolchie et aliis personis prenominatis sunt reginae et principi maxime favorabiles cum totis suis viribus . . . Item, bonum esset quod iuvenis dux Suffolchie cum suis militibus et armigeris uteretur suis calcaribus et iam probaretur in bello cui esset fidelis, an caro vel piscis.*"
6. *PL* Davis 231.
7. *PL* Davis 58.
8. *PL* Davis 636, 160. For Margaret's presence at Hellesdon in late June and early July, see *PL* Davis 635 and 159.
9. *PL* Davis 59.
10. *PL* Davis 117.
11. *PL* Davis 163.
12. *PL* Davis 163.
13. *PL* Davis 167.

14. *PL* Davis 168.

15. *PL* Davis 168.

16. *PL* Davis 169.

17. *PL* Davis 662.

18. *PL* Davis 677. Davis suggests a date of 1463 for this letter, but the issue of leasing land at Boyton, which Playter mentions in the middle of the letter, connects it with *PL* Davis 653, written at the end of December 1461. Playter was therefore writing in January 1462.

19. *PL* Davis, 661.

20. *PL* Davis 644. Davis placed the whole of the Cotton episode in the autumn of 1461, but it has since been redated to 1462 by reference to the King's Bench proceedings that resulted from the incident: see Richmond, *Paston Family: Endings,* pp. 199–200n. The letters redated to 1462 as a result are *PL* Davis 166, 644, 645, 647, 648, and 737.

21. *PL* Davis 645.

22. *PL* Davis 647. The John Paston who went with Richard Calle to Cotton has previously been taken to be John Paston II, the eldest son of the family, but the evidence suggests that it was in fact John Paston III. John Paston's later petition to the duke of Norfolk on the subject of the conflict at Cotton (*PL* Davis 65, redated to some time after March 1463 because of the redating of the incident itself from 1461 to 1462) remarks that the son John sent with Calle to Cotton was "a servant of my lord's." It was John III, not John II, who was by that stage in the service of the duke of Norfolk. John's instruction to Calle and his son to go to Cotton is given in *PL* Davis 66 (which must, therefore, date from before 8 October 1462), and it is "*John Paston the younger*" to whom he refers. It was John III who called himself John Paston junior, or the younger (see *PL* Davis 318, 319), whereas John II signed himself John Paston the older (see *PL* Davis 231, 232, 234, 235). The "*John Paston junior*" to whom Calle addressed his letter about events at Cotton (*PL* Davis, 737) was therefore John III.

23. *PL* Davis 648.

24. *PL* Davis 737. There is one apparent difficulty with redating this letter to 1462: Calle refers to "the day after All Saints, which shall be on Tuesday next coming." Davis took Calle to mean that the day *after* All Saints' day was a Tuesday, which would fit his suggested date of 1461. However, if Calle meant that All Saints' day itself was a Tuesday, as it was in 1462, the difficulty disappears—and the substance of his comments about the conflict at Cotton clearly place the letter in the autumn of that year.

25. *PL* Davis 166.

26. *PL* Davis 120 (redated to 16 March 1462: see Richmond, *Paston Family: Fastolf's Will,* pp. 150–51).

27. *PL* Davis 680.

28. *PL* Davis 652. Davis was uncertain of the year, but the substance of the letter best fits 1463.

29. *PL* Davis 88.

30. "*iste iuratus non intellexit in tota vita sua tantam liberalitem in dicto domino Johanne Fastolf*": *PL* Gairdner 565.

31. *PL* Davis 119.
32. *PL* Davis 118.
33. *PL* Davis 177.
34. *PL* Davis 671. The precise date of this letter is uncertain, beyond the fact that it was written between 1462 and 1466. However, Russe's comments best fit the circumstances of 1464.
35. *PL* Davis 72. For the redating of John's quarrel with his eldest son, see chapter 9.
36. *PL* Davis 688.
37. *PL* Davis 73. The letter was written on "the Thursday before St. Peter's Day." Davis took this to be the feast of Saints Peter and Paul, on 29 June, and therefore dated the letter to 27 June. However, internal evidence suggests it was written much earlier in the year—especially its closeness in tone to *PL* Davis 72 (written 15 January), and the fact that John says that he hopes to make progress in the probate case "before Easter." It seems much more likely that he was writing on 21 February, the day before the feast of St. Peter's Chair.
38. *PL* Davis 180.
39. *PL* Davis 181, 180.
40. *PL* Davis 184.
41. *PL* Davis 690.
42. *PL* Davis 188.
43. *PL* Davis 74.
44. *PL* Davis 190, 191.
45. *PL* Davis 323. In 1465 Elizabeth Venour was embroiled in a protracted legal battle with a rival claimant, William Babington, over her right to the wardenship—a fight that became a cause célèbre as a result of her colourful love life. As a wealthy heiress and widow, Elizabeth was an appealing prospect as a potential wife, and in 1462 she was allegedly abducted and forcibly married by a man named Robert Worth. Worth was outlawed for the offence and took sanctuary at Westminster Abbey, but Elizabeth's decision to join him there allowed Babington to claim that she had colluded in her own kidnapping, and that she should forfeit her possessions as a result. When the case went to trial, Elizabeth initially refused to leave Worth, but divorced him when it became clear that she otherwise risked losing her inheritance. Babington subsequently won the case, but Elizabeth launched an appeal, and in 1466 an out-of-court settlement was agreed by which Elizabeth kept the wardenship, on condition that Babington would inherit the office after her death if (as proved to be the case) she remained childless. Worth then petitioned the pope for an annulment of their divorce, and the couple lived out the rest of their days together. For Elizabeth Venour and the Fleet Prison itself, see M. Bassett, "The Fleet Prison in the Middle Ages," *University of Toronto Law Journal* V, no. 2 (1944).
46. *PL* Davis 77.
47. *PL* Davis 192.
48. *PL* Davis 180.
49. *PL* Davis 194.
50. *PL* Davis 196.
51. *PL* Davis 196.

52. *PL* Davis 196.
53. *PL* Davis 688.
54. *PL* Davis 30.
55. "pro Johannes Fastolf milite ditissimo qui egit contra istud concilium."
56. C. F. Bühler (ed.), *The Dicts and Sayings of the Philosophers* (London: Early English Text Society, 1941), pp. xxiv, 54; Richmond, *Paston Family: First Phase,* pp. 259–60.

CHAPTER 9: a drone among bees

1. *PL* Gairdner 637.
2. *PL* Davis 153.
3. *PL* Davis 116.
4. *PL* Davis 231.
5. *PL* Davis 231.
6. See chapter 8.
7. *PL* Davis 116.
8. *PL* Davis 643.
9. *PL* Davis 232.
10. *PL* Davis 172.
11. *PL* Davis 680.
12. *PL* Davis 175.
13. *PL* Davis 176.
14. *PL* Davis 72.
15. *PL* Davis 72.
16. *PL* Davis 73 (redated to 21 February 1465).
17. *PL* Davis 234. Davis suggests a date of March 1464 for this letter, but its contents best fit the situation a year later, when John II had been barred from home by his father.
18. *PL* Davis 178. Margaret says that the time of year when John II was banished from the house was "about St. Thomas's mass." The difficulty in interpreting her comment is that there was more than one St. Thomas, and more than one feast for each one. Nevertheless, it is possible to narrow down the options because the major feasts of the most prominent saints of that name—St. Thomas the apostle and St. Thomas Becket—were concentrated in December and July. Given the intensity of John Paston's anger at his eldest son in January 1465, it seems likely that the breach between them had taken place not long before, which suggests that Margaret was referring to one of the feasts of St. Thomas in December 1464.
19. *PL* Davis 179.
20. *PL* Davis 690.
21. *PL* Davis 897, 896. In the mid-sixteenth century John Paston III's great-grandson Sir William Paston named one of his sons Wulstan in honour of this Norman "ancestor." R. Hughey (ed.), *The Correspondence of Lady Katherine Paston, 1603–1627* (Norwich: Norfolk Record Society, 1941), pp. 19, 36–37.
22. *PL* Davis 896.
23. *PL* Davis 198.

24. *PL* Davis 279.

25. *PL* Davis 329. Davis tentatively suggests a date of 1468 for this letter. However, John III's comments about a man named Hugh Fenn link it with *PL* Davis, 749, which must have been written before George Neville lost the chancellorship in June 1467. Both letters can therefore be dated to March 1467.

26. *PL* Davis 236.

27. Letter now lost; extract quoted in headnote to *PL* Davis 236.

28. *PL* Davis 236.

29. *PL* Davis 327.

30. *PL* Davis 745.

31. *PL* Davis 323.

32. *PL* Davis 330, 329. Margaret mentions a "little John" in her household in two letters before this date, without further comment on his identity. In 1472, John III also mentions "little Jack" as one among a list of people to whom John II should send greetings in London: see *PL* Davis 187, 194, 354).

33. *PL* Davis 327.

34. *PL* Davis 325.

35. *PL* Davis 720. John Paston and John II were together in London when this letter was written, which rules out Davis's suggested date of February 1465, given that the two were estranged at that point. It is much more likely that the letter was written a year later, on 6 February 1466.

36. *PL* Davis 748.

37. *PL* Davis 741, 748.

38. C. Ross, *Edward IV* (London: Eyre Methuen, 1974), p. 63n.

39. *PL* Davis 199.

40. *PL* Davis 199.

41. *PL* Davis 901A.

42. *PL* Davis 237.

43. *PL* Davis 330.

44. *PL* Davis 902.

45. *PL* Davis 752.

46. For the last three years of his life, Howes was rector of Pulham Market, in south Norfolk. He commissioned a stained-glass window for the church there depicting Sir John Fastolf and his wife, Millicent, with an inscription asking onlookers to pray for their souls, and declaring that Fastolf "did many good things during his lifetime" ("*multa bona fecit in tempore vitae*"): Richmond, *Paston Family: Fastolf's Will,* pp. 184–86.

47. *PL* Davis 238.

48. *PL* Davis 759.

49. *PL* Davis 200.

50. *PL* Davis 752.

51. Quotation from the *Annales Rerum Anglicarum:* Ross, *Edward IV,* p. 93.

52. *PL* Davis 764. The letter is undated, but a reference to a man named Roger Ree as sheriff of Norfolk and Suffolk means that it cannot have been written earlier than his appointment to office in November 1468. The king visited Norfolk in June 1469, and the dramatic events that followed his visit mean that the letter cannot

have been written after that point. The most likely dating is therefore sometime in the early months of 1469, when John II's relationship with the Hautes was already established.

53. *PL* Davis 200, 201.
54. *PL* Davis 904.
55. *PL* Davis 201.
56. *PL* Davis 331, 332, 333.
57. *The Plumpton Letters and Papers,* ed. J. Kirby, Camden Society Fifth Series (Cambridge: Cambridge University Press, 1996), p. 40.
58. *PL* Davis 240.
59. *PL* Davis 333.
60. *PL* Davis 333.
61. *PL* Davis 333.
62. *PL* Davis 333.
63. Myers (ed.), *English Historical Documents,* p. 300; Scofield, *Edward the Fourth,* I, p. 495.
64. *PL* Gairdner 719.
65. *PL* Davis 762.
66. *PL* Davis 763.

CHAPTER 10: till better peace be

1. J. H. Harvey (ed.), *William Worcestre: Itineraries* (Oxford: Oxford University Press, 1969), p. 187. Worcester reported that the duke's army numbered three thousand men, but such figures were used to give an impression of imposing scale rather than an accurate headcount, and it is clear, by comparison with what is known about armies fighting on international campaigns, that a single nobleman could not have mustered a force of that size. It is impossible to be sure how many men the duke had at his disposal during the siege, but by extrapolation from Worcester's list of local knights and esquires who offered him their support (*Itineraries,* p. 189), a total of two or three hundred is not implausible.
2. *PL* Davis 202.
3. *PL* Davis 241.
4. *PL* Davis 242.
5. *PL* Davis 242.
6. *PL* Davis 204.
7. *PL* Davis 204.
8. *PL* Davis 243.
9. *PL* Davis 243.
10. *PL* Davis 244.
11. *PL* Davis 786.
12. *PL* Davis 334.
13. *PL* Davis 335.
14. *PL* Davis 335.
15. *PL* Davis 205.
16. *PL* Davis 245.

17. *PL* Davis 328 (redated to October 1469 by reference to *PL* Davis 335 and 205; cf. Richmond, *Paston Family: Endings,* p. 135n).
18. *PL* Davis 201.
19. *PL* Davis 332.
20. *PL* Davis 861.
21. *PL* Davis 861.
22. *PL* Davis 203.
23. *PL* Davis 203.
24. *PL* Davis 203.
25. *PL* Davis 335.
26. *PL* Davis 208 (redated to 1469 by reference to *PL* Davis 328—see chapter 10, note 17).
27. *PL* Davis 336.
28. *PL* Davis 245.
29. *PL* Davis 248.
30. *PL* Davis 337.
31. *PL* Davis 337.
32. *PL* Davis 338.
33. *PL* Davis 248, 339.
34. *PL* Davis 912.
35. *PL* Davis 252.
36. *PL* Davis 248.
37. *PL* Davis 787.
38. From a report by Sforza di Bettini, the Milanese ambassador to France: Myers (ed.), *English Historical Documents,* p. 304; and see Scofield, *Edward the Fourth,* I, p. 529.
39. Proclamation quoted in Scofield, *Edward the Fourth,* I, p. 537.
40. G. E. Cokayne, *The Complete Peerage,* ed. V. Gibbs *et al.,* 13 vols. (London: St. Catharine Press, 1910–1940), vol. IX, p. 91.
41. *PL* Davis 345.
42. *PL* Davis 217 (redated to 1470 by reference to *PL* Davis 345).
43. *PL* Davis 248.
44. *PL* Davis 258.
45. *PL* Davis 213 (redated to 1470: see *PL* Davis, vol. II, p. xxv).
46. *Calendar of the Close Rolls, 1468–76,* pp. 163–65.
47. *PL* Davis 727. Davis's suggested date of 1468 is too early, since the letter must have been written after Bishop Wainfleet's intervention in the dispute. The year 1471 is the most likely, although it is not impossible that Worcester was writing a year earlier, in 1470.
48. Quotation from the *Arrival of Edward IV*—an exactly contemporary, largely eyewitness account, albeit a partisan Yorkist one. See Ross, *Edward IV,* pp. 157, 162n.
49. Ross, *Edward IV,* p. 162.
50. Quotation from the *Arrival of Edward IV:* see Ross, *Edward IV,* p. 165.
51. Quotation from the *Great Chronicle of London:* see Ross, *Edward IV,* p. 166.
52. *PL* Davis 261.
53. *PL* Davis 346. John III signed the letter "your humblest servant, J. of Geldeston"—

using his birthplace to identify himself to his mother rather than his name—in case the paper fell into unfriendly hands. See also chapter 2.

CHAPTER 11: the matter of Caister

1. *PL* Davis 263.
2. *PL* Davis 347.
3. *PL* Davis 263.
4. *PL* Davis 267.
5. *PL* Davis 266.
6. *PL* Davis 264.
7. *PL* Davis 266.
8. *PL* Davis 263.
9. *PL* Davis 209.
10. *PL* Davis 256 (August 1470).
11. *PL* Davis 394.
12. *PL* Davis 395.
13. *PL* Davis 353.
14. *PL* Davis 353.
15. *PL* Davis 395.
16. *PL* Davis 263.
17. *PL* Davis 268.
18. *PL* Davis 216.
19. *PL* Davis 221.
20. *PL* Davis 209.
21. *PL* Davis 83.
22. *PL* Davis 209.
23. *PL* Davis 212 (29 November 1471). Margaret's much calmer letter of 20 November (*PL* Davis 211), which does not mention the issue of the loan, seems likely to have been addressed to John III, rather than John II as Davis suggests.
24. *PL* Davis 212.
25. *PL* Davis 266.
26. *PL* Davis 350 (written shortly before Christmas 1471).
27. *PL* Davis 355.
28. *PL* Davis 214 (which Davis dates "about 1472," but the substance of the letter makes clear that it must have been written shortly after John III's letter no. 355 of 16 October).
29. *PL* Davis 354.
30. *PL* Davis 354.
31. *PL* Davis 269.
32. *PL* Davis 270.
33. *PL* Davis 271.
34. *PL* Davis 357.
35. *PL* Davis 358.
36. *PL* Davis 358.
37. In fact, the legal situation was a great deal more complicated even than this. It was

true that, in the absence of a male heir, daughters had equal rights to a share of the estate irrespective of seniority. However, the earldom of Warwick itself was the inheritance of the earl's wife, Anne Beauchamp, who was still alive, and whose rights should therefore have taken precedence over those of her daughters. Many of the earl's own Neville estates, meanwhile, were held in "tail male"—in other words, the right of inheritance was limited to male heirs—and should have passed to his nephew, John Neville's son George. Nevertheless, neither the widowed countess of Warwick nor George Neville was in any position to insist on their rights, and the claims of Isabel and Anne Neville (and therefore of their husbands, Clarence and Gloucester) were ratified in parliament once the settlement had been agreed.

38. *PL* Davis 274. John II's difficulties were compounded by the fact that, although he had not sold the timber at Sporle, he had mortgaged the manor for a year to a local lawyer, Roger Townsend, thinking that he would be able to redeem it with the hundred pounds he believed Margaret had promised him. Now that she was withholding the money, the whole manor was potentially at risk.

39. *PL* Davis 264.

40. *PL* Davis 212.

41. *PL* Davis 274.

42. *PL* Davis 279.

43. *PL* Davis 277.

44. *PL* Davis 275.

45. *PL* Davis 282.

46. *PL* Davis 275.

47. *PL* Davis 277.

48. *PL* Davis 275.

49. *PL* Davis 272.

50. *PL* Davis 354.

51. *PL* Davis 355.

52. *PL* Davis 356.

53. *PL* Davis 355.

54. *PL* Davis 282.

55. Certainly, John III had been deeply committed to ensuring that John Daubeney's will was dealt with properly and promptly. In March 1470, he reported to John II that Daubeney's executors could not act until they received confirmation that he had owed no money to his employers, and was clearly much exercised at the prospect that his brother might not get around to producing the document with any urgency: "You may do it well enough, so God help me, for I know well you owe him money and he not you, if so be that he were true when he died, and I know well we found him never untrue in his life. But his friends and other of the country put great default in me that there is nothing done for him, saying that he might do no more for us but lose his life in your service and mine, and now he is half forgotten among us; wherefore I pray you let this be sped." *PL* Davis 339. Another possibility—not mutually exclusive with this one—is that John III made the journey to Santiago in the retinue of Earl Rivers (Lord Scales), who was said to have visited the shrine at some point in 1473.

56. *PL* Davis 282.

57. *PL* Davis 284.
58. *PL* Davis 286.
59. *PL* Davis 770.
60. *PL* Davis 285 (which must have been written before 26 October 1474—compare with the opening of *PL* Davis 286).
61. *PL* Davis 221.
62. *PL* Davis 221.
63. *PL* Davis 291.
64. *PL* Davis 221.
65. *PL* Davis 291.
66. Ross, *Edward IV,* p. 218.
67. *PL* Davis, 224.
68. *PL* Davis 289.
69. *PL* Davis 293.
70. *PL* Davis 365.
71. *PL* Davis 366.
72. *PL* Davis 365.
73. *PL* Davis 293.
74. *PL* Davis 365.
75. *PL* Davis 366.
76. *PL* Davis 294.
77. It has always been assumed that the duke died at his home at Framlingham in Suffolk, but there seems to be no concrete evidence to confirm the supposition. John II and John III were both nearby when he died, since they reported the news to Margaret the next morning (*PL* Davis 295), but it seems unlikely that they would have been at Framlingham given their breach with Norfolk two months earlier. However, John III had previously reported that the duchess intended to spend her pregnancy at Norwich (*PL* Davis 365), and certainly both John II and John III were there on 20 January, three days after the duke's death (*PL* Davis 367). It therefore seems probable that the duke and members of his household were staying in Norwich with his wife when he died.
78. *PL* Davis 295.
79. *PL* Davis 368.
80. *PL* Davis 296.
81. *PL* Davis 298, 372.
82. *PL* Davis 371.
83. *PL* Davis 299.
84. *PL* Davis 299.
85. *PL* Davis 300.

CHAPTER 12: I pray get us a wife somewhere

1. *PL* Davis 379. It was presumably because of his shortage of money that, in the same year, the duke sold a magnificent jewel to his brother-in-law King Edward for £160 ("an image of Our Lady, of gold, with Our Lord in her arms, and the images of St. John the Baptist and St. Catherine on either side of Our Lady, and two other

images with seven angels thereto pertaining, the same image of Our Lady sitting upon a cushion of silver and over-gilt in a pavilion of gold garnished with six sapphires, six rubies, twenty-four great pearls upon five cushions of gold, twenty small pearls upon the crown, four little pearls in little diamonds, a ruby and two emeralds, thirteen very little pearls set in other places, and a ruby set in Our Lady's breast"): Scofield, *Edward IV,* II, p. 433.

2. *PL* Davis 782.

3. *PL* Davis 297.

4. *PL* Davis 302.

5. Quotation from the rolls of parliament: Ross, *Edward IV,* p. 242.

6. *PL* Davis 312.

7. *PL* Davis 278.

8. *PL* Davis 774.

9. *PL* Davis 316, 755.

10. *PL* Davis 228.

11. *PL* Davis 366.

12. *PL* Davis 298.

13. *PL* Davis 227.

14. *PL* Davis 227. This was the second time John II had mortgaged Sporle to the local lawyer Roger Townsend. He had successfully redeemed the manor after the first mortgage in 1472 (for which, see chapter 11, note 37), but was now concerned about whether he would again be able to recover the property.

15. *PL* Davis 371.

16. *PL* Davis 311.

17. *PL* Davis 228.

18. *PL* Davis 227.

19. *PL* Davis 270.

20. *PL* Davis 209.

21. *PL* Davis 283.

22. *PL* Davis 282.

23. *PL* Davis 236. Sir Geoffrey Boleyn bought the manor of Blickling from Sir John Fastolf in 1452. Boleyn's great-granddaughter Anne married King Henry VIII in 1533.

24. *PL* Davis 339.

25. *PL* Davis 369.

26. *PL* Davis 791.

27. *PL* Davis 374.

28. *PL* Davis 773 (and see also *PL* Davis 376). The word *cousin* denoted a much less specific family relationship than it does in modern usage. Given the extent of inter-marriage among the gentry of any region, it was always likely that some form of kinship existed between families from the same area, and *cousin* was therefore often used as a term of respectful address.

29. *PL* Davis 415, 416. Margery's letters are the earliest surviving Valentine messages in the English language. Her mother had invited John III to stay for St. Valentine's Day itself, when "every bird chooses him a mate," she said: *PL* Davis 791.

30. *PL* Davis 226.

31. *PL* Davis 236.
32. *PL* Davis 303.
33. *PL* Davis 304.
34. *PL* Davis 306.
35. *PL* Davis 305.
36. *PL* Davis 312.
37. *PL* Davis 302, 381.
38. *PL* Davis 220.
39. *PL* Davis 404.
40. *PL* Davis 381.
41. *PL* Davis 397.
42. *PL* Davis 245. John Paston's youngest brother Clement had died in the late 1460s, soon after John himself. By the 1470s, therefore, William Paston was the only surviving son of Judge William and Agnes.
43. *PL* Davis 315.
44. *PL* Davis 383. John II was buried in the church of the White Friars, just off Fleet Street. John III had intended to bring his brother's body back to Norfolk along with that of his grandmother, who had also died in London. In the end, of course, it was just Agnes's coffin that was brought back, for burial in the Lady Chapel of the White Friars' Church in Norwich, beside her parents and her youngest son, Clement.

CHAPTER 13: our trusty and wellbeloved knight

1. *PL* Davis 222. The right to private worship was one that held social cachet, and the Pastons must previously have secured such permission when James Gloys was their resident chaplain. Nevertheless, the fact that Margaret couched her request this time in terms of her own infirmity seems significant.
2. *PL* Davis 793.
3. *PL* Davis 384.
4. Anne Beaufort's oldest brother, Henry, was executed in 1464 for his part in leading the Lancastrian resistance against Edward IV in the north of England. Her second brother, Edmund, was captured and beheaded after the Battle of Tewkesbury in 1471.
5. *PL* Davis 383.
6. *PL* Davis 417.
7. *PL* Davis 418.
8. *PL* Davis 417, 418.
9. *PL* Davis 417.
10. *PL* Davis 417.
11. *PL* Davis 386.
12. *PL* Davis 230.
13. *PL* Davis 123.
14. *PL* Davis 230.
15. *PL* Davis 230.
16. *PL* Davis 230.

17. *PL* Davis 795.
18. *PL* Davis 796.
19. Quotation from the contemporary accounts of Edward's funeral rites compiled by his heralds: see Scofield, *Edward IV*, II, p. 366.
20. *PL* Davis 796.
21. Henry's father, Edmund Tudor, was the son of Henry V's queen, Catherine de Valois, by her second marriage to the Welsh esquire Owen Tudor. Edmund and his brother, Jasper, were therefore half-brothers of King Henry VI, but they had no claim to the throne in their own right, since their relationship with King Henry came through their French mother rather than through the royal line of England.
22. *PL* Davis 799.
23. A. Crawford (ed.), *The Household Books of John Howard, Duke of Norfolk, 1462–71, 1481–3* (Stroud: Alan Sutton, 1992), p. 183.
24. *PL* Davis 387.
25. *PL* Davis 801.
26. *PL* Davis 807.
27. *PL* Davis 810.
28. *PL* Davis 811.
29. *PL* Davis 813 (and see chapter 4, for Thomas, Lord Scales addressing Sir John Fastolf as "father" as a term of respect). The three women—Alice Fitzhugh, Catherine Hastings, and Margaret de Vere—were all members of the large Neville brood, sisters of the kingmaking earl of Warwick and of the Pastons' former patron Archbishop Neville.
30. *PL* Davis 823, 816, 420. By law, half of the whale belonged to the local men who found it, and the other half to the crown—"fish royal" being a technical legal term that included sturgeon and porpoise as well as whales. There was initial uncertainty about whether the crown's share should be taken by the king himself or by Oxford in right of the admiralty, but the earl graciously abdicated his claim.
31. *PL* Davis 830. Henry Heydon was married to Anne Boleyn, whose sister Alice had refused John III's suit more than twenty years earlier (see chapter 9).
32. Agnes made no mention of any Paston connections when she wrote her own will after John III's death, for example. She asked to be buried beside her first husband, John Harvey: *PL* Davis 930.
33. *PL* Davis 839.

EPILOGUE: letters of good consequence in history

1. *PL* Davis 848. The earl himself was both concerned and solicitous: "your brother William, my servant, is so troubled with sickness and crazed in his mind that I may not keep him about me, whereof I am right sorry, and at this time send him to you," he told John III; "praying especially that he may be kept surely and tenderly with you to such time as God fortune him to be better assured of himself, and his mind more sadly disposed, which I pray God may be in short time."
2. Sir William's choice of name for his eldest son was an unusual one, which probably derived from a family connection to the great Dutch scholar Desiderius Erasmus. John Paston III was a friend of the wealthy London merchant Henry

Colet, whose son John was one of the leading English humanists in the early six-teenth century. John Colet developed a close relationship with Erasmus during the years that the latter spent living in England, and the friendship between the Paston and Colet families may therefore have meant that Sir William Paston also knew Erasmus well.

3. It was this William Paston who named his second son Wulstan, after the family's fictional Norman ancestor (see chapter 9).

4. Cokayne, *Complete Peerage,* vol. XII part 2, p. 890.

5. *PL* Davis 350.

6. Quotation from the Norfolk antiquarian Thomas Martin, 1744: see R. W. Ketton-Cremer, "The Treasure of Oxnead," in R. W. Ketton-Cremer, ed., *Norfolk Assembly* (London: Faber & Faber, 1957), p. 214.

7. *PL* Davis, vol. I, p. xxvi.

8. *PL* Davis, vol. I, p. xxiv.

9. D. Stoker, " 'Innumerable Letters of Good Consequence in History': The Discovery and First Publication of the Paston Letters," *The Library: Transactions of the Bibliographical Society* xvii (1995), p. 119.

10. J. Fenn (ed.), *Original Letters, written during the reigns of Henry VI, Edward IV, and Richard III by various persons of rank or consequence . . . ,* 2 vols (London: G. G. J. and J. Robinson, 1787). There had been some discussion between Fenn and his publishers about the timing of publication—whether to wait until the spring, when the members of fashionable society would return to London from their country estates, or whether the fact that most books were published in the spring for that very reason would provide unhelpful competition. Fenn's brother-in-law John Frere, who was acting as his agent and adviser in London, saw no reason to delay publication: ". . . I should think its coming out before other works might find it purchased among people who don't care to buy everything that comes out, which it might lose if it had to stand the market with four or five other books. I have often heard people say—'Bless me! What number of guinea-quartos are come out this spring—'tis impossible to buy them all!' ": Stoker, " 'Innumerable Letters,' " p. 136.

11. *PL* Gairdner, vol. I, p. 1.

12. Stoker, " 'Innumerable Letters,' " p. 143.

13. Stoker, " 'Innumerable letters,' " p. 108.

14. M. Serpell, "Sir John Fenn, his friends and the Paston Letters," *Antiquaries Journal* 63 (1983), p. 111. Fenn's publishers had been sceptical about the com-mercial value of a royal dedication: "they will not allow that they shall sell one copy more on that account," Fenn's brother-in-law reported (Stoker, " 'Innumerable Letters,' " p. 136).

15. *PL* Davis, vol. I, p. xxiv.

16. *PL* Davis, vol. I, p. xxvi.

17. Huizinga, *Waning of the Middle Ages,* p. 25.

SELECT BIBLIOGRAPHY

This bibliography lists the main primary and secondary sources for the lives of the Pastons themselves, followed by a selection of further reading on fifteenth-century England. Some of the more specialist works cited in the notes have not been repeated here.

THE PASTONS

UNPRINTED PRIMARY SOURCES

London: National Archives
C1: Early Chancery Proceedings
KB9: King's Bench, Ancient Indictments
KB27: King's Bench, *Coram Rege* Rolls

Oxford: Magdalen College
Fastolf MSS
Hickling MSS

PRINTED PRIMARY SOURCES

Calendar of the Close Rolls, 1399–1509. 18 vols. (London: H. M. S. O., 1927–1963).
Calendar of the Fine Rolls, 1399–1509. 11 vols. (London: H. M. S. O., 1931–1962).
Calendar of the Patent Rolls, 1399–1509. 17 vols. (London: H. M. S. O., 1903–1916).
Davis, N. (ed.). *Paston Letters and Papers of the Fifteenth Century,* 2 vols. (Oxford: Oxford University Press, 1971–1976).
———. *The Paston Letters: A Selection in Modern Spelling* (Oxford: Oxford University Press, 1983).
Fenn, J. (ed.). *Original Letters, written during the reigns of Henry VI, Edward IV, and Richard III by various persons of rank or consequence . . . ,* 5 vols. (London: G. G. J. and J. Robinson, 1787–1823).

Gairdner, J. (ed.). *The Paston Letters*. 6 vols. (London, 1904; reprinted Gloucester: Alan Sutton, 1983).

Harvey, J. H. (ed.). *William Worcestre: Itineraries* (Oxford: Oxford University Press, 1969).

List of Sheriffs for England and Wales. P.R.O. Lists and Indexes, 9 (London: H. M. S. O., 1898).

Rotuli Parliamentorum. 6 vols. Record Commission, London.

Williams, C. H. (trans. and ed.). *Year Books of Henry VI (1 Henry VI)* (London: Selden Society, 1933).

SECONDARY SOURCES

Barron, C. "Who Were the Pastons?" *Journal of the Society of Archivists* 4 (1972): 530–35.

Bennett, H. S. *The Pastons and Their England* (Cambridge: Cambridge University Press, 1922).

Blomefield, F. *An Essay Towards a Topographical History of the County of Norfolk*. 11 vols. (London: W. Miller, 1805–1810).

Britnell, R. H. "The Pastons and their Norfolk." *Agricultural History Review* 36 (1988): 132–44.

Castor, H. *The King, the Crown, and the Duchy of Lancaster: Public Authority and Private Power, 1399–1461* (Oxford: Oxford University Press, 2000), part II.

Cokayne, G. E. *The Complete Peerage,* ed. V. Gibbs et al., 13 vols. (London: St. Catharine Press, 1910–1940), vol. XII part 2, 889–93 (earldom of Yarmouth).

Davis, V. *William Waynflete* (Woodbridge: Boydell & Brewer, 1993).

Gies, F., and J. Gies. *A Medieval Family* (New York: HarperCollins, 1998).

Hughey, R. Introduction to *The Correspondence of Lady Katherine Paston, 1603–1627.* (Norwich: Norfolk Record Society, 1941).

Lewis, P. S. "Sir John Fastolf's Lawsuit over Titchwell, 1448–55," *Historical Journal* 1 (1958): 1–20.

McFarlane, K. B. "The investment of Sir John Fastolf's Profits of War," and "William Worcester: A Preliminary Survey." In his *England in the Fifteenth Century* (London: Hambledon Press, 1981), pp. 175–97 and 199–224.

Rawcliffe, C., and R. Wilson. (eds.). *Medieval Norwich* (London: Hambledon & London, 2004).

Richmond, C. *The Paston Family in the Fifteenth Century: The First Phase* (Cambridge: Cambridge University Press, 1990).

———. *The Paston Family in the Fifteenth Century: Fastolf's Will* (Cambridge: Cambridge University Press, 1996).

———. *The Paston Family in the Fifteenth Century: Endings* (Manchester: Manchester University Press, 2000).

Serpell, M. "Sir John Fenn, His Friends and the Paston Letters," *Antiquaries Journal* 63 (1983): 95–121.

Smith, A. R. "Litigation and Politics: Sir John Fastolf's Defence of His English Property." In A. J. Pollard (ed.), *Property and Politics* (Gloucester: Alan Sutton, 1984), 59–75.

————. " 'The Greatest Man of That Age': The Acquisition of Sir John Fastolf's East Anglian Estates." In R. E. Archer and S. Walker (eds.), *Rulers and Ruled in Late Medieval England* (London: Hambledon Press, 1995), pp. 137–54.

Stoker, D. " 'Innumerable Letters of Good Consequence in History': The Discovery and First Publication of the Paston Letters." *The Library: Transactions of the Bibliographical Society* xvii (1995): 107–55.

Virgoe, R. *Private Life in the Fifteenth Century: Illustrated Letters of the Paston Family* (London: Macmillan, 1989).

FIFTEENTH-CENTURY ENGLAND: POLITICS AND THE WARS OF THE ROSES

Carpenter, C. *The Wars of the Roses: Politics and the Constitution in England, c. 1437–1509* (Cambridge: Cambridge University Press, 1997).

Chrimes, S. B. *Henry VII* (London: Eyre Methuen, 1972).

Curry, A. *The Hundred Years' War* (London: Macmillan, 1993).

Goodman, A. *The Wars of the Roses: Military Activity and English Society, 1452–97* (London: Tempus, 1981).

Griffiths, R. *The Reign of Henry VI* (London: A. & C. Black, 1981).

Gunn, S. J. *Early Tudor Government, 1485–1558* (London: Macmillan, 1995).

Haigh, P. A. *The Military Campaigns of the Wars of the Roses* (Stroud: Alan Sutton, 1995).

Harriss, G. L. (ed.). *Henry V: The Practice of Kingship* (Oxford: Oxford University Press, 1985).

————. *Shaping the Nation: England, 1360–1461* (Oxford: Oxford University Press, 2005).

Hicks, M. A. *False, Fleeting, Perjur'd Clarence: George, Duke of Clarence, 1449–1478* (Gloucester: Alan Sutton, 1980).

Horrox, R. *Richard III: A Study of Service* (Cambridge: Cambridge University Press, 1989).

Laynesmith, J. L. *The Last Medieval Queens: English Queenship, 1445–1503* (Oxford: Oxford University Press, 2004).

McFarlane, K. B. *England in the Fifteenth Century: Collected Essays* (London: Hambledon Press, 1981).

Maurer, H. E. *Margaret of Anjou: Queenship and Power in Late Medieval England* (Woodbridge: Boydell & Brewer, 2003).

Pollard, A. J. (ed.). *The Wars of the Roses* (London: Macmillan, 1995).

————. *Late Medieval England, 1399–1509* (Harlow: Longman, 2000).

Ross, C. *Edward IV* (London: Eyre Methuen, 1974).

————. *Richard III* (London: Methuen, 1981).

Scofield, C. L. *The Life and Reign of Edward the Fourth*, 2 vols. (London: Longmans, Green, and Co., 1923).

Watts, J. L. *Henry VI and the Politics of Kingship* (Cambridge: Cambridge University Press, 1996).

FIFTEENTH-CENTURY ENGLAND: SOCIETY, ECONOMY, AND CULTURE

Bailey, M. (ed.). *The English Manor, c. 1200–c. 1500* (Manchester: Manchester University Press, 2002).

Barker, J.R.V. *The Tournament in England, 1100–1400* (Woodbridge: Boydell & Brewer, 1986).

Bolton, J. L. *The Medieval English Economy, 1150–1500* (London: J. M. Dent & Sons, 1980).

Duffy, E. *The Stripping of the Altars: Traditional Religion in England, 1400–1580* (New Haven and London: Yale University Press, 1992).

Dyer, C. *Standards of Living in the Later Middle Ages: Social Change in England, c. 1200–1520* (Cambridge: Cambridge University Press, 1989).

———. *Everyday Life in Medieval England* (London: Hambledon and London, 1994).

Hanawalt, B. *The Ties That Bound: Peasant Families in Medieval England* (Oxford: Oxford University Press, 1986).

Harding, A. *The Law Courts of Medieval England* (London: Allen and Unwin, 1973).

Harriss, G. L. *Shaping the Nation: England, 1360–1461* (Oxford: Oxford University Press, 2005).

Horrox, R. (ed.), *The Black Death* (Manchester: Manchester University Press, 1994).

———. (ed.). *Fifteenth-Century Attitudes: Perceptions of Society in Late Medieval England* (Cambridge: Cambridge University Press, 1994).

Keen, M., *Chivalry* (New Haven and London: Yale University Press, 1984).

———. *English Society in the Later Middle Ages, 1348–1500* (London: Penguin, 1990).

Labarge, M. W. *Medieval Travellers: The Rich and Restless* (London: Hamish Hamilton, 1982).

Marks, R. and P. Williamson (eds.). *Gothic: Art for England, 1400–1547* (London: V. & A., 2003).

Orme, N. *Medieval Children* (New Haven and London: Yale University Press, 2001).

Platt, C. *The English Medieval Town* (London: Secker and Warburg, 1976).

Rawcliffe, C. *Medicine and Society in Later Medieval England* (Stroud: Alan Sutton, 1995).

Reeves, C. *Pleasures and Pastimes in Medieval England* (Stroud: Alan Sutton, 1995).

Webb, D. *Pilgrimage in Medieval England* (London: Hambledon and London, 2000).

Woolgar, C. M. *The Great Household in Late Medieval England* (New Haven and London: Yale University Press, 1999).

INDEX

Joan of Arc, 86
John, king of England, 283–84

Kent, 251–52
King's Lynn, 103, 105, 106, 272, 284

Lancaster, duchy of, 29, 149, 152
Lancaster, Henry, Bolingbroke, duke of,
    29, 30
  See Henry IV, king of England
Lancaster, John of Gaunt, duke of, 20,
    26, 29, 359
Lancastrian dynasty, 30–31. See also
    Henry IV, Henry V, Henry VI;
    Margaret of Anjou; Wars of the
    Roses
Langham, Simon, archbishop of
    Canterbury, 21
Langstrother, Jane (Witchingham Boys),
    124–25, 384n. 20
Langstrother, Robert, 124–25
law
  career of William Paston, 28, 32–44
  court calendar, 25–26
  courts at Westminster, 24–25, 27, 95
  "distraint," 197
  enforcement, thirteenth century, 27
  English legal system, 26–27, 33
  inheritance and "tail male," 396n. 37
  Inns of Court, 26, 49, 218
  inquisition post mortem, 173–74,
    178–79
  judicial commission of 1453, 126–27
  King's Bench, 196, 203
  landownership, disputes over, 28,
    33–34, 36, 38–42, 68–70, 75, 93–98,
    100, 101–7, 110, 111, 116, 117–30,
    141–42, 154–57, 188–215, 227, 231,
    239, 241–45, 249, 250, 253, 274, 276,
    278, 286, 287–88, 291, 294, 296,
    301–2, 304, 309, 311–12, 313, 316,
    319–20, 325–29, 331–32, 344–45,
    361–62, 369–70, 396n. 37 (see also
    Caister Castle)
  "outlawry," 77, 203, 224

"oyer et terminer" commission, 95
  political control of, 111–12
  training in, 24–26, 218
  trial by combat, 33–34, 380n. 10
  Year Book, 32–33
Ledham, Robert, 118–19, 122, 123, 124,
    125, 127, 134, 135
Leicester, 148–49, 364
Leiston, 198
Lincoln, John de la Pole, earl of, 366–68
Lipyate, Philip, 206, 207, 208–9, 227
Litster, Geoffrey, 13, 20
Lomnor, William, 89
London, 22–23, 317
  Black Swan Inn, 298, 300
  Bridge, 90, 91, 92
  economics and trade, 23, 129–30
  Edward IV's return, 1469, 272
  Farringdon and Inns of Court, 26
  Fastolf's Southwark townhouse, 90–91,
    93, 95, 96, 108, 111, 135, 138, 165,
    241
  Fleet Prison, 210–11
  George Inn, 320
  Guildhall, 91
  housing, 23–24
  John Paston's lodgings, Inner Temple,
    108, 195, 216, 218
  Newgate Prison, 92
  plague in, 345
  Tower of, 23, 29, 73, 88, 91, 133, 177,
    237, 248, 252, 284, 290, 293, 296,
    333, 358–59, 372
  Wars of the Roses, support for York,
    176, 177, 181–82, 290, 291
  White Friars, 399n. 44
"London Lickpenny," 24, 26
Losecoat Field, Battle of, 279
Louis XI, king of France, 237, 248
  alliance brokered between Warwick
    and Lancastrians, 279–82, 289
  alliance with Oxford, 303, 312, 313
  death of, 362
  truce with England (Treaty of
    Picquigny), 1475, 324–25, 355